SORCERY OR SCIENCE?

THE MAGIC IN HISTORY SERIES

FORBIDDEN RITES
A Necromancer's Manual of the Fifteenth Century
Richard Kieckhefer

CONJURING SPIRITS
Texts and Traditions of Medieval Ritual Magic
Edited by Claire Fanger

RITUAL MAGIC
Elizabeth M. Butler

THE FORTUNES OF FAUST
Elizabeth M. Butler

THE BATHHOUSE AT MIDNIGHT
An Historical Survey of Magic and Divination in Russia
W. F. Ryan

SPIRITUAL AND DEMONIC MAGIC
From Ficino to Campanella
D. P. Walker

ICONS OF POWER
Ritual Practices in Late Antiquity
Naomi Janowitz

BATTLING DEMONS
Witchcraft, Heresy, and Reform in the Late Middle Ages
Michael D. Bailey

PRAYER, MAGIC, AND THE STARS IN THE ANCIENT AND LATE ANTIQUE WORLD
Edited by Scott Noegel, Joel Walker, and Brannon Wheeler

BINDING WORDS
Textual Amulets in the Middle Ages
Don C. Skemer

STRANGE REVELATIONS
Magic, Poison, and Sacrilege in Louis XIV's France
Lynn Wood Mollenauer

UNLOCKED BOOKS
Manuscripts of Learned Magic in the Medieval Libraries of Central Europe
Benedek Láng

ALCHEMICAL BELIEF
Occultism in the Religious Culture of Early Modern England
Bruce Janacek

INVOKING ANGELS
Theurgic Ideas and Practices, Thirteenth to Sixteenth Centuries
Edited by Claire Fanger

THE TRANSFORMATIONS OF MAGIC
Illicit Learned Magic in the Later Middle Ages and Renaissance
Frank Klaassen

MAGIC IN THE CLOISTER
Pious Motives, Illicit Interests, and Occult Approaches to the Medieval Universe
Sophie Page

REWRITING MAGIC
An Exegesis of the Visionary Autobiography of a Fourteenth-Century French Monk
Claire Fanger

MAGIC IN THE MODERN WORLD
Strategies of Repression and Legitimization
Edited by Edward Bever and Randall Styers

MEDICINE, RELIGION, AND MAGIC IN EARLY STUART ENGLAND
Richard Napier's Medical Practice
Ofer Hadass

PICATRIX
A Medieval Treatise on Astral Magic
Translated by Dan Attrell and David Porreca

MAKING MAGIC IN ELIZABETHAN ENGLAND
Two Texts of Early Modern Vernacular Magic
Frank Klaassen

THE LONG LIFE OF MAGICAL OBJECTS
A Study in the Solomonic Tradition
Allegra Iafrate

KABBALAH AND SEX MAGIC
A Mythical-Ritual Genealogy
Marla Segol

The Magic in History series explores the role magic and the occult have played in European culture, religion, science, and politics. Titles in the series bring the resources of cultural, literary, and social history to bear on the history of the magic arts, and they contribute to an understanding of why the theory and practice of magic have elicited fascination at every level of European society. Volumes include both editions of important texts and significant new research in the field.

MAGIC *in* HISTORY

SORCERY OR SCIENCE?

CONTESTING KNOWLEDGE AND PRACTICE IN WEST AFRICAN SUFI TEXTS

ARIELA MARCUS-SELLS

THE PENNSYLVANIA STATE UNIVERSITY PRESS
UNIVERSITY PARK, PENNSYLVANIA

Library of Congress Cataloging-in-Publication Data

Names: Marcus-Sells, Ariela, 1985– author.
Title: Sorcery or science? : contesting knowledge and practice in West African Sufi texts / Ariela Marcus-Sells.
Other titles: Magic in History.
Description: University Park, Pennsylvania : The Pennsylvania State University Press, [2022] | Series: Magic in History | Includes bibliographical references and index.
Summary: "Examines the works of two Sufi Muslim scholars, Sīdi al-Mukhtār al-Kuntī (d. 1811) and his son Sīdi Muḥammad (d. 1826), focusing on their cosmology and metaphysics of the realm of the unseen, in relation to the history of magical discourses within the Hellenistic and Arabo-Islamic worlds"—Provided by publisher.
Identifiers: LCCN 2021054031 | ISBN 9780271092294 (cloth) | ISBN 9780271092300 (paper)
Subjects: LCSH: Kuntī, al-Mukhtār ibn Aḥmad, 1729 or 1730–1811. | Kuntī, Muḥammad bin al-Mukhtār, 1765–1826. | Islamic magic—Sahara—History. | Sufism—Sahara—History.
Classification: LCC BP190.5.M25 M36 2022
LC record available at https://lccn.loc.gov/2021054031

Printed in the United States of America
Published by The Pennsylvania State University Press,
University Park, PA 16802–1003

The Pennsylvania State University Press is a member of the Association of University Presses.

It is the policy of The Pennsylvania State University Press to use acid-free paper. Publications on uncoated stock satisfy the minimum requirements of American National Standard for Information Sciences—Permanence of Paper for Printed Library Material, ANSI Z39.48–1992.

To my parents,
Janet and Michael

CONTENTS

LIST OF ILLUSTRATIONS / ix

ACKNOWLEDGMENTS / xi

LIST OF ABBREVIATIONS / xv

ORTHOGRAPHY / xvii

Introduction / 1

1. The Visible World / 27
2. The Realm of the Unseen / 62
3. The Sciences of the Unseen / 87
4. Bridging the Worlds in Prayer / 127

Conclusion / 161

NOTES / 169

BIBLIOGRAPHY / 187

INDEX / 201

ILLUSTRATIONS

FIGURES

MAP

ACKNOWLEDGMENTS

This is a book about the power of invisible and intangible forces, and so it is only appropriate to begin by thanking the often unseen but always deeply felt network of institutions and people who supported me throughout the years and made this research possible. I want to begin by thanking the many teachers whose guidance and encouragement led me down this path. This book has its origins in my work at Stanford University, where I benefited from the guidance and support of Shahzad Bashir. Shahzad was, and continues to be, a patient, caring, and expert mentor, and I am profoundly grateful for all the insight and wisdom that he has shared with me over the years. I still hope to inspire and support my own students as he has inspired and supported me. Sean Hanretta was also a dedicated teacher and mentor, and his advice over the years has been invaluable. I am still discovering all the subtle and profound ways in which his guidance has shaped my scholarship. I am also grateful to my undergraduate professors at Barnard College and Columbia University, and particularly to Peter Awn, whose course on classical Sufi literature first captivated me and whose loss is deeply felt. I am forever indebted to Issam Eido, and to the faculty and staff of the Qasid Arabic Institute in Amman, Jordan, for so patiently nurturing my interest in classical Arabic.

The primary research for this project was conducted with the support of an IIE Graduate Fellowship for International Study, while preliminary research was funded by grants from the Stanford Abbasi Program in Islamic Studies and the Stanford Center for African Studies. Additional work on the project was supported by a fellowship from the Andrew W. Mellon Foundation through the Stanford Humanities Center, and the process of writing the book was generously funded by a fellowship from the National Endowment for the Humanities.

I conducted research in several libraries and archives in Mali, Morocco, France, and the United States. During preliminary research in the summer of 2010, I visited the Mama Haidara Library, the Kati Library, and the Institut des Hautes Études et de Recherches Islamiques–Ahmed Baba in Timbuktu. My primary research in 2012 was spent at the Bibliothèque des Manuscrits de Djenne in Mali; the Bibliothèque Nationale du Royaume du Maroc in Rabat; the Royal Library, or al-Maktaba al-Ḥasaniyya, in Rabat; the library of the Great Mosque in Meknes; the Bibliothèque nationale de France, and the archives of the University of Illinois at Urbana-Champaign. I owe thanks to the staff at all of these institutions, but particularly to the archivists and digitalization team at the Bibliothèque des Manuscrits de Djenne: Yelpha Djeite, Garba Yaro, Sidi Mohamed Toure, Al-Foussein Abba Maiga, and Soumaila Gomeda. I owe special thanks to Mamadou Samake, the cultural director, for acting as my liaison to the library and to him and his wife, Koumba, for serving as my generous hosts during my stay in Djenne. Sophie Sarin Keita provided invaluable hospitality and support for my research during my stay. I would like to thank Muhammad Lahbib Nouhi, in Rabat, for making items from his personal library available to me, and Valerie Hoffman, at the University of Illinois at Urbana-Champaign, for hosting me during my research there. Charles Stewart, in Chicago, also made numerous Kunta texts from his personal collection available to me and provided insightful advice on my research throughout this process. Yousef Casewit offered valuable advice for contacting manuscript libraries in Rabat.

I am overwhelmed by the hospitality that I have been shown during my studies in, and research trips to, Mali over the years. I owe special thanks to the Malians who have hosted me over the years, including Fatimata Sididi Mohamed, Aichatou Wallet, and Abdramane Guisse. Fatimata and her daughters, Alkahidatt and Ayatou, have been like a second family to me over the years. I am thankful to Modibo Coulibaly and all of the instructors and staff of the SIT Mali program for introducing me to their country and providing me with innumerable contacts and support. I am particularly thankful to Mahamadou Lamine Bagayoko for his help in learning Bambara.

I am indebted to numerous colleagues in the fields of Islamic studies and African history for their insight at various stages of the research and writing process and for their support and encouragement over the years, including Jessica Chen, Michael Cooperson, Alireza Doostdar, Carl Ernst, Bruce Hall, Matthew Hotham, Mbaye Lo, Matthew Lynch, Wendell Marsh, Candace Mixon, Ahoo Najafian, Oludamini Ogunnaike, and William Sherman. Years of discussions with Joshua Gentzke and Alexander Hamilton have inspired and shaped my thinking as a scholar. I am deeply thankful to Xiaolin Duan, Pablo Celis-Castillo, Raj Ghoshal, Waseem Kasim, and Pamela Winfield for reading drafts of my work and supporting me as a writer. Special thanks to Bryan Rusch for his editorial assistance.

My partner, Ryan Scadlock, has been my traveling companion for so many journeys. He was there at every stage of this process and a constant source of love and support across countries and continents. Our daughter, Tamzin, was born just as this book went to press. Her presence brings us deep joy and reminds us of all the journeys ahead. I also feel deep gratitude for Ryan's parents, Cheryl and David Scadlock, his sister, Sara Throndson, brother-in-law, Rob Throndson, and their children, Rylee and Darby, for welcoming me into their family, and for the memory of Pat Lee and her love and wisdom. And throughout my life and across all the distances that I have traveled, I have felt the presence of my parents, Janet Marcus and Michael Sells. They have offered insight and encouragement and supported me through the many challenges and anxieties of the years. This book is dedicated to them, for their love made everything possible.

ABBREVIATIONS

BnF	Bibliothèque nationale de France, Paris
BNRM	Bibliothèque Nationale du Royaume du Maroc, Rabat, Morocco
EI2	*Encyclopaedia of Islam*, 2nd ed., edited by P. Bearman, Th. Bianquis, C. E. Bosworth, E. van Donzel, and W. P. Heinrichs. https://referenceworks.brillonline.com/browse/encyclopaedia-of-islam-2
EI3	*Encyclopaedia of Islam*, 3rd ed., edited by Kate Fleet, Gudrun Krämer, Denis Matringe, John Nawas, and Everett Rowson. https://referenceworks.brillonline.com/browse/encyclopaedia-of-islam-3
EIr	*Encyclopaedia Iranica*, online ed. https://iranicaonline.org/
EQ	*Encyclopaedia of the Qurʾān*, edited by Johanna Pink. https://referenceworks.brillonline.com/browse/encyclopaedia-of-the-quran
MH	Al-Maktaba al-Ḥasaniyya, Rabat, Morocco

ORTHOGRAPHY

For the transliteration of Arabic words, I have followed a slightly modified version of the system used by the *International Journal of Middle East Studies.* Proper nouns and technical Arabic words that have come into English usage are fully transliterated. The definite article is transcribed as written, rather than according to pronunciation (e.g., *al-shams* rather than *ash-shams*). I have used the Arabic versions for place-names in the Azawād and those specifically referenced in the texts used for this study. For other place-names, I have followed the orthographies represented most frequently in the academic literature. For the individual and group names of people who spoke Arabic (or an Arabic dialect) or produced written works in Arabic, I have followed Arabic orthography and included full diacritics. Exceptions occur for authors who have provided their own individual spellings in published literature. For the names of individuals and groups who did not speak or produce written works in Arabic (such as names in Tamasheq), I have sought to make it easier for the reader by following the past practice of academic writing.

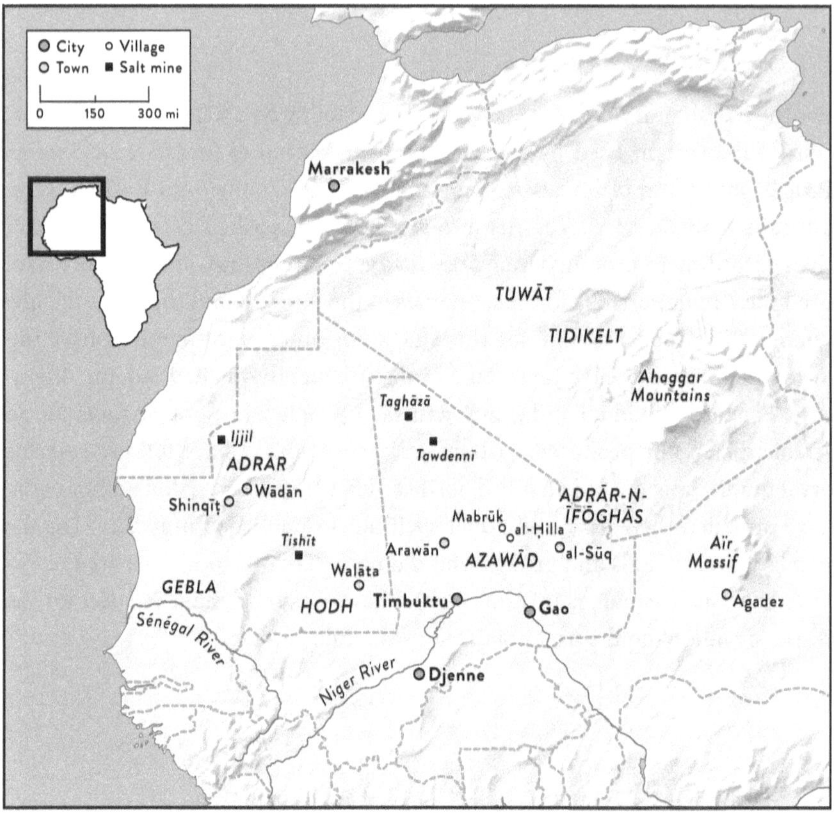

The Azawād and surrounding region, ca. 1800. Map by Erin Greb Cartography.

INTRODUCTION

This is a book about two Sufi Muslim scholars who lived, taught, and wrote in the West African Sahara Desert at the turn of the nineteenth century. These scholars, Sīdi al-Mukhtār al-Kuntī (d. 1811) and his son, Sīdi Muḥammad al-Kuntī (d. 1826), composed numerous works across multiple genres that discuss contested and controversial practices related to a vast unseen realm (*ʿālam al-ghayb*) that surrounds, and interpenetrates, the visible world. Sīdi Muḥammad in particular acknowledged that other Muslim scholars might consider these practices to be acts of sorcery (*siḥr*), but he rejected this categorization and argued that they should instead be considered "the sciences of the unseen" (*ʿulūm al-ghayb*). The descendants of Sīdi al-Mukhtār and Sīdi Muḥammad, known collectively as the Kunta, are still associated with these practices today, which Muslims in West Africa—like Muslims in many other parts of the world—continue to perform, even as their legitimacy remains contested. This book demonstrates why the Kunta family became associated with these practices by situating the sciences of the unseen within the thought of Sīdi al-Mukhtār and Sīdi Muḥammad as well as within the social and historical context that gave those sciences shape and meaning.

To give one example, a text by Sīdi Muḥammad, called the *Fawāʾid nūrāniyya wa farāʾid sirriyya raḥmāniyya* (The Illuminated Benefits and Secret Pearls of the Compassionate), offers to reveal God's secret, greatest name. According to the text, the universe itself is crafted out of the various names of God, each of which controls a specific function in the world. The greatest name controls all of the lesser names, and anyone who manages to "connect to" this name can accordingly manipulate all aspects of the world. Ultimately, the narrator reveals the greatest name of God to be a string of unvoweled consonants: AHM SQK ḤLʿ YṢ and then provides a table and a supplicatory prayer associated with that name. Specific instructions tell the reader how to inscribe the table on a tablet and recite the prayer to gain control over "any thing that includes the property of existing"—in other words, complete mastery over the universe. This one text makes claims about the structure of the world, powerful knowledge about that world, and correlating practices that would allow a user to master his surroundings. The text also places individuals who study or search for knowledge of the letters and names along a moral spectrum, discrediting those who would use these practices solely in fulfillment of their individual desires. Indirectly, the text asserts that those who have fully mastered these practices have done so on the basis of a moral and spiritual superiority that serves as the foundation for those individuals' social authority. The text thus elaborates a complex cosmology, presents practices that draw on that cosmological structure, and links those practices to hierarchies of social authority and power.

Texts like the *Fawāʾid nūrāniyya* are difficult for scholars to read, because they relate to a sphere of human activity—ritual practice—that is difficult to reconstruct from textual sources alone. Unlike an ethnographer, I cannot ask eighteenth-century Saharan Muslims how (or whether) they put Sīdi Muḥammad's instructions into practice. And although Muslims in West Africa continue to both use and produce similar texts today, the Kunta scholars and their followers are separated from our current context by two hundred years and the epistemic ruptures of colonization and postcolonial nationalization. Oral histories have proved useful in examining the recent past and have extended our understanding of regional contexts as far back as the end of the nineteenth century. But oral histories cannot reliably reconstruct the lives and contexts of people who—like Sīdi al-Mukhtār and Sīdi Muḥammad—have passed from living memory into legend, and attempting such reconstructions on the basis of oral sources risks projecting present debates and contestations into the past. As a result of this theoretical position, this project does not attempt to describe what the Kunta or their followers did with these texts, or what rituals they may or may not have performed. Instead, I first demonstrate how the Kunta scholars attempted to leverage discussions of the sciences of the unseen specifically, and devotional practice in general, to shape the religious landscape of the Sahara Desert, and to claim social authority within that space. Second, I argue that attention to the content and circulation of these works reveals changing attitudes toward devotional practice in the Sahara Desert, as Muslims increasingly came to understand practice as connected to changing forms of textuality.

Texts like the *Fawāʾid nūrāniyya* are also difficult for historians to read because they implicate categories of knowledge and practice whose meanings have been contested at almost every period in history. Sīdi al-Mukhtār's and

Sīdi Muḥammad's defense of their practices against charges of sorcery recalls contemporaneous efforts in western Europe to distinguish science from both religion and magic. Those European discussions were shaped by colonialist analyses that pejoratized African practices as superstitious and resulted in the excision of the study of these texts and practices from the field of religious studies for generations. Today, scholarship on historical African and Islamic societies takes place within an academy that has inherited these colonial-era categories, and is practiced by scholars living in societies where terms like "magic" have taken on additional meanings ranging from whimsical entertainment to the diabolic. As a result, scholarly literature on discussions of sorcery in Islamicate contexts occasionally conflates the epistemological understandings of historical Muslim writers with either colonial or current understandings of magic practices. In order to understand how the Kunta scholars understood the sciences of the unseen, and how their discussions responded to and shaped both synchronic and diachronic discourses about knowledge and practice, we must first examine our own presumptions and categories.

Therefore, although texts like the *Fawāʾid nūrāniyya* are difficult, it is crucial that we read them. This book performs just such a reading. It tells the story of Sīdi al-Mukhtār and Sīdi Muḥammad al-Kuntī, the first two leaders of the Kunta network, through the prism of their writings on the sciences of the unseen. Through close and sustained analysis of these texts, I demonstrate (1) that the Kunta scholars rooted their description and defense of the sciences of the unseen in an epistemology informed by Sufi cosmology and metaphysics, and (2) that the relationship between knowledge and practice that they posit was inextricably related to the structures of social authority under which they lived. This reading thus leads to the reconstruction of the matrix of epistemology, practice, and authority of a particular Muslim society. At the same time, even as this book offers a window into a West African Muslim society at the turn of the nineteenth century, it also puts that particular history into dialogue with scholarship on the development of discourses about legitimate and illegitimate knowledge and practice that reached from ancient Greece to modern Europe. And while some of this scholarship has acknowledged the role of Islamic traditions in the development of these discourses, other scholars have asserted the uniqueness of the western European framing of magic as illegitimate knowledge and superstition. Ultimately, this book aims to demonstrate that the Kunta participated in an epistemic process that cannot be limited to western European history but rather characterizes all societies in which an elite attempts to define and limit access to legitimate and true knowledge and practice.

The Kunta Scholars and the Sahara Desert

Situating the history of Sīdi al-Mukhtār and Sīdi Muḥammad involves tracing two lines of historical inquiry—the history of the Kunta family and that of the desert in which they lived. Of these two, the latter has received much more attention. Within the Sahara, desert peoples built and maintained elaborate systems of wells that allowed them to cultivate date palms. These oasis towns served as nodes in regional networks of interconnectivity and provided transhumanant pastoralists and merchants with places to store and defend their stocks. While many of the regional networks that connected these nodes responded to the economics of scarcity that governed desert life, the development of these networks and life in the oases also represented great individual and collective investment in both the physical and the human landscape.[1] The Kunta scholars rose to prominence in a particular region of the Sahara known as the Azawād, which was linked by regional networks to the Ahaggar Mountains and the Aïr Massif to the east, the Mauritanian Hodh and Adrār to the west, and the oases of Tuwāt and the Tidikelt to the north. At the social, economic, and political levels, these desert communities were connected to the desert edge (Sahel) and savanna lands to the south and the political entities that governed them.[2]

Recent scholarship on the Sahara and the greater region indicates that Sīdi al-Mukhtār built his economic and pedagogical network during a period of great social change marked by cultural and political realignments both within the desert and between desert and desert-edge communities. These changes resulted in the increasing dominance of nomadic desert pastoralists over settled agriculturalists in the Sahel and savanna lands to the south. Meanwhile, desert communities developed new racial and religious idioms to express this realignment in power. Previously Berber-speaking populations adopted the Arabic dialect of Ḥassāniyya and produced new family histories that tied them to an Arab lineage and to the family of the Prophet Muḥammad.[3] Increasingly, groups who identified as Arab came to refer to themselves as "white" (*biḍān*) and to distinguish between different lineages of white "nobles." These lineages were often divided into "warrior" groups that claimed political and military authority and "clerical" lineages that (in theory) renounced military force and dedicated themselves to learning and providing religious services. Both warrior and clerical groups came to describe the settled people whom they dominated as "black" (*sūdān*) and, in a context of increasing violence and slave raiding, whiteness became associated with Muslimness and free status and blackness with permanent enslaveability.[4]

As slave raiding and violence increased during the seventeenth and eighteenth centuries, "warrior" lineages and military rulers—both Muslim and non-Muslim—could no longer guarantee protection to their tributary populations and increasingly came to prey upon and sell their own people into slavery. This cycle of violence and insecurity led in turn to new forms of political organization, as Muslim scholars began to claim political power and establish new states.[5] Beginning in the Senegambia, a wave of military campaigns led by Muslim intellectuals established "Almamates" in Bundu in the 1690s, in the Futa Jallon in the 1720s and 1730s, and in the Futa Toro in the 1770s and 1780s.[6] Linked to these movements by religio-political ideology, student-teacher networks, and a common ethnic identity, another set of campaigns then began in Hausaland, in the Inner Niger Delta at the beginning of the nineteenth century. In 1804, a Sufi Muslim teacher named ʿUthmān ibn Fūdī rallied a movement that ultimately deposed all of the Hausa states and established a Muslim-ruled empire often referred to as the Sokoto Caliphate.[7] The establishment of Sokoto was soon followed by the campaign of Aḥmad Lobbo, a pastoral Muslim scholar from the Niger River Valley who established the state of Macina, centered on the new city of Hamdullahi. Finally, in 1852, al-Hājj ʿUmar Tāl began a sweeping campaign that originated in the Futa Jallon, defeated both the Bambara kingdom of Segou and the state of Macina, and reached north to threaten Timbuktu.[8]

Sīdi al-Mukhtār rose to prominence in the Azawād roughly contemporaneously with the movement to establish the Almamate along the Senegal River, but decades before ʿUthmān ibn Fūdī rallied his followers in Hausaland. Indeed, the Kunta family of scholars appears to have provided some of the intellectual foundations for the second "wave" of *jihāds*, even as they entered into competition with many of the new Muslim states. ʿUthmān ibn Fūdī claimed Sīdi al-Mukhtār as a teacher, and Ibn Fūdī's successor, Muḥammad Bello, received Sīdi Muḥammad's son Aḥmad al-Bakkāʾī as a visitor. During the first half of the nineteenth century, the Kunta leaders managed a tense series of negotiations between Sokoto and Macina. And when ʿUmar Tāl defeated Macina and marched toward Timbuktu, he was opposed and ultimately defeated by Aḥmad al-Bakkāʾī al-Kuntī.[9] However, while the Kunta leaders engaged, in diplomacy or in war, with the leaders of Islamic states in the region, they carefully distanced themselves from the political ideologies of these rulers. Sīdi al-Mukhtār and Sīdi Muḥammad drew on a long-standing current of Islamic political ethics that distinguishes the morally suspect rulership of princes (*ʿumarāʾ*) from the legitimate authority of scholars (*ʿulamāʾ*). In Islamicate contexts throughout the premodern period, Muslim scholars used a genre known as "mirrors for princes" to offer advice to rulers, attempting to guide political policy while simultaneously asserting their greater moral and ethical standing.[10] Sīdi al-Mukhtār and Sīdi Muḥammad very much understood themselves as *ʿulamāʾ* and attempted to use their social and religious authority to direct various neighboring *ʿumarāʾ*, including the leaders of the Barābīsh and the Iwellemmedan Tuareg. Notably, Sīdi Muḥammad wrote letters to both Muḥammad Bello and Aḥmad Lobbo in the form of a "mirror for princes,"[11] thus suggesting that both leaders had ceded their status as scholars by claiming political rulership.

In contrast to direct political rule, Sīdi al-Mukhtār used the voluntarist model of submission to a Sufi shaykh to attract and retain followers. Louis Brenner argues that this model represented a new form of political formation in the region, one that explicitly rejected military force as the foundation of political legitimacy; instead, the Kunta shaykhs asked followers to willingly submit to the authority of a pious Sufi leader.[12] The Kunta leaders based their claims to the voluntary devotion of their followers on both their Islamic learning and an assertion of their particular proximity to God, as manifested through the spontaneous occurrence of marvelous events. In the context of the late eighteenth century, as the moral legitimacy of military leaders decreased in inverse correlation to the rise of military violence, the growth of the Kunta movement represented a new political and social experiment. Of course, the "voluntary submission" of individuals and groups to the authority of Sīdi al-Mukhtār and his successors was a rhetorical fiction—the Kunta often resorted to military force to assert or maintain their authority. Nevertheless, this fiction offered the possibility of a political formation whose legitimacy was based on something other than rule by force. Moreover, scholars agree that the success of the Kunta model established the Sufi lineages as a mode of political organization in the region.[13]

Indeed, the appeal of the Kunta model led directly to the development of at least one other Sufi community in the desert. Shaykh Sīdiyya al-Kabīr, a student first of Sīdi al-Mukhtār and then of Sīdi Muḥammad, established his own Sufi community in the Mauritanian Gebla in the early nineteenth century, following the model of his Kunta teachers.[14] During the same time period, another Sufi community developed in the Mauritanian Hodh around the shaykh Muḥammad Fādil, whose hagiography imitates the content and structure of Sīdi Muḥammad's hagiography of his father.[15] Descendants of these figures influenced the development of the region throughout the nineteenth century and perpetuated the memory and legacy of the Kunta model. Sons of Muḥammad Fādil and a grandson of Shaykh Sīdiyya rallied followers either in opposition to, or in collaboration with, French colonial rule in the late nineteenth century.[16] And while the names of Kunta leaders, their descendants, and their students appear most frequently in historical studies of the late eighteenth to the early twentieth century, Saharan communities in Algeria, Mali, and Mauritania continue to consider Kunta descendants to be the bearers of both religious authority and particular knowledge of the sciences of the unseen.[17]

However, although the significance of the Kunta network to the development of the political and intellectual history of the region has been established, there is comparatively little original research devoted to the lives and work of Sīdi al-Mukhtār and Sīdi Muḥammad. ʿAbd al-ʿAzīz Baṭrān's book *The Qadiryya Brotherhood in West Africa and the Western Sahara: The Life and Times of Shaykh al-Mukhtar al-Kunti (1729–1811)*, an abridged version of his 1971 doctoral dissertation, remains the only published monograph on either of these two scholars. Baṭrān's impressive research draws on dozens of manuscript works by Sīdi al-Mukhtār and Sīdi Muḥammad, relying primarily on two family chronicles composed by Sīdi Muḥammad to reconstruct the life of Sīdi al-Mukhtār. The first, *Al-Ṭarāʾif wa'l-talāʾid min karāmāt al-shaykhayn al-wālida wa'l-wālid* (Original and Inherited Knowledge Regarding the Miracles of the Two Shaykhs, My Mother and My Father), is Sīdi Muḥammad's hagiography of his father (a final chapter, theoretically devoted to his mother, is not extant). The second, *Al-Risāla al-ghallāwiyya* (The Letter to the Aghlāl), is a long letter that denounces the aggression of the Aghlāl against a branch of the Kunta family in the Mauritanian Hodh, while rejecting the claims to religious authority made by the Aghlāl leader ʿAbd Allāh wuld Sīdi Mahmūd. Baṭrān also draws on the earlier work of the colonial scholar and administrator Paul Marty, whose voluminous publications on West African peoples emerged as part of the colonial government's attempt to classify and categorize the Africans under their rule. Marty's book on the history of the Kunta follows the narrative trajectory of Sīdi Muḥammad's *Risāla al-ghallāwiyya* almost point by point.[18]

Because Baṭrān draws primarily from the work of Marty and the Kunta chronicles, and because Marty relies on those same chronicles, the internal Kunta narrative presented by Sīdi Muḥammad in the *Ṭarāʾif wa'l-talāʾid* and the *Risāla al-ghallāwiyya* has become deeply ingrained in subsequent scholarship concerning the Kunta family. This literature acknowledges the hagiographic quality of Sīdi Muḥammad's depictions of his family's earliest history, which he traces back to the legendary Arab conqueror of North and West Africa, ʿUqba ibn Nāfiʿ, and from him to the Prophet Muḥammad's tribe of Quraysh.[19] Both Baṭrān and Marty argue that the family lineage emerges from "legend" into "history" with the late fifteenth-century figure Sīdi Muḥammad al-Kuntī al-Kabīr and his son, Sīdi Aḥmad al-Bakkā'ī.[20] These scholars then trace the split of the Kunta patrilineage into two branches, with a "western branch" moving into the Hodh and Adrār, in contemporary Mauritania, and an "eastern branch" moving first into the northern Saharan regions surrounding the city of Tuwāt, now in Algeria, and from there into the Azawād, in contemporary Mali. The story continues with the rise of Sīdi al-Mukhtār al-Kabīr among the Azāwad Kunta in the late eighteenth century. Again, drawing on the internal Kunta chronicles, Baṭrān recounts how a young Sīdi al-Mukhtār studied with various teachers across the Sahara before meeting his Sufi shaykh, Sīdi 'Alī ibn al-Najīb (d. 1757), who initiated him into the Qādiriyya Sufi order. At some point, Sīdi al-Mukhtār claimed for himself the title of head of the Qādiriyya order. In this role, Sīdi al-Mukhtār consolidated the diffuse branches of the Kunta family, established his family's control over important material resources, particularly livestock and salt, and accumulated wealth through the management of crucial Saharan trade routes. Baṭrān also records Sīdi al-Mukhtār's establishment of a school at al-Hilla, where he trained followers and managed the organizational structure of the Qādiriyya order.[21]

This book approaches the pre-eighteenth-century history of the Kunta family with hermeneutic suspicion while acknowledging that some documentary evidence does support the broad outlines of the received Kunta history from the fifteenth through the nineteenth century (see chapter 1). And while 'Abd al-'Azīz Baṭrān's work on Sīdi al-Mukhtār al-Kuntī brought this important family into the work of modern historians, his reliance on Paul Marty's publications and Sīdi Muḥammad's hagiographies has reinscribed a narrative meant to assert a long history of Kunta authority over other West African Muslims. This study accepts that Sīdi al-Mukhtār was a historical figure who lived and taught in the Azawād, and the textual evidence is sufficient to support the broad outlines of his life. However, the importance of the Kunta family to both regional politics and the development of Sufi intellectual and social traditions owes much to the role played by Sīdi Muḥammad in cultivating and promulgating the legacy of his father. This book thus presents a revised version of the history of the Kunta scholars set within recent scholarship on the social and economic history of the eighteenth-century Sahara.

Sufism

Sīdi al-Mukhtār and Sīdi Muḥammad argued for their social authority within the Azawād on the basis of their status as Sufi friends of God (*awliyā'*), and they presented their mastery over the sciences of the unseen as a critical element of that status. As a result, most of their discussions of the sciences of the unseen occur in texts that fall under the discursive rubric of Sufism. This general category was coined by Islamic studies scholars to refer to the diverse array of social, cultural, and intellectual traditions related to people who called themselves "Sufis," a category of identity that emerged in, and then spread out from, Baghdad as early as the ninth century.[22] As a neologism, the category of Sufism represents neither a term internal to historical Muslim societies nor a unified and coherent domain. The Kunta, for example, refer to people and ideas as "Sufi" (*ṣūfī*), or to Sufis as a collective group (*al-ṣūfiyya*), but never to "Sufism" as a unifying system. Rather, they participate in a large array of literary genres associated with Sufi Muslim writers, including cosmological, metaphysical, and hagiographical works, and they refer to practices and modes of piety developed and debated by Sufi lineages, including the recitation of the names of God (*dhikr*) and spiritual retreat (*khalwa*). Some of these works fall into a genre known in Arabic as *taṣawwuf*, which translates literally as "how to make oneself into a Sufi." This term refers to an internal discussion by Sufis of how best to perfect their ethical development and devotional practice, and as such represents only one component of the broader sociocultural and intellectual world of Sufism.[23]

As the movement developed in ʿAbbāsid Baghdad in the ninth and tenth centuries, early Sufis gathered around particularly revered teachers who focused on developing an ethic of ascetism coupled with a totalizing focus on loving and being loved by God. Early Sufis understood these valorized figures as particularly close to God, so close that they earned his particular friendship (*wilāya*) and became known as the friends of God (*walī*, pl. *awliyāʾ*).[24] These figures are still sometimes referred to in scholarly literature as Sufi "saints," based on a comparison to Catholic sainthood. As the tradition developed in the ʿAbbāsid period, Sufi writers described the friends of God as responsible for guiding their students along a path (*ṭarīq[a]* or *sabīl*) to God articulated in terms of a series of internal or psychological states. The goal of the Sufi path was often described as extinction (*fanāʾ*), in which the individual consciousness of the believer is annihilated in a direct experience of the divine, followed by a period of abiding (*baqāʾ*), when the now-inspired worshipper returned as a leader and teacher for his community. By the twelfth century, important Sufi figures had appeared across the breadth of the ʿAbbāsid empire, from Iran to the Iberian Peninsula.

The twelfth and thirteenth centuries witnessed important developments within the growing cultural current of Sufism. The focus on divine love and love of the divine combined with poetic traditions to produce Sufi love poetry in both vernacular and transregional languages. Meanwhile, Sufi scholars engaged with and absorbed Neoplatonic Islamic philosophy, resulting in the widely influential philosophical syntheses of Abū Hamīd Muḥammad al-Ghazālī (d. 1111)[25] and Muḥyī al-Dīn ibn al-ʿArabī (d. 1240).[26] In the works of these two scholars and contemporaneous figures, the friends of God adopt roles of critical cosmological importance as figures who allow for the existential flow of being from God to his creation. Meanwhile, increasingly complex and widespread Sufi teaching circles developed into full-scale social institutions with hierarchical leadership structures, distinctive rituals, and physical structures that served as lodges, schools, and gathering places for members. These institutionalized Sufi networks, or "orders" (*ṭarīqa*, pl. *ṭurūq*), traced their founding to an eponymous or authenticating friend of God and focused on the transmission of spiritual authority in an unbroken chain (*silsila*) from each pupil back through the founder of the lineage and ultimately to the Prophet Muḥammad and God.[27] Although all of these developments involved people identified as Sufis, not all Sufis participated simultaneously in all these discursive, social, or institutional registers. Thus throughout Islamic history there have been Sufi teachers and poets who did not belong to institutionalized Sufi networks, members of those networks who had no interest in Neoplatonic philosophy or cosmology, and philosophers who rejected the erotic or drunken imagery of love poetry.

Sīdi al-Mukhtār and Sīdi Muḥammad participated in almost all of these discursive realms of Sufism. They presented themselves and their ancestors as friends of God with particular proximity to the divine, gathered students in teaching circles, and traced their spiritual chain back through a valorized Sufi predecessor—ʿAbd al-Qādir al-Jīlānī (d. 1166)[28]—to the Prophet Muḥammad. They composed poetry and produced extensive treatises detailing their particular Neoplatonic Sufi philosophy and cosmology. However, my research indicates that they did not understand their pedagogical circle as an institutionalized Sufi order. By positioning the Kunta scholars outside the structures of institutionalized Sufi orders, I differ from A. A. Baṭrān, who described Sīdi al-Mukhtār as the founder of the Qādiriyya Sufi order in West Africa, and from more recent scholars who have described either Sīdi al-Mukhtār or Sīdi Muḥammad as the head, or "pole," of the Qādiriyya order in the region.[29] As I discuss at greater length in chapter 1, the Qādiriyya appears to have coalesced as a regional institution in reaction to the proliferation of Tijānī Sufis following the *jihād* of al-Hājj ʿUmar Tal. Prior to this historical moment, Sufis in the region understood themselves as members of a community following a particular shaykh and as individual links in a chain (*silsila*) extending back to the Prophet Muḥammad.[30] Sufi leaders often understood themselves as spiritually linked to important earlier members of their lineage. For example, Sīdi al-Mukhtār positioned himself as the living heir of ʿAbd al-Qādir al-Jīlānī, and Sīdi Muḥammad described his father's teachings as a "path" (*ṭarīqa*), but neither of these discourses provides evidence for an institutional, corporate identity as members of a "Qādiriyya Sufi order."

Miracles and Magic

Two other debates of importance to this study developed alongside, and interpenetrated, the growth of Sufi identities and traditions. The early ʿAbbāsid empire brought together people from Arabia, Persia, and Byzantium and witnessed the elaboration of new scholarly disciplines, including Islamic law and theology. As Muslim scholars worked to classify the textual and ritual traditions of this diverse population, theologians found themselves confronted with two sets of practices that infringed on the ontological space of prophetic miracles (*muʿjizāt*). First, members of early Sufi communities claimed that the friends of God were themselves surrounded by miraculous occurrences (*karāma*, pl. *karāmāt*). Important Sufi synthesizers from the tenth through twelfth centuries defined these *karāmāt* as gifts from God that indicated the elevated spiritual status of one of his friends.[31] Because the Kunta scholars use this same definition for the *karāmāt* in their own works, I have chosen to translate this term as "the charismata," to retain the sense of both a divine gift and a compelling presence that inspires devotion. Second, as Muslim scholars discussed the astrological, alchemical, divinatory, thaumaturgic, and medicinal practices of peoples stretching from the Indus Valley to Iberia, they began to classify some of these practices under either the Arabic term *siḥr* or the Persian term *nirānj*—"sorcery," or perhaps "magic."[32] Theologians who discussed these practices did so under the new category of *khawāriq al-ʿādāt*, "breakings of the norm," or events that appeared to reverse the usual sequence of events.[33] When Sīdi al-Mukhtār and Sīdi Muḥammad argue for the legitimacy of the "sciences of the unseen," they do so by referencing these earlier debates about breakings of the norm by positioning the sciences in relation to both sorcery, on the one hand, and the charismata, on the other.

The Islamic studies scholarship on textual-ritual traditions related to sorcery and the sciences of the unseen is still haunted by the unanswered question "is it magic?" The difficulty in answering this question stems partly from the semantic ambiguity of the word "magic" itself and partly from a long history of Western elites' using this term to discredit the traditions of colonized people, the poor and working classes, and women. On the one hand, in Western contexts today, practitioners claim to perform magic and identify themselves as magic practitioners; others profess the existence of magic but consider it a form of evil or at least amoral behavior, while yet others think of magic as a fantastical form of entertainment.[34] On the other hand, during the formative period of the field of religious studies, scholars associated "magic" with "superstition." When these scholars, and other Western elites, applied the term "magic" to colonized peoples, they defined it as either an irrational, corrupt version of a rational religiosity or a sort of flawed science. Many of these scholars specifically cited African traditions and practices as examples of "primitive" or "superstitious" thinking.[35] These elites simultaneously used the terms "magic" and "superstition" to discredit the practices of both the working classes and women within their own borders, in this case defining "magic" as surviving traces of primitive societal and cognitive stages of development that needed to be purged from a "rational" society.[36]

An early push against defining magic as the result of deficient or irrational thinking came from the anthropologist E. E. Evans-Pritchard, whose work portrayed magic and divination as logical within the epistemic world of his Azande interlocutors in east-central Africa. Evans-Pritchard did not, however, question whether the terms "magic" and "witchcraft" were appropriate translations of Azande terminology.[37] Within Islamic studies, the hiving off of "magic" from "religion" resulted in the long neglect of these traditions within the field.[38] Finally, scholars of Islam in Africa long considered "magic" to represent surviving elements of local African traditions, or, more recently, to reflect an unquestioning mimesis of textual-ritual traditions originating in North Africa or the Middle East. The colonial baggage that weighs down this term has led several scholars to argue for dropping the word altogether. Wouter J. Hanegraaff, for example, has likened "magic" to "a kind of wastebasket" filled with forms of knowledge and practices that do not fit easily into Enlightenment definitions of "religion" and "science."[39] Meanwhile, Randall Styers has accused scholars of magic of "culling diverse forms of behavior, modes of knowledge, social practices, and habits from an indiscriminate range of cultural systems and historical epochs and transmogrifying them into a unified phenomenon."[40]

Styers's argument accurately criticizes scholarship that unreflectively applies the label of "magic" to textual or ritual traditions without interrogating the relationship between their sources and the history of that particular term. However, work by scholars across various subfields has demonstrated that the word "magic" has its own history and that is it possible to isolate and identify the growth and spread of specific magic discourses through time, across geographical regions, and into and between different religious communities. Kimberly B. Stratton has demonstrated compellingly that the discourse of magic and witchcraft emerged within ancient Greek texts in the fourth century BC as a result of changing citizenship laws and wars with the Persians. Within these texts, depictions of magic users and witches served to highlight anxieties about sexually deviant women and threatening foreigners.[41] Bernd-Christian Otto has labeled this kind of magic discourse a "discourse of exclusion," which pejoratively marginalizes people associated with threatening practices. As a discourse of exclusion, accusations of magic practice position the accused beyond the bounds of a particular community and its construction of orthodoxy, morality, and/or rationality.[42] However, Otto has also pointed out that people have identified themselves as "magicians" and referred to their own practices as "magic" from almost the earliest uses of the term. Recently, Otto has argued compellingly that there might be a continuous, if constantly changing and heterogenous, textual-ritual tradition of "Western learned magic" from antiquity to the present.[43] Magic in this sense operates as a "discourse of inclusion," in which individuals and groups identify themselves as magic practitioners. Because the polysemous term "magic" resists definition, this book asserts that the operating question should be rephrased as "whose magic is it?" and that research into these textual-ritual traditions must begin by locating specific actors and thinkers within the larger history of this term.

Indeed, recent publications by scholars in Islamic studies have clarified the outline of the growth and spread of inclusive discourses of Islamicate magic in the early medieval period. This scholarship demonstrates that the Arabic term *siḥr* served the same discursive functions in the premodern Arabophone world that the term "magic" did in Greek and Latinate contexts. The first written texts of self-identified *siḥr*/magic practitioners were produced during the ninth and tenth centuries, even as theologians and Sufis were debating the existence and legitimacy of the charismata. These works included the letters of the enigmatic Brothers of Purity (Ikhwān al-Ṣafā') and the *Ghāyat al-hakīm* (The Goal of the Sage), attributed to Maslama ibn Qāsim al-Qurṭubī (d. 964).[44] Arabic-language works on astral magic synthesized Neoplatonic understandings of the relationship between individual souls and the "World Soul," Aristotelian ideas of causation, and a neo-Pythagorean mathematization of the cosmos.

By the twelfth and thirteenth centuries, Muslim scholars writing in Arabic were much less likely to describe their own works as *siḥr*, as discussions of that term shifted to a discourse of exclusion. However, this period also saw the elaboration of a "science of names and letters" by Sufi writers, who posited a lettrist cosmology by which the names of God, and the letters that made up those names, corresponded to both numbers and specific properties and components of the universe. Renowned Sufi philosophers such as Ibn al-ʿArabī discussed the sciences of names and letters and occasionally mentioned their thaumaturgic applications, particularly in the construction of talismans.[45] The articulation of both the theoretical and applied aspects of this science reached a decisive formulation in the works of Aḥmad al-Būnī (d. ca. 1232). The historical al-Būnī was a Sufi philosopher and teacher who developed esoteric reading circles in Cairo. His works focused on elaborating a Neoplatonic Sufi cosmology in which the names of God and letters serve as agents of creation and on the practical application of those names and letters to attain both divine mysteries and this-worldly benefits. Al-Būnī's reputation became associated almost entirely with the practical application of the sciences and resulted in the proliferation of textual forgeries and imitations attributed to him after his death. The most important of these, the *Shams al-maʿārif al-kubrā* (*The Suns of Knowledge: The Longer Version*), was produced in the seventeenth century and achieved widespread appeal across North Africa and the Middle East.[46] The *Shams al-maʿārif al-kubrā* and other pseudo-Būnian works eventually acquired a reputation as works of *siḥr*, and it was through the circulation of texts such as these that magic discourses became deeply associated with the realm of Sufism.

Scholars have also traced the transmission of Islamicate magic discourses into western Europe. Liana Saif in particular has demonstrated how the translation of Arabic texts on astral magic into Latin in the eleventh and twelfth centuries stimulated the growth of Western "occult philosophy" in the fifteenth and sixteenth centuries.[47] The occult philosophy of Renaissance magicians such as Marsilio Ficino, Giovanni Pico, and John Dee "present[ed] this 'natural magic' as part of one single, supreme tradition of *religious* wisdom derived from sages such as Zoroaster or Hermes Trismegistus."[48] This "occult philosophy" of the Renaissance then became the "wastebasket" of rejected magic and superstition of the Enlightenment. However, even as new categories of "science" and "religion" gained coherence in modern Europe, a countermovement that rejected the "philosophical rationalism and mechanical philosophy" of the Enlightenment resulted in the emergence of a new set of "esoteric" or "occult sciences."[49] This period saw a broad range of groups combine "a drive to recover a hidden God" with attempts to establish a scientific study of the spirit realm.[50] Unlike the occult sciences of the Renaissance, these movements drew on Enlightenment-era conceptions of a rational, scientific process, even as they attempted to reposition the spiritual within the scientific. From these western European developments, scholars such as Peter Pels have concluded that "magic *belongs* to the modern," because "modern discourses position[ed] magic as their antithesis, reinventing it in the process."[51] Bever and Styers have since described this process as a "double gesture," in which attempts to banish and delegitimize magic discourse only reinforce and reinscribe magic as an alternative "potent resource."[52] European and North American discussions of magic in the nineteenth and twentieth centuries clearly involved reconceptualizing magic discourses inherited from the past and repositioning them relative to forces such as industrialization, education, consumerism, and new media, among others. However, Bever and Styers's "double gesture" essentially describes a process by which elites attempt to claim authority over a sphere of legitimate knowledge while invalidating and marginalizing the textual-ritual traditions of various marginalized others. That basic process also describes the twin magic discourses of exclusion and inclusion described by Otto—the process of defining and categorizing a "rejected" body of knowledge and practice ironically opens up that sphere for powerful reinterpretation and reappropriation.

This book engages this recent scholarship by positioning the Kunta's distinction between the sciences of the unseen and sorcery at the intersection of magic discourses and the particular history of the eighteenth-century Sahara. The resulting picture is simultaneously Saharan and Islamic and yet connected to a longer transregional, multireligious tradition that began in ancient Greece and connects people across the world today. Specifically, this book argues that Sīdi al-Mukhtār's and Sīdi Muḥammad's defense of their sciences of the unseen responded to both Arabo-Islamic traditions of self-professed sorcery and social expectations that Sufi leaders should offer powerful practices that yield tangible results. The Kunta scholars responded to this textual-ritual landscape by offering a set of powerful practices—their sciences of the unseen—while rejecting their categorization as sorcery. In doing so, they participated in a magic discourse of exclusion, rejecting sorcery qua magic as illegitimate practice. Moreover, the Kunta's discussion of sorcery and the sciences of the unseen very much participates in the double gesture of disavowal and inscription. Sīdi Muḥammad in particular classified knowledge and practice in an attempt to delegitimize and disavow the knowledge and practices of racialized others living to the south. However, in the process, he simultaneously reinscribed and reinforced the theoretical and cosmological basis of knowledge that draws on the structure of the realm of the unseen and wove himself and the legacy of his family into the history of Islamic magic discourses. The salience of this argument depends, first, on its framing within a specific set of historical discourses about science and sorcery and, second, on its careful attention to the semantic meanings of terms within the Kunta's texts. For example, Sīdi Muḥammad explicitly defines sorcery as a manipulation of the normal order of the world, in contrast to the miracles of the prophets and the charismata of God's friends. Thus any understanding of *siḥr* as related to the "supernatural" or to "ideas and actions that alter the natural course of events"[53] reflects an inaccurate conflation of modern and historical epistemological categories.

Attention to the emic meanings of terms as they emerged from the Kunta's works also led me to avoid the labels of "the occult," "the occult sciences," and "the esoteric sciences" as translations for the Kunta's sciences of the unseen. Islamic studies scholars have applied the rubric "the occult sciences" on the basis of the apparent semantic overlap with the Arabic *ʿulūm al-gharība* (the strange sciences) or *ʿulūm al-kāfī* (the sciences of the hidden).[54] Neither of these terms appears in the works of Sīdi al-Mukhtār or Sīdi Muḥammad. The Arabic phrase used by the Kunta scholars—*ʿulūm al-ghayb*—does not suggest that the sciences themselves are hidden or obscured; rather, they are the sciences *of that which is hidden*. Moreover, while the terms "esoteric" and "occult" might accurately highlight a distinct sphere of knowledge and practice within some contexts, they do not provide useful heuristic distinctions when discussing precolonial West African history. Louis Brenner has argued compellingly that precolonial West African society was characterized by "an esoteric *episteme*" in which *all* Islamic knowledge required some degree of initiation. While the sciences discussed by the Kunta were imbued with a rhetoric of secrecy, they may not have been, in fact, less accessible to Saharan Muslims than training in the procedures of Islamic jurisprudence. Moreover, this esoteric and initiatory approach to Islamic knowledge developed out of a context in which all crafts were governed by a caste system composed of professional guilds, who guarded and handed down knowledge of leatherworking, weaving, blacksmithing, and epic storytelling (among other crafts).[55] In a context where the knowledge of how to tan a hide into leather was as closely guarded a secret as the practice of making amulets, the term "esoteric" offers little explanatory force. Ultimately, the terminological choices used by a particular author represent the goals and methodology of her study. This book is rooted in a methodology that begins by identifying the internal, emic terminology used by the Kunta so that those categories can then be usefully connected to recent scholarship on the history of magic discourses. With this goal in mind, I have decided to avoid the terms "esoteric" and "occult." These terms not only obscure the finer distinctions that the Kunta scholars made among the various sciences but also artificially separate them from other sets of knowledge and practice that bridge the visible and invisible worlds, particularly the use of ritual practices such as supplicatory prayer.

Texts and Textuality

The analysis in this book is based on a selection of Arabic texts attributed to Sīdi al-Mukhtār and Sīdi Muḥammad al-Kuntī that are themselves part of a vast Saharan manuscript legacy that has defied attempts to quantify.[56] Through examinations of the catalogues of more than a dozen manuscript libraries across West and North Africa, I identified several hundred separate titles of works attributed to Sīdi al-Mukhtār and another several hundred attributed to Sīdi Muḥammad al-Kuntī. These works cover almost the entire range of the classic Islamic disciplines, including commentaries on the Qur'ān and *ḥadīth* traditions, stories of the prophets, works on Arabic grammar, Islamic jurisprudence, and theology, and a sizeable and diverse body of works related to Sufism, including hagiographies, works defending the friends of God, descriptions of the Sufi path, treatments of the relationship between teachers and their students, and many others. Moreover, this book examines a set of devotional aids, a genre of Islamic textual production rarely examined in formal scholarship. Manuscript catalogues attribute dozens of these texts to Sīdi al-Mukhtār, and they include supplicatory prayers and poems in praise of the Prophet. Some of these texts stand on their own and are only one or two folios long, while others are collected in longer compendia.

These works represent a small segment of a precolonial West African manuscript tradition that remains understudied, even as new scholarship begins to pay attention to the written legacy of this region. Attention to the written form and features of these texts does not discount their oral aspects or the context of textual transmission in the region, in which written works were often memorized by students and "read" back to an instructor.[57] Indeed, the textual devotional aids in particular contain elements—including formulaic and rhythmic qualities, repetition, and the use of rhyming prose—that indicate that they were composed in a fashion intended to aid memorization and point to a context of oral performance and transmission. Memorization and oral performance can be used to transmit ideas and texts to a wide array of audiences, including those who might not be fully literate in written Arabic or have access to manuscript texts. These components of orality, inscribed into these written works, demonstrate what Ruth Finnegan has described as the "multi-modal" interconnectedness of written and oral forms of literature.[58] This study draws on a theory of textuality developed by Karin Barber that includes both oral and written production.[59] However, while in some cases practices of oral transmission have left traces in the manuscript record, much of the context and content surrounding the oral transmission and interpretation of these texts prior to the late nineteenth century has been lost. Accordingly, this study addresses the oral performative features of these texts when possible, but also depends on a methodology of reading written texts—including devotional aids—in historical contexts by carefully addressing their location relative to a body of intertexts.

Specifically, my approach to the vast Kunta manuscript corpus is based on a methodology developed by literary theorists and anthropologists who attempt to "read related texts together, to read across genres, and to read for discursive systems." Recently, Brinkley Messick has used the work of Bakhtin and other literary theorists to criticize "the tendency . . . to view texts in isolation, as individual 'monuments.'" Instead, Messick advances "a 'dialogic' conception [in which] individual writings could be understood as responding to and as anticipating responses from other texts."[60] This methodology begins by locating texts within an intertextual context composed of other works connected across the boundaries of genre. Specifically, this study focuses on discussions of the realm of the unseen and the bodies of knowledge and practice associated with that realm across different genres and registers of texts aimed at different audiences. Such a reading presumes that claims to authoritative knowledge and effective action are based on deeper epistemological frameworks, and that these in turn are rarely contained or concisely laid out in one work or even one genre.

A small number of works by Sīdi al-Mukhtār and Sīdi Muḥammad have been published, including the aforementioned *Risāla al-ghallāwiyya* and *Ṭarāʾif waʾl-talāʾid*. With the exception of these two texts and one collection of supplicatory prayers, all the other works by Sīdi al-Mukhtār and Sīdi Muḥammad referenced in this study exist only in manuscript form. The research in this book references manuscripts held by the Bibliothèque des manuscrits de Djenne in Mali; the Cheik Zani Baye Library, also in Mali;[61] the Bibliothèque nationale du royaume du Maroc in Rabat; the Royal Library, or al-Maktaba al-Ḥasaniyya, in Rabat; the library of the Great Mosque in Meknes; and the Bibliothèque nationale de France in Paris, which holds the contents of the former library of Segou,[62] while the archives of the University of Illinois at Urbana-Champaign provided reproductions of their microfilm copy of the Boutilimit Collection, from Mauritania.[63] I accessed and obtained reproductions of these texts during nine months of research in Mali, Morocco, and France in 2012.

At the most elite register, this project draws on two long treatises by Sīdi al-Mukhtār aimed at other highly educated elite Muslim scholars: the *Kitāb al-minna fī ʿitiqād ahl al-sunna* (The Book of Grace Concerning the Belief of the People of the Sunna),[64] a long theological treatise dedicated to the concept of declaring the unity of God (*tawḥīd*) that demonstrates Sīdi al-Mukhtār's understanding of the relationship of God to his creation; and the *Sharḥ al-qaṣīda al-fayḍiyya* (The Explanation of the Overflowing Poem),[65] a line-by-line commentary on one of Sīdi al-Mukhtār's own poems.[66] The commentary does not explain the literal meanings of the words or lines, but rather uses them as evocative headings for lengthy discussions of the Sufi path to God, the degrees of love for God, and the heart of the believer. In their absence of local referents, the complexity and richness of their classical Arabic prose, their adherence to genre conventions, and their length, these long treatises can be considered "cosmopolitan texts." Sheldon Pollock defined a cosmopolitan text as one that "thinks of itself as unbounded, unobstructed, unallocated," and Brinkley Messick has recently expanded on this definition by focusing on the transportability of these texts, which, "by means of their distinctive discursive horizons . . . thought beyond any local frame."[67]

In contrast to these "generalizing" texts, the Kunta scholars also produced works related to the unseen directed at a more localized, although still elite, audience. These include the *Risāla al-ghallāwiyya* and the *Ṭarāʾif wa'l-talāʾid* by Sīdi Muḥammad, both of which assert and defend the authority of the Kunta family lineage within a Saharan context. No complete copies of the *Ṭarāʾif wa'l-talāʾid* have been found—the longest extant witnesses stop midway through chapter 5—suggesting that the work may never have been completed and thus may have been composed toward the end of Sīdi Muḥammad's life. While the *Ṭarāʾif wa'l-talāʾid* contains bio-hagiographical content throughout, certain chapters more closely resemble other genres of Islamic literature and could be read as self-contained treatises on specific topics. For example, the long introduction could stand alone as a treatise on the defense of God's friends, while chapter 3 discusses the various types of human knowledge, with a specific focus on the sciences of the unseen. Both of these works explicitly name, and respond to, other regional leaders and scholars. Sīdi al-Mukhtār's *Jidhwat al-anwār fī dhabb ʿan munāṣib awlīyāʾ allāh al-khiyār* (The Torch of Lights in Defending the Offices of the Friends of God, the Best of [Men]) directs itself at a similarly local audience.[68] The work itself is a long defense of the friends of God, and in the preface Sīdi al-Mukhtār claims that he composed this text in response to another regional scholar, Mukhtār ibn al-Būnā al-Jakānī, who supposedly pronounced anybody convinced by the words of the *awliyāʾ* to be an unbeliever.[69]

This book draws on two other works in this category, Sīdi al-Mukhtār's *Kitāb zawāl al-ilbās wa ṭard wasāwas al-khannās* (The Book of Dispelling Confusion and Banishing the Whispering of the Slinking One),[70] and Sīdi Muḥammad's *Fawāʾid nūrāniyya wa farāʾid sirriyya raḥmāniyya* (Illuminated Benefits and Secret Pearls of the Compassionate).[71] The *Kitāb zawāl al-ilbās* begins with the idea that God sent down the last two suras of the Qurʾān, Sūra al-Falaq and Sūra al-Nās, specifically as refuges against sorcery (*siḥr*) and evil whisperings. It then argues that both the prophets and the friends of God are protected (*maʿṣūm*) from these whisperings, before enumerating all the different ways that Satan can deceive and lead Muslims astray. Finally, the work concludes by describing those who perfect their devotions to God and discussing the importance of formal ritual prayer (*ṣalāt*). Meanwhile, as described above, the *Fawāʾid nūrāniyya* details specific instructions for using the greatest name of God to make the cosmos submit to the will of the supplicant. Additionally, this work includes a lengthy introduction explaining the relationship between the names of God and cosmology, defending the practice of using the greatest name of God, providing a sacred history for the sciences of letters and names, explaining the theory behind those sciences, and illustrating specific uses for each letter of the greatest name, such as defeating one's enemies or healing the sick. Although the *Kitāb zawāl al-ilbās* and the *Fawāʾid nūrāniyya* do not inscribe the names of Saharan figures, their shorter length and narrow focus position them within a more localized set of concerns than more expansive treatises such as the *Kitāb al-minna*.

Finally, this book examines a selection of devotional aids attributed to Sīdi al-Mukhtār. Several of the freestanding supplicatory prayers consulted here are named *ḥizb*, including *Ḥizb sīdī al-mukhtār al-kuntī* (The Prayer of Sīdi al-Mukhtār),[72] *Ḥizb al-nūr* (The Prayer of Light),[73] and *Ḥizb al-isrāʾ* (The Prayer of the Night Journey).[74] One of the most copied devotional texts attributed to Sīdi al-Mukhtār was the *Nafḥat al-ṭīb fī'l-salāt ʿalā'l-nabī al-ḥabīb* (Sweet Breath Concerning Prayer for the Beloved Prophet), a collection of prayers to the Prophet.[75] Unlike the other genres of texts used in this study, these devotional aids contain no explanatory material. On their own, detached from a narrative, ideological superstructure, they resist interpretation. Who used these texts, and under what conditions? Were they read and recited aloud or silently, on their own or in combination with other practices? Unlike anthropologists, historians cannot ask people what meanings texts held for them, or what uses they put them to, and this study is based on the theoretical position that it is not possible to draw observations from the present back into the past. Rather, evidence about the past needs to be independently confirmed in order to demonstrate continuities and ruptures with the present. Instead of attempting to use the practices of contemporary communities to make inferences about the meanings of Kunta devotional materials, I propose an alternative method for examining devotional texts in historical contexts. Specifically, this book connects these texts to other works by the same authors, and to other examples of the genres by other authors to reveal how elite Muslim scholars both attempted to shape and were shaped by the devotional landscape of the Sahara.

When reading these texts, I draw on the conceptual ground laid out by Talal Asad, who focused on the relationship between the religious meanings produced in any given present and the historical conditions of their production. In an essay originally published in 1986, Asad famously defined Islam "as a discursive tradition that connects variously with the formation of moral selves, the manipulation of populations (or resistance to it) and the production of appropriate knowledges."[76] Asad understood this discursive tradition as the process, at every historical moment, in which individuals and groups interpreted, selected, and rejected practices from the reservoirs of the past, and he sought in particular to call attention to the institutional power structures that informed these choices. This book follows in Asad's path by examining the institutional forces at work in the Kunta's production of the sciences of secrets as a form of social knowledge, and it understands those sciences both as part of the discursive tradition of Islam and as part of the production of orthodoxy in the Sahara. For when Sīdi al-Mukhtār and Sīdi Muḥammad, as Saharan elites, sought "to regulate, uphold, require, or adjust *correct* practices, and to condemn, exclude, undermine, or replace *incorrect* ones," they established the "relationship of power to truth" that constitutes orthodoxy.[77]

Approach and Position

It has become standard practice in works of anthropology to outline how the position of an author affects a particular study; however, reflections of this kind in historical scholarship are still rare. Anthropologists who include these reflections do so in response to the contributions of scholars working within the discipline of postcolonial studies, who have dismantled the idea of a value-neutral or "objective" observational position and pointed out that decisions made by scholars about what methods to use, what questions to pose, and what to publish are enmeshed in ethical considerations. The choices made throughout this book, particularly concerning the methodology I used to interrogate the textual base for this study and the decision to publish the litanies, prayers, magic squares, and names of God referenced in these texts, reflect the unique combination of my academic training, personal interests, and social position. Other scholars might make, and have made, different choices when dealing with similar materials. But another insight from postcolonial studies has been to highlight the value of including within the academy works that represent views formed by different social locations.

In order to research this book, and for various academic and professional engagements over the past fifteen years, I traveled to Mali and Morocco (in 2010 and 2012) and Senegal (in 2016). While the bulk of my research time in West Africa was spent in manuscript libraries, my travels included extended stays with host families and friends, discussions with students engaged in religious training, archivists, librarians, Qur'ān teachers, and people I met on public transport, in cafés, and in airport lounges as well as scholars in local universities. In all three countries, and also during extended Arabic language training in Jordan and Syria, I met members of transnational Sufi orders and their students. When I was able to visit Timbuktu in 2010, I spoke to several contemporary practitioners of "the sciences of the unseen," who today both identify themselves, and are identified by others, using the French term "marabout," which has now come into English as well.[78] I spoke with friends in Bamako and Timbuktu about their own visits to marabouts. After my first visit of several weeks to Timbuktu, my research plan for 2012 was to return to the city for an extended period of six months. The beginning of the conflict in northern Mali in 2011 made this plan untenable, and although I was able to spend several weeks in Djenne, conditions of warfare and violence have made it impossible for me to return to northern Mali or to consider entering the desert. In 2016, during a faculty development seminar in Senegal sponsored by the Council on International Educational Exchange, I had the pleasure of meeting with a contemporary descendant and student of the Kunta scholars in the town of Ndiassane. But I did not deliberately seek out the current representatives of this community in Senegal or southern Morocco as part of my research, and my analysis in this book does not draw on discussions with contemporary West African Muslims or my observations of current practices.

I had multiple reasons for this decision. First, my academic training cautions me strongly against reading the interpretations of contemporary communities back into the distant past. Perceptions of Muslim orthodoxy and heterodoxy, both in West Africa and around the world, have changed greatly over the past two hundred years and have been influenced by global trends, including increasing travel, migration, and study abroad, the rise of the Salafi movement, and the growing prominence of transnational Sufi networks. Indeed, contemporary Kunta students are understood today as members of an organized Sufi order, which represents a shift from late eighteenth-century understandings of Sufism in West Africa (see chapter 1). Second, contemporary shaykhs in the Kunta lineage—those who have been authorized to transmit Kunta texts, have their own private manuscript collections, and who teach and train students—represent a very specific set of authoritative social positions. Reading historical documents according to the interpretations of contemporary Kunta leaders thus risks inscribing the current positions of a particular group with social and institutional authority back into the past. Interviews with the contemporary readers and transmitters of these texts would be invaluable for determining the reception history of the works composed by Sīdi al-Mukhtār and Sīdi Muḥammad, for tracing the development of the sciences of the unseen and Sufi identities over the past century, and for examining the ongoing impact of this community in West Africa. I certainly hope that future research will pursue these lines of inquiry.

My methodological decision not to interview contemporary followers of Sīdi al-Mukhtār al-Kuntī stemmed primarily from my theoretical position on the usefulness of such sources in answering the questions posed in this study. But I also found throughout my travels that networks of Muslim and Sufi religious learning were largely unavailable to me as a non-Muslim woman. This applied mostly to contact with local scholars who held authority within the historical textual tradition. In contrast, discussions with Malian marabouts and their clients were often effortless. Many people were eager to connect me with their marabout or one they knew, and the marabouts with whom I spoke often surprised me in their openness. They willingly discussed their training and the training of their students, and the types of practices they used. My discussions with Malian friends and marabouts impressed on me the degree to which the practices discussed in this study are contested in West Africa today. The marabouts whom I met invested these disciplines with highly varying degrees of secrecy, and while some of these practitioners were connected to Sufi orders, others were not. Moreover, there is evidence that the perceived heterodoxy or orthodoxy of these practices has changed greatly since the late eighteenth century. Members of transnational Sufi orders must maintain their reputations and the respectability of their organizations on a global stage, where criticisms and rejections of magic squares and amulets often predominate, even as these practices continue to attract widespread popularity in local contexts from Indonesia to India to Senegal.

It is not my place to intervene in these debates or to uphold the perspective of one group of West African Muslims over another. Accordingly, I have been willing to publish anything that Sīdi al-Mukhtār and Sīdi Muḥammad felt comfortable committing to writing, including the magic squares, litanies, and names of God that are found in their works. This decision reflects the goals, the intellectual stakes, and the primary audience of this study. This book aims to add a history of a West African Muslim community to discussions within the fields of Islamic studies and religious studies, where scholarship in precolonial African contexts remains rare. I also hope that illuminating the trajectory of magic discourses in this Islamic African context will destabilize some of the assumptions concerning the uniqueness of the western European experience of contesting the boundaries of legitimate knowledge and practice. Sharing the details of the Kunta's understanding of sorcery and the sciences of the unseen allows for collaborative work toward these goals while opening new possibilities for understanding the location of West African Muslims within local, regional, and transregional debates over acceptable practice. However, while these have been my choices, I recognize and respect the work of scholars whose theoretical and methodological choices differ from my own, and I acknowledge the benefit gained from the multiple positions and perspectives highlighted by our collective research.

Outline of the Book

This book demonstrates that Sīdi al-Mukhtār and Sīdi Muḥammad al-Kuntī understood human life as governed by the interactions between the visible and invisible worlds. Chapter 1 thus begins with the visible world by situating the Kunta scholars within the sociohistorical context of the Sahara Desert at the turn of the nineteenth century. The first section of this chapter connects primary sources by the Kunta scholars to the rich scholarship regarding the social, cultural, and economic history of the region to demonstrate how the Kunta's new model of authority, based on Sufi friendship with God, responded to the changing sociopolitical context of the region. The chapter then presents a revisionist account of the role and influence of Sufism on the organization and intellectual foundations of the Kunta family and updated biographies of Sīdi al-Mukhtār and Sīdi Muḥammad.

The Kunta scholars understood the visible world of the senses as only one component of created existence. In the hagiographies, the other, unseen parts of the world are always breaking through into the human realm in the form of marvelous events that occur in the vicinity of the friends of God. In various stories, a needed water flask breaks, only to suddenly reappear intact. A friendly campsite appears where none was expected. Bandits and tyrants unexpectedly surrender to the authority of a Sufi shaykh. In all of these stories, an apparently dire situation resolves into unexpected salvation because of the presence of a Kunta family member. And while these unexpected reversals affect the social realm, the Kunta texts locate their source beyond the social, human world, in a vast invisible realm that surrounds and permeates perceptible reality—the subject of chapter 2. The realm of the unseen presented in the Kunta texts is composed of an afterlife, various cosmological realms, unseen entities, and invisible components of the human body. According to Sīdi al-Mukhtār and Sīdi Muḥammad, all believing Muslims experience the realm of the unseen to some degree, but certain elite individuals succeed in traveling through the various layers of this realm back to the divine presence at its source. In the Kunta texts, the physical body assumes a central role in this process, for only a heart and body perfected through devotional practice will reach this ultimate goal. Moreover, when the elect friends of God reach the end of this path and are annihilated in knowledge of the divine, their perfected bodies are then re-created as the source of all existence. As a result, the friends of God assume a position of ultimate cosmological importance in the Kunta texts, simultaneously allowing creation to proceed from the unseen into the manifest realms and offering a pathway for believing Muslims to return to God.

The Kunta's understanding of the "realm of the unseen" provides the epistemological framework for a group of practices that they refer to as the "sciences of the unseen" (*ʿulūm al-ghayb*) or the "sciences of secrets" (*ʿulūm al-asrār*). Chapter 3 examines these "sciences," which include the crafting of amulets, communicating with the jinn, and reciting various types of litanies for healing and protection. As this chapter demonstrates, the Kunta scholars acknowledged that other (unnamed) Muslim scholars might reject these practices as acts of sorcery (*siḥr*); however, they explicitly reject this label and argue strenuously for the categorization of these acts as legitimate devotional practices. Moreover, their texts provide explicit instructions for how to perform these actions to accomplish specific goals. This chapter situates the debate over the classification of knowledge and practice as sorcery or science within a longer history of the development of magic discourses in the region. Specifically, I demonstrate that the Kunta participated actively in a magic "discourse of exclusion," as they rejected sorcery as illegitimate practice. Nevertheless, the Kunta texts also demonstrate an awareness of works that embrace the category of *siḥr* as a positive designation. Their categorization of the sciences of the unseen thus reflects the presence of a magic "discourse of inclusion" in the region. In reaction to this discourse of inclusion, Sīdi Muḥammad argues that his "sciences" are *just as effective* as acts of sorcery, but also categorically distinct in their legitimacy and legality.

When the Kunta scholars argue for the legitimacy of the sciences of the unseen, they do so by associating them with devotional practices, particularly supplicatory prayer (*duʿāʾ*). In chapter 4, I take this association seriously and engage with the Kunta's understanding of supplicatory prayer as another method of connecting the realm of the unseen to the material and human world. Moreover, this chapter investigates the relationship between the elite intellectual frameworks developed by the Kunta scholars and the larger social body of their followers by examining the short nonnarrative devotional aids attributed to Sīdi al-Mukhtār. First, the chapter situates these works against other works by the same authors to show how the Kunta used these texts to encode their complex teachings for oral transmission. Next, I compare these works to other devotional aids that were becoming increasingly popular during this period. This reading shows how the Kunta adapted their works in response to the increasing popularity of textual devotional aids. Ultimately, this chapter argues that both of these readings are equally correct and equally necessary—practice shapes ideology even as ideology shapes practice. Whether read in one direction or another, these texts reveal that both the Kunta specifically and Saharan Muslims generally understood Arabic texts as a fundamental component of efficacious religious practice. For eighteenth-century Saharan Muslims, prayer was based in, and driven by, textuality.

This final point returns us to the social landscape addressed in chapter 1. But whereas the first chapter dealt with the social world of the Sahara as it emerges from both historical scholarship and Kunta hagiographies, the end of chapter 4 reveals the connection between that idealized representation of Saharan society and the larger Kunta project of consolidating their authority as Sufi friends of God. The chapters of this book thus reveal different ways that the Kunta leaders argued for the authority of God's friends: as teachers of students and transmitters of devotional prayers, as the cosmological underpinnings of the invisible and manifest realms, and as the source of the only legitimate practices with tangible and predictable outcomes. Finally, in returning to the material remnants of historical Muslim practices, I argue that the Kunta directed these arguments for their authority as friends of God toward a greater landscape of devotional religious practice. Ultimately, the discursive works produced by Sīdi al-Mukhtār and Sīdi Muḥammad acquire their meaning only in reference to a larger discussion about practice in the region, but this larger discussion becomes legible only when situated against the larger conceptual context embedded in the textual production of these scholars.

1

THE VISIBLE WORLD

Sīdi al-Mukhtār and Sīdi Muḥammad al-Kuntī lived, wrote, and taught in the western part of the Sahara Desert at the end of the eighteenth century and the beginning of the nineteenth. This period in Saharan history occurred between the fall of the Songhay Empire and the onset of European colonization and saw the rise and development of many of the social and cultural institutions that continue to characterize desert life. While the desert was long considered a mostly empty space whose significance lay in connecting its southern and northern "shores," a new field of Saharan studies has focused on illuminating the desert as a place in its own right. This new focus on Saharan society and history has yielded a much richer picture of historical desert life and permits a reassessment of the received history of the Kunta family itself. A reassessment is needed, as scholarship on the Kunta family in the western Sahara has reproduced a standard narrative that has remained unrevised and uncontested for more than four decades. This chapter provides a revisionist account of the first two generations of the Kunta scholars that fully situates them within the context of the western Sahara Desert.

This chapter begins with the physical environment of the Sahara, which comprises both material and human elements and the interactions between the two. The human ecology and culture of the desert served as both the arena and the foundation for different organizations of power in the region. The emergence of the Kunta family signaled the development of a new model of religious and political authority in the region, one based, in theory, on voluntary submission to a teacher whose moral and spiritual superiority placed him in greater proximity to God. In Arabic, these individuals were known as "the friends of God" (*awliyā'*). Devotion to the friends of God emerged as part of the cultural stream within Islam known as Sufism, and both Sīdi al-Mukhtār and Sīdi Muḥammad al-Kuntī composed texts that positioned them squarely within the Sufi tradition. This chapter treats Sufism within the context of the development of Islamic institutions in the desert, particularly law and learning. The rise of the Kunta scholars occurred as part of the growth and increasing influence of Sufi teaching lineages across the desert and marked a pivotal shift in regional understandings of the nature and role of the Sufi friends of God. However, this chapter rejects previous descriptions of Sīdi al-Mukhtār as either the "pole" (*quṭb*) or "head" (*khalīfa*) of the Qādiriyya Sufi order in West Africa. These descriptions represent an anachronistic use of terms that developed later in the nineteenth and twentieth centuries. Rather, Sīdi al-Mukhtār and Sīdi Muḥammad understood themselves as following a spiritual path, or "way" (*ṭarīqa*), that included the recitation of devotional prayers (*awrād*) handed down from their predecessors, and specifically from the twelfth-century Sufi ʿAbd al-Qādir al-Jīlānī. Finally, I present the biographies of Sīdi al-Mukhtār and Sīdi Muḥammad as they emerge from the available sources.

Ecology and Economy

The hagiographies and family chronicles composed by Sīdi Muḥammad locate his father's life and his family's activities within the desert region known as the Azawād, now located in northern Mali. Including the salt mines of Taghāzā and Tawdennī in the north, the town of Arawān marks a rough center of the region, the city of Timbuktu anchors the southern boundary, and the mountains of the Adrār-n-Īfōghās (the "Malian Adrār") define the eastern edge. However, while these landmarks constitute the formal designations of the Azawād, the territory imagined by Sīdi Muḥammad extends farther, reaching into the oases of the Algerian Tuwāt and the Tidikelt to the north, the Ahaggar Mountains and the Aïr Massif to the east, and the "Mauritanian" Hodh (with the important trading town of Walāta) and "Mauritanian Adrār" (including the town of Wādān) to the west. Connections to these western territories, and control over the salt mine at Ijjil, linked the Kunta family to the political and cultural sphere of the Mauritanian emirates, including the Trārza and Brakna in the Mauritanian Gebla, and entered them into economic and political relationships with Morocco. Meanwhile, their connections to Timbuktu and the peoples of the Aïr Massif enmeshed them in webs of economic, social, and political relationships with the desert-edge and savanna peoples of the Niger River Valley.

This complex web of relationships that connected the Azawād of the Kunta to peoples throughout, above, and below the desert, has become the focus of new lines of inquiry into desert life, history, and society. Critics have argued that earlier approaches to the Sahara treated the desert as either an obstacle to be surmounted or a bridge connecting the spaces on either side, rather than a dynamic space in which contemporary and historical people lived, worked, and moved. These scholars have called for a new approach that examines the Sahara from the inside out and that seeks out the "historically deep and enduringly vigorous aspects of life in the region which arguably not only connect, but *create* the various, complementary, and interdependent spaces of northwest Africa."[1] This approach recasts the empty space of the desert as a vibrant place of densely overlapping networks that link microregions of highly specialized production in complex and flexible but enduring patterns of interdependence.[2] Historians, anthropologists, and sociologists are productively framing the desert as a place that both shapes and is shaped by the people who live there in patterns that join the ideological articulation of authority to the production, control, and movement of physical and human resources.[3] Following this approach, the Azawād of the seventeenth and eighteenth centuries emerges as a place very much at the center of desert life, at once rooted in a specific geographical location, with an associated physical and human ecology, and connected via a regional web of economic, cultural, social, and political ties to other Saharan communities.

As part of the desert proper, life in the precolonial Azawād was tied to specific environmental features that provided sharp limits on population growth and forced Saharans into webs of commercial interdependence with communities across the region. The environment of the greater region of northwestern Africa is characterized by narrow ecological zones that run horizontally across the continent from the Atlantic Ocean to Lake Chad. The northern regions receive progressively less rain than the southern latitudes, generating ecological "strips" of desert, desert edge (Sahel), savanna grasslands, and forest lands.[4] Within the desert proper, most pasturelands allow only for the herding of camels. As pasture increases along the Sahel, pastoralists prefer to herd cattle, which require watering every day and can thus browse at most half a day from a water source. However, in the savanna lands, the higher humidity allows for the survival of the tsetse fly, which carries trypanosomiasis, or sleeping sickness, an illness that leads to the deaths of large mammals such as camels, cattle, and horses. Below the northern limit of the tsetse, transhumanant pastoralism becomes less productive and settled agriculture dominates. This line of aridity demarcating the range of the tsetse fly has thus proved crucial in the history of the region. As aridity increases and the desert moves south, the range of this fly also decreases, allowing both cattle herders and horse-mounted warriors to expand their range.[5]

Despite low desert rainfall, mountainous regions, such as the Mauritanian and Malian Adrār, the Ahaggar Mountains, and the Aïr Massif, along with the large basin of the Hodh, accumulate and retain water over the course of the year. For desert populations like the Kunta community, these areas produce prized pastureland, which can support goats and sheep in addition to camels and even seasonal cereal crops.[6] Moreover, digging deep enough in desert soil eventually produces water, and throughout the precolonial period and into the present, Saharan peoples have invested the time, capital, and "constantly renewed labor" needed to create and maintain wells and irrigation systems.[7] Oasis agriculture depends on the production of long underground canals called *fagāgīr*, which begin to silt up as soon as they are constructed and which continually drain the water table. In addition to a large initial capital investment, *fagāgīr* require constant maintenance and extension to continue functioning. As Judith Scheele has pointed out, the large oases, including Tuwāt, Agadez, and Ghadames, were not a given; rather, each represented a collective and enduring human investment.[8]

Oases and towns supported by wells and date palm groves provided bases of support, safe areas in which to store supplies, and schools for religious communities such as the Kunta. Once created and maintained, wells and canals allowed for the cultivation of date palms, and the presence of defendable towns provided areas of safe storage for nomadic and transhumanant peoples. Although in some years the date palm oases could yield significant surpluses for export, in other years harvests barely sustained the resident population, and in others were utterly insufficient. Characterized by an economy of extreme scarcity, the desert was never capable of reliably feeding its inhabitants. Saharan peoples thus depended on imports of cereals in addition to the manufactured goods needed for material culture, including cotton cloth, durable wooden tent poles, calabash bowls, and forged metal products. Saharan traders paid for these commodities primarily in salt, the desert's most valuable commodity, for export to the savanna lands to the south.[9]

Salt, livestock, and trans-Saharan commerce formed the cornerstone of the Kunta's wealth. According to the Kunta's own accounts, Sīdi al-Mukhtār managed some of his camel herds himself and located others with tributary clients identified as the Ladīm, the Mashzūf, and the Ibd'l-Kel. The pack camels raised in these herds were put to work in caravans that moved between Tuwāt and Timbuktu, while riding camels were sold and exchanged for cattle, grain (millet and rice), honey, butter, tobacco, and gold. While Sīdi al-Mukhtār sanctioned the trade in slaves and owned slaves whom he received as gifts, he does not appear to have participated directly in the slave trade.[10] The major salt mines in the region in the eighteenth century were at Taghāzā, Tawdennī, and

Ijjil. At Taghāzā and Tawdennī, the Qā'id Aḥmad al-Ḥayūnī, and then his son, 'Abd al-Mālik, served as deputies of the Moroccan sultan Mawlāy Muḥammad ibn 'Abd Allāh (r. 1757–90). During this period, others could extract salt from the mine if they paid a fee of 10 to 25 percent of the value of the mined salt to the Moroccan deputy. The deputies also sold salt directly to customers, including Sīdi al-Mukhtār. Ann McDougall's research indicates that the Kunta family gained control of salt production at the Ijjil mine in the third quarter of the eighteenth century.[11] In addition to salt, by at least the early nineteenth century, the trade in tobacco had become an essential part of the Kunta's wealth. Tobacco became so crucial to the fortunes of the Kunta family that when the caliph of Macina, Aḥmad Lobbo, forbade and disrupted the tobacco trade in the Middle Niger Valley, Sīdi Muḥammad found his economic interests in the region threatened, leading to a rift between the two leaders.[12]

The entanglement of Kunta and Moroccan interests in the Saharan salt mines and the dependence of Saharan and Sahelian peoples on the salt and cereal trade indicate the involvement of the Kunta in wider patterns of regional economic connectivity. Scheele's analysis of legal registers from southern Algeria reveals that Saharan residents from across the region maintained astonishingly diverse and far-flung investments. Owners and investors in water rights, date palms, homes, and gardens in southern Algerian oases might live in southern Morocco, the Ahaggar Mountains, or Aïr. Meanwhile, residents of these oases often borrowed against or leased out usufruct rights to their properties to generate capital, which they then reinvested across the region, buying herds pastured in the Sahel, investing in savanna harvests, and acquiring interregional trading goods such as tobacco and cotton cloth. By the late nineteenth century, the webs of debt within the Algerian oases were so great that one moneylender suggested to the French that they could acquire the region peacefully by simply buying all the debt owned by local landlords. Scheele emphasizes that these networks of debt, investment, and exchange were based on relationships between families connected by marriage, clients bound to patrons, and students attached to religious teachers. Although driven in part by an "economy of scarcity," these networks were never determined by ecological or economic considerations alone, but rather reflected generations of human investment in the material and interpersonal landscape.[13]

Moreover, although fluid and flexible, these networks of exchange depended on relationships of social and economic inequality best indicated by the substantial dependence of the precolonial economy on slave and servile labor.[14] Excellent research has demonstrated how precolonial Saharan peoples came to articulate the relationship between language, economic role, and social status in the vocabulary of race and ethnicity. Many of these patterns reflect long-term gradual changes in the human geography of the region. Throughout the sixteenth and seventeenth centuries, the Sahara and Sahel experienced "a realignment of language, cultural practice, and genealogy,"[15] in which formerly Berber-speaking populations adopted an Arabic dialect called Ḥassāniyya and sought to tie themselves, genealogically, to the Prophet Muḥammad. This process developed unevenly across the region, with Ḥassāniyya coming to predominate in the western part of the region and Berber-speaking peoples in the east. Eventually, peoples who continued to speak the Berber language of Tamasheq became known by the ethnic name "Tuareg." These cultural and linguistic changes occurred simultaneously with a shift in the regional balance of power. In the fifteenth and early sixteenth centuries, powerful Sahelian and savanna-based empires, including Songhay and Bornu, extended their authority deep into the Sahara and over desert-based pasturalists. But the 1591 Moroccan invasion of Timbuktu marked a turning point, after which nomadic pastoralists, whether Ḥassāniyya speakers or Tuareg, increasingly came to dominate agricultural communities of the desert edge and savanna who spoke a variety of languages, including Wolof, Soninke, Pulaar, and Hausa.[16] By the seventeenth century, Ḥassāniyya-speaking and Tuareg pastoralists identified themselves as "white" (*biḍān*) in contrast to the "black" (*sūdān*) agriculturalists living to the south. James Webb has argued that a long-term trend of regional desiccation beginning in the late sixteenth or early seventeenth century led to the increasing dominance of camel nomads and pastoralists over agriculturalists, as the descending desert frontier gave the former added advantages in terms of mobility and military force. The increasing ability of pastoral populations to raid, pillage, and enslave settled communities then drove the development of racialized identities that posited white pastoralists as superior to black agriculturalists.[17]

Bruce Hall's research on the history of racial ideologies in the region largely confirms Webb's thesis, while highlighting the ideological tools used to create and maintain the superiority of white identities.[18] These tools also developed gradually, beginning in the seventeenth century with the production of family genealogies and local chronicles. Both of these textual genres were produced by white-identifying Muslim scholars who crafted "improved" genealogies for their families that granted them sharifian status as descendants of the Prophet Muḥammad.[19] Meanwhile, scholars also produced histories that served as "social charters," articulating "a set of idealized relationships" between various white and black desert groups.[20] These narratives provided a set of historical rationales for the dominance of pastoralists over subservient black agriculturalists, while legal opinions increasingly associated blackness with non-Muslim status and thus with permanent enslaveability. The chronicles also rationalized the divisions within white society that classified lineages as either "warrior" (Arabic: *ḥassān*, Berber: *imajaghen*) or "clerical" (Arabic: *zwāya*; Berber: *ineselman*) in status. The most widely analyzed of these charters was produced in the Gebla (now in Mauritania) in the eighteenth century by a scholar named Muḥammad ibn al-Mukhtār al-Yadālī al-Daymānī (d. 1753). His chronicle recounts the events of the seventeenth-century conflict known as Shurr Bubba, in which a messianic religious leader called Nāṣir al-Dīn rallied (mostly Berber-speaking) factions and launched a war against, first, the Senegambian states to the south, and then later against rival lineages in the desert. Al-Yadālī focuses mostly on this latter part of the conflict and casts Nāṣir al-Dīn's defeat and the subsequent relinquishing of political and military power by his allies as the origin of the warrior/clerical divide in the western Sahara.[21]

Shurr Bubba was a historical conflict recorded by both Arabic chroniclers and French observers in St. Louis and likely developed from centuries-long processes of local migration coupled with long-term changes in linguistic, cultural, and religious patterns.[22] However, scholarship has emphasized the ideological purposes served by the narrativization of the conflict by eighteenth- and nineteenth-century chroniclers. These chronicles portray a hierarchical desert culture organized as a pyramid, with nobles, both warrior and clerical, at the top and slaves (Ḥassāniyya: *ʿabīd*; Tamasheq: *iklan*) at the bottom. Freed slaves (*ḥaratīn*; *irewelen*) were often settled in agricultural villages, where they paid a part of each harvest to their original owners. Meanwhile, nobles could lose status, through either military defeat or loss of their herds, and become vassals (*znaga*; *irewelen*) by entering into a tributary relationship with another noble group. Nobles often placed supplemental livestock in the care of pastoral vassals, who gained the use (in exchange for an annual fee) of the herds but had to surrender them in times of scarcity. The rationale for these social classes in historical chronicles masked the fluidity of these social categories. As Lovejoy and Baier have demonstrated, in times of plenty, agriculturalists along the desert edge could acquire livestock from nobles and "become" Tuareg, while pastoral groups with vassal status could save capital and ultimately invest as nobles by acquiring herds, cereal stocks, and trading goods of their own. Meanwhile, in times of scarcity, the desert economy contracted, and nobles appropriated their herds from pastoral vassals, who often fled south and settled in villages as farmers. Each of these shifts in economic "niche" was accompanied by a corresponding shift in ethnic and racial identification, and at the higher levels these shifts were rationalized or justified by the production of new genealogies or new histories.[23] Thus, while changing ecological conditions necessitated human adaptation, economic change took place according to patterns laid out by processes of cultural production.

The rise to prominence of Sīdi al-Mukhtār al-Kuntī and his family in the late eighteenth century both reflected and helped determine these long-term patterns of economic and cultural development across the desert. The family chronicles produced by Sīdi Muḥammad reflect the integration of the family's economic role as nobles who managed an intraregional trading network and owned herds pastured either by themselves or by tributaries. Meanwhile, the Kunta scholars justified their family's elite economic and ethnic status through the production of multiple genealogies that tied their family to the tribe of the Prophet Muḥammad and to notable Muslim scholars in the region. The absence of these genealogies in the biographical works of other regional scholars suggests that they were produced at the turn of the nineteenth century, as the family gained economic status. These genealogies, along with historical chronicles that documented the migration of the family into the region and their dominance over other groups, then served as ideological tools that Sīdi al-Mukhtār and Sīdi Muḥammad employed in disputes over authority with other regional groups. These social and political maneuvers took place amid reconfigurations of political power and authority in the region during the seventeenth and eighteenth centuries.

Political Formations

Scholars have tied the development of a regional culture distinguishing between warrior and clerical classes of "nobles," tributary peoples, and slaves back to both large-scale environmental shifts in the region and the development of specific political formations. The successful Moroccan invasion of Timbuktu in 1591, which destroyed the last vestiges of the Songhay Empire, acted as a temporal boundary demarcating a series of environmental, cultural, and political changes across the region. Prior to this moment, the region had been dominated by a series of empires (Ghana, Mali, and Songhay) that traced their origins to peoples of the savanna and expanded to impose their authority into the desert. However, the end of the sixteenth century inaugurated a period of increasing desiccation, causing a gradual expansion of the desert and the lowering of the northern limit of the tsetse fly. As the northern limit of the tsetse fly moved south into what had been savanna lands, the use of large mammals—including horses and camels—became increasingly viable, giving mounted troops an advantage over settled adversaries.

This advantage, in turn, allowed for the rise of the "cavalry states" of the savanna, particularly the Wolof kingdoms of Waalo and Kajoor in the Senegambia. While the southward movement of the tsetse fly permitted the southern expansion of horses, camels, and cattle, the large horses imported from North Africa still could not survive long in the savanna lands. But since these horses proved the most advantageous in war and raiding, the new cavalry states of the savanna imported them continually across the desert to replenish herds constantly depleted by sleeping sickness and other diseases. The nobles of the cavalry states imported these horses in exchange for slaves, and then put the horses to work in warfare and raids that in turn produced more slaves. James Webb has posited, contentiously, that as many slaves were traded into and across the desert as into the Atlantic slave trade.[24] Estimates of the size of the Saharan slave trade remain preliminary, and the impact of the Atlantic trade should not be discounted.[25] Indeed, the history of the greater region—stretching from the Senegal to the Niger River Valley—indicates that periods of great warfare and instability began at the Atlantic coast in the sixteenth and seventeenth centuries and moved gradually inland, affecting the central Sudan to the east of the Niger by the turn of the nineteenth century. This regional trend suggests that the greatest instability occurred in areas impacted simultaneously by the Atlantic and Saharan slave trades. As the impact of the Atlantic trade moved deeper into the interior, progressively eastern regions fell into the vicious cycle of near-constant slave raiding and warfare.

The rise of the cavalry states of West Africa developed concurrently and in concert with the domination of desert and desert-edge life by nomadic warriors (*ḥassān* or *imajaghen*) who survived by raiding or by levying taxes on various tributary groups. The cultural division of desert society between warrior or clerical nobles, tributary groups, and slaves has been studied most thoroughly in relation to the western Sahara, where these divisions appear to have developed earlier and become more firmly rooted. Louis Brenner has posited that these occupational divisions developed as part of a "larger regional political economy" that was "organized as a collection of various hereditary occupation groups."[26] These occupations included blacksmiths, bards/historians, and warriors whose occupation was to bear arms and govern.[27] According to this model, Islam was thought of as another "craft," and Muslims living in majority non-Muslim societies were expected to provide religious services to Muslims and non-Muslims alike. However, in the context of the majority-Muslim societies of the Sahara and desert edge, these "Muslim lineages became clerical or *maraboutic* lineages; whose members act[ed] as Muslim intellectuals."[28]

In the western Sahara, the emergence of lineages of Muslim intellectuals also corresponded to political developments of the seventeenth century. Prior to this period, the desert was dominated by loose confederations of groups that traced their genealogical origins to a common ancestor (tribes). However, beginning in the seventeenth century, these confederations developed into the four "emirates" of Brākna, Trārza, Adrār, and Tagnīt. The organization of the emirates offered more political structure than the previous tribal confederations, with the *amīr* controlling and representing multiple lineage groups in addition to his own. Abdel Wedoud Ould Cheikh first described the emirates as "embryos of political power" and credited Islamic principles with providing an organizing structure and granting legitimacy to these "proto-states."[29] Alternatively, Pierre Bonte argued that Islamic principles were involved in the formation of the emirates only in that "conversion" to clerical status offered defeated warriors a method of saving face during succession disputes. While the emirates offered some degree of political organization, the territorial boundaries of each emirate remained vague, and with no accepted principle of succession, each new *amīr* was determined by internecine warfare following the death of the previous officeholder.[30] Moreover, the emirates' control over tributary warrior groups often proved fragile, and these warriors continued to conduct raids without the permission or sanction of the *amīr*.[31]

By the dawn of the seventeenth century, the desiccation of the region had opened up a dangerous, uninhabited stretch of desert known as the Majābat al-Kubrā, or "Empty Quarter," that separated the western Sahara from the region known as the Azawād.[32] Directly to the north of the Niger bend, the Azawād fell under the domination of the Songhay Empire, with its capital at Gao and its geographic and intellectual center in Timbuktu. After the invasion in 1591, the soldiers of the Moroccan sultan remained in the city and became culturally and linguistically assimilated into the Songhay milieu. Nevertheless, they and their descendants, known locally as the Ruma or Arma, retained an identity as soldier-governors ("pashas"), who nominally ruled Timbuktu and the Niger bend on behalf of the Moroccan sultan.[33] Despite the rise and fall of successive Songhay dynasties, followed by the nominal rule of the Arma pashalic, Elias N. Saad has argued that the local Muslim intelligentsia provided and maintained the key governing institutions of the city from the fifteenth through the eighteenth century. This local "patriciate" actively asserted—with varied success—the autonomy of Timbuktu from the various political entities that attempted to rule the city, and built large and enduring institutions of Islamic learning that reached outward into both the desert and the savanna.[34]

To the north, the Azawād was dominated by the Barābīsh and various Tuareg factions in the century following the Moroccan invasion of Timbuktu. Like the western Saharan peoples who formed the Mauritanian emirates, the Barābīsh traced their origins to the intermixture between an Arabic-speaking group that relocated from the northern Sahara in the sixteenth century and a local Berber-speaking people, the Massūfa.[35] The names for the Tuareg factions of this region in the late seventeenth and early eighteenth centuries relate to geographic markers, such as the Kel Ahaggar (the people of the Ahaggar Mountains) and the Kel Aïr (the people of the Aïr Massif), although one group, the Kel Intasār, apparently identified as the descendants of the "helpers" (*anṣār*) who welcomed Muḥammad in Medina. One particular faction, the Kel Tadamakkat, took its name from the ancient city of Tadamakkat or al-Sūq in the Malian Adrār.[36] In the early seventeenth century, the Kel Tadamakkat became the heart of an emerging new political entity, the Iwellemmedan confederation, which at its peak in the mid-nineteenth century dominated the Saharan/Sahelian region between Timbuktu and the Aïr Massif and between the Ahaggar Mountains in the north and the fertile lands of the Niger River Valley to the south. Like the Mauritanian *ḥassān*, the Iwellemmedan confederation traced its origins to the arrival of an "outsider from the West," an Arabic-speaking cultural hero who distinguished himself in battle and then married into the matrilineal Tadamakkat. His succession by his youngest son, Karidenna, serves as a cultural marker of the transition from a matrilineal to a patrilineal descent system. Internal narratives from the eighteenth century portray Karidenna as the agent who simultaneously defeated Tadamakkat rivals from his matrilineage and united various Tuareg lineages into one political formation. He became the first *amenoukal* (leader or sultan) of this confederation, his office symbolized by the *eṭṭebel*, or war drum.[37]

The office of *amenoukal* among the Tuareg greatly resembled that of the *amīr* in the western Sahara: both offices established leadership over a group of lineages, were symbolized by a war drum, and were legitimated through origin stories linked to Arabic-speaking groups or individuals from outside the region. The Tuareg also developed a hierarchical culture similar to that predominating in the western Sahara, with the warriors or free nobles at the top, tributaries and "occupation groups" such as blacksmiths and leatherworkers in the middle, and slaves at the bottom. Among the Tadamakkat, the Kel al-Sūq—who trace their origin to the same ancient city—became known as a clerical lineage of Muslim intellectuals who studied and wrote works in Arabic and worked among the Barābīsh and the Iwellemmedan. The Kel al-Sūq provided one of the deepest reservoirs of Islamic learning in the region. They maintained contact with scholars in Agades and Aïr to the west and Sijilmāsa and the Atlas Mountains in southern Morocco. Many of the central towns of the Azawād, including Arawān and Bū Jbayha, attribute their founding to friends of God from the Kel al-Sūq.[38] Sīdi al-Mukhtār's own teacher, Sīdi ʿAlī al-Najīb, was a member of the Kel al-Sūq, and the Kunta scholar and his descendants maintained close contact with this group of scholars.

The Kunta also participated actively in Tuareg politics in the region, occupying a location midway between the major Tuareg confederations in the region, the Kel Ahaggar (or Huqqār) in the Ahaggar Mountains to the northeast and the Iwellemmedan to the southeast.[39] In the mid-seventeenth century, a dissident branch of the Kel Tadamakkat broke away from the Iwellemmedan confederation. Around 1690, the leader of the Iwellemmedan, Karidenna, led his forces to the Niger and asked the pashas of Timbuktu to invest him as ruler—thus locating himself as a tributary client. In contrast, the dissident Kel Tadamakkat refused to pay tribute to the pashas and suffered raids by them as a consequence. Over the course of the eighteenth century, the Kel Tadamakkat expanded their influence under the leadership of ʿUwar (or Ughmar) ibn Alād and retaliated against the Timbuktu pashas in a series of raids from 1720 to 1737. In 1737, the "Tadhkirāt al-nisyān" recounts that a Kunta family member named ʿAbd al-Muʾmin ibn Sīdi Muḥammad al-Muṣṭafā left Timbuktu to negotiate with ʿUwar, but he was unsuccessful, and the Arma pashalic crumbled beneath the assault of the Kel Tadamakkat.[40] The Kel Tadamakkat then ruled Timbuktu until the death of ʿUwar ibn Alād in 1755, when the pashalic briefly regained control of the city. However, in 1770 the Iwellemmedan captured Gao and the Kel Tadamakkat once again besieged Timbuktu. Sīdi al-Mukhtār intervened and attempted, unsuccessfully, to negotiate an agreement between the Kel Tadamakkat and the city. He then twice supported claimants more favorable to the Kunta to the office of *amenoukal* of the Tadamakkat, and in one instance asked the Iwellemmedan to intercede in support of his candidate. Ultimately, the Iwellemmedan captured Timbuktu in 1787, marking the end of the Arma pashalic.[41]

In his work on education and political formation in West Africa, Louis Brenner outlines a series of "models" of precolonial Islamic political formations in the region. The developments surveyed thus far correspond to three of these models: first, the model of "descent-based forms" of organization characterized by warrior and clerical lineages, which Brenner understands as an Islamic formulation of a West African political economy that predates the arrival of Muslims in the region. The second model—that of the Muslim state—was represented in West Africa by the early empires of Mali and Songhay and by "the emirates of the Western Sahara, in which political authority was retained by 'rulers' who were distinct from the Muslim scholars who advised them and legitimated their rule in Islamic terms." In contrast with these "states," which consolidated authority in the hands of one ruler and sought to impose their political domination on surrounding territories, Timbuktu serves as a third model of religio-political formation—that of "a Muslim 'free city.'" Organized and run by autonomous Muslim scholars, Timbuktu during this period more closely resembled the "small, self-contained Muslim communities which have appeared across time and space in West Africa in which Muslim leaders have attempted to establish a kind of utopian Muslim order isolated from mundane influences and temporal political interference."[42]

Scholars have shown that in the period of the seventeenth through nineteenth centuries, these models of political formation had started to break down in the wake of ever-rising levels of warfare and slave raiding. The authority of warrior lineages and military rulers rested partly on their ability to guarantee and enforce the safety of their tributaries or subjects. As these leaders lost the ability to protect weaker groups—or actively traded their subject populations into slavery—Muslim intellectuals began to assume roles of political authority or power themselves.[43] These efforts took two forms. In the first, a wave of military movements led by Muslim intellectuals established new states and polities across the region. These movements were linked by a common Islamic ideology of warfare, a common project of establishing direct rule by Muslim intellectuals, and by the common Fulbe (Pulaar) ethnic identity of their leaders. Beginning in the Senegambia, these movements established Muslim-ruled "almamates" in Bundu in the 1690s, in the Futa Jallon in the 1720s and '30s, and in the Futa Toro in the 1770s and '80s. In addition to the close links that established teacher-pupil or familiar relationships between the founders of these movements, all three tied themselves to Nāsir al-Dīn's war along the Senegal River in the mid-seventeenth century.[44] The momentum, and the consolidation of a Fulbe ethnic and religious identity, established by these movements was next manifested in the Hausa states of the central Niger River Delta at the turn of the nineteenth century. There, in the state of Gobir, ʿUthmān ibn Fūdī began a campaign that ultimately deposed all of the Hausa states and established a Muslim-ruled empire often referred to as the Sokoto Caliphate.[45] After the establishment of Sokoto, a Fulbe Muslim herder named Aḥmad Lobbo launched his own campaign and founded the state of Macina, centered on the new city of Hamdullahi.[46] These movements, stretching from the Senegal to the Niger River Valleys, established a series of states connected by a common political ideology and ethnic Fulbe identity, but all of these leaders focused their campaigns around local peoples and against local rulers. In contrast, in 1852, al-Ḥājj ʿUmar Tāl gathered Fulbe soldiers from across the region and launched a *jihād* with a much wider, transregional horizon. Tāl's ambitious goals led to the collapse of Kaarta and the Bambara Kingdom of Segou and then pitted him against Macina. In response, as Tal's forces marched toward Timbuktu, Aḥmad al-Bakkāʾī, a grandson of Sīdi al-Mukhtār, rallied the dispossessed Macina leadership and in 1864 launched a counter-*jihād* that finally brought ʿUmar Tāl's war machine to a halt.[47]

The rise of the Kunta family in the Azawād occurred contemporaneously with this wave of state formation led by Muslim intellectuals in the Sahel and savanna lands. Indeed, the political success of Sīdi al-Mukhtār and Sīdi Muḥammad in the desert may have inspired Muslim scholars in the Middle Niger Valley and Inner Niger Delta to abandon their previous roles as advisors and seek leadership themselves. Certainly, the end of both Sīdi al-Mukhtār's and Sīdi Muḥammad's careers involved political debates and maneuverings with the new governments of Sokoto and Macina.[48] However, the Kunta leaders drew on a very different rhetoric of Islamic authority than the Muslim leaders of these new states. Rather than position themselves as political leaders and rule directly, they borrowed: first from the idiom of the autonomous Muslim communities, which rhetorically distanced themselves from the corrupting influence of political authority, and second from the Sufi lineages (*ṭuruq*). The latter "were founded, at least ideologically, upon the voluntary association of followers, or disciples, to the religious Way (*ṭarīqa*) of the *shaykh* or leader of the order."[49] The Kunta thus pioneered a new model of political formation in the region, one that explicitly rejected military force as the foundation of political legitimacy in favor of a voluntarist model of submission to a Sufi shaykh. And although the "voluntary association" of individuals and groups with the Kunta was rhetorical, this fiction nonetheless offered the possibility of a political formation whose legitimacy was not based on military force. Moreover, the success of the Kunta model established the Sufi lineages as a possible mode of political organization in the region.

Islamic Institutions and Identity

Rock inscriptions in the western Sahara indicate the presence of Muslims in the region from as early as the eleventh century.[50] By the time Sīdi al-Mukhtār rose to prominence in the late eighteenth century, Islamic religious traditions and institutions had pervaded desert life. Accordingly, the Kunta writers seem unconcerned with measuring Muslimness—the process of determining which individuals and groups qualified as Muslim—that so concerned Askia Muḥammad in the fifteenth century, Aḥmad Bābā in the sixteenth, and Sīdi al-Mukhtār's contemporary ʿUthmān ibn Fūdī in the late eighteenth and early nineteenth.[51] Rather, the writings of the Kunta scholars across all genres presume not only a uniformly Muslim audience but also an audience highly familiar with the Qurʾān and *ḥadīth*, along with sacred history, Islamic law, and Islamic gender norms such as patrilinear descent and gender segregation.

Scholarship on Islamic institutions during this period of Saharan history has stressed three themes: (1) the function of Islamic law in generating forms of social organization, (2) the importance of educational institutions for the transmission of learning, and (3) the growth and consolidation of Sufi lineages from the eighteenth century onward. The careers of Sīdi al-Mukhtār and Sīdi Muḥammad al-Kuntī played a crucial role in developing and sustaining all three of these patterns of Saharan Islamic life.

In the past two decades, scholars such as Ghislaine Lydon, Bruce Hall, and Ismail Warscheid have contributed to Saharan social history through investigations of West African legal institutions and their literary products, including contracts and legal opinions.[52] The last of these, known as fatwas, were collected in volumes called *nawāzil*. Saharan scholars began producing their own fatwas and *nawāzil* in the late seventeenth century. Warscheid has argued that the development of local legal traditions in the seventeenth through nineteenth centuries served as a site for mediating between local customs and Islamic legal norms and provided Saharans with a new avenue for issuing complaints and seeking resolutions. As such, Islamic law in the Sahara was simultaneously normatizing and generalizing while also very local and diverse.[53] Lydon's meticulous research on the nineteenth-century trans-Saharan caravan trade demonstrates that the production of this literature—and the fact that Saharans followed the edicts contained therein, even in the absence of a state—helped produce a uniquely Saharan culture. Lydon argues that Islamic law provided not only the tools (contracts for sale and lease, etc.) but also the authority and trust necessary to maintain a widespread economy in the absence of a state.[54]

Substantive scholarship has also pointed to the importance of desert institutions of learning, which Sīdi Muḥammad describes vividly in the *Ṭarāʾif wa'l-talāʾid*. According to this hagiographic portrayal, Sīdi al-Mukhtār "grew up among the other boys of his folk [*qawm*] of the Kunta and was raised in the fashion of the desert. He read the Qurʾān in the *kuttāb*, and sometimes he shepherded, and sometimes he did nothing."[55] The *kuttāb*, or local school where children memorized the Qurʾān, served as the initial form of education across the premodern Muslim world, and it continues today in many regions.[56] This passage portrays Sīdi al-Mukhtār as expressing no more interest in learning as a young boy than his peers, and describes him as committed equally to memorizing the Qurʾān, shepherding, and simply passing the time. The hagiography then depicts a series of charismata, or marvelous occurrences, that jolt the young Kunta from his disinterest and energize him in his quest for knowledge. The narrative voice of Sīdi al-Mukhtār thus relates that when he was around thirteen years old, he and a group of boys came across a group of slaves braiding alpha grass into strands and joined them in this activity as a form of amusement. The text identifies one of the slaves as "Nubian" and specifies that although he neither spoke nor understood the language of the region, he suddenly looked at Sīdi al-Mukhtār and said, "eloquently," "you were not made for this, nor were you commanded to do this." Reflecting on this moment, Sīdi al-Mukhtār says, "[His words] hit me like an arrow and I said to him, 'Why was I created and to what have I been commanded?' He replied: 'You were created for knowing [*maʿrifa*] your lord and worshipping him [*ʿibādatihi*], and you have been ordered to teach knowledge and to seek it'" (1:223). When the spring rains arrived, the young Sīdi al-Mukhtār mounted one of the camels from his herd, asked God to return the rest to their owners, and departed (1:223).

According to the *Ṭarāʾif wa'l-talāʾid*, Sīdi al-Mukhtār began this journey by traveling to one of the divisions of the Kel al-Sūq, called the Kel Inbalbūsh, to study with their young men. At this point, the text does not mention a specific teacher or topic of study, only that the young Kunta drives himself to study "such that no one took up a book save that [Sīdi al-Mukhtār] had preceded him in learning what was in it" (1:224). Sīdi al-Mukhtār then leaves the Kel Inbalbūsh to study jurisprudence (*fiqh*) with a teacher named Āḥḥ al-Kalḥurmī, a scholar of the Kel al-Sūq. The narrative emphasizes al-Kalḥurmī's kindness toward his Kunta pupil and contrasts that concern with the harsh treatment that Sīdi al-Mukhtār received from the other students, "who would wrong [him] in the worst ways" (1:225). The text suggests that jealousy might have motivated this cruelty, as Sīdi al-Mukhtār quickly outstripped his peers, not only studying what "the leaders of the lessons" assigned him but also taking the initiative to attend and absorb other lessons. According to the hagiography, he would then dictate these "outside lessons" to the leaders of his own lessons, so that all his peers benefited from his exceptional abilities. Indeed, the *Ṭarāʾif wa'l-talāʾid* depicts the extraordinary pace of the young Kunta scholar's learning as another charism. The narrative voice of Sīdi al-Mukhtār thus declares, "I never finished a book in a lesson. Rather, whenever I had read half or one-third of a book I would [suddenly] know the rest of it with complete knowledge [*maʿrifa*], and so I would move on to another" (1:223).

According to the *Ṭarāʾif wa'l-talāʾid*, the pace of Sīdi al-Mukhtār's learning caused him to grow ill. When the seasonal inundation of the river began, Āḥḥ al-Kalḥurmī worried for his young pupil's health and suggested that he relocate to Timbuktu. However, Sīdi al-Mukhtār expressed disapproval of the status of learning in Timbuktu, stating that he was frustrated in his attempts to find someone to learn or benefit from. The young Kunta scholar noticed a gathering of turbaned men of upright appearance in a mosque, but when he eavesdropped on them, he found that they were comparing the merits of women slave singers (*qaynāt*). In disgust, he departed and spent several nights without shelter, until finally one of the notables of Timbuktu found him and put him up in a house with his personal library.

Emerging one day from his self-enforced solitude, the young Kunta encounters a relative who reproaches him for living alone in poverty and insists that Sīdi al-Mukhtār accompany him out of Timbuktu (1:225–27). It is after parting ways with this relative that Sīdi al-Mukhtār meets and joins the circle of the man who will be his primary teacher, Sīdi ʿAlī al-Najīb. "Then I came to the lordly shaykh Sīdi ʿAlī ibn al-Najīb, who was a knower [*ʿārif*] of God, an ascetic [*nāsik*], and a devotee [*mutaʿabbid*], an artly scholar, the possessor of noble states and pure, correct deeds. So I accompanied him and I took from him the *qādirī* litanies [*awrād*] and performed exercises [*riyāḍāt*]" (1:228). This passage designates Sīdi ʿAlī unequivocally as a Sufi shaykh and specifically as Sīdi al-Mukhtār's Sufi shaykh—who both supervised the spiritual exercises of his training and granted him access to the *awrād*, or specific litanies, ascribed to the twelfth-century Sufi master ʿAbd al-Qādir al-Jīlānī.[57]

Scholarship on Saharan institutions of learning has focused primarily on the Mauritanian context and tends to draw on sources from later in the nineteenth century, or even the twentieth. The account of Aḥmad ibn al-Amīn al-Shinqīṭī (d. 1911) in his *Wasīṭ fī tarājim udabāʾ shinqīṭ* (The Conveyer of the Biographies of the Authors of Shinqīṭ) has been particularly influential.[58] The fact that the *Ṭarāʾif waʾl-talāʾid* largely parallels these late nineteenth- and early twentieth-century descriptions allows us to confirm both the presence of these institutions of learning in the late eighteenth century and their extension eastward into the desert interior. Thus Sīdi Muḥammad's hagiography portrays a process of learning that began with the memorization of the Qurʾān in a local Qurʾānic school (the *kuttāb*), after which point the stages of learning depended on traveling, often over great distances and for long periods of time. While the image of a young shaykh-to-be "traveling in search of learning" developed as a Sufi hagiographic trope in Muslim societies around the world, in the context of the western Sahara these travels were also very much a lived experience.[59] As portrayed in the *Ṭarāʾif waʾl-talāʾid*, education past the memorization of the Qurʾān was largely an optional activity in which students chose their own teachers and subjects of study, leaving one teaching circle and moving to another as they pleased. As one point of difference, it must be noted that the Kunta do not use (at least in writing) the Ḥassāniyya terminology that dominates current scholarship on desert institutions of learning, including *maḥāḍra* (from the Arabic *ḥāḍara*) and its variants for the teaching circle around a shaykh or *dawla* for a group of students studying the same text or topic together.[60]

Apart from the technical vocabulary, Sīdi Muḥammad's *Ṭarāʾif wa'l-talāʾid* portrays the process of education in these nomadic desert teaching circles in much the same fashion as his later Mauritanian counterparts. Thus, just as al-Shinqīṭī says in his *Wasīṭ*, desert scholars might accept students studying a variety of different topics and at different levels. To manage large numbers, teachers grouped students according to their level and the text under study and assigned their advanced students to lead these study groups.[61] Sīdi Muḥammad refers to a study group of this sort as a *majlis* and to the student leaders as the "lords of the lessons" (*arbāb al-durūs*). Meanwhile, the shaykh himself would work directly with the most advanced students and offer a general lecture available to any and all students. When the narrative voice of Sīdi al-Mukhtār claims to attend and master "outside" lessons and bring them back to the leaders of his own study group, he is probably claiming to have attended the lessons of more advanced study groups. The method of learning consisted of copying sections of a book onto wooden tablets (*lawḥ*, pl. *alwāḥ*) and then memorizing them until a student could recite the entire text correctly from memory and discuss its meaning with his teacher (1:226).[62] When a teacher was satisfied with a student's mastery, he provided the student with a certificate, called an *ijāza*, that allowed him to teach that text or topic himself. Each *ijāza* contained a chain of transmission (*isnād*) that linked the recipient back to the original author of the work.

The *Ṭarāʾif wa'l-talāʾid* lists Sīdi al-Mukhtār's *ijāza*s and their chains of transmission for works in Islamic jurisprudence (*fiqh*), legal theory (*uṣūl*), *ḥadīth*, grammar (*naḥw*), the "sciences of meanings" (*ʿulūm al-maʿānī*), and Qurʾānic commentary (*tafsīr*). Sīdi al-Mukhtār's chains of transmission indicate that he received *ijāza*s from three teachers: Sīdī Aḥmad ibn al-Shaykh al-Hīyūnīkal al-Sūqī (also identified as Sīdi ʿAlī's direct teacher, who might be the unnamed teacher from the Kel Inbalbūsh), Āḥḥ al-Kalḥurmī, and Sīdi ʿAlī al-Najīb (1:241–44). All three of these teachers are identified, either by the narrative or by their *nisba* (a surname indicating geographic or ethnic origin), as members of the Kel al-Sūq, which demonstrates the degree to which the Kunta family's education derives from their contact with this understudied group of Saharan Muslims. These *isnād*s support the argument that, while urban centers such as Timbuktu, Walāta, and Shinqīṭ had served as the wellsprings of Saharan scholarship from the fifteenth to seventeenth centuries, by the eighteenth century desert learning had become a nomadic and decentralized activity.[63] Sīdi ʿAlī's lineage in particular stretches back through the most prominent scholars of Timbuktu and Walāta in the sixteenth century. A typical *isnād* from Sīdi ʿAlī reads: "he [Sīdi al-Mukhtār] read them with Sīdi ʿAlī, who read them with his shaykh Sīdi Aḥmad ibn al-Shaykh [al-Hīyūnīkal al-Sūqī],[64] who read them with And-Agh Muḥammad ibn And-Agh ʿAbd Allāh [al-Walātī],[65] who read them with Sīdi Aḥmad Bābā al-Timbuktī, who read them with his uncle Sīdi Maḥmūd, who read them with his shaykh [Muḥammad] Baghayuʿu, until the end of the chain" (1:242). The relationship between Aḥmad Bābā al-Timbuktī and Muḥammad Baghayuʿu (or Baghayughu) in Timbuktu is well attested,[66] and their presence in the links of the Kunta's teaching lineage testifies to the ongoing authority of these figures in the eighteenth-century Sahara.[67]

Scholarship on Islamic institutions of learning in the western Sahara has also emphasized the role of women, particularly in teaching children numbers and the letters of the alphabet and how to count, and beginning their instruction in the Qurʾān and *sira* (biography) of Muḥammad.[68] Al-Shinqīṭī's nineteenth-century account attributes these educational roles to women and even claims that among the *zwāya*, all women and men learned to read and write.[69] Recent scholarship, particularly by Britta Frede, has demonstrated that some Saharan women in the eighteenth and nineteenth centuries became known as scholars. One notable example is Khadīja bint Muḥammad al-ʿĀqil al-Daimāniyya (d. 1835 or 1836), a Mauritanian contemporary of the Kunta scholars who composed her own works on logic and even counted Mukhtār ibn Būnā al-Jakanī, a prominent critic of Sīdi al-Mukhtār, among her students.[70] Ghislaine Lydon has also demonstrated that many nineteenth-century trans-Saharan caravans were managed by literate women.[71] The *Ṭarāʾif wa'l-talāʾid* does not portray women in any educational role, but one woman scholar does appear as a rival to the young Sīdi al-Mukhtār. According to Sīdi Muḥammad's hagiography, Sīdi ʿAlī al-Najīb had a daughter named ʿĀʾisha, who was a scholar in her own right. The narrative voice of Sīdi al-Mukhtār recounts that "she had a husband called Abū Bakr, whom she was teaching. And when he was in the aforementioned gathering [of the students] he would say: "ʿĀʾisha said to me . . .' So I found fault with him and said: 'I would not be pleased, having a beard like your beard, if a woman were my teacher and I traced traditions to her.' That reached ʿĀʾisha and she urged the shaykh to bring us together for a debate" (1:235). This narrative reinforces gender roles surrounding the relationship between women and men in institutions of learning. The passage continues by describing a debate, with Sīdi al-Mukhtār sitting with Sīdi ʿAlī inside his house and ʿĀʾisha sitting outside behind a screen. Sīdi al-Mukhtār recounts that he responded to every question that she posed to him, while she proved "incapable of responding" to a single one of his own questions. Finally, Sīdi al-Mukhtār says to her, "not every man is Abū Bakr," at which point she became "aware of her incapacity." In this fashion, the text denigrates ʿĀʾisha, depicting her as an incapable woman married to a simpleton.

Unfortunately, the texts used as the source base for this study rarely refer to women and cannot be used to analyze the ideology or role of gender within the Kunta's writings or community. Notably, Sīdi Muḥammad appears not to have composed the final chapter of the *Ṭarāʾif waʾl-talāʾid*, which, according to the introduction, would have been dedicated to the life and career of his mother. However, the report of conflict between Sīdi al-Mukhtār and Sīdi ʿAlī's daughter, ʿĀʾisha, adds to evidence suggesting that the Kunta family were not known in the region for their scholarship or learning at the beginning of Sīdi al-Mukhtār's career. No Kunta family members prior to Sīdi al-Mukhtār are listed in the major biographical dictionaries of the region. The *Ṭarāʾif waʾl-talāʾid* presents many Kunta ancestors as Sufi friends of God and claims that Sīdi al-Mukhtār is descended from a daughter of the great scholar Aḥmad al-Raqqād of Tuwāt (1:216).[72] However, the same text provides no evidence that Sīdi al-Mukhtār's parents or grandparents were known, or had any training, as scholars. Rather, the teaching lineages of Sīdi Muḥammad's hagiography indicate that the most notable scholars of the region during the mid-eighteenth century were found among the Kel al-Sūq, and that Sīdi al-Mukhtār, a relative outsider, had to struggle against other students to establish his authority as the successor of his teachers. Moreover, while the *Ṭarāʾif waʾl-talāʾid* repeatedly mentions rivalries between the young Sīdi al-Mukhtār and other students in the circles of both Āḥḥ al-Kalḥurmī and Sīdi ʿAlī al-Najīb, the text mentions only ʿĀʾisha and Abū Bakr by name. This evidence suggests that Sīdi ʿAlī's spiritual and scholarly authority had been poised to pass to his daughter, and through her and her husband to his grandchildren—a model that holds particular salience owing to its resemblance to the life of the Prophet. The Kunta scholars had to present Sīdi ʿAlī's daughter and son-in-law as "incapable" of succeeding him in order to argue that his authority was handed down to someone outside his family.

Sufis and Sufism

As mentioned above, the *Ṭarāʾif waʾl-talāʾid* identifies Sīdi ʿAlī not only as Sīdi al-Mukhtār's shaykh but specifically as his *Sufi* shaykh, from whom he received litanies traced back to ʿAbd al-Qādir al-Jīlānī. On the basis of this description and other, similar references to al-Jīlānī, academic scholarship on the life of Sīdi al-Mukhtār has univocally portrayed him as the leader of an institutionalized Sufi order, which in Arabic is known as a *ṭarīqa*.[73] This description stems from the scholarship of ʿAbd al-ʿAzīz Baṭrān, who describes the Kunta's Sufi order as composed of four organizational levels.[74] Since the 1970s, Baṭrān's work has proved invaluable to research on the history of the Kunta family, but his portrayal of the Kunta scholars' role as Sufi shaykhs needs to be revised. This revision takes into account two pointed criticisms of research on Sufism in West Africa. First, in his study of Muḥammad Fādil and his followers in the early nineteenth century, Glen McLaughlin argued against describing the Fādiliyya as a "Sufi order," positing that *ṭarīqa*, in this context, referred to "a spiritual way" rather than an institutionalized brotherhood.[75] Ten years later, Benjamin Soares argued that an overemphasis on the history of Senegal—where institutionalized Sufi orders have dominated social and political life from the nineteenth century to the present—has led scholars to read the presence of institutionalized Sufism both anachronistically back into history and into regions where this form of Sufism has little contemporary salience (Mali, for example).[76] Both of these studies point to the fact that the word *ṭarīqa* had no stable meaning, and that its use was subject to great changes from the seventeenth to the nineteenth century. The polysemic shifts in how this term was used regionally have been overlooked in scholarship that seeks to chronicle the history of "the Sufi orders" in West Africa. In contrast, the texts consulted for this study provide no evidence that Sīdi al-Mukhtār and Sīdi Muḥammad understood themselves as the heads of an institutionalized Sufi order, or that they organized their network of students into a hierarchy of any complexity. Indeed, Baṭrān's evidence for such an institutional hierarchy comes from the writings of Sīdi al-Mukhtār's grandson Aḥmad al-Bakkāʾī, whose career unfolded in the late nineteenth century, when the campaign of ʿUmar Tāl had provoked changes in how local Sufi leaders described their own communities.

The work of Sīdi al-Mukhtār and Sīdi Muḥammad significantly influenced the development of Sufi traditions of learning in the region and shaped how later generations of West Africans understood Sufi social organization and the role of Sufi shaykhs. Work on the development of Sufi traditions in precolonial West Africa is still nascent, but there is evidence that networks of Sufi teaching lineages connected communities of mystics and ascetics within and across the desert in the seventeenth and early eighteenth centuries. Indeed, the Moroccan invasion of Timbuktu in 1591 under the reign of Sultan Ahmad al-Manṣūr inaugurated a period of increased trade in gold, salt, and slaves across the Sahara—a development that stimulated an intellectual and cultural resurgence in southern and southeastern Morocco. As discussed above, religious centers and teaching communities both followed and shaped Saharan trade routes. Thus this period of increased economic activity also witnessed the rise of influential Sufi lodges in rural areas of southern Morocco. These lodges included the Zāwiya al-Dilāʾiyya, which was founded by Abū Bakr al-Dilāʾī (d. 1612) in the Middle Atlas, and the Zāwiya al-Nāṣiriyya in Tamgrūt, which was originally founded in 1575 but then transformed and expanded by the *shādhilī* Sufi Muḥammad ibn Nāṣir al-Darʿī (d. 1674) and his son Aḥmad ibn Nāsir (d. 1717).[77] Moreover, the Sufi lodges of the Algerian Tuwāt trace their founding to the end of this period, in the late seventeenth and early eighteenth centuries. Indeed, the lodge known as the Zāwiya Kunta was founded during this period by Aḥmad al-Raqqād, whom Sīdi al-Mukhtār claims as a maternal ancestor.[78]

In the Sahara, H. T. Norris has described the development of the Maḥmūd-iyya, a community of ascetic mystics in the Aïr Massif—a complex of rocky outcroppings in what is now northern Niger. While oral and written traditions trace the foundation of this community to a sixteenth-century teacher called Sīdī Maḥmūd al-Baghdadī, the evidence for this figure does not precede the eighteenth century. Nonetheless, Norris's research provides documentation for a network of interconnected Sufi communities across the length of the Sahel and Sahara Desert in the seventeenth century. Thus Aḥmad al-Yamanī, born in 1630 in a village in what is now Sudan, was initiated by a *qādirī* shaykh in Arbajī and in 1664 began a westward journey that took him across the length of the Sahel. He visited a community of mystics in Belbelec—also known as Kulumfardo or Kulumbardo—about eighty kilometers north of the capital of Bornu. The leader of this community at the time was ʿAbdullah al-Burnāwī, who is described as establishing his own "way" but also as well versed in *qādirī* practices. After his stay with al-Burnāwī's community, Aḥmad al-Yamanī continued his travels, reaching Agadez in 1670, where he met the then leader of the Maḥmudiyya community, Aḥmad al-Ṣadiq ibn Uwāyis al-Lamtunī, whom he described as *suhrawardī*. Al-Lamtunī then recommended that he visit a shaykh in al-Maghrib al-Aqsā (now in Mauritania) named Abū Bakr al-Dilāʾī. The name al-Dilāʾī suggests that this teacher migrated to al-Maghrib al-Aqsā after the destruction of the Zāwiya Dilāʾiyya and the dispersal of its community by the sultan Mawlāy Rashīd in 1668.[79] In 1680, al-Yamanī and al-Dilāʾī traveled together to Aïr and Bornu, only to find that both al-Burnāwī and al-Lamtunī had died, the former killed during a Tuareg raid that dispersed his community throughout Niger and northern Nigeria.[80]

Aḥmad al-Yamamī's travels between connected Sufi communities across the Sahel and Sahara indicate the presence of Sufi communities with *shādhilī* and *qadirī* lineages. And although the sources for the Maḥmudiyya in Aïr that date from the nineteenth century or later refer to an institutionalized hierarchy and specific bureaucratic roles, the earlier sources refer only to the "way" of each teacher. As Mohamed Lahbib Nouhi has argued, these earlier Sufi leaders understood the word *ṭarīqa* to refer to a personal and pious endeavor based on a combination of solitary introspection and the transmission of devotional prayers, called *awrād*, from earlier friends of God.[81] This understanding of a Sufi "path" or "way" accords with the description of al-Burnāwī as versed in *qādirī* practices, but as the leader of his own *tarīqa*. In other words, he had received and knew the *qādirī* litanies and exercises but had developed his own as well. Al-Yamamī's visits to communities with *qādirī*, *shādhilī*, and *dilā'i* lineages demonstrate that while a community might adopt practices handed down through a particular chain or attributed to a specific founding figure, its members did not see their paths as exclusive, nor did they demand formal or exclusive membership in order for students to study with them. Indeed, Sīdi al-Mukhtār's own Sufi lineage demonstrates exactly the kind of spiritual mélange indicated by al-Yamamī's travels, combining a claim to *qādirī* descent with a *silsila* populated with members of the *shādhilī* lineage, including Abū Ḥasan al-Shādhilī, his student Aḥmad Abū 'Abbās al-Mursī, and Jalāl al-Dīn al-Suyūṭī (1:290–91, 299–307). Sīdi Muḥammad refers to Abū Ḥasan al-Shādhilī as "the pole [*al-quṭb*], the knower, the inheritor, the lordly realizer," and writes that "he is the teacher of this fellowship [*ustādh ḥadhah'il-ṭā'ifa*] and the deputy [*muqaddam*] of their way after the shaykh 'Abd al-Qādir al-Jīlānī" (1:299, 303). This statement demonstrates how the Kunta scholars used terms like "pole" (*quṭb*) and "deputy" (*muqaddam*) to both honor and rank illustrious Sufi predecessors, rather than to organize members of their living community. Indeed, Sīdi al-Mukhtār's own work was more concerned with the appearance of "renewers" (*mujaddadūn*) who would usher in a revival of Islamic learning and devotion. It was this title—the renewer of the thirteenth century—that Sīdi Muḥammad bestowed on his father (2:236).[82]

In addition to linking Sīdi al-Mukhtār to both *qādirī* and *shādhilī* figures of authority, the Sufi lineage provided by Sīdi Muḥammad deliberately encompasses authoritative personas of the Saharan past as well as famous early Sufis from other regions. The *silsila* thus includes, improbably and in some cases impossibly, the Saharan scholars Sīdi Aḥmad al-Khalīfa al-Raqqād, of Tuwāt, and Muḥammad ibn 'Abd al-Karīm al-Maghilī, of Tlemcsen, the renowned Sufi philosophers Abū Ḥamīd al-Ghazālī and Muḥyī al-Dīn ibn al-'Arabī, the influential North African teacher Ibn Mashīsh, and Abū Najīb al-Suhrawardī, the uncle of the famous Persian Sufi Shihāb al-Dīn Abū Hafs 'Umar al-Suhrawardī (1:281, 288–90, 299–314). Stretching back further, the *silsila* includes the names of founders of the Sufi movement in Baghdad, such as Abū Bakr al-Shiblī and Abū Qāsim al-Junayd, and extends from him to al-Ḥasan al-Basrī, and then to 'Abī ibn Abī Ṭalib, the Prophet Muḥammad, and the "faithful Spirit" (*al-rūḥ al-amīn*), which other Kunta texts identify with the angel Jibrīl (see chapter 2) (1:324–35). Sīdi Muḥammad concludes the account of his father's Sufi lineage with a statement that plays with the multiple meanings of the word "way" or "path." "Thus we have devoted ourselves to precisely demarcating this lineage [*silsila*]," he writes, "and providing information about its men because of how greatly it is needed in this path [*ṭarīq*] . . . for success is only achieved in one of two ways [*bi-aḥad al-ṭarīqayn*]: by divine attraction [*jadhb ilāhī*] or by wayfaring under [the guidance] of a shaykh . . . indeed the way of becoming a Sufi [*ṭarīq al-taṣawwuf*] is a knowledge and a practice and their destination is the two sanctuaries [*al-ḥaramān*] and refuge with God" (1:335). This statement refers to *ṭarīqa* not as an institutional and hierarchical organization but rather as a *process*, a means of becoming a Sufi by joining a lineage of teachers on the path to God.

In *al-Kawkab al-waqqād fī dhikr faḍl al-mashāyik wa ḥaqīqat al-awrād* (The Burning Stars in Remembrance of the Excellence of the Shaykhs and the Truth of the Litanies), Sīdi al-Mukhtār elaborates on his understanding of the word *ṭarīqa*, using it to describe the process of following the prophets. Specifically, he writes that the hearts of the friends of God follow "the heart" of a particular prophet, so there are friends "whose hearts are like the heart of Moses . . . and those whose hearts are like the hearts of Noah . . . and those whose hearts are like the heart of Ibrāhīm."[83] He concludes that "there is no prophet save that on his path [*ṭarīqatihi*] is a friend from this community [*umma*] who follows it until the day of judgment." Sīdi al-Mukhtār then describes the importance of adhering to the guidance of a shaykh, writing that "whoever has the rope of the shaykhs and preserves the creeds and fulfills the covenants, then for him is the best of the two abodes." In this text, holding to "the rope of the shaykhs" means reciting the litanies, or devotional prayers (*awrād*), handed down from the Prophet and the friends of God. Sīdi al-Mukhtār describes these litanies as both the means and the result of communication with God, specifying that the origin of each *wird* is in "prophetic revelation or unseen inspiration" (*al-ilhām al-ghaybī*).[84] Thus, when Sīdi Muḥammad writes that "the paths [*ṭuruq*] . . . of the folk have intermediaries of links, whose ways [*ṭarāʾiq*] are known by affiliation to those intermediaries—like the *ṭarīqa al-qādiriyya*, and the *ṭarīqa al-shādhiliyya*, and the *ṭarīqa al-naqshibandiyya*, and the *ṭarīqa al-badawiyya* (i.e., the Aḥmadiyya)—and our *ṭarīqa* from among them is the *ṭarīqa al-qādiriyya*," he understands the meaning of *ṭarīqa* in terms of the inheritance of *awrād*, writing, "its *awrād* are the loftiest in value, the most abundant in treasure, the most plentiful in rewards, and the most widely recollected . . . and its *sanad* is the strongest *isnād*, with the highest and most perfect men, and the most complete connection" (1:259). When Sīdi al-Mukhtār and Sīdi Muḥammad al-Kuntī claimed to be *qādirī*, they understood this "way" in much the same fashion as their predecessors in the region—as members of a community modeled around submission to a Sufi shaykh and the transmission of litanies from a specific friend of God.

Sīdi al-Mukhtār and Sīdi Muḥammad did not distinguish themselves from earlier West African Sufis in terms of organizational structure. Rather, they differed from earlier Sufi shaykhs in West Africa by practicing active social and political engagement rather than ascetic withdrawal from the world. Their writings also represent the beginning of an explosive growth in the composition of Sufi literature in the region. Prior to the rise of Sīdi al-Mukhtār, local Sufis had produced only a few written works of their own. H. T. Norris located a work called the *Qudwat al-muʿtaqid fī siyar al-ajwād* (The Believer's Model for Exemplary Conduct), attributed to a follower of Sidi Maḥmūd named Aḥmad Uwāyis al-Lamtūnī. Norris dated the first three or four folios of the *Qudwat*, a section dedicated to the signs presaging the arrival of the *mahḍī*, to the eighteenth century, while admitting that the rest of the document was produced much more recently.[85] The eighteenth-century scholar al-Yadālī, who composed the primary chronicle for the war of Nāṣir al-Dīn, mentioned above, also composed a short work called "Khātima fī al-taṣawwuf" (The Seal of Becoming a Sufi), which describes the world as divided into the apparent (*ẓāhir*) and the hidden (*bāṭin*) and counsels aspiring Sufis to avoid vices while cultivating moral virtues.[86] Zachary Wright has recently located and described what may be the earliest Sufi work composed in the region, a text dedicated to devotional prayers and secrets (*asrār*) called the *Bustān al-fawāʾid wa l-manāfiʿ* (The Garden of Excellences and Benefits) by the fifteenth-century Timbuktu scholar Muḥammad al-Kābarī.[87] In contrast, Sīdi al-Mukhtār and Sīdi Muḥammad each composed dozens of long treatises related to Sufi philosophy, hagiography, and practice as well as their own devotional prayers and litanies, short summaries, and responses to students. This explosion of written production corresponds to an overall growth in the composition of works by regional Muslim scholars beginning in the eighteenth century and continuing into the nineteenth.[88]

The large-scale production of their own works in Arabic allowed Sīdi al-Mukhtār and Sīdi Muḥammad to extend their reputations far beyond the Azawād, and they attracted students from the Mauritanian Gebla to the west and the Sahel states to the south. These students engaged with other regional scholars and leaders and spread the reputation of their teachers. Thus one of Sīdi al-Mukhtār's students, Nūḥ ibn Ṭāhir, traveled to Hausaland, where he advised ʿUthmān ibn Fūdī before becoming an advisor to Aḥmad Lobbo, whose local authority and reputation he helped to build.[89] The Kunta "model" of a socially and political engaged Sufi community dedicated to both practice and learning also inspired one of their students, the *shaykh* Sīdiyya al-Kabīr, to establish his own Sufi community in the Mauritanian Gebla along similar lines.[90] In the early nineteenth century, the Torobbe scholars of Futa Toro sent many of their students to study with Shaykh Sīdiyya.[91] During the same time period, another Sufi community developed in the Mauritanian Hodh around the shaykh Muḥammad Fādil. While there is no evidence for a direct connection between the Fādiliyya and the Kunta, the main hagiography of Muḥammad Fādil intentionally imitates the content and structure of Sīdi Muḥammad's *Ṭarā'if wa'l-talā'id*.[92] In yet another example of the wide-ranging influence of the Kunta shaykhs, when Uthmān ibn Fūdī began his *jihād* in Hausaland at the turn of the nineteenth century, he claimed Sīdi al-Mukhtār as one of his teachers.[93]

Indeed, David Robinson has suggested that the monopoly of the Kunta leaders and their students over lineages of intellectual authority by the nineteenth century may have motivated a young 'Umar Tāl to seek another source of Sufi initiation.[94] Tāl found this source in the Tijāniyya lineage, which Muḥammad al-Ḥāfiz brought to the western Sahara in the early eighteenth century. Al-Ḥāfiz spent several years in Fez, where he was initiated into the lineage by Aḥmad al-Tijānī and assisted in the composition of the latter's hagiography before making the pilgrimage to Mecca. After his return to the region of Shinqīṭ in 1805–6, he began spreading the Tijānī lineage and *awrād* among the Idaw 'Alī.[95] A student of the Ḥāfiziyya community in Mauritania named 'Abd al-Karīm al-Nāqil eventually returned home to the Futa Jalon, where he met and initiated a young 'Umar Tāl. Tāl decided to undertake the pilgrimage to Mecca, where, by his own account, he met another teacher, a direct disciple of al-Tijānī named Muḥammad al-Ghālī, who appointed him to the rank of *khālifa*, or head, of the Tijāniyya in West Africa. Upon his return to West Africa, Tāl transmitted the teachings of Aḥmad al-Tijānī and demanded that his own initiates into the Tijāniyya abandon any other Sufi initiations or allegiances.[96] 'Umar Tāl understood himself as the head of a hierarchical Sufi institution, which he organized through the appointment of *muqaddams* and *amīrs* as deputies of administrative units.[97] By the time Aḥmad al-Bakkā'ī launched his counter-*jihād* against the 'Umarian forces in 1864, the pressure of Tāl's movement had provoked other regional Sufis to reimagine their communities along similar lines—as institutional and hierarchical organizations with an exclusive corporate identity.[98] Al-Bakkā'ī's description of the "Qādiriyya-Mukhtāriyya" as a hierarchical Sufi organization thus emerged in reaction and opposition to the growth of 'Umar Tāl's Tijāniyya in the region, but it does not reflect his father's or grandfather's understanding of their teaching networks or their roles as Sufi shaykhs.

Scholars of Sufism have called attention to the fact that "Sufism" itself is a neologism coined by Western academics to capture the various literary genres, cultural traditions, and religious practices related to people who called themselves "Sufis."[99] However, as an internal Muslim category of identity, the meaning of the word "Sufi," like the meaning of associated terms such as *ṭarīqa*, has changed drastically in different historical and geographical contexts. The Kunta were actively involved in a shift in the understanding of the role and identity of Sufi leaders in the region. Whereas Sufi shaykhs had previously been ascetic teachers who transmitted the devotional prayers handed down from the founders of their lineage, after the rise of the Kunta, Sufi leaders in the region adopted more socially and politically active roles. And while previous West African Sufi scholars had produced some philosophical and devotional literature, the Kunta's outpouring of new written compositions on these topics inaugurated a new phase in regional Sufi textual production. After the rise of Sīdi al-Mukhtār al-Kuntī, Sufi leaders sought direct political power and justified their claim to leadership by demonstrating intellectual mastery through written composition.[100] After the death of Sīdi Muḥammad, his son Aḥmad al-Bakkāʾī did come to reimagine the Kunta "way" as an organized Qādiriyya Sufi order. However, Sīdi al-Mukhtār and Sīdi Muḥammad predated that development and instead understood themselves as following and handing down the spiritual way of ʿAbd al-Qādir al-Jīlānī.

The Kunta Family

As Sīdi al-Mukhtār and Sīdi Muḥammad rose to prominence in the Sahara, they produced family histories that portrayed themselves as the most recent descendants of an illustrious and authoritative Saharan lineage. These genealogies present the Kunta family as descending from the Prophet Muḥammad's tribe of Quraysh through the legendary conqueror ʿUqba al-Mustajab. Drawing on observations by H. T. Norris, Mauro Nobili has demonstrated that both the Kel al-Sūq and the Kunta family developed myths about this legendary figure in the eighteenth and nineteenth centuries as a means of asserting Arabized genealogies. The Kunta version of this persona conflates two historical figures: ʿUqba ibn Nafiʿ al-Fihrī (d. 683), the Umayyid-era general responsible for conquering much of North Africa, and ʿUqba ibn ʿAmīr al-Juhanī, who governed Egypt from 665 to 667. Although there is no record of either of these figures traveling farther south than the oasis of Kawar (in what is now Libya), in the *Risāla al-ghallāwiyya* Sīdi Muḥammad claims that ʿUqba al-Mustajab's campaign reached the empire of Ghana before returning to North Africa, where ʿUqba was assassinated and buried in Qayrawān. According to the chronicle, one of his descendants, named Dawmān, later migrated to the Algerian oasis of Tuwāt, establishing the Kunta family line in the Sahara.[101] The family histories then describe the Kunta patrilineage splitting into a "western branch" that moved into the Hodh and Adrār, in contemporary Mauritania, and an "eastern branch," that moved first through the regions surrounding Tuwāt and then into the Azawād.[102] These chronicles focus particularly on the late fifteenth-century figure Sīdi Muḥammad al-Kuntī al-Kabīr and his son, Sīdi Aḥmad al-Bakkāʾī.[103] Both of these personas are presented as Sufi friends of God, and the tomb of Sīdi Aḥmad al-Bakkāʾī in Walāta served as a physical marker that anchored the Kunta's claims to authority over that important town and its associated trans-Saharan trading networks.[104]

Some documentary evidence supports the broad outlines of the Kunta history from the fifteenth through the nineteenth centuries. The colonial-era French historian Alfred Georges Paul Martin published translations of three documents, including a letter dated 1440 from the sultan of Bornu addressed to descendants of Sīdi Muḥammad al-Kabīr in Tuwāt,[105] and an unnamed and undated "local chronicle" that refers to the arrival of a Kunta-led army in the city in 1551.[106] More recently, Thomas Whitcomb published a two-part article detailing a text composed by a Kunta family member, al-Ḥājj ʿAbd Allāh ibn Sīdi Aḥmad, at the turn of the eighteenth century. After a genealogy that survives only in fragments (but that makes no mention of ʿUqba al-Mustajab), this text quotes part of another work attributed to Sīdi Aḥmad al-Bakkāʾī.[107] All three documents need to be located, but if verified they would provide good evidence for the association of the Kunta family with the city of Tuwāt by the late fifteenth century and for the importance of Sīdi Aḥmad al-Bakkāʾī in Kunta family histories by the turn of the eighteenth century.

At the same time, however, there are significant reasons to question elements of this received history. The *Fatḥ al-shakūr* of al-Bartilī (d. 1805) recognizes Sīdi al-Mukhtār as a friend of God and lists some of his major works, but it does not mention any of his supposedly illustrious ancestors or his teacher Sīdi ʿAlī al-Najīb.[108] Meanwhile, Aḥmad ibn al-Amīn al-Shinqīṭī's *Wasīṭ fī tarājim udabāʾ shinqīṭ* accepts the Quraysh ancestry of the Kunta family but implies that Sīdi al-Mukhtār belonged to a tributary group and was not himself a Kunta family member.[109] While al-Shinqīṭī's account may represent an attempt to delegitimize the leaders of an authoritative network, it raises the possibility that Sīdi al-Mukhtār and Sīdi Muḥammad descended from a client group and reimagined their lineage and genealogy only after rising to political power. This possibility accords with Timothy Cleaveland's demonstration of how precolonial Saharan Muslims manipulated genealogies to make different claims to patron or client status.[110] The received history of the Kunta family in academic literature stems from the combination of family chronicles provided by Sīdi al-Mukhtār and Sīdi Muḥammad and the works of the colonial scholar and administrator Paul Marty, whose works on West Africa took part in the colonial administration's efforts to classify the peoples under its rule. Marty's *Les Kunta de l'est* follows the same narrative trajectory as Sīdi Muḥammad's *Ṭarāʾif wa'l-talāʾid*.[111] Marty's publications thus represent a moment in which the hagiographic projections of the Kunta family entered into and became authorized by colonial historiography.[112]

The only sources to provide details about Sīdi al-Mukhtār's childhood and education are the Kunta's own texts, specifically Sīdi al-Mukhtār's *Kitāb al-minna* and Sīdi Muḥammad's *Ṭarā ʾif wa'l-talāʾid*. According to the latter, Sīdi al-Mukhtār was born in 1142/1729–30 to a branch of the Kunta in the Azawād. The narrative testifies that his mother, Lalla Ambārikah (or Mbarka) al-Hāmiliyya, died when he was four or five and that his father died when he was ten years old, at which point he passed into the care of his half brother, Sīdī Muḥammad, known as Abū Ḥāmiyya (1:211–12, 216–17). The hagiography provides almost no information about Sīdi al-Mukhtār's father, Aḥmad ibn Abī Bakr, and instead lingers on the importance of his maternal grandfather, "the *sayyid* ʿAbd al-Qādir," known as Sīdi Bādī (1:212–15). As mentioned above, the *Ṭarāʾif wa'l-talāʾid* records that Sīdi al-Mukhtār left his family at the age of thirteen to study among the Kel Intasār and the Kel al-Sūq, and that he ultimately found his Sufi shaykh in the person of Sīdi ʿAlī al-Najīb, who died in 1757 (1:260). Sīdi al-Mukhtār's account in his *Kitāb al-minna* states that after finishing his studies in 1747, he moved to Walāta, where he became the custodian of the shrine of his ancestor Aḥmad al-Bakkāʾī al-Kuntī. At this point, he began his trading business and used the proceeds in part to host and offer hospitality to pilgrims visiting the shrine. According to Baṭrān, this position at the main point of pilgrimage for Kunta across the region raised Sīdi al-Mukhtār's profile and reputation. From Walāta, Sīdi al-Mukhtār moved to the Taqānt, where he successfully negotiated an end to a feud between the Kunta and the Awlād Bu-Sayf; as a result, both the Kunta of the Taqānt and the Bu-Sayf acknowledged his authority as a Sufi friend of God. With a retinue of students and notables from the various Kunta families, Sīdi al-Mukhtār returned home to the village of Mabrūk in the Azawād in 1753, at the age of twenty-four.[113]

From this point forward, the biography of Sīdi al-Mukhtār comes primarily from his epistolary exchanges with other regional leaders, which Sīdi

Muḥammad includes as the fourth chapter of the *Ṭarāʾif wa'l-talāʾid*. According to these letters, the most prominent family of the Kunta of the Azawād during this period were the descendants of Sīdi al-Ḥājj Abū Bakr, but internal divisions and infighting had caused them to lose so much prestige that they had surrendered leadership of Mabrūk to an immigrant from Tuwāt, Mawlāy ʿAlī ibn Sīdi Ḥamū. Sīdi al-Mukhtār began by resolving the conflicts among the Awlād Sīdi al-Ḥājj Abū Bakr and by marrying into the al-Ḥammāl branch of the Kunta family. The *Ṭarāʾif wa'l-talāʾid* presents Sīdi al-Mukhtār's wife, Lalla ʿĀʾisha bint Sīdi al-Mukhtār ibn Sīdi al-Amīn al-Azraq, as a Sufi friend of God in her own right, and provides her full maternal lineage. According to this text, Lalla ʿĀʾisha was born in 1747, married Sīdi al-Mukhtār in 1757, and died in 1810, one year before her husband (1:216–17). Ultimately, Sīdi al-Mukhtār claimed leadership of all the branches of the Kunta, including his own family of the Awlād al-Wāfī, his wife's family the al-Ḥammāl, the Awlād Sīdi al-Ḥājj Abū Bakr, and others. He symbolically ratified the consolidation of the Kunta under his authority with the construction of a new camp at al-Ḥilla, where he dug numerous wells and established his school.[114]

When Sīdi al-Mukhtār arrived home from his travels in 1753, the Azawād was under the influence of the Barābīsh, an Arabized "warrior" group that collected taxes on all caravans that passed through their territory as representatives of the Iwellemmedan. The letters preserved in the *Ṭarāʾif wa'l-talāʾid* indicate that the next fifty years witnessed an expansion of the Kunta's authority under Sīdi al-Mukhtār's leadership until, by the end of the century, he exercised authority over the Iwellemmedan, the Kel Tadmakkat, and the Barābīsh. Sīdi al-Mukhtār began this consolidation by paying a tribute to the leaders of the Iwellemmedan, the brothers Amma and Muḥammad ibn Ag al-Shaykh ibn Karidenna. This gift would have established the Kunta as tributary clients of the Iwellemmedan, but Sīdi al-Mukhtār recast this offering as a *baraka*, an extension of his blessing to the Tuareg leaders. He then claimed that Amma, Muḥammad, and their successors, Kāwa and Ukadadu, were under his spiritual direction, and that anyone under his protection had security from being raided by or paying tribute to the Iwellemmedan.

Then, in 1770, the Ruma of Timbuktu assassinated Abtītī, the leader of the Kel Tadmakkat. The assassination led to two political crises: a succession dispute and a blockade of Timbuktu. Sīdi al-Mukhtār intervened in both issues. First, he negotiated a pact between the Ruma and the Kel Tadmakkat. Next, he supported a series of contenders for leadership of the Kel Tadmakkat. Because Abtītī's son Ghumayrī was still a young child, Sīdi al-Mukhtār invested Abtītī's uncle Khumayka as leader of the Kel Tadmakkat instead. However, Khumayka immediately besieged Timbuktu and rejected Sīdi al-Muktār's attempts to negotiate. Sīdi al-Mukhtar then drew on his relationship with the Iwellemmedan, asking them to depose Khumayka and invest Bāsha ibn Intiqād in his stead. However, Bāsha refused to recognize the authority of the Kunta leaders and pay them the "voluntary" gift (*hadāya*) that signals deference to a shaykh. Sīdi al-Mukhtār thus asked the Iwellemmedan to intercede again and return Khumayka, now appropriately chastised, to power. When Khumayka died in 1786, al-Ghumayrī appealed to Sīdi al-Mukhtār, who invested him as leader of the Kel Tadmakkat.

Sīdi al-Mukhtār applied this same method of calling on his influence with the Iwellemmedan to interfere in succession disputes among the Barābīsh. Thus when the leader of the Barābīsh, Muḥammad ibn Yūsuf, died in 1753, Sīdi al-Mukhtār asked the Iwellemmedan to invest Muḥammad ibn Riḥāl ibn Daḥmān ibn al-Ḥājj as the new leader. In return for his assistance, all of Sīdi al-Mukhtār's caravans, along with the caravans of those under his protection, traveled tax-free through Barābīsh territory. When Muḥammad ibn Riḥāl died, his son ʿAlī also asked for Sīdi al-Mukhtār's support, and upon his investiture extended this immunity from taxation to the caravans of all Kunta family members and their clients. Thus, while Sīdi al-Mukhtār began his career by paying tribute to the Iwellemmedan, by the end of the century the Iwellemmedan responded to his requests, which he used to determine the leadership of both the Kel Tadmakkat and the Barābīsh. However, this method was not foolproof. When the agreement between the Kunta and the Barabīsh leader, ʿAlī ibn Muḥammad, broke down in 1791, the Iwellemmedan refused to intervene in a dispute between their allies (the Kunta) and their tributaries (the Barābīsh). The situation reached the point of crisis and was only resolved when ʿAlī was assassinated.[115]

The growing influence of the Kunta in the region threatened the positions of other "clerical" lineages and scholars. The letters preserved in the *Ṭarāʾif wa'l-talāʾid* thus record a conflict between the Kunta of the Azawād and the *zwāya* of Tishīt, who were allied with the Awlād Bella, a warrior confederation that operated between Walāta and Tishīt in the second half of the eighteenth century. In reponse to the conflict with the Awlād Bella, Sīdi al-Mukhtār mobilized the resources of several direct tributary clients: the Awlād al-Nāṣir, the Awlād al-Faḥfāḥ, the Daʾūd ibn ʿAruq, and the Mashẓūf. Together, this coalition defeated the Awlād Bella and established a treaty under which the Awlād Bella acknowledged the authority of the Kunta shaykhs. This agreement threatened the position of the *zwāya* of Tishīt, and two of their leaders—Sīdiyya ibn al-Ḥājj al-Amīn al-Tuwātī and Sīdi Muḥammad ibn al-Ḥājj ibn Abū Radda al-ʿAlūshī—persuaded al-Bāsha Bū Farīra, the leader of the Awlād Bella, to break the peace treaty. Once again, Sīdi al-Mukhtār rallied the forces of his tributaries, but this time they destroyed the Awlād Bella and absorbed their survivors as new clients of the Kunta. The clerical families of Tishīt then lost their status as *zwāya* with the destruction of those who recognized their authority.[116]

Similarly, although Sīdi al-Mukhtār studied with the scholars of the Kel Intasār and the Kel al-Sūq, as noted above, the growth of his family's influence threatened the authority of these established *zwāya* lineages. Thus, in the third quarter of the eighteenth century, two groups of Kunta began to move into the territory of the leader of the Kel Intasār, Ḥammāda ibn Muḥammad ibn Amalan. Sīdi al-Mukhtār's third son, Sīdi Bābā Aḥmad, led one group of tributary clients and their herds eastward toward the lake of Rās al-Mā', while a second group, led by Sīdi al-Mukhtār himself, moved toward Atlāq. In response to this incursion, Ḥammāda assembled a force, intercepted the Kunta migrants, raided their herds and possessions, and pushed them back toward the Azawād. According to the *Ṭarā'if wa'l-talā'id*, Sīdi al-Mukhtār called on the Maghāfra to attack Ḥammāda's forces on his behalf. Ḥammāda died in the conflict, and with no children who equaled him in either learning or spiritual status, the authority of Ḥammāda's confederation died with him. However, Ḥammāda's son Muḥammad al-Amīn (nicknamed Dua-Dua) did successfully expel Sīdi Bābā Aḥmad from Rās al-Mā'. Sīdi Bābā Aḥmad then led his migrants west and settled in the Mauritanian Hodh.[117]

In addition to these disputes, narrated in the *Ṭarā'if wa'l-talā'id*, al-Shinqīṭī records a series of hostile epistolary exchanges between Sīdi al-Mukhtār and a Mauritanian scholar named al-Mukhtār ibn Būnā al-Jakanī. Indeed, Sīdi al-Mukhtār's *Jidhwat al-anwār fī dhabb 'an munāṣib awlīyā' allāh al-khiyār* is written as a refutation of Ibn Būnā's alleged rejection of the charismata, or marvels, of the friends of God.[118] Ibn Būnā appears to be the source of a school of anti-Sufi scholarship in the region, as his students continued to oppose the teachings of the first Tijānī leaders in the region in the first half of the nineteenth century.[119]

According to the *Ṭarā'if wa'l-talā'id*, Sīdi al-Mukhtār died in 1226/1811 at the age of eighty-four (1:211). He had ten sons and was succeeded by his fifth son, Sīdi Muḥammad (called al-Khalīfa, to distinguish him from his ancestor of the same name). Information about Sīdi Muḥammad's life stems from the works of his most famous student, Shaykh Sīdiyya al-Kabīr, and from a corpus of forty-seven letters that he exchanged with other leaders of Saharan and Sahelian states.[120] According to these sources, Sīdi Muḥammad's only teacher was his father, Sīdi al-Mukhtār, and he appears never to have left the Sahara. He did, however, leave the Azawād and establish himself in Timbuktu in 1818.[121] From Timbuktu, as from the desert, he managed the growing wealth and influence of his family and communicated regularly with his allies, tributaries, and neighbors. The French explorer René Caillié met Sīdi Muḥammad while studying Arabic in the Mauritanian Gebla in 1824—referring to him as "the Sherif Sidy Mohammed, belonging to the Koont nation."[122] The writings of Shaykh Sīdiyya record that he had eight sons and died in 1826.[123]

Sīdi Muḥammad sent long letters to Aḥmad Lobbo and to the leaders of Sokoto, ʿUthmān ibn Fūdī, his brother ʿAbd Allāh, and his son Muḥammad. In some of these cases he positioned himself in the classic role of a moral "advisor" to princes and in others he advocated on behalf of former students who had taken up residence in these territories. He likewise communicated with the Tuareg leaders of the Iwellemmedan and the Kel Away' of the Aïr Massif. Some of his correspondence indicates the growth of other Muslim revivalist movements during this period. For example, he wrote to Kāwa ibn Amma of the Iwellemmedan to alert him to the presence of a man named al-Jaylanī, who had appeared among the Kel Dinnig in the Azawaq and claimed to be the *mahdī*.[124] Similarly, he wrote his *Risāla al-ghallāwiyya* to the Aghlāl in the Mauritanian Hodh to reject the attempts of ʿAbd Allāh wuld Sīdi Maḥmūd (d. 1839) to establish an imamate and to denounce the aggression of his followers and the Idaw al-ʿIsh against the Kunta of the Taqānt.[125] In addition to managing the trading business and defending the Kunta's interests across the region, Sīdi Muḥammad established and spread the reputation of his father as a Sufi friend of God and the renewer of the thirteenth century through his hagiographies and family histories. Many of his own works comment on or summarize his father's texts or systematize and organize the principles of his father's thought. It was thanks to the efforts of Sīdi Muḥammad that both Sīdi al-Mukhtār and the Kunta family acquired their final and long-lasting reputations as Sufi friends of God.

Sīdi al-Mukhtār and Sīdi Muḥammad did not understand themselves as the heads of an institutionalized Qādiriyya Sufi order. Instead, they positioned themselves as the inheritors of devotional prayers and practices handed down within the Sufi lineage of ʿAbd al-Qādir al-Jīlānī. This understanding of the role of Sufi leaders developed from the context of the seventeenth and early eighteenth centuries, which saw the rise of autonomous Sufi communities that practiced ascetic devotion under the guidance of a shaykh. However, Sīdi al-Mukhtār broke with the ascetic model of these earlier communities by asserting the importance of "earning a living" and taking an active role in desert and desert-edge politics. The social and political context of the eighteenth century was characterized by (1) the association between economic niche and ethnic or racial identity, and (2) experiments in new modes of political organization, as cycles of increasing violence and slave raiding destroyed the legitimacy of previous rulers. The desire for protection against rulers who preyed on their people stimulated a wave of campaigns to establish Muslim-ruled states in the Sahel and savanna lands. However, in the desert, the Kunta adopted a different model. Drawing on the Sufi rhetoric of voluntary submission to a shaykh, the Kunta positioned themselves as "advisors" rather than rulers. Sīdi al-Mukhtār and Sīdi Muḥammad were able to maintain their rhetorical distance from the corrupting influence of political power by drawing on the tributary system of the desert. Accordingly, they used the wealth they acquired from trans-Saharan trade to establish alliances by sending gifts to powerful factions like the Iwellemmedan, and to acquire camel herds, which they placed with tributary groups such as the Awlād al-Nāṣir and Mashẓūf, who gained a percentage of the products of the camel herds in exchange for their labor and military assistance. They then called up the military power of their tributaries in response to direct attacks by the Awlād Bella or Ḥammāda ibn Muḥammad ibn Amalan of the Kel Intasār. Meanwhile, they used their influence with the Iwellemmedan to effectively choose the next leaders of the Kel Tadamakkat and the Barābīsh, thus consolidating their authority over these large factions. With every victory, the Kunta could offer greater security for those under their protection, increasing the desirability of submitting to their authority as Sufi friends of God. The rise and influence of Sīdi al-Mukhtār and Sīdi Muḥammad contributed to the ongoing development of Sufi identity and leadership in the region. Their careers inaugurated a period of active and direct social and political leadership by Sufi scholars, even though the scholar-leaders who followed them chose not to maintain the same rhetorical distance from power but directly claimed rulership. However, following the example of the Kunta, these leaders were expected to demonstrate their mastery of the Sufi intellectual tradition through the production of their own written works.

The dynamics that gave rise to the Kunta illuminate a West African region simultaneously destabilized by continuous raiding and stabilized by networks of trade and diplomacy. These networks of violence and security joined populations from Morocco and the Algerian Tuwāt in the north to the states of Sokoto and Macina to the south, and from the Aïr Massif and Ahaggar Mountains in the east to the Mauritanian Hodh and Gebla in the west. Positioned at the center of this web, the history of Sīdi al-Mukhtār and Sīdi Muḥammad tells a very Saharan story. Responding to an economics of scarcity, they developed a trading business based around camel herds, salt, and, later, tobacco. When Sīdi al-Mukhtār succeeded in consolidating the branches of the Kunta family, he embodied that new social configuration by digging new wells to establish a school and town at al-Ḥilla. This investment in the physical landscape rerouted caravans, which continued to generate wealth even as they brought along social capital in the form of students. With material and social capital at their disposal, the Kunta inserted themselves into the socioreligious and political developments of the late eighteenth and early nineteenth centuries. They disputed with the Moroccan sultan, cast the Sokoto caliphs as corrupted princes, and argued with the rulers of Macina. Their letters also indicate the presence of other, shorter-lived religious movements in the desert and suggest the skepticism of non-Sufi scholars. Ultimately, these scholars left a lasting impression on the physical and human geography of the West African desert—a permanent imprint on the visible world.

2

THE REALM OF THE UNSEEN

In Sīdi Muḥammad's hagiographic account of his father, marvelous events are always occurring in the vicinity of Kunta family members. In one story, Sīdi al-Mukhtār's brother Abū Bakr had reached the midpoint of a long journey when, in the sweltering heat, the last water flask falls from a camel, breaks, and spills its contents. Sīdi Abū Bakr runs forward and grabs the flask, which instantly reverts to its unbroken, unspilled condition. In another story, while traveling with Sīdi ʿAlī and his other students, a young Sīdi al-Mukhtār scares the pack camel, causing it to spill all their remaining water. In the face of this crisis, Sīdi ʿAlī says that, improbably, only good will come from Sīdi al-Mukhtār's mistake, and then suddenly they see the lights of a campsite where none was expected. In yet another narrative, enemy bandits attack Sīdi al-Mukhtār and his traveling companion, only to unexpectedly surrender and acknowledge the authority of the shaykh as a friend of God.[1] The hagiography portrays these endings as marvelous and improbable reversals, in which apparently dire situations are resolved in unexpected salvation because of the presence of a Kunta family member. Specifically, these are moments when proximity to God becomes visible, when the divine authority with which these individuals are invested manifests itself in the material world of the senses. In the *Ṭarāʾif wa'l-talāʾid* and other treatises, Sīdi al-Mukhtār and Sīdi Muḥammad explain that the humbling of oppressors partakes in a special category of improbable events that occur around the friends of God. Other examples include making fruit bloom out of season, causing water to appear from the desert or dead rock, traveling great distances instantaneously, and speaking to the dead.[2] The Kunta scholars, like Sufi writers before them, refer to these marvelous events as *karāmāt*, a term I translate as "charismata" to indicate both a divine gift and a compelling presence. The charismata are gifts bestowed by God to single out and highlight the extraordinary status of his friends. For Sīdi al-Mukhtār and

Sīdi Muḥammad, the charismata represent one type of relationship between the world as perceivable to the human senses, and another, invisible world that extends around and interpenetrates it: the *ʿālam al-ghayb*, or realm of the unseen. Ultimately, it is their access to and position within this unseen realm that give the friends of God their legitimate socioreligious authority in the human realm and differentiate them from the bandits and tyrants of the hagiography. This chapter thus reconstructs the architecture of this invisible world in order to illustrate how the Kunta argued for their authority as Sufi Muslim leaders.

In the Kunta texts, discussions of the unseen draw on a mélange of vocabulary from the Qurʾān, *ḥadīth*, and sacred history mixed with cosmological and philosophical terminology stemming from both the Greco-Arabic tradition and medieval Sufi philosophy. The term *al-ghayb* (the unseen) entered the Qurʾān from pre-Islamic Arabia. In her work on the context of the Qurʾānic revelation, Jacqueline Chabbi describes the *ghayb* as "the world of the invisible, which has to do with the future or the hidden present. . . . The *ghayb* used to designate an absence to the eye that masked a presence simultaneously overwhelming and terrifying."[3] In the Qurʾān, where the word occurs forty-nine times, some verses stress that the *ghayb* is known exclusively by God, while others indicate that God occasionally gifts knowledge of the unseen to his believers.[4] The *ghayb* of the Qurʾān is populated by invisible entities, including angels, devils (*shayāṭīn*), and jinn. The jinn are often understood as beings made of fire, and the Qurʾān indicates that some of them will hear and heed the revelation of God, while others will become devils and ultimately be cast into the fire.[5] In the works of later commentators and philosophers, the *ghayb* came to mean both the invisible world and its inhabitants, as well as everything invisible to human knowledge and reason. For these scholars, as for the Kunta, the counterpart to the realm of the unseen is the perceptible world, *ʿālam al-shahāda*.[6] In Kunta texts, the angels, devils, and jinn of the Qurʾān are placed within a greater cosmological imaginary inspired by Greek philosophy. In their cosmological discussions they use a technical vocabulary that can be traced back to Aristotle, while positioning those terms within a Neoplatonic framework in which all existence emanates from God.[7] The cosmology of the Kunta texts is also based on the principles of what scholars refer to as lettrism and Muslim writers in Arabic call the science of letters (*ʿilm al-hurūf*), the idea that the letters of the Arabic alphabet, and their numerical equivalents, constitute the building blocks of the universe.[8]

That said, the *ʿālam al-ghayb* is rarely the direct topic of sustained discussion in the Kunta texts, but rather forms an intellectual backdrop that occurs across different discussions and categories of texts. Attention to this metaphysical framework reveals that the Kunta scholars organized different human bodies into a sociospiritual hierarchy according to their differential access to the realm of the unseen. According to these scholars, all believing Muslims acquire some knowledge of the invisible through the mediating role of the human heart. Devotional Muslim practices purify the heart and prepare individuals for travel within the unseen, but they also provide a dangerous opening for attacks by devils and other unseen entities. Ultimately, only those with perfect bodies, as demonstrated by extraordinary acts of devotion, will successively navigate these threats and achieve mastery over the unseen. It is this claim—to master the invisible world—that serves as the basis for the Kunta scholars' understanding of their authority as Sufi friends of God. The first section of this chapter lays out the architecture of the realm of the unseen as it appears in the Kunta's writings, with a particular focus on the role of the heart as the bridge between the visible and invisible worlds. The next section discusses how certain valorized individuals acquire particular knowledge of God and the unseen, and thus become the site for the manifestation of all created existence. Because this process occurs within and through the heart of believing Muslims, the final section discusses the relationship between knowledge of the unseen and the perfection of the heart and the physical body through devotional practice.

The Invisible World

In the Kunta texts, the visible world and the realm of the unseen are imagined as conjoined opposites—two sides of one coin. On one register, the visible world (*ʿālam al-shahāda*) and the unseen (*al-ghayb*) correspond to the opposition between this world (*al-dunyā*) and the next (*al-ākhira*). In the Kunta imaginary, the next world refers both to a set of places—the garden and the fire—and to a time, the eschatological period when God destroys the world and then resurrects and judges its inhabitants.[9] In one passage from the *Jidhwat al-anwār*, Sīdi al-Mukhtār quotes a description of the end-times attributed to Ibn ʿAbbās, one of the companions of the Prophet. The scene begins by describing the tightly packed crowd of resurrected people assembled for judgment, and then depicts an invisible voice that summons groups of people to escape from the crowd and pass directly into the garden. These groups include "those who praised God at all times," "those whose minds drew them from their beds, calling to their lord in fear and longing, and giving away in alms what we gave them as sustenance," "those who were not distracted from the remembrance of God by trade or commerce, and undertook prayer and gave alms, fearing the day that hearts and fates would reverse," and finally "those who obeyed [God] and preserved [His] compact, not because of the unseen (*la li'l-ghayb*)." Earlier in the same text, Sīdi al-Mukhtār refers to this last group of believers as those whose "minds stop seeking the garden and no longer fear, through avoidance of the fire, being denied it; rather, they worship Him for the sake of His glory and His might and His greatness." Thus, in this particular scene, Sīdi al-Mukhtār uses the term *al-ghayb* to refer specifically to heaven and hell. Those who obeyed and worshipped God, not out of fear of hell or desire to reach heaven but for the sake of God alone, will escape from the packed crowd. This group "will stand up and their faces will be full moons, made up of the best parts of light, to which a red ruby will adhere and by which they will fly to the head of the martyrs and continue, by means of it, into the presence of God. . . . So they will pass onto the dazzling road of lightning and then the gates of the garden will open up for them and they will glorify in it as they will."[10]

Although the Kunta scholars often locate the garden and the fire in the specific temporal frame of the end-times, these locations also inform their understanding of the invisible world as a separate cosmological realm. In this register, the visible world and the realm of the unseen are distinguished spatially, as higher and lower planes of existence. Thus both Sīdi al-Mukhtār and Sīdi Muḥammad refer to the unseen as *al-malakūt*, the higher, invisible, or immaterial plane, and to the lower, material world as *al-mulk*. For example, in one passage from the *Jidhwat al-anwār*, Sīdi al-Mukhtār describes the process of traveling between these planes to reach God as a dissolution of boundaries: "His sleeping enters into his waking and his waking into his sleeping, and his life into his afterlife and his afterlife into his life, and his secret into his publicness (*ʿilāniyya*) and his publicness into his secret, and his *mulk* into his *malakūt* and his *malakūt* into his *mulk*."[11] Other passages from Kunta texts also mention a third realm, *al-jabarūt*. The terms that the Kunta use for these three realms have a long history within Sufi cosmological discussions, with different systems proposing different orders for the various realms, and some systems adding the realms of *al-nāsūt* and *al-lāhūt* to these three.[12] The Kunta's presentation of the three cosmological realms of *al-malakūt*, *al-mulk*, and *al-jabarūt* most closely resembles that of the late eleventh-century Sufi philosopher al-Ghazālī. According to al-Ghazālī's schema, *al-jabarūt* acts as the intermediary realm that sits between and binds together the heavenly *malakūt* and the physical *mulk*. In this configuration, *al-jabarūt* acts as the most important realm, allowing the other two to fulfill their function by giving each access to the other. In this fashion, *al-jabarūt* lies, spatially, between the other two, while representing the completion of the universe by uniting and permitting congress between the unseen and material realms.[13] The Kunta scholars do not focus on elaborating the relationship between these realms to the same degree as al-Ghazālī, but in his *Sharḥ al-qaṣīda al-fayḍiyya*, Sīdi al-Mukhtār describes the ascent through the realms to God in these terms: "He [God] opens upon them three secrets from the secrets of the unseen [aspects] of the Real [*ghayūb al-ḥaqq*]. So with the first secret they see *al-mulk*, and with the second *al-malakūt*, and with the third *al-jabarūt*—which is the talisman of the two preceding secrets, because it turns you away from them and is the veil for them; indeed, their affair is only completed by means of it."[14] At first, this passage appears to place *al-jabarūt* as the highest realm, as it is the last of the three secrets revealed as the believer ascends toward God. However, the final line indicates that *al-jabarūt* in fact mediates between the other two, completing them by separating each from the other. If the realm of the unseen and the visible world represent two sides of one coin, then *al-jabarūt* is the substance of that coin, binding the two together.

On yet another register, the realm of the unseen includes the invisible inhabitants of the various cosmological realms—primarily angels, devils, and jinn. Various Kunta texts portray the friends of God interacting with unnamed angels. In one passage from the *Jidhwat al-anwār*, Sīdi al-Mukhtār describes how, when a pious believer dies, God raises his spirit to a "high place," which he refers to with the Qur'ānic term *ʿIllyīn* (83:18–19). Then "God creates angels faster than the blink of an eye" to protect him on the journey. "Then He loves him, so when He loves him He orders Jibrīl to cry out among the people of the heavens [*ahl al-samawāt*][15] and the martyrs that God loves so-and-so—so love him!"[16] In addition to the unnamed ranks of angels and other inhabitants of the heavens, Sīdi al-Mukhtār also refers here to Jibrīl, whom the Kunta identify with "the faithful spirit" (*al-rūḥ al-amīn*) of the Qur'ān, and who appears often in their texts in the role of a messenger between God and both the prophets and the people of the heavens.[17] In addition to Jibrīl, the Kunta texts reference other specific angels, including Mīkā'īl, Isrāfīl, and ʿAzrā'īl; the archangels (*al-karūbiyyūn*); "those who are brought near" (*al-muqarrabūn*),[18] those who carry and circle God's throne (*al-ḥāffīn*, Qur'ān 39:75), "the spiritual entities" (*al-rūḥāniyyūn*), the angel of death (*malak al-mawt*) (Qur'ān 32:11), the two angels who question the believer in the grave, and the punishing angels (*al-zabāniyya al-ʿadhāb*).[19] Indeed, angels fill the Kunta texts, and although they belong primarily to the realm of the unseen, they often descend into and interact with the visible world. Thus stories recounted in Sīdi Muḥammad's hagiography of his father indicate that angels can and do interact directly with the bodies of believing Muslims. One story from the *Ṭarāʾif wa'l-talāʾid*, for example, claims that an angel punished Sīdi al-Mukhtār for looking at an unrelated woman by slapping his left eye, blinding it for a time.[20]

The direct counterparts to the angels of the Kunta texts are the devils (*shayāṭīn*). The word *shayāṭīn* is associated with the Qurʾānic story of Iblīs, who refused God's order to bow before Adam and as a result was cast from heaven and forced to wander the earth as *al-Shayṭān*, the Satan, or the Devil. Theologians debated whether Iblīs was an angel, and whether angels were capable of disobeying God. The Kunta specifically identify angels as protected from sin (*maʿṣūm*) and suggest that Iblīs was instead a member of a third race known as the jinn.[21] While the Kunta do not explain the relationship between devils and *the* Devil, various passages suggest that "devils" refer to humans and jinn who fall under the sway of *Shayṭān*.[22] In *Khalwa*, for example, Sīdi al-Mukhtār describes how jinn appear to Muslims who undertake a spiritual retreat and attempt to distract them from their devotions to God. These jinn try several different methods of misleading a secluded believer. First, they "show him their faces" in an attempt to frighten him, but if he succeeds in adhering to his devotions and ignoring his assailants, then they

> bring forth evil whisperings [*al-waswās*]. But if they find his heart inhabited by remembrance of God, then the lights of that remembrance burn them and they flee out of self-preservation. . . . Then they lose hope for the one whose heart is inhabited [with remembrance], so they change their approach to him and glorify him as one of the righteous and they tell him their names and bring him news about unseen things [*al-mughayyibāt*] . . . and they say to him: "Go to so-and-so and tell him that he is one of the people of the garden because of such-and-such deed," which only he knew about. And so he is deceived by that news . . . and people come to him, thinking that he is a friend, but he is a *shayṭān*, ensnared. The *shayāṭīn* have seduced him.[23]

By the end of this passage, the narrator is referring to both the jinn *and* the secluded believer as *shayāṭīn*: the jinn for tricking a Muslim into abandoning his quest for God, and the human for falling into their trap. However, the jinn/*shayāṭīn* in this passage do not lie to their target. They truly do bring him knowledge of the unseen, including true information about the actions of others. The deception here consists of enticing the believer away from God by means of this secret knowledge.

While it is useful to think of the realm of the unseen in the separate registers of time, space, and inhabitants, these registers collapse when the Kunta texts address the human body. In the anthropological imagination of these texts, the human body, and specifically the heart, partakes of both the visible and invisible worlds and serves as the gate allowing passage between the two. Indeed, in the Kunta texts the heart plays a role within the human body similar to that which the realm of *al-jabarūt* plays on a cosmic scale. Just as the middle realm lies between and permits congress across the lower and higher planes, so too does the heart connect a corporeal body to the unseen realm. And just as the visible world acts as a barrier to the realm of the unseen, so does the inclination of a believer to the *dunyā*, the world of the body, prevent the heart from accessing the world of the spirit. In this role, the heart represents *al-jabarūt*, the cosmological realm that both separates and permits congress between *al-malakūt* and *al-mulk*. Thus in the *Sharḥ al-qaṣīda al-fayḍiyya*—the same work that describes *al-jabarūt* as the talisman that completes the other two realms—Sīdi al-Mukhtār describes the human body as a "talisman" that each believer must break to "win the treasure of his heart."[24] In the Kunta imaginary, the human heart acts as the organ of perception of the unseen, just as the five senses provide information about the visible world. In the *Kitāb zawāl al-ilbās*, Sīdi al-Mukhtār writes, "There is for the hearts of the prophets and the friends an acquaintance with [*maṭālaʿa ʿalā*] the unseen realm, just as for the senses there is an acquaintance with the visible world."[25] Communication with the invisible world is thus easier during sleep, when the five senses are stilled. Indeed, the text identifies "abundance of being occupied in the world of sensory perception and inclining toward it" as the primary veil between a believer and both the realm of the unseen and the divine presence at its heart.[26]

In addition to the heart, which lies in both the visible and invisible worlds, these texts assign every human body two fully invisible components: a self (*nafs*) and a spirit (*rūḥ*). The Kunta scholars explicitly identify the *nafs* of the believer with both the aforementioned "inclination" for the world of the senses and the "whisperings" of the devils. The *nafs* of the Kunta texts is an exclusively negative force. The seat of carnal passions and trivial desires, the self distracts a believer from God and leads her into evil and corruption. Thus an individual's moral character is determined by the extent to which she resists and controls the desires of her *nafs*. According to Sīdi al-Mukhtār and Sīdi Muḥammad, the self requires constant surveillance and training. Once a believer joins the ranks of the friends, however, God takes control of his *nafs*. Thus, in the *Jidhwat al-anwār*, Sīdi al-Mukhtār quotes another scholar as saying, "The true friend is whomever God brings close to Him, and repels from him his devil [*shayṭānihi*], and takes possession of his self and does not allow it power over him."[27] In contrast, the spirit (*rūḥ*) is neither good nor evil; rather, people use their spirits as tools for good or evil purposes. The spirit inhabits and animates the body, but, unlike the *nafs*, it can leave and travel forth from it.[28] Indeed, one of the primary properties of the human spirit is its ability to detach itself from the human body. Moreover, the Kunta are very clear that a person's spirit has the ability to interact with and alter both other human bodies and material objects in the perceptible world. For example, Sīdi Muḥammad tells a story about a group of people who can remove the seeds from a pomegranate without opening it and another about a group who use their spirits to repel an enemy army from a fortress.[29] As the mirror of the macrocosm, the human body draws together the cosmological, temporal, and interpersonal aspects of the unseen. Just as the larger cosmos contains a material realm, a spiritual realm, and one that mediates between them, so too does the human body contain an aspect that inclines to the material (the *nafs*), a component that partakes of the spiritual (the *rūḥ*), and a heart that mediates between the two. The body partakes in temporal life and death but will be miraculously resurrected on the Day of Judgment. And, as we will see below, it is through the actions of the body in ritual devotion that a believer encounters and interacts with angels, devils, and jinn.

Finally, at the heart of the realm of the unseen lies the most important of invisible entities—God. Following Neoplatonic Sufi traditions, the Kunta scholars understand all of creation as emanating from God, the wellspring of all existence. In his *Kitāb al-minna*, Sīdi al-Mukhtār explains his understanding of God by drawing on the Ashʿarī theological categories of the essence (*dhāt*), attributes (*ṣifāt*), and acts (*afʿāl*) of God.[30] In this text, the Kunta scholar explains that God alone does not depend on the process of creation, that he is the only being "for whom existence [*al-wujūd*] is necessary [*yujiba lahu*]." That is, God is the only entity whose existence itself is absolute, independent, and uncreated. Moreover, what is true for God's essence (*dhāt*) is true for both his attributes (*ṣifāt*) and his acts (*afʿāl*). Just as he exists before the creation of existence, he also has knowledge (and life, speech, sight, etc.) and *knows* (lives, speaks, sees, etc.) even before the creation of things to know, words to speak, and sights to see. Finally, it is from God's real, essential existence, attributes, and acts that created beings gain their own existence, attributes, and acts. Sīdi al-Mukhtār refers to these derivative human components as "metaphorical" (*majāzī*): "Know that God Most High made for us a metaphorical existence, within which His real existence acts. . . . And he made for us a metaphorical power that we might infer from it His true power acting within our metaphorical power. And He made for us a figurative will that we might infer from it His true will. . . . And He made for us a figurative knowledge, that we might infer by it our true, eternal knowledge, for all is from Him and toward Him. And He made for us a figurative life that we might infer by it His true life." Thus people both exist and can be described as "powerful," "willing," "knowing," and "alive" only because they have been granted extensions of God's own properties and because he himself works within them. The passage continues in this vein for the properties of hearing, sight, and speech ("and He made for us a metaphorical hearing"), with the addition that human perceptions depend on physical properties, such as sensory organs and directionality. In contrast, God's perceptions have no need of these corporeal limitations; they function only through his essence.[31] According to Sīdi al-Mukhtār and Sīdi Muḥammad, God creates the universe from himself—his own essence, attributes, and acts—and then works within these ontological echoes. As a result, God's own life exists within every created metaphorical life.

In a passage from the *Fawāʾid nūrāniyya*, Sīdi Muḥammad describes the process by which God creates the various realms of the cosmos from his own essence, attributes, and acts by means of his "most beautiful names" (*al-asmāʾ al-ḥusnā*).

> Know that God Most High created *al-malakūt* of the lights and established its parlors [*maqāʿid*] by means of His noble names . . . just as He created the realm of *al-mulk* and the realm of *al-jabarūt* and established their parlors by means of His noble names. Then He created the angels of *al-malakūt* from the lights of the throne [*al-ʿarsh*] because the throne was created from the names of the essence [*al-dhāt*] by means of the secret of secrets. Then He created the angels of *al-jabarūt* from the light of the footstool [*al-kursī*] because it stands upon the names of the characteristics. . . . Then He created the angels of the realm of *al-mulk* from the light of the tablet [*al-lawḥ*] because it is based on the names of the actions.[32]

The divine throne, footstool, pen, and preserved tablet are all terms drawn from the Qur'ān that have been ascribed symbolic importance by various Muslim and Sufi interpreters.[33] In the Kunta's interpretation, these terms find their roles in a cosmogonic process in which the various realms of the world are created directly from different aspects of God. Thus, for the Kunta writers, the nature of God is not merely a point of contention in a theological argument; rather, God's essence, attributes, and actions form the metaphysical substance from which he created the universe and its components.

The Return to God

While sense perceptions allow all humans access to the manifest material world, the unseen aspects of creation become apparent only to the hearts of believing Muslims. Sīdi al-Mukhtār explains that believing Muslims "become acquainted" with the unseen "in [one of] two ways: the first is God Most High informing them [of the unseen] and the other is God creating faith in their hearts and creating in them an inborn disposition for it and beautifying it in their hearts and making them to love it."[34] Thus believers know about the unseen in the first place because of references in the Qurʾān and *ḥadīth* to various aspects of the invisible world, such as the afterlife, angels, jinn, and devils. However, beyond information about the unseen communicated directly by God through prophetic revelation, believers also become acquainted with the unseen because of the faith in their hearts. That is, by acknowledging God, they also acknowledge the unseen foundation of their own existence, and thus they acquire knowledge of the invisible realm by existing in it, just as created beings gain knowledge of the manifest realm by living in it. Sīdi al-Mukhtār emphasizes that only those who hear, but disbelieve, God's revelation to Muḥammad have no acquaintance at all with the realm of the unseen. The senses of these unbelievers might provide them information about the material world, but by rejecting God they reject the source of all existence and are cut off from all things concealed.

However, while the Kunta allow that all believing Muslims experience the unseen realm to some extent, Sīdi al-Mukhtār emphasizes that this experience varies "in accordance with the rank [*manzila*] of the informed heart."[35] For the Kunta scholars, all believing Muslims occupy a hierarchy arranged according to the purity of their hearts and thus their proximity to God. Indeed, Sīdi al-Mukhtār and Sīdi Muḥammad present the process of training at the hands of a Sufi shaykh as a purification of the heart and ascent toward the divine: as each believer's proximity to God increases, so too does his knowledge of the unseen realm. And although many believers will achieve some stage along this path, only a select few will reach the ultimate goal. These valorized few go beyond acknowledging God and the unseen as the foundation and framework for their existence and directly experience all of creation as an extension of God. The Kunta texts depict this process as a sequence of destruction and re-creation. First, the believer experiences the destruction of the created world, which disappears into the unity of the divine; then the process is reversed, as the heart and body of the new friend of God become the site for the re-creation of the universe.

As discussed in the preceding section, the Kunta scholars locate the ascent toward God within the human heart, the organ through which Muslims come to know God and in which God manifests himself to them.[36] But the inclination of a believer's self to the *dunyā*, the world of the body, prevents the heart from accessing the world of the spirit. Thus, in order to control the inclination of the self toward the manifest world, a believer must submit to the training of a Sufi shaykh, himself a friend of God. This shaykh engages the seeker, his disciple (*murīd*), in a series of exercises (*riyāḍāt*) designed to tame and control the *nafs*, clearing the way to knowledge of God. These texts associate controlling the self with Sufi training to such an extent that Sīdi Muḥammad compares the devotion of Sufis to legal scholars' devotion to the law, or the *ḥadīth* folk to the sayings of the Prophet: "So the judges undertook renewal of the provisions of judging and the *amīrs* the renewals of ruling, and the exegetes the fulfilling of the judgments of the Qur'ān and its etiquette and the *ḥadīth*-folk the preservation of the *ḥadīth* and their accuracy, and the legal scholars the reporting of the *ḥalāl* and the *ḥarām* and its preservation, and the Sufis [*al-ṣūfiyya*], the science of struggling with the self, and training it, and curing its illnesses and pruning its hidden thickets."[37] Only when the self is trained, cured, and pruned by following a Sufi shaykh will God manifest his love for his servant by "lifting the veil from his heart until he sees Him with it."[38]

When Sīdi al-Mukhtār and Sīdi Muḥammad describe the believer's ascent through various stations toward God, they speak of increasing love (*maḥabba*) between God and his servant, who receives lights (*anwār*) in a series of manifestations (*tajallīyāt*) and disclosures (*mukāshifāt*). Like Sufi writers before them, the Kunta understand these disclosures as moving a believer through a progression of states (*aḥwāl*) and stages (*maqāmāt*), most of which come in contrasting pairs, such as awe and intimacy, hope and fear, enrichment and poverty, and expansion and contraction.[39] Moreover, in one passage, which recurs almost verbatim in both the *Jidhwat al-anwār* and the *Sharḥ al-qaṣīda al-fayḍiyya*, Sīdi al-Mukhtār relates the rankings of these various stations to the actions, attributes, and essence of God.

> All those who arrive at the purity of certainty by the way of tasting [*dhawq*] and ecstasy [*wijdān*] have achieved a degree from the degrees of arriving. . . . Included among them are those who define God in the path of acts [*af'āl*]—which is a degree in the manifestation [*al-tajallī*]. So they are annihilated, by means of that, from their actions and the actions of others by undertaking the actions of God. So in this state he leaves planning and choice.
>
> And among them are those who stand in the station of awe and intimacy by means of acquaintance with the glory and perfection that their hearts disclose to them. And this is manifested through the path of the attributes [*ṣifāt*], which is a degree in arriving.
>
> And among them are those who rise to a station of annihilation in which the light of certainty and witnessing encloses their hearts, washed away by their witnessing from their existing. And this is a blow from the

> manifestation of the essence [*dhāt*] to the elite who are brought near. And this is a degree in arriving, and above this degree is the truth of certainty and there they are in effacement and it is the flowing of the light of witnessing in the entirety of the servant until his spirit and his heart and his self and his form [*qālibuhu*] obtain it.[40]

The idea of the extinction (*fanā'*) of the conscious self of the believer in the totality of the divine goes back to the earliest Islamic mystical writings.[41] This passage describes a series of annihilations correlated to different ranks of believers as they "arrive at" different degrees of knowing God. Some will come to know God through his actions and find their own actions effaced, others will connect to his attributes, and still others will witness the divine essence, which will annihilate even their sense of existing (*wujūd*).

However, the passage also hints at yet a higher station, beyond annihilation in the essence of God. Sīdi al-Mukhtār refers to this last degree as a light that flows into the believer until it suffuses every aspect of her being: her spirit, her heart, her self, and her physical form. Elsewhere, the Kunta refer to this last station as abiding (*baqā'*), which both complements and fulfills the purpose of extinction. Indeed, these two stations—annihilation and abiding—are the most frequently discussed within the Kunta's works and represent their understanding of the goal of the Sufi path. Sīdi Muḥammad even defines friendship with God by saying, "In the understanding of the Sufis, it [friendship] is annihilation in God and abiding with him. Annihilation is sinking into witnessing him with the heart [*al-mushāhidihi al-qalbiyya*] until he is unaware of anything but Him; rather, he is annihilated from himself and from the rest of his kind. And [the state of] being unaware of anything but Him is the end of traveling to Him. Then he abides with Him because he is the site of manifestation [*maẓhar*] of God's actions and wishes, without choice in the wellspring [*'ayn*] of His choice."[42] Thus, for Sīdi Muḥammad, friendship with God can be summarized by the twin processes of annihilation and abiding—which he once again situates within the heart of the believer. Moreover, according to this passage, a believer who reaches the station of abiding with God becomes "the site of the manifestation of God's actions and wishes." This statement is crucial because, as described above, God's actions, along with his attributes and essence, are the very substance out of which he created the universe. Thus, at the highest stage of the Sufi path, the heart of the believer becomes the location of God's creation, and the macrocosm of the universe is revealed to inhabit the body of the believer.

In one of the most elaborate descriptions of this process, the *Sharḥ al-qaṣīda al-fayḍiyya* traces the ascent of a believer to the highest stage of the path, where he becomes the site of, and source for, all of created existence. Over the course of six manuscript pages, Sīdi al-Mukhtār describes the entrance of the believer into the presence of God, resulting in the annihilation of the individual and created existence, followed by the subsequent abiding of the believer and the internal re-creation of the universe. The path begins with the training of the self: "The first rank by which he reaches the presence is the training of the self with exercises until it results in knowing it and at that point the lights shine upon it." At this stage the self does not pass away but rather becomes completely comprehended, illuminated, and indeed visible to the believer in a series of visions. Moreover, once the believer understands his own self, he comes to see clearly the selves of others as well: "he sees the self of the believer, pure whiteness, and he sees the self of the corrupted, clouded muddiness, and he sees the self of the unbeliever and the hypocrite, intensely dark black." From this understanding of human selves, the seeker then progresses to the stages of the heart and then the spirit: "And the second stage is the heart. So he becomes occupied with its training and knowing it. . . . Then he rises to the third stage, which is the spirit [*rūḥ*]. So when he knows it [the spirit] and his knowing of it is complete, then the winds of certainty blow upon him and the sides of the expanse swell and water flows, running, the rays of perception separated by flashes of lightning . . . and he comprehends nothing of what has come to him from the three stages, and there he is bewildered as God wills."[43] This stage of bewilderment in the love of God marks the end of the process of training and coming to know the various components of the believer. The believer's intellect is bewildered and "comprehends nothing," and nevertheless he fully knows his own self, heart, and spirit.

At this point, the seeker moves beyond the limits of human characteristics and begins to acquire knowledge of the cosmos and then of God himself: "Then God supports him by the light of the original Intellect [*al-ʿaql al-aṣlī*] in the lights of certainty and he sees a being [*mawjūd*] with no border or limit in addition to this servant. Then all of the existing entities [*kāʾināt*] dwindle away but this being remains." The seeker then hears the voice of a concealed speaker, who "says to him that this being is the Intellect [*ʿaql*] by means of which God takes and gives and it is the outpourer [*al-sāqī*] and the created before any creation."[44] In another work, Sīdi al-Mukhtār mentions this moment as a particularly dangerous point along the Sufi path, when a believer risks conflating this vast being with God himself.[45] Only a true friend of God will receive the guidance necessary—here represented as a voice from an invisible speaker—to correctly identify this being as "the Intellect." While Sīdi al-Mukhtār refers to this being as "the original Intellect" here, later in the same text he uses the specific term "the Active Intellect" (*al-ʿaql al-faʿaliyya*).[46] The idea of "the Active

Intellect" entered Sufi cosmology from Greek philosophy and is often considered one of the agents mediating between the celestial and material, or human, realms.[47] Sīdi al-Mukhtār's description of "the Intellect" also serves to highlight the parallels between the microcosm of the human and the macrocosm of the universe. Thus, just as a person has a specific intellect, so too is there a cosmic, original "Intellect." And just as a person has an individual spirit, so too is there a universal, macrocosmic Spirit: "[God] supports him with the light of the lordly Spirit. . . . Then God Most High enlivens him with the light of his attributes and they bring him by degrees into this life, so by means of them he knows this lordly being. . . . Then God supports him with the light of the secret of the Spirit. And when he is sitting at the gate to the field of the secret then he loses consciousness, for all of his attributes are destroyed until he becomes as if he were nothing."[48] As the seeker becomes illuminated by the divine Spirit, he ascends into the sphere of God's attributes, and then, illuminated by the secret of the Spirit, he achieves annihilation and all of his own attributes disappear. This moment marks the point where the believer has returned to the nonexistence that preceded creation. The passage begins with the revelation of all the created forms as the believer came to know the components of his own being. The multiplicity of these created beings then disappeared, replaced by the singularity of "the Active Intellect," as the seeker rose to the level of the cosmos. Finally, as the seeker is brought into the divine presence, both "the Active Intellect" and all of his own attributes are annihilated—leaving nothing at all. Thus, as the believer moves upward toward God, he also moves backward through time in a process of de-creation.

From this point of nonexistence, extinction, and annihilation, Sīdi al-Mukhtār reverses the process, describing the re-creation of the world through the believer. First, the annihilation of the seeker becomes abiding as God illuminates him with the divine essence: "Then, at that moment, God supports him with the light of His essence and so He brings him to life at that moment with an abiding life that has no limit. Then, at that moment, he looks at all the known things with the light of this life. Thus he becomes the source of the beings [*aṣl al-mawjūdāt*], a light shining in everything, nothing but it is known."[49] According to this passage, the re-created life of the abiding believer serves as the singularity from which all other creations come into being. Later in the same text, Sīdi al-Mukhtār elaborates on this process, describing how the various components of both the cosmos and the seeker gradually reappear. Rather than a direct, linear unfolding, the internal elements of the seeker (such as his heart, spirit, and self) and external features of the cosmos (such as God's throne, pen, and tablet) are created by and within one another, interpenetrating and entangling to the point where the order of events and sequence of causation become indecipherable:

> Then this servant is brought to life . . . thus he becomes the first thing to appear, with nothing appearing before him. Then [all] things become existent by means of his qualities and appear through his light by his decree [*qadarihi*]. So the first thing that appears is his secret [*sirruhu*]; then by means of it his pen [*qalamuhu*] appears, then his command [*amruhu*] appears by means of his secret in his secret and it appears by means of his command in his command. Then by means of it his throne [*ʿarsh*] appears in the light of his footstool [*kursī*] by means of the light of his throne. Then his heart appears by means of his spirit in his spirit and it appears by means of his heart in veils [*ḥujub*] by means of the light of his footstool in the light of his footstool. Then his self [*nafs*] appears by means of his heart in his heart and it appears by means of his self in his evilness and his goodness by means of the light of his veils.[50]

All of these entangled elements, both cosmic and human, partake of the invisible realm, and as Sīdi al-Mukhtār describes their re-creation, he also positions them definitively within the physical body of the believer: "Then [his heart] appears in his body by means of his self and by means of his body [*jismhi*] [all] the bodies of the manifest realm [*al-ʿālam al-kashīf*], from earth or heaven, appear, and all together, every thing is manifest by the light of *al-mulk* in the light of *al-mulk*."[51] Thus, as creation of the unseen cosmos proceeds both from and within the unseen parts of the believer, so finally does the manifest realm, *al-mulk*, appear by means of his physical body. Creation thus proceeds from the invisible to the visible realm through the body of a Muslim who arrives at the highest point of the Sufi path.

The unseen realm that emerges from the Kunta texts consists of both the higher, spiritual realms—the sites of manifestation of God's attributes and essence—and the interior, invisible components of the believer, such as her self, spirit, and heart. The Sufi path illustrates the fundamental interdependence of these two aspects of the unseen as the invisible cosmic realms are revealed within the seeker. Finally, the last stage of the Sufi path demonstrates the relationship between the invisible and manifest realms, *al-malakūt* and *al-mulk*, the *ʿālam al-ghayb* and *ʿālam al-shahāda*, as the believer's body becomes the source for the creation of *all* bodies. However, these descriptions of the Sufi path within the Kunta texts also highlight the vast gulf between the general "acquaintance with the unseen," available to all believers, and the intimate knowledge of the *ʿālam al-ghayb* bestowed only upon the friends of God. For while the masses of believing Muslims might learn that all existence originates in God, those who reach the end of the Sufi path will directly experience this unity, as the created world extends outward, through the macrocosm/microcosm of their perfect hearts, and from there to all material bodies.

Perfect Bodies

Sīdi al-Mukhtār and Sīdi Muḥammad al-Kuntī ascribe a great deal of cosmic importance to the physical heart and body of the believing Muslim. When a seeker reaches the highest point of the Sufi path, the entire unseen realm is manifested within, and the entire physical realm through, her body. Thus, the Kunta texts dedicate a significant amount of attention to how Muslims use their bodies, and in particular to their engagement in various devotional practices, from reading or listening to the Qurʾān, to fasting, to ritual prayer. The Kunta writers clearly understand Muslim devotional practice as intimately concerned with the *ʿālam al-ghayb*, and they insist that access to the unseen realm and advancement along the path to God come only through correct use of a believer's own body. Moreover, while engaging in both required and supplemental devotional practices provides benefits to all Muslims, Sīdi al-Mukhtār and Sīdi Muḥammad understand the level of physical exertion necessary to reach the pinnacle of the path as beyond the capacities of most people. Not everyone will attain annihilation and abiding in God's essence or become the source of all created beings. That role they reserve for the perfect hearts and bodies of the prophets and their successors, the friends of God.

As demonstrated above, the Kunta understanding of the unseen includes the Sufi path and the ascension of believers through various degrees of knowing God. According to the Kunta shaykhs, the various ranks of believing Muslims along this path correspond to perceivable changes to their bodies. Thus, in his *Sharḥ al-qaṣīda al-fayḍiyya*, Sīdi al-Mukhtār writes:

> And the people who love God are of two types: the first type love Him for the sake of the good that He brings them and His kindness to them, and this is the love of the masses . . . and the second type loves Him for the sake of His greatness and His majesty and His might and His power, and whether they are tried or spared does not alter the love of Him in their hearts . . . and this is the love of the elite . . . and the people of this degree in love are also of two types. So the first type, their bodies shrivel up from the heat of their love and their color changes from its blaze and its burning. The second type, their bodies fatten up when rejoicing in witnessing Him intermingles with [their bodies].[52]

The passage goes on to explain that the shriveling of the body and the unhealthy hue of the skin correspond to the state of fear of God, while the fattening of the body corresponds to the state of hope and rejoicing in being brought near.[53] Thus as believers move from a station of fear and distance to one of hope and proximity, their bodies undergo perceptible changes. Moreover, just as the physical condition of the believer corresponds to different stages along the Sufi path, so too can the realization of God in the heart of a believer have direct and noticeable effects on her external body. Sīdi al-Mukhtār relates a story about a famous early Sufi, Abū Yazīd al-Bisṭāmī: "Abū Yazīd al-Bisṭāmī, was, on a Friday, facing the pulpit when the speaker was making his address, and he read, *They measured not God with His true measure* [Qur'ān 6:91], and when it [the verse] fell upon the ear of Abū Yazīd, blood flowed from his eyes until it hit the pulpit, and that was because he was immersed in the sea of might and majesty. So when that majestic address passed by his ears, the winds of might stirred in his heart until the blood flowed from his eyes."[54] In this story, a Qur'ānic verse that refers to the greatness of God causes two of the divine attributes—might and majesty—to awaken in Bisṭāmī's heart, a process that becomes visible as blood runs from his eyes. These references to processes that begin in the heart of a believer and then affect her physical condition follow from the interpenetrating of the manifest and unseen realms. If God and all the cosmos are contained in the heart of a believer, then changes to that cosmos will affect the believer's heart, and thus her body.

Moreover, the Kunta texts demonstrate that this process works in reverse as well; just as events in the unseen realm can affect human bodies, so can the actions of those bodies travel through the heart into the unseen realm. Thus when Muslims engage in correct devotional practice (ritual prayer, fasting, and remembrance of God), those actions elicit a direct response from the *ʿālam al-ghayb*. "God Most High said *to Him good words go up and righteous deeds rise* [Qur'ān 35:10]. This means that good words appear from the good heart and go to God themselves, having no goal save Him. And righteous deeds are raised by the angels to *Illyīn*. . . . And if his spirit is seized, it is raised to that high place. Then God creates angels faster than the blink of an eye from that *takbīr*, they repulse from him the restrained jinn, and in their hands are whips of light."[55] Once again, the heart serves as the connection between the actions of the believer—in this case the pronouncement of the *takbīr* (God is great) and the higher realm. Moreover, if that believer's spirit also returns to God, those words become the substance from which God creates angels to defend the spirit from attacks by the jinn. This process of creating angels from words evokes God's creation of the three realms of existence from his own names, discussed earlier. Indeed, the Kunta often imagine words and speech as traveling through and interacting with the unseen realm. In the *Sharḥ al-qaṣīda al-fayḍiyya*, for example, Sīdi al-Mukhtār explains that the phrase "'in the name of God, the compassionate, the merciful' is a veil between those who take refuge in it and the punishing angels [*zabāniyya al-ʿadhāb*], because the punishing angels have nineteen leaders and [the phrase] has nineteen letters—each letter subdues one of the angels."[56] This passage depicts the letters that form this phrase as traveling outward to interpose themselves between a believer and the leaders of these angels.

The physical body of the believer contains a direct connection to the realm of the unseen through his heart, but this does not mean that the Kunta valorize the manifest realm or encourage aspirants on the Sufi path to engage in it. On the contrary, as noted earlier, it is occupation with the physical world that prevents a believer's heart from accessing the realm of the unseen. Thus, in the *Kitāb zawāl al-ilbās*, Sīdi al-Mukhtār states that "unseen things appear to the sleeper that do not appear to the one who is awake because of the stilling of the realm of his senses. Because it is abundance of being occupied in the world of sensory perception and inclining toward it, and especially those parts of it that are legally prohibited, that creates in the heart doubts and delusions and thoughts that veil him from being informed of the unseen."[57] Passages like this one often depict the believer as torn between love of the material realm, perceptible to the senses, and love of God and the unseen realm, perceptible to the heart. Indeed, in the Kunta texts, the physical human body performs a dual function. On the one hand, the implication of the body in the material world acts as a barrier between the believer and the *ʿālam al-ghayb*; on the other hand, however, it is only through the engagement of the body in ritual action that a seeker can purify his heart and attain any knowledge of God. In this fashion the body serves in the same dual role as a gate—it both prevents and permits access to the heart. And it is because of this gatelike function that Sīdi al-Mukhtār refers to the body as a "talisman": "and whoever does not break the talisman of his body will not win the treasure of his heart."[58]

In the Kunta texts, breaking the talisman of the body requires the performance of various "exercises" under the guidance of a Sufi shaykh, with the ultimate goal of pulling the self away from its obsession with the material world. These exercises involve corporeal "devotions" (*ʿibādāt*), including both obligatory practices, such as ritual prayer and fasting during Ramaḍān, and supererogatory practices such as ritual seclusion (*khalwa*) and additional prayers or fasts. Thus, in one section of the *Sharḥ al-qaṣīda al-fayḍiyya*, Sīdi al-Mukhtār discusses the practice of fasting for forty days:

> And the shaykh Abū ʿAbd Allāh al-Sāṭī,[59] may God have mercy on him, said, "I saw [several] men, none of which broke their fast except at the head of forty days," so it was said to him, "where did the burning of their abdomens go?" And he said: "the light of witnessing and the flowing nectar of love extinguish it. Then the rays of the light of his heart are reflected and the self is pulled out from the manifest realm [*ʿālam al-kashīf*] to the subtle realm [*ʿālam al-laṭīf*], like iron is pulled by magnetic stones, and thus it becomes tranquil."[60]

In this story, the act of fasting out of devotion to God eliminates the physical sensation of hunger and pulls the self entirely out of the manifest realm, causing it to grow calm. Sīdi al-Mukhtār and his son insist that these devotional exercises are an absolutely necessary part of the approach to God, with Sīdi Muḥammad writing that anyone who "directs his face toward the Real without looking at his practice [*sunna*] in his devotions [*ʿibādihi*]—then there is doubtless error in his deeds, straying in his states, and calamity in his statements, thus he is either destroyed or he destroys."[61] Similarly, Sīdi al-Mukhtār devotes the majority of the *Kitāb zawāl al-ilbās* to listing various ways in which Muslims can become "deceived" by Satan—many of which involve failing to perform or understand the importance of one or another type of devotional action.

Finally, after listing all the categories of deceived believers, Sīdi al-Mukhtār attributes the root cause of all forms of deception to "the lack of presence with God in prayer, because it repeats many times during the day. And if they are present with God during all of them—or most of them—then Satan does not lodge firmly within their hearts and whisper to them."[62] This statement indicates the centrality of formal, ritual, prayer (*ṣalāt*)[63] to the Kunta leaders' understanding of the Sufi path, and evokes their description of remembrance of God as filling the heart and thus protecting it from attacks by the jinn and *shayāṭīn*. To emphasize the importance of *ṣalāt* to his understanding of Muslim devotional practice and the path to God, Sīdi al-Mukhtār writes:

> The messenger of God, may the prayers and peace of God be upon him, said: The servant is in no state closer to his lord than in prayer [*ṣalāt*], because it is the location of those arranged in ranks [*al-maṣāfāt*] and the pulpit of intimate conversations and the core of the disclosures, and the spring of the blessings, and the gathering place of the greetings, and the ladder by which one climbs into the presence of the lord of the heavens and the earth. It is the ointment for every wound that distresses, and a panacea for every known poison.[64]

As we have seen, though, as beneficial as ritual prayer may be, it can also be dangerous, offering an opportunity for Satan to whisper to the heart of the believer multiple times a day. A believer in prayer can stave off these whisperings and realize the potential of his prayer to raise him "into the presence of his lord" only "if he stands to pray with a heavenly heart" and maintains "presence with God" through the entirety of each (or at least most) of his prayers.[65]

In the *Kitāb zawāl al-ilbās*, Sīdi al-Mukhtār explains exactly what he means by "being present with God" during prayer, and he makes it clear that not all believers will succeed in "breaking the talisman of the body." Correctly performing prayer requires a believer to "conceive in his mind the might and majesty [of God], and that he is preparing to enter into the presence of a king" at each stage of the prayer—during the ritual ablutions that proceed it, in pronouncing the *takbīr*, in raising and lowering his hands, in praising God, in reciting the selected verse from the Qur'ān, and so forth. Moreover, at various stages of the prayer, the believer may receive inspirations regarding his relationship to God, and each one of these inspirations requires a proper response. For example, when he reads the selected verse, "should he be present at that moment, then his lord Most High will address him about what it contains concerning commands and prohibitions or promises or compacts or glad tidings or warnings . . . and He will inform him of his lot from them. So let him thank God if it is glad tidings and let him ask for forgiveness and for improvement and for guidance if it is a warning . . . and if he does not do so then his lot will be failure and lack of joy."[66] These detailed instructions continue for each possible inspiration from God to the believer in prayer and extend into the bowing, prostrating, and supplicating section of the prayer, with the narrator noting at each stage that failing to maintain the proper mental state or to provide the correct response to an inspiration will result in failure and "sorrow." The accumulated effect of all these instructions is to suggest that maintaining presence with God throughout the entirety of even one prayer, and thus fending off the whisperings of Satan, is an almost impossible task, which only a very select few will accomplish. The difficulty of correctly performing the prayer recalls Sīdi al-Mukhtār's story, in the *Sharḥ al-qaṣīda al-fayḍiyya*, of al-Sāṭī fasting for forty days and thus succeeding at calming his *nafs*. The Kunta clearly do not expect all believers to successfully go without food for forty days or to "maintain presence with God" at each stage of every ritual prayer; they reserve these feats of devotional practice—and their association with the pinnacle of the Sufi path—for a very select few. In the words of Sīdi Muḥammad, "not all those who go wayfaring arrive at the presence of the king of the universe, for that is a presence none take refuge in save the well raised, and a station none acquire save those brought close, well-trained."[67]

Within the Kunta texts, the role of the paradigmatic perfect body is filled by the Prophet Muḥammad. At various points, the Kunta point out differences between Muḥammad's body and the bodies of most Muslims, indicating, for example, his particular relationship to food and fasting: "The messenger of God—prayers and peace be upon him—said: 'I am not like any one of you, for I remain with my lord who gives me food and drink, and this food is not like corporal food [*al-ṭaʿām al-jismānī*]; rather, it is spiritual food [*al-ṭaʿām al-rūḥānī*], which does not ruin a fast because it is a breaking [of the norm], and the judgments of the law don't apply to breakings.' But he only said that to them so that the strong might imitate him and the weak ones might walk in a higher path."[68] This passage once again emphasizes the antithetical nature of the corporeal and the spiritual and indicates the degree to which Muḥammad's body partook of the spiritual world, since it could be nurtured even by noncorporeal food. Indeed, in the *Kitāb zawāl al-ilbās*, Sīdi al-Mukhtār claims that while the scholars receive news of the unseen through "reports," and the friends "in a sleep that is like waking and in a waking that is like sleep," the prophets gaze directly at the unseen with their eyes, a process that caused Muḥammad physical pain because of the opposing nature of the physical and spiritual realms.[69] And because the heart and body of a believer who ascends into God's presence serve as the connection between God's light and all created bodies, Muḥammad, the archetypal believer, is also the archetypal source for knowledge of God. In one metaphor, Sīdi al-Mukhtār compares knowledge of God to a vast flood, filling first the heart of Muḥammad and then the hearts of those closest to him, and so forth, out to the masses of believers:

> And one of the knowers said: knowledge has the rank of the sea, out of which a river extends, then from the river extends a stream, then from the stream extends a creek, then from the creek extends a rivulet. And were the sea to flow into the river, or the river into the stream, it would flood it and ruin it. . . . And the Creator indicated that with His statement: *He sends down out of heaven water, and the rivers flow each in its measure* [Qurʾān 13:17], and the meaning of the water is: what God sent down on his messenger—may the prayers and peace of God be upon him—is a sea, and the hearts of his companions are rivers, and the hearts of the followers [of the companions] are streams, and the hearts of the legalists are creeks, and the hearts of the masses are rivulets.[70]

Sīdi al-Mukhtār's point in this passage is that most human hearts could not contain the totality of knowledge of God; rather, believing Muslims each acquire a particular share of knowledge of the divine through their connection to the Prophet, and according to the particular capacity of each individual heart.

However, this passage also states that knowledge of God grows increasingly attenuated the further one gets from the Prophet, and the first three ranks mentioned—the Prophet, his companions, and the generation that followed them—had long since passed away by the time of Sīdi al-Mukhtār. This analogy would suggest that knowledge of God ceased to flood into the hearts of the believers after the death of Muḥammad and the end of the period of prophecy. Does this leave the world with only the "water" contained in the remaining creeks and rivulets? For the Kunta, the answer to this question was a decided "no." Sīdi al-Mukhtār states unequivocally that "the friends are the heirs of the prophets and the inheritor has what the bequeather had."[71] This allows both him and his son to claim that, like the prophets, the friends of God are "inviolable" (*maʿṣūm*), that they too have the potential to receive a direct vision of God, and that the *ḥadīth qudsī* "Neither my earth nor my heaven encompasses me, but the heart of my believing servant encompasses me" refers specifically to God's friends.[72] As a result, when Sīdi al-Mukhtār and Sīdi Muḥammad describe the paired states of annihilation and abiding by which the heart and body become the source of all creation, they are referring specifically to the heart and body of God's friends: "His friends . . . with their light the created beings are illuminated and with their knowledge the religions were penned, and with their blessings the blessings descended and the hidden treasures appeared, and with their sanctity and illustriousness before God the sorrows were lifted."[73] Moreover, just as the hearts of the friends allow light from God to reach downward, so too can the process be reversed. Thus Sīdi al-Mukhtār explains the importance of loving the friends of God: "For their hearts are like mirrors, and whoever loves them, their names appear in those polished hearts. And God, may He be exalted and glorified, looks into the hearts of His friends every day with a merciful gaze, and whoever loves them, their names are etched in their hearts and thus they obtain their share of the mercy by which their master looks at them."[74] Like the talisman, the metaphor of the mirror works in two directions. While most believers will never ascend into the divine presence, they can broadcast an "image" of themselves onto the divine gaze by becoming inscribed in the hearts of the friends. In return, the gaze of God, reflected back through the same heart, will confer upon these lower-ranking believers a portion of God's love for his friends.[75]

Indeed, for the Kunta scholars, the continued presence of the friends of God amounts to the continuation of revelation, even after the passing of the last prophet. Thus Sīdi Muḥammad begins his introduction to the *Ṭarāʾif wa'l-talāʾid*, a work devoted to one particular friend, with this statement: "Know, oh sincere brother . . . that there is never a period without a friend of the friends of God Most High, through which he preserves the countries and the servants. . . . Their number is never deficient and their support never decreases. And if one of them was to be deficient, then the light of prophethood would be deficient."[76] The guarantee of the constant presence of the friends ensures that the light of God's revelation to humankind will continue to flood out into the hearts of the believers. To the constancy of the friends and their number, the Kunta also add a specific hierarchy, adding to the sense that the friends form part of the cosmic scaffolding underlying the universe. Thus, in his *Jidhwat al-anwār*, Sīdi Muḥammad ascribes the following statement to al-Khidr:

> Know that when He took the messenger of God—peace and prayers be upon him—the earth wept, so she said to Him, "O my master, I will remain without a prophet walking upon me until the day of resurrection!" So God revealed to her, "I shall place upon your back from among this *umma* those whose hearts are according to the hearts of the prophets—upon them be peace—I shall not make you empty of them until the day of resurrection." She said, "how many are they?" He said, "three hundred—and they are the friends; and seventy—and they are the nobles; and forty—and they are the pegs; and ten—and they are the chiefs; and seven—and they are the chosen; and three—and they are the poles; and one—and he is the succor [*al-ghawth*]. So if the *ghawth* dies, then one of the three moves and becomes the *ghawth*, and one of the seven moves to the three, and from the ten to the seven, and from the forty to the ten, and from the seventy to the forty, and from the three hundred to the seventy, and from the rest of the created beings to the three hundred, and thus until *the day the trumpet is blown* [Qurʾān 6:73]."[77]

The Kunta scholars are not the first to refer to a constant hierarchy of variously ranked friends grouped according to numbers. Various versions of this hierarchy appear in Sufi intellectual traditions.[78] Within the rhetorical world of the Kunta texts, this tradition allows Sīdi Muḥammad to acknowledge the existence of a vast number of friends of God while maintaining that, at all times, one will sit at the top of the pyramid—a position he ascribes to his father.[79] Together, these passages claim that the light of God will continue to pass into the created realm through the hearts of the friends of God—who serve as replacements for the hearts of the prophets. Moreover, they imply that as believers connect to higher and higher ranks of God's friends, they will move progressively closer to the source of the light—to God himself. Finally, in one passage, Sīdi al-Mukhtār explicitly states the reverse corollary of this claim—that rejecting the friends amounts to abandoning the search for God, writing: "Among [the things necessary for the believer to know] is having a good opinion of the friends of God, that he might draw near to their presence and be ennobled by their goals, for whoever has a poor opinion of them is expelled from their presence and whoever is expelled from their presence is expelled from the presence of God and the prophet."[80] The stakes of this claim could not be higher. The flow between God and the manifest realm goes both ways, and in both directions it passes through the hearts of the *awliyāʾ*—and in particular the highest of the friends, the *ghawth*. Flowing outward, the hearts of the friends allow the light of God to pass from the unseen to the manifest realm, assuring the continued re-creation of all existent beings. And in the other direction, these same hearts provide the *only remaining path* back toward God. Therefore, rejecting God's friends amounts to rejecting God.

Although only the hearts of the prophets and the friends of God can attain the purity and clarity necessary to become the source of all existence, the Kunta do not go so far as to say that *all* knowledge of the unseen realm must pass through these specific individuals. Such a claim would effectively render prayer (or fasting, reading the Qurʾān, etc.) futile for anybody outside the hierarchy of friends. As discussed earlier, Sīdi al-Mukhtār explains that all believers have some experience of the *ʿālam al-ghayb* according to the rank of their heart. This statement accords with the Kunta's presentation of the unseen realm as concealed aspects of the created universe, and the created universe as an extension of God. Thus anyone who acknowledges God as the foundation of existence and engages in devotional practices to control the *nafs* and clear the heart will acquire some knowledge of the realm of the unseen. However, according to Sīdi al-Mukhtār, this basic level of knowledge does not include "the category of knowledge of the unseen by which God singles [someone] out."[81] The Kunta texts identify this second category of knowledge as the particular access to the unseen granted to a select few individuals. These elite few ascend the Sufi path, experience the various components of God, and ultimately achieve annihilation in the unity of God before being re-created as the source of created existence. Finally, at the end of the *Kitāb zawāl al-ilbās*, Sīdi al-Mukhtār explicitly links this ascent to devotional practice. As believers control their selves and purify their hearts through devotions, they gain increasing knowledge of the unseen, with the pinnacle of the path reserved for those perfected hearts and bodies of the friends of God. These perfect bodies thus assume cosmological and soteriological significance. With the end of the period of prophecy, the hearts of the friends allow divine light and the process of creation to continue flowing into the manifest realm, while offering the rest of believing Muslims a path back toward God. For the Kunta scholars, the unseen realm provides the structure that gives the friends of God both significance and purpose. As Sīdi Muḥammad puts it, "whoever believes in a thing that he has not reached has believed in the unseen, and that is the key of happiness and the place of ascension of friendship."[82]

3

THE SCIENCES OF THE UNSEEN

Sīdi al-Mukhtār and Sīdi Muḥammad al-Kuntī understood Muslim devotional practice to be intimately connected to the realm of the unseen (*ʿālam al-ghayb*), the invisible world that exists above, alongside, and within the world of the senses. And just as all believing Muslims acquire some access to the realm of the unseen through God's revelation to Muḥammad, so too can they engage in devotional practices such as formal prayer, fasting, spiritual retreat, and reciting the Qurʾān. However, beyond this general knowledge of the unseen, the Kunta scholars single out the friends of God for special experiences within this realm, and they understand one of the results of this unique access to include the acquisition of certain powerful practices that they refer to as the sciences of the unseen (*ʿulūm al-ghayb*) or the sciences of the secrets (*ʿulūm al-asrār*). These "sciences" include the crafting of amulets, communicating with the jinn, and reciting various types of litanies for healing or protection, activities that have most often been addressed as practices in scholarly literature. However, the Kunta scholars clearly understood these engagements both as practices and also as the discrete bodies of knowledge on which those practices are based, and they cannot therefore be reduced to either rituals or intellectual products. In what follows, I use the joint term "knowledge/practice" interchangeably with "disciplines" to refer to this connection between intellectual forms and specific modes of behavior.

Unlike the rest of this book, this chapter focuses solely on the works of Sīdi Muḥammad al-Kuntī. For while Sīdi al-Mukhtār refers to the sciences of the unseen in his writings, it was his son who performed the apologetic work of defending these practices against detractors. In the process of defending his family's engagement in the sciences, Sīdi Muḥammad explained how the sciences worked and categorized them in relation to other bodies of knowledge/practice. For Sīdi Muḥammad, the sciences of secrets were related to other disciplines and actions that appeared similar in terms of their effects on the world of the senses. These groups included the miracles of the prophets (*muʿjizāt*), the charismata of the friends of God (*karāmāt*), sorcery (*siḥr*), false charismata (*istidrāj*), and medicine (*al-ṭibb*). The enactment of each of these categories resulted in a material change to the visible world, and many had overlapping uses and goals, such as healing, protecting, or extending the powers of the body (allowing someone to fly, walk on water, or travel instantly through time or space). The categorization of these disciplines in the works of Sīdi Muḥammad thus reveals the epistemological structure by which his family grouped together, or separated, related bodies of knowledge and their associated practices.

I use the terms "knowledge/practice" and "disciplines" to anchor a methodology that begins by determining the meanings of the "sciences of the unseen" in Sīdi Muḥammad's own writing. As discussed in the introduction, scholarship on these disciplines often begins by taking such terms as "magic" and "the occult," which are laden with pejorative meanings in the contemporary West, and applying them to non-Western cultures and, anachronistically, to other historical contexts. Scholars who attempt to avoid this practice often resort to abandoning second-order categories in their entirety and dealing exclusively with first-order disciplines (alchemy, astrology, etc.). While the former method obfuscates the emic terminology used by Muslims, the latter leads to a fragmentation of knowledge about these disciplines while failing to address the relationship between different disciplines in any given context. This chapter avoids the perils of both approaches by clarifying both the first- *and* second-order *emic* categories used in Sīdi Muḥammad's apologetic and didactic works.

It is only after clarifying the landscape and ordering of knowledge and practice in these texts that I continue—in the third section of the chapter—to situate Sīdi Muḥammad's classifications within two interrelated *etic* contexts. First, I locate the Kunta's discussion of these disciplines within the precolonial history of the sciences of the unseen in West Africa. This examination reveals Sīdi Muḥammad as one of the first Muslim scholars in the region to begin classifying the sciences in writing and to integrate them into a Sufi cosmological and metaphysical framework. This discussion, moreover, links Sīdi Muḥammad's classification of certain disciplines as either sorcery or prohibited sciences to the racialized context of the region, which sought to delegitimize the knowledge/practices of people living in "the land of the blacks." Second, I connect this discourse of legitimization to research on the history of the pejorative applications of the word "magic" that stretches back to ancient Greece. Scholars working in this vein, such as Kimberly Stratton, Bernd-Christian Otto, and Birgit Meyer, no longer consider magic a defined and stable set of practices or epistemological positions; rather, they understand magic as a set of related discourses with their own particular historical trajectory. Otto in particular has posited that magic discourses can be divided into "discourses of exclusion" that reject "magic" as the domain of marginalized and threatening "others," such as foreigners, gender-nonconforming women, and sexually deviant men, and "discourses of inclusion" in which self-identifying practitioners of magic lay claim to knowledge/practices rejected by normative discourse.[1] This chapter argues that Islamic discussions of sorcery and disciplines related to the unseen function in the same way as the discourses of "Western learned magic" outlined by these scholars, and we can thus refer to them as Islamic magic discourses. Positioning Sīdi Muḥammad's categories within this history of Islamic magic discourses indicates that he was aware of the presence of Islamic magic discourses of inclusion and that he accordingly engages in a discourse of exclusion meant to distance himself from those traditions. These discourses of inclusion and exclusion are further related to a discursive pattern that scholars such as Peter Pels, Edward Bever, and Randall Styers have previously described for western European modernity. According to these scholars, the codevelopment of magic and science is characterized by a "double gesture" that ironically reinforces the power and saliency of those disciplines rejected as magic.[2] This chapter concludes by arguing that such a "double gesture" cannot be limited in scope to modern European history but characterizes all epistemologies that attempt to distinguish between legitimate and illegitimate knowledge and practice.

First-Order Disciplines

The third chapter of the *Ṭarāʾif waʾl-talāʾid* opens with a concise synopsis of Sīdi al-Mukhtār's education and learning, stating that "he was well versed in all of the branches of knowledge [*ʿilm*]: whether in terms of Qurʾānic exegesis, *ḥadīth*, or jurisprudence. Possessing expertise in both the sciences of language [*ʿulūm al-lisān*]—including syntax, conjugation, and rhetoric; as well as in the sciences of the hidden [*ʿulūm al-bāṭin*]—including *al-taṣawwuf*, revealed knowledge [*ʿulūm al-manāzila*], and the secrets of the hidden—he would speak perfectly about the sciences of the knowers [*al-ʿārifīn*]."[3] This passage serves as an overview of Sīdi Muḥammad's classification of human knowledge. The younger Kunta first credits Sīdi al-Mukhtār with mastery of *all* knowledge, and then divides that encompassing category into three groups: (1) the interpretation of prophetic revelation through the genres of Qurʾānic exegesis, *ḥadīth* commentary, and jurisprudence; (2) the study of language in both its grammatical construction and its rhetorical deployment; and (3) the "sciences" of the hidden (*al-bāṭin*). The passage associates the sciences of the hidden with the process of becoming a Sufi (*al-taṣawwuf*) and mystical knowledge (*maʿrifa*), the subject and goal, respectively, of the Sufi path. Positioned here between the Sufi path and its supposed goal, these "sciences" are described as both "hidden" and "revealed" in the sense of "sent down by God." And while this passage positions the sciences as one of three parts of Sīdi al-Mukhtār's education, Sīdi Muḥammad indicates that his father "considered the science of *taṣawwuf* and knowledge of the illnesses of spirits [*ʿilal al-nufūs*] and their treatments and the modalities of the *dhikrs* . . . to be a personal obligation [*farḍ al-ʿayn*] that was more important than all of [the other disciplines]" (2:156).

The challenge facing the Kunta scholars when advocating for these disciplines was their similarity to prohibited groups of knowledge/practice. One of the Kunta scholars' most famous students, Sīdiyya ibn al-Mukhtār, explicitly poses this question by asking Sīdi Muḥammad to "distinguish between the blameworthy and the praiseworthy" among the many sciences he mentions (2:166). In response, Sīdi Muḥammad provides a list of practices that might be "confused with sorcery," namely, "*sīmā*, *hīmā*, talismans, magic squares, properties corresponding to the realities and properties corresponding to the spirits, *ruqiyya*, adjurations [*ʿazāʾim*], and evocations [*al-istakhdāmāt*]," and specifies that only three of them constitute sorcery: *sīmā* (or *sīmiyāʾ*),[4] or the use of "earthly properties such as special fats, fluids, or words that produce special imaginings or perceptions of the five senses" (2:168); *hīmā*, defined as identical to *sīmā* but "related to heavenly effects" (2:168); and "some of the properties of the realities" (2:169). While Sīdi Muḥammad organizes his discussion loosely around these eight categories, he also treats disciplines not found in this list, and he often circles back to discuss a previously mentioned practice. In what follows, I have imposed stricter order on these contested disciplines as they appear across Sīdi Muḥammad's writings. Accordingly, in this section I address bodies of knowledge/practice that Sīdi Muḥammad considered permissible in almost all circumstances, while the next section addresses disciplines considered prohibited and those whose legal status changes under different conditions.

Sīdi Muḥammad defends many disciplines by subsuming them under the umbrella of what he calls, alternately, "the science of letters and names" (*ʿilm al-ḥurūf wa'l-asmāʾ*) or the "science of forms and names" (*ʿilm al-ashkāl wa'l-asmāʾ*). These disciplines draw on the principles of lettrism, the idea that the universe is built from the names of God and the letters that make up those names. In defending these practices, Sīdi Muḥammad refutes the position of one of his contemporaries, a Saharan legal scholar named ʿAbd Allāh ibn al-Ḥājj Ibrāhīm al-ʿAlawī (d. 1818).[5] According to Sīdi Muḥammad, al-ʿAlawī prohibited the use of the most beautiful names of God "to gain knowledge of the unseen" or "in order to obtain a worldly purpose" (2:177–78). Sīdi Muḥammad explicitly rejects this position, stating that "longing for knowledge of the unseen" is not, in and of itself, illicit. Moreover, he explains that certain types of knowledge of the unseen involve "polishing insight and illuminating the self and perfecting the connection to the lordly names and the Qurʾānic verses—so they are not blameworthy nor detested, rather [they are] laudatory and coveted" (2:178). These laudatory and coveted types of knowledge of the unseen include two types of insight (*baṣīra*). The first, "perception" (*al-firāsa*), relates to the ability to see things as they really are and to perceive the hidden feelings of others (2:179).[6] Sīdi Muḥammad defines the second, "consultation" (*istikhāra*), as "the close examination of the self [for the purpose of discovering] what has been fated for it" (2:179), and he connects this practice to both the Prophet Muḥammad and to his father, Sīdi al-Mukhtār.

Among the sciences of the unseen, Sīdi Muḥammad valorizes above all what he refers to as the "science of letters and names." He even wrote a short treatise—*Fawāʾid nūrāniyya wa farāʾid sirriyya raḥmāniyya* (The Illuminated Benefits and Secret Pearls of the Compassionate), sometimes listed in catalogues as *Ism allāh al-aʿẓam* (The Greatest Name of God)—dedicated specifically to the properties of the letters, the names of God, and particularly the greatest name of God.[7] On the one hand, Sīdi Muḥammad presents the sciences of letters and names as a secret teaching at the heart of Sufism. In this mode, the Kunta writer links the letters and the names of God to the divine process of creation and the subsequent cosmological structure of the world. Thus he explains that God created the three realms, *al-malakūt*, *al-jabarūt*, and *al-mulk*, along with the divine throne (*ʿarsh*), the divine footstool (*al-kursī*), and the tablet (*al-lawḥ*) by means of his names (see chapter 2). God then created the angels of *al-malakūt* from the light of the throne, the angels of *al-jabarūt* from the light of the footstool, and finally the angels of *al-mulk*—the visible human realm—from the light of the tablet, with each set of angels assigned a specific task.[8] This cosmological structure establishes a correspondence between angels and realms and names such that the angels act as stand-ins for the names from which they were created. Sīdi Muḥammad puts this succinctly when he writes, "the shaykh, my father, may God be pleased with him, used to say, 'every name of the names of the Exalted is an agent [*fāʿil*] [for what He wishes] in existence.'"[9] Moreover, each name occupies a role in the material and spiritual worlds and governs specific actions, such as making the rain fall or the wind die down, or allowing someone to walk on water or cure the blind.[10]

On the other hand, Sīdi Muḥammad presents the sciences of names and letters as an operational body of knowledge linked to specific practices. He writes explicitly that people who "become connected to the names" can assume the role and powers of a particular name. In this fashion, people can insert themselves into the cosmological order and gain control over the world and its processes. Moreover, Sīdi Muḥammad explains that all of the names of God are controlled by, and subsumed under, the greatest name (*Ism allāh al-aʿẓam*). An individual who succeeds in connecting to this name thus assumes control over the role and powers of all the names: "Whenever a servant connects to the greatest name and comes to possess its form, the lights of the names flood out [*istifāḍat*] from the form to the angelic spirits[11] and so they cry to their lord and say: 'oh our god and our lord, why has the light of the form poured out?' So He says: 'I know, oh my angels, that my servant, so-and-so, has connected to this noble name out of a need he has asked me about. Oh you, satisfy his need, whatever it may be.'"[12] Sīdi Muḥammad adds that if the believer's need is "illuminated [*nūrāniyya*] and pure," then the angels respond to the request directly, but if it is unjust or oppressive (*ẓulmāniyya*), then they force the devils to do the work.[13] By positing that individuals can co-opt the power of the greatest name to accomplish any task at all—even one that is oppressive or corrupt—the *Fawāʾid nūrāniyya* implies that by connecting to God's agents, individuals are capable of assuming for themselves the agency of God. Sīdi Muḥammad puts this succinctly when he quotes one of "the knowers" (*al-ʿārifīn*) as saying, "*bismillāh* [in the name of God] from the knower has the rank of *kun* (Be!) from Him."[14]

Discussions of the names of God in early Islamic traditions centered on the Qurʾānic proclamation "to God belong the most beautiful names, so call him by them" (7:180, 20:8), along with *ḥadīth* reports that God has ninety-nine names.[15] Speculation about one "greatest" divine name pointed to *ḥadīth* in which the Prophet refers to a man as "praying to God by His greatest name—whoever prays to God by it is answered, and whoever asks God with it is given [that which he asked]."[16] Some interpreters posited that this greatest name might be one of the known ninety-nine, while others suggested that there might be a secret one-hundredth name. Prominent Sufis in northwestern Africa were often associated with knowledge of the greatest name, ranging from Abū Ḥasan al-Shādhilī (d. 1258) to Aḥmad al-Tijānī (d. 1815), a Moroccan contemporary of Sīdi al-Mukhtār al-Kuntī.[17] But Sīdi Muḥammad is the only writer I know to have revealed the secret, greatest name of God in writing. He refers to this name as that "which, if one calls by it, He answers, and if one asks by it, He gives, and if one asks for help by it, He helps."[18] In the *Fawāʾid nūrāniyya*, Sīdi Muḥammad cites twenty different opinions concerning the greatest name, ranging from the claim that there is no greatest name—because all the names are equally great—to the belief that it is a secret known only to God, to many variations on Allāh (*Allāh al-Raḥmān al-Raḥīm*, *Allāh al-Ḥayy al-Qayyūm*, *Allāh lā ilāha illā huwa*, etc.), to Lord, Lord (*rabb rabb*), and finally to *alif lām mīm*, the three letters that open six chapters of the Qurʾān.[19]

According to Sīdi Muḥammad, his father declared "that the greatest name of God is Allāh, on its own, or with another [name] joined to it, or with its numerical strength extracted and pronounced."[20] This stance equivocates by subsuming as many of the options as possible, accepting not only any of the standard variations of Allāh but also anything that can be derived by performing numerological operations on Allāh. Ultimately, Sīdi Muḥammad reveals the greatest name to be AHM SQK ḤLʿ YṢ, which consists of four "words" of unvoweled consonants. Presumably, the Kunta shaykhs kept the short vowels necessary to pronounce this word as an oral tradition, an initiatory secret. Sīdi Muḥammad explains that this name was derived through numerological operations from the name Allāh (see below). Moreover, each "word" of the name itself represents one of the other names of God; "thus the meaning of *AHM* is God the Everlasting [*Allāh al-Dāʾim*], and the meaning of *SQK* is the Alive, the Self-Subsisting [*al-Ḥayy al-Qayyūm*], and the meaning of *ḤLʿ* is the possessor of Majesty [*Dhū al-Jalāla*], and the meaning of *YṢ* is the Generous [*al-Ikrām*]." Indeed, the symbolic associations of the greatest name expand further as Sīdi Muḥammad proceeds to address each of the eleven letters in turn. He associates each of the letters with other names of God and also with the four elements (earth, air, water, and fire) and other properties. For example, he writes that "*alif* is a letter of fire, of light, of elevation, and the name from it, in regard to its interior [aspect] is 'the Concealed [*Kāfī*]' and in regard to its exterior [aspect] is 'Allāh.'"[21]

The correspondences hidden within the letters and words of the greatest name relate to Sīdi Muḥammad's theory behind the science of the names and letters. God created the universe from speech itself, and thus the twenty-eight letters of the Arabic alphabet form the fundamental building blocks of the universe. Sīdi Muḥammad focuses in particular on the fourteen letters (which he calls "the illuminated letters") that appear, disconnected, at the beginning of some suras of the Qurʾān. The greatest name, AHM SQK ḤLʿ YṢ, is composed of eleven of these fourteen mysterious letters. It is also an anagram of the eleven letters that make up the opening "words" *alif lām mīm*, which begin six chapters of the Qurʾān (2, 3, 29, 30, 31, 32); *kāf hāʾ yāʾ ʿayn ṣād*, which begins Sūra Maryam (19:1); and *ḥaʾ mīm ʿayn sīn qāf*, which begins Sūra al-Shūra (42:1). Moreover, the letters of the alphabet correspond to other elements of the natural world, including the four elements (earth, water, air, and fire), the four humors of the body (phlegm, blood, yellow bile, and black bile), the twelve signs of the zodiac, and the seven "planets" (Mercury, Venus, Mars, Jupiter, Saturn, the sun, and the moon) (2:176). The text even provides a table illustrating these correspondences (see fig. 1). Moreover, following the neo-Pythagorean roots of this discipline, Sīdi Muḥammad understands each letter to correspond to a number, in accordance with the *abjad* system. He describes numbers as inhabiting the letters as spirits (*arwāḥ*) inhabit bodies.[22] This correspondence results in the efficacy of numerology, as users apply mathematical operations to manipulate letters and thus the material bodies built upon them.

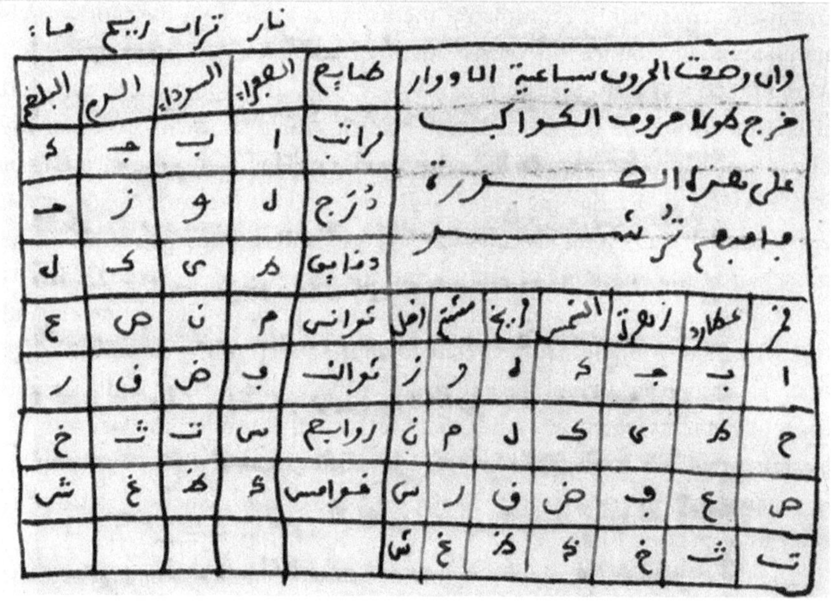

Fig. 1 Two side-by-side charts demonstrating correspondences with the letters of the Arabic alphabet. In the chart on the left, the top row reads (*right to left*): fire, earth, wind, water. The next row reads (*right to left*): yellow bile, black bile, blood, phlegm. The rightmost column reads (*top to bottom*): ranks, degrees, minutes, twos, threes, fours, fives. In the chart on the right, the top row reads (*right to left*): the moon, Mercury, Venus, the sun, Mars, Jupiter, Saturn. The caption in the top right corner reads, "In this fashion, if you put the letters seven at a time, the letters [corresponding to] the planets will emerge along their length according to this image." Sīdi Muḥammad al-Kuntī, *Fawāʾid nūrāniyya wa farāʾid sirriyya raḥmāniyya*, MH 12211, fol. 32b.

In the *Fawāʾid nūrāniyya*, Sīdi Muḥammad provides several examples of how to extract different numerical properties from each letter. For example, the letter *jīm*: "Its total is 3 and its specification is 6—the product of multiplying 3 by what precedes it, which is 2. And its strength in the hidden aspect of high things is 53—and that is the sum of the letters of its pronunciation, which are *jīm* and *yāʾ* and *mīm*—3 with *jīm*, 10 with *yāʾ*, and *mīm* with 40, and the sum of those is 53. And its strength in the hidden aspect of low things is 159, which is the product of multiplying its total (3) by its strength in the hidden aspect of the high things (53)."[23] The numbers 3, 6, 53, and 159 are thus some of the most important numbers associated with the letter *jīm*. In another method, Sīdi Muḥammad writes that each letter has a number; a body, which is the written form of that letter; a spirit, which is the number squared; a self, which is the number cubed; a heart, which is the number to the fourth power; and a mind, which is the sum of the body, spirit, self, and heart multiplied by four; a total strength, which is the mind multiplied by four; and a natural strength, which is the total strength multiplied by ten. Thus, for the letter *bāʾ*, its number is 2, its body is ب, its spirit is 4, its self is 12, its heart is 16, its mind is 136 ([2 + 4 + 12 + 16] × 4), its total strength is 544 (136 × 4), and its natural strength is 5,440 (544 × 10).[24] Although Sīdi Muḥammad demonstrates how to find the hidden numerical associations of the letters, he does not provide instructions for the discipline of combining letters and words (*tarākīb*), nor does he explain exactly how to draw on their associations with the four elements, the humors of the body, or the planets.

Instrumentalizing the science of letters and names often involved writing or inscribing them on various surfaces (paper, lead tablets, glass bowls, city walls, etc.). This practice brings together numerous other terms in a combined semantic field. For example, when corporealized in writing or inscription, the letters and names are referred to as "the forms" or "the shapes" (*al-ashkāl*) and can be used in the construction of talismans (*al-ṭilasmāt*). When discussing the creation of powerful forms and talismans, Sīdi Muḥammad makes repeated references to the use of tables (*jadāwil*). These "tables" are charts filled with numbers, letters, and symbols. In one example from the *Ṭarāʾif waʾl-talāʾid*, Sīdi Muḥammad provides instructions for using a table and a talisman to treat a person under attack by a bloodsucking sorcerer. He tells the reader to write out a series of Qurʾānic verses (4:141, 17:45–46, 83:36, and 60:13) along with a certain table on two pieces of paper, and then to "put one of them in the fire and fumigate [the smoke] in his nose and hang the other upon [his body]. . . . Then God Most High shall heal him with his power" (2:189). Manuscript copies of the *Ṭarāʾif waʾl-talāʾid* provide the

Fig. 2 A seven-by-seven table containing symbols sometimes referred to as "the seven seals of Solomon," with each row offset by one character. Sīdi Muḥammad al-Kuntī, *Al-Ṭarāʾif wa'l-talāʾid min karāmāt al-shaykhayn al-wālida wa'l-wālid*, Manuscrits Orientaux, Arabe 6755, BnF, fol. 208b.

necessary table, a seven-by-seven square containing a specific set of symbols, with each row offset by one character (see fig. 2). These seven characters have been identified in both Islamic and Jewish manuscripts from as early as the thirteenth century, where they are sometimes identified as the greatest name of God.[25]

In many cases, the table is also a magic square (*wafq*, pl. *awfāq*)—a specific algebraic construct of subdivided squares in which all the columns, rows, and diagonals add up to the same number. Mathematical treatises in Arabic detailing the construction of magic squares date back to the tenth century, and later became incorporated into medieval Neoplatonic treatises on talismans and astrology.[26] Regarding the functioning of the magic squares, Sīdi Muḥammad quotes his father as explaining that God "bound the managers of existence [*al-tadabburāt al-kawniyya*] to his holy names" and then "determined for them realities that operate in the world of *al-malakūt*, the realm of existence and corruption, through normal connections" (2:175). This explanation mirrors the Kunta writers' understanding of the names of God as the agents of existence and of the sciences as working according to "normal" processes. In the *Fawāʾid nūrāniyya*, Sīdi Muḥammad refers to the process of turning a letter or name into a three-by-three square as "cubing" (*taʿkīb*), and of creating a four-by-four square as "quad-ing" (*tarrabaʿ*). He also provides examples of magic squares associated with particular letters, along with instructions on how to use them to achieve specific effects. Thus, for the letter *mīm*, he provides a three-by-three square in which all of the rows, columns, and diagonals add up to 333 (see fig. 3), writing, "whoever engraves it on a lead tablet . . . will be protected from the deceit of enemies and the envious."[27] In this fashion, he endorses the creation and use of talismans that make use of verses of the Qurʾān, the names of God, the letters of the Arabic alphabet, the numbers that correspond to the names and letters, and the various squares, tables, and shapes that represent the names and letters (2:174).

The sacred history that Sīdi Muḥammad provides for the greatest name of God brings together all of these possible uses and permutations of the science

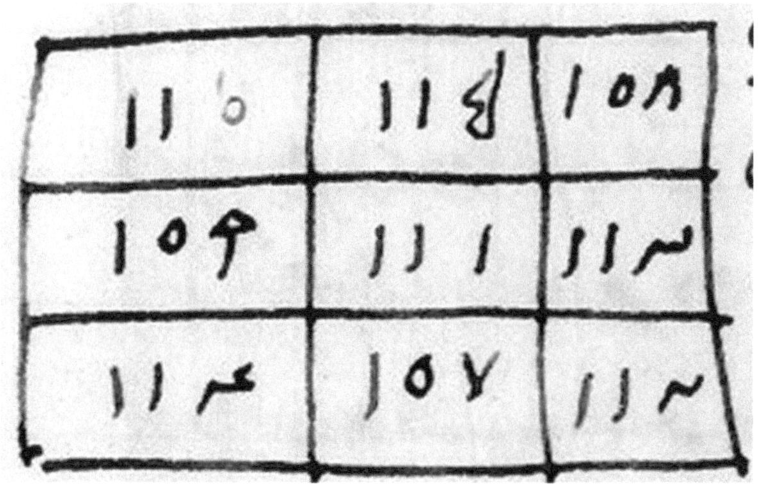

Fig. 3 A three-by-three magic square for the letter *mīm*. All the rows, columns, and diagonals add up to 333. Sīdi Muḥammad al-Kuntī, *Fawāʾid nūrāniyya wa farāʾid sirriyya raḥmāniyya*, MH 12211, fol. 32b.

of letters and names. Thus he explains that knowledge of the names of God and their uses was sent down by God to his prophets, most notably Adam and Idrīs. Idrīs received "the sciences of letters and the appointed secrets and the subtleties of the numbers and the effects of the spheres." Idrīs passed his teachings on to his followers, a group of "forty men" called the "Harāmisa."[28] Plato received from the Harāmisa a book relating the teachings of their leader—identified as Hermes in one passage and Idrīs in another—which allowed him to extract the numerological value of the name Allāh, create from it a four-by-four magic square, and derive the eleven letters of *AHM SQK ḤLʿ YṢ*.[29] The text then provides that square, with the four "words" of the greatest name forming the top row. Substituting the numerical equivalents of each word (by adding up the values of their letters) produces a magic square in which the rows, columns, and diagonals all add up to 644 (see fig. 4). The text then instructs the reader to inscribe the table on a lead tablet, take it to a place of retreat (*khalwa*), fumigate it with aloewood, perform ritual ablutions (*wuḍūʾ*) and, finally, recite a specific supplicatory prayer. This prayer begins by addressing God by his greatest name—"O AHM SQK ḤLʿ YṢ!"—and concludes with a request for total control over the universe: "O God! . . . Compel the forms [*al-ashbāḥ*] to me[30] and

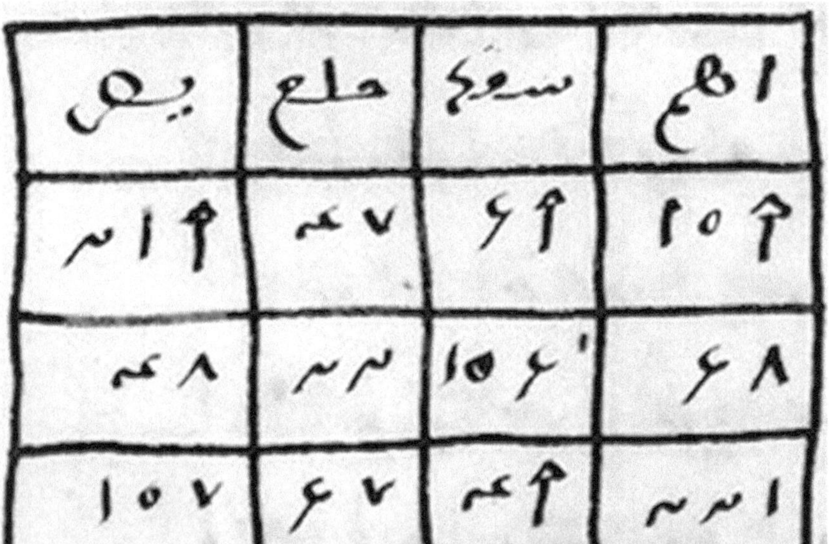

Fig. 4 A table for the greatest name of God. From right to left, the top row reads: AHM SQK ḤLʿ YṢ. When the letters of each "word" in the name are added up according to the *abjad* system, all of the columns, rows, and squares add up to 644. Sīdi Muḥammad al-Kuntī, *Fawāʾid nūrāniyya wa farāʾid sirriyya raḥmāniyya*, MH 12211, fol. 40a.

strengthen me from the register of the spirits until neither human nor jinn nor angel from the agents nor benefit nor power nor seeker nor devil nor time nor place—nor any thing that includes the property of existing is beyond the encompassing of my freedom of action [*taṣrīfī*] or emerges from the grip of my imposing."[31] Sīdi Muḥammad provides variations for the supplicatory prayer that accompanies the greatest name. He also explains how to use the greatest name in combination with other practices, such as retreat, the repetition of the names of God (*dhikr*), and the crafting of amulets, to achieve more specific purposes, such as healing the sick, destroying an enemy, making someone love you, and expelling a ruler from his own country or devils (*shayāṭīn*) from a human body.[32]

These passages link knowledge of the greatest name of God to Hermes Trismegistus, the protagonist of a series of texts on medicine, alchemy, and astrology produced in late antique Roman Egypt. Over the course of the ʿAbbāsid period, Muslim writers in Arabic developed two Hermes traditions; the first identified Hermes with both Enoch of the Hebrew Bible and Idrīs of the Qurʾān, and the second elaborated a history of "three Hermeses" (*al-Harāmisa*), who together preserved and transmitted secret and ancient knowledge through human history.[33] In Sīdi Muḥammad's reception of these legends, Hermes is once again identified as Idrīs and associated with the reception of scientific knowledge through revelation. Moreover, the identity of the *Harāmisa* has changed once again, with that term now indicating the group of people to whom Hermes/Idrīs brought his revelation. According to Sīdi Muḥammad, Plato later received this wisdom from the *Harāmisa* in the form of a book, allowing him to extract the numerical values of Allāh, determine the eleven Arabic letters of *AHM SQK ḤLʿ YṢ*, and produce the four-by-four magic square connected to the name. In this fashion, Sīdi Muḥammad establishes the greatest name of God and its accompanying table as a derivation of the name Allāh. Moreover, the instructions for using the greatest name—by inscribing it on a tablet, taking it to a place of retreat, and reciting a supplication—tie the sciences of the names and letters to more established Muslim devotional practices such as spiritual retreat (*khalwa*) and supplicatory prayer (*duʿāʾ*).

Over the course of chapter 3 of the *Ṭarāʾif waʾl-talāʾid*, Sīdi Muḥammad repeatedly emphasizes the permissibility, and even the desirability, of disciplines that involve the divine names, the letters of the alphabet, verses of the Qurʾān, and supplications handed down from the greatest shaykhs. Thus he thoroughly endorses the use of *ruqyā* (the plural of *ruqiyya*), which he defines as a kind of "speech by which every illness is healed" (2:214). The meaning of this term in Muslim societies has varied, and in West Africa today it is often linked specifically to curing those possessed by the jinn.[34] In one passage, Sīdi Muḥammad explains that his paternal uncle Abū Bakr was able to heal people possessed by a female jinn (*qarīna*), without having to use *ruqiyya*—thus implying that one *could* use *ruqiyya* for such a purpose (1:222). However, more typically, the Kunta writers refer to *ruqiyya* as a general healing practice and describe it as a medicine (*adwiyya*). Thus Sīdi Muḥammad writes, "[Sīdi al-Mukhtār] said, '*ruqiyya* is spiritual medicine [*al-ṭibb al-rūḥānī*] and making use of it is not incompatible with trusting in God [*al-tawakkul*] . . . because the prophet (may the prayers and peace of God be upon him) is the master of those who trust in God and it is verified and established that he used to perform *ruqiyya* and have it performed'" (2:204–5). Sīdi Muḥammad elaborates on the Prophet's use of spiritual medicine as a healing practice, writing that Muḥammad used three methods to treat the sick: "The first of them was with divine, spiritual medicines [*bi'l-adwiyya al-ilāhiyya al-rūḥāniyya*], and the second was with natural medicines [*al-adwiyya al-ṭabīʿiyya*], and the third was with a combination of the two" (2:217). Like the use of talismans, the permissibility of the *ruqyā* relies on their connection to valorized forms of speech, and specifically to "the book of God and His names and to what has been established and verified from the prophet of God" (2:217). Indeed, Sīdi Muḥammad specifically contrasts these approved *ruqyā* with Sīdi al-Mukhtār's disapproval of those that depend on foreign, non-Arab words (*ʿajamī*) (2:215, 217; see also 2:199–200). Similarly, Sīdi Muḥammad permits the use of magic squares and talismans only on the condition that "they are constructed and filled with the most beautiful names of God and the verses of his cherished book," and he specifies that "if not," then the practice is sorcery and is only applied at the hands of an unbeliever or corrupt person" (2:202). This same caution also applies to "increasing something paltry" (*takbīr al-qalīl*), which falls under the permitted sciences if it is accomplished "by means of the most beautiful names and the noble verses and the good speech, but if not then it is a type of sorcery" (2:203). In this fashion, Sīdi Muḥammad uses the valorized speech of the Qurʾān, the names of God, and the Arabic language as one marker of the boundary between permitted and prohibited knowledge and practice.

Categories and Classification

Sīdi Muḥammad classifies the various disciplines that could be confused with sorcery into three second-order categories: the charismata of God's friends, the sciences of the unseen, and sorcery. His definition of the charismata, the first of these categories, relies on Ashʿarī theological positions that developed during the ʿAbbāsid period. In the face of textual and ritual traditions from regions as disparate as the Iberian Peninsula and the South Asian subcontinent, theologians developed the category of acts that "broke the normal course of events" (*khawāriq al-ʿāda*). For Muʿtazīli theologians, a central concern was upholding the proof value of prophetic miracles (*muʿjizāt*). Consequently, they asserted that only prophets could break the normal course of events, and that any apparent manifestation from the realm of the unseen after the death of Muḥammad amounted to nothing but trickery and deception.[35] In contrast, early Ashʿarī theologians emphasized God's transcendent power and argued that neither the charismata of the friends nor acts of sorcery compromised the proof value of the prophetic miracles. If anyone attempted to use a charism or act of sorcery to make a false claim to prophecy, God would simply cause that act to fail. These theologians developed the doctrine of acquisition (*kasb*) by asserting that all acts originate ultimately with God, who allows humans to "acquire" them.[36] Theologians who followed this line of thought located the legitimacy of an act not in the practice itself (as all acts originate with God), but rather in the relationship between a person and God. Thus an act (such as producing fruits out of season) that a friend of God acquired as a charism could be acquired as an act of sorcery by someone else.

Like Ashʿarī writers before him, Sīdi Muḥammad distinguishes between two primary types of "breakings of the norm" (*khawāriq al-ʿāda*), or acts that run counter to the "normal course of events": the miracles of the prophets, the *muʿjizāt*, and the extraordinary events that occur in the presence of the friends of God, the *karāmāt*. The former are defined as miracles that confirm the veracity of a message from God and the latter as unexpected charismata, or gifts, conferred by God to confirm the rank of one of his friends (1:58–87). However, unlike Ashʿarī theologians before him, Sīdi Muḥammad specifically includes sorcery within the category of the "normal" (*al-ʿāda*), writing, "and included among the normal is sorcery, even if its normal cause is rare, in opposition to whoever would label it a 'breaking'" (1:90). The stipulation that sorcery belongs to the realm of the normal distinguishes sorcery from the *istadrāj*, which Sīdi Muḥammad defines as "the creation of a breaking at the hands of the wretched, like the anti-Christ and Pharaoh" (1:94; see also 1:99).[37] He even provides examples of the normal, writing, "included among the normal are the special properties [*khawāṣṣ*—see below] found in some bodies, like the attraction of iron with magnetic stones, and the like" (1:90). According to the Kunta scholar, the miracles of the prophets and the charismata of God's friends share the quality of rupturing the normal state of affairs, while sorcery occupies a normal—if rare—corner of everyday life. This categorization positions sorcery, on the one hand, and miracles and charismata, on the other, as occupying opposing ends of a spectrum that runs from corrupt and ordinary to righteous and extraordinary.

Sīdi Muḥammad positions the sciences of the unseen between the charismata of the friends of God and the acts of sorcerers. In the introduction to the *Ṭarāʾif wa'l-talāʾid*, he lists nine practices that theologians have included under the heading of sorcery: gossiping; deluding the mentally ill into believing that they have special powers; "making use of the special properties [*khawāṣṣ*] of instruments and singular objects—like iron's attraction to magnets and the like"; amazing works of engineering "like the revolving of clocks and the moving of weights"; "illusions and tricks of the eye"; harnessing and controlling the jinn; using one's thoughts or spirit to effect a material change in a person or an object; making use of the stars; and *al-sīmā*, the "use of something with a special set of properties, such as special fats and fluids or special words, that results in special envisioning and perceptions of the senses" (1:95–96). Sīdi Muḥammad agrees with the anonymous theologians that none of these acts should be included among the charismata but says that, of all of them, *al-sīmā* "has the greatest right to be called sorcery" and that controlling the jinn, making use of the stars, and focusing one's spirit absolutely do not deserve that label (1:97). Because the Kunta assert that all acts of sorcery are legally prohibited, Sīdi Muḥammad's failure to categorize these practices as sorcery opens up space between the prohibited category of sorcery and the charismata. Effectively, in the introduction to his *Ṭarāʾif wa'l-talāʾid*, Sīdi Muḥammad suggests that certain practices might appear to break the normal course of events but still be both *legal* and *controllable.*

In the third chapter of the *Ṭarāʾif wa'l-talāʾid*, he returns again to the classification of practices as sorcery. In this chapter he provides a list of eight practices—"*sīmā*, *hīmā*, talismans, magic squares, properties corresponding to the realities and properties corresponding to the spirits, *ruqiyya*, adjurations [*ʿazāʾim*], and evocations [*al-istakhdāmāt*]"—and then states definitively that "three of them are sorcery" (2:167–68). These three are *sīmā*, *hīma*, and "some of the properties of the realities" (2:169). He addresses *hīmā* only briefly, saying that it is identical to *sīmā*, except that while *sīmā* pertains to "earthly properties," *hīmā* "is related to heavenly effects" (2:168). For acts of sorcery that draw on the properties of the realities, Sīdi Muḥammad provides a series of examples, including the practice of taking a stone bitten by a dog and submerging it in water or in a well in order to affect those who drink it. He immediately clarifies that, while sorcery can induce health or sickness in someone, "medicines and nourishments from solids, plants, and animals recorded in the books of physicians, herbalists, and naturalists" are "from the science of medicine, not from the science of sorcery" (2:169). Of the greater category of sorcery and the three component practices of *sīmā*, *hīmā*, and the use of "some of the properties of the realities," Sīdi Muḥammad declares that "all of them are forbidden and among the great offenses. . . . And [practicing them] might be an act of disbelief [*kufr*] or it might not be disbelief but rather a great disobedience . . . and learning and teaching it are prohibited [*ḥarām*]" (2:173). So, while learning or practicing sorcery always entails disobedience toward God, it does not necessarily constitute an act of disbelief that ejects the practitioner from the community of Muslims. Like most classification schemes, the boundaries that separate these three categories of knowledge/practice are permeable, and the rest of this section discusses the pastiche of rationales that Sīdi Muḥammad uses to maintain the border between these second-order categories. Specifically, the *Ṭarāʾif wa'l-talāʾid* attempts to separate the charismata from the sciences of the unseen, and the sciences from sorcery; however, Sīdi Muḥammad also maintains that there are disciplines within the sciences of the unseen that are prohibited but *do not* constitute acts of sorcery.

To begin with the difference between the charismata and the permitted sciences of the unseen, Sīdi Muḥammad distinguishes between these two categories according to the means by which a practitioner obtains the desired effect. He explains that some actions—such as folding up space (*ṭayy al-arḍ*) in order to travel instantly between two points—can be accomplished by relying on the types of valorized speech discussed above: "one of the *sayyids*, when he wants to fold up space, would recite His Most High's statement: *They do not measure God with His true measure. The earth altogether will be His handful on the Day of Resurrection, and the heavens will be rolled up in His right hand* (39:67). He repeats it and gestures with his hand to the side on which he wants to fold up space. Then he recites the number of His two names, the Grasping [*al-Qābiḍ*] and the Swift [*al-Sarīʿ*]" (2:203). This example evokes the image of one of Muḥammad's descendants (a *sayyid*) folding up space by reciting a specific verse of the Qurʾān, along with the numbers related to two of the divine names. However, this example includes the caveat that, "for most of the friends, [space] is folded up with no cause or request save for the directing of their intention [*al-himma*], and that is the truth of the charism [*ḥaqīqat al-karāma*]" (2:203). Sīdi Muḥammad makes a similar pronouncement for protecting against woodworms and locusts, explaining that "the righteous used to do it by [making use of] causes [*asbāb*] and stations [*maqāmāt*] and without those it is a charism" (2:204). Thus, while believers might draw on the principles of cause and effect that drive the sciences of the unseen, the friends of God are able to achieve the same effect simply by directing their thoughts and intentions toward the goal.

Sīdi Muḥammad suggests that his father went through a similar process, in which he ceased to need the sciences of the unseen as he grew into his role as a friend of God. Thus he writes that at one point his father was especially adept in the science of magic squares and that his skill in this area grew until he received a visit from two angels with a message from God, who said, "'if you wish, I will inspire you from the science of tables with that which I have not gifted to anyone before you, and then I will put you in charge of it. And if you wish I will make you free of needing anything other than remembrance of me and being present with me'" (2:196–97). Sīdi Muḥammad relates that his father chose the second option and asked his lord to make remembering and being present with God sufficient for him. The ambiguities of this passage center on the terms "remembering" (*dhikr*) and "sufficient"; the former term could refer either to the general recollection of God or to the specific Sufi practice of *dhikr*, the ritual recitation of God's names.[38] Meanwhile, asking that remembrance of God "suffice him" could refer to either a desire that God's presence nullify any material needs or desires, or a request to effect the same results as the science of magic squares merely by mentioning God's name(s). While the symbolism of the passage evokes both readings simultaneously, other passages in the text add salience to the latter. Thus, in a rare description of his own talents, Sīdi Muḥammad writes that he himself followed a path similar to his father's: "Through the revelation [*fatḥ*] of God and his inspiration, I myself realized knowledge of the magic squares and the forms that is only realized by someone supported with a revelation and a perfect inspiration from God. Then, when I enlarged the scope [of my knowledge] . . . I received the sign to dispense with them by means of nothing more than remembrance [*dhikr*] and the transmitted supplications [*ʿadiyāʾ*] and the prayers [*aḥzāb*] and the directions toward which the shaykh, my father, may God be pleased with him, devoted himself" (2:197). In this passage, Sīdi Muḥammad claims to have received direct revelations concerning the science of magic squares until a day when he received a sign that he no longer needed them. His language parallels his description of his father's choice to have "remembrance" (*dhikr*) of God suffice for him. However, in describing his own journey, the younger Kunta places remembrance of God in the same category as various types of supplicatory prayer (*ʿadiyāʾ* and *aḥzāb*; see chapter 4). This semantic field indicates that "remembrance of God" in this context refers to calling on God by performing ritual recitation of the divine names. Thus Sīdi Muḥammad suggests that both he and his father reached a point where they could achieve the same effects gained by using magic squares merely by supplicating God directly. In this fashion, Sīdi Muḥammad positions the sciences of the unseen as merely one stage along the Sufi path to God, a stage, moreover, that the most advanced practitioners will ultimately abandon as they move further along that path.

In the *Ṭarāʾif wa'l-talāʾid*, Sīdi Muḥammad also repeatedly rejects the argument that the sciences of the unseen should be prohibited because they depend on effects (*asbāb*) and that use of them indicates a failure of trust in God. The effects that Sīdi Muḥammad refers to in these passages are the principles of causation that drive the functioning of the natural world. For the Kunta, these principles include the *khawāṣṣ*, the sympathetic or antithetic properties that connect all material bodies.[39] These properties include examples that stem from Peripatetic philosophy, such as the attraction of iron to magnets (e.g., 1:95), as well as the relationships between the letters of the alphabet and both the human body and the celestial world (see above). These causes are considered "secondary," in contrast to the primacy of God's direct action in the world. Sīdi Muḥammad's authorization of the use of secondary causes depends on maintaining a theological line established by earlier Ashʿarī writers. As demonstrated, he rejects the belief that entities other than God have effects in and of themselves, but he also describes someone who "abandons the causes and depends upon the fate that preceded him" as a "senseless idiot" who does not "realize that God Most High arranged the matters of the world according to causes," and who must not "eat when he hungers, nor drink when he thirsts, nor dress when he is cold, nor take medicine when he sickens" (2:195). Instead, Sīdi Muḥammad advocates a path between these two positions, writing, "abandoning causes to [the will of] God is bad etiquette and believing in them is idolatry, and the path between the two is to make use of causes without depending on them" (2:205). The Kunta shaykhs' endorsement of *ruqiyya* walks this middle path between depending on causes to act of their own accord and abandoning them entirely in favor of predestination. Thus Sīdi Muḥammad rules that *ruqyā* are permitted as long as they fulfill three conditions. The first two, consisting of "the speech of God Most High or His names and His attributes" and occurring "in the Arabic language, from that which has a known meaning," both refer to the distinction discussed above between valorized and pejoratized speech. The third condition, "the belief that the *ruqiyya* does not effect in itself but rather by the determination of God Most High" (2:215), demarcates the line between permitted sciences and idolatry.

Sīdi Muḥammad's categorization of sciences as illegitimate because of their reliance on both foreign speech and idolatry is clearest during his discussion of different ways of controlling spirit beings and the jinn. He refers to a discipline from the sciences of the unseen called "evocations" (*istakhdāmāt*), for which he specifies two subtypes, employment of the planets (*al-kawākib*) and employment of the jinn. He explains that the former refers to the practice of worshipping the planets in order to obtain the obedience of the spirit-beings of the planetary spheres: "Its practitioners claim that the planets have perceptive faculties and spirits and so, if a planet is offered special incense and special clothes and is presented with specific acts from among those that are prohibited in the law [*sharʿ*]—like sodomy—as well as those that are true acts of disbelief—like prostrating to them—along with addressing the planet with pronouncements that are outright disbelief, like calling it a god and the likes of that . . . then they claim that the spirit of one of the planetary spheres will be obedient to them" (2:218–19). Similarly, evocation of the jinn involves using specific actions and oaths to bind these beings to the will of the practitioner (2:219). Making offerings and prostrating oneself before beings other than God constitute idolatry. Moreover, the binding oaths often involve pronouncing the secret, foreign names of the jinn (2:219). The reference to sodomy (*al-liwāṭ*) also evokes the historical link between stereotypes of magicians and sexual deviance. For all of these reasons, Sīdi Muḥammad prohibits these practices, writing that these are "affairs that make the skin crawl and that the rulings and limits of the law deny" (2:219). However, although he prohibits believing Muslims from "the evocations," he permits them to make use of the jinn with what he terms "adjurations" (*al-ʿazāʾim*), which he defines as "short or long words" that originate with the example of the prophet Solomon. According to the Kunta's version of this story, Solomon saw the jinn "toying with people and abducting them from the roads," so "he asked God Most High to make an angel rule over each tribe from the jinn to restrain them from corruption and interfering with people. Then Solomon, peace be upon him, compelled them to the wastelands and ruins in uninhabited lands in order to spare people from their evil" (2:218). As a result, anyone with knowledge of the divine names can use them to "engage the service of the angels" to control the jinn (2:218). The "adjurations" can thus be categorized as a subset of the science of letters and names. For this reason, Sīdi Muḥammad quotes his father as emphasizing that "what banishes the rebellious jinn is not from sorcery; rather, it is from wisdom [*al-ḥikma*] and from the most beautiful names of God Most High or the secret of the letters" (2:200). The narrative voice of Sīdi al-Mukhtār only cautions that someone employing the jinn in this fashion should distance himself from the illicit and legally suspicious (*al-shubhāt*), as proximity to such practices will cause "the angels and the spirits of the names and letters [to] desert him and at that time the jinn will overpower and then destroy him" (2:200).

In addition to acts that involve foreign speech or idolatry, Sīdi Muḥammad prohibits divination (*al-kahāna*), astrology (*ʿilm al-nujūm*), and "[sand] writing" (*al-khaṭṭ*)[40] because of their roots in the practices of the pagan Arabians in the period before the advent of Islam (*al-jāhiliyya*) (2:181). This prohibition includes the subset of divination that Sīdi Muḥammad refers to as *al-zajr*: the reading of omens from the flights of birds and wild animals (2:183).[41] In this case, Sīdi Muḥammad clarifies that in some cases practices are not only illicit but also ineffective. He explains that the divination of the pre-Islamic Arabians relied on establishing friendships with the jinn, who would then eavesdrop on the inhabitants of the heavens and the earth and bring this news back to the diviner (*al-kāhin*) (2:182). He follows the interpretation of verses of the Qurʾān that depict the jinn as cut off from the unseen to argue that using the jinn to obtain news about the heavens became impossible with the beginning of Muḥammad's prophetic mission. However, he argues that the jinn retain the ability to access and bring news of unknown goings-on throughout the earth, and that humans can employ them for these functions either legally, with the adjurations, or illicitly, with the evocations (2:182). Regarding the astrological practice of "[sand] writing" (*al-khaṭṭ* [*al-raml*]), which is often translated as "geomancy," the Kunta explain that this science was among those revealed to the prophet Idrīs and that it relates to "the [heavenly] spheres [*al-aflāk*] and their natures and the means of their progression [across the sky] and the traveling of the bright stars in the constellations" (2:186). However, beginning in the period of the prophet Yūshaʿ, this knowledge became confused and riddled with flaws—as a result, there is no longer any way to practice "writing" correctly, according to its prophetic precedent (2:186–87).

The Kunta texts categorize these various forms of divination, along with evocations of the planets and the jinn, as illicit practices; however, Sīdi Muḥammad does not classify them as acts of sorcery. Indeed, he writes that "employment of the jinn is not truly called sorcery, and likewise making use of the stars; rather it is 'astrology' [*al-tanjīm*]" (1:97). As we have seen, in the list of eight practices that he provides in the third chapter of the *Ṭarāʾif wa'l-talāʾid*, he specifies that only three deserve the label of sorcery: *sīmā*; *hīmā*, and some of the properties (*khawāṣṣ*) (2:169). Apart from providing definitions for *sīmā* and *hīmā*, he does not discuss them at all. For the special properties, he clarifies that these are properties that God has deposited "in parts of this world" and that they include properties that are generally known, "like the quenching of water and the burning of fire," and properties that are secret: "And among them are those that harm, and among them are those that are an antidote to those afflicted by harm . . . and among them are those that act upon bodies and among them are those that act upon selves [*al-nafūs*]" (2:187). Ultimately, Sīdi Muḥammad uses only vague criteria to demarcate the line between prohibited sciences and acts of sorcery. He writes that each kind of sorcery produces "an effect in [people's] hearts, like love or hatred, or deposits goodness or evil in [their] bodies, like pain or sickness" (2:173), and that some kinds of sorcery affect an individual's self (*nafs*) (2:169). However, many of the examples he provides for the permissible sciences of the unseen also have the goal of producing effects in people's hearts or depositing goodness in their bodies. Although imprecisely defined, the line between science and sorcery carries legal ramifications. For while someone who has become overly preoccupied with astrology has erred, and someone who propitiates the spirits of the planetary spheres has committed the greater sin of idolatry, acts of sorcery are considered crimes with determined punishments. Specifically, Sīdi Muḥammad writes that according to Malikī law, acts of sorcery that also constitute disbelief are punished with execution, while similar acts that do not rise to the level of disbelief are punished by flogging (2:173).

The criteria that Sīdi Muḥammad uses to distinguish between the charismata and the sciences of the unseen, between the permitted and prohibited sciences, and between prohibited sciences and sorcery reflect a series of different rationales: causality, valorized and derogated types of speech, prophetic precedent, and association with non-Muslim Arabian practices. As demonstrated above, a given action (for example, the inscription of a talisman or controlling the jinn), or an effect (such as healing the body or predicting the future), can move from one category into another depending on the method used, the understanding of the practitioner, and the personal and social effects of the practice. Moreover, Sīdi Muḥammad's classification system is not only fluid but also, at times, inconsistent. Thus, although he emphatically describes sorcery as part of the normal functioning of the world in the introduction to the *Ṭarāʾif waʾl-talāʾid*, elsewhere he contradicts this statement. In the third chapter of the same work, he says that "*sīmā*, *hīma*, talismans, magic squares, properties corresponding to the realities and properties corresponding to the spirits, *ruqiyya*, adjurations [*ʿazāʾim*], and evocations [*al-istakhdāmāt*]" are "confused [*taltabis*] with sorcery in that [*min ḥaythu*] their performance is in the breaking of norms" (2:167). In this passage, he thus suggests that these categories of practice (which include the three that he has labeled "sorcery") subvert, rather than partake in, the normal.

In his classic book *Map Is Not Territory*, Jonathan Z. Smith describes classificatory systems that absolutely and perfectly order the world as "imperial systems" and suggests that scholars stop trying to explain away logical inconsistencies and instead view them as arising from an "incongruity that gives rise to thought."[42] Following Smith's example, I read the inconsistencies in Sīdi Muḥammad's classifications of knowledge/practice as reflecting the incongruity between the theological tenet of God's ultimate agency and the desire, even the necessity, of maintaining that people can alter their personal and material circumstances through actions that have predictable results. Finally, as I discuss in the next section, tensions between different categories of knowledge/practice are not restricted to the Kunta's texts but reflect common difficulties in any system that seeks to distinguish among human disciplines.

Etic Engagements

The previous two sections began with the Kunta scholars as interlocutors and examined the emic, second-order categories that emerged from within their own texts. This section illustrates how uneasily the terms "religion," "science," and "magic" that developed in early modern western Europe map onto the Kunta's categories of "breakings of the norm," "sciences of the unseen," and "sorcery." First, European scholars used "magic" to designate a degraded or vestigial form of religion, and then to refer to a kind of flawed science. Meanwhile, in popular parlance, "magic" has come to designate an appeal to supernatural forces other than God. However, as we have seen, the Kunta scholars understood both the sciences of the unseen and sorcery to depend on the appropriate functioning of the "normal" operations of the world. It is the miracles of the prophets and the charismata of the friends of God, by contrast, that break free of the constraints of normalcy and the natural. The terminology developed in western Europe fails to work for this Muslim context in part because of an epistemic divide that separated western European elites from the knowledge/practices of their Renaissance counterparts. Max Weber's theory of "disenchantment" described a historical process in which Europeans came to understand God and religion as belonging to a spiritual place distinct and separate from the physical, knowable world. Science came to occupy the role of informing people about the physical world of the senses, while religion was confined to the spiritual realm and—because the spiritual was reconceived as fundamentally unknowable—was presented as a matter of faith and doubt.[43] In that the Kunta scholars understand the visible and invisible realms to be intimately and inextricably connected, their categories of knowledge/practice stand on the other side of the epistemological divide from the so-called Enlightenment elites. However, the idea of a disenchanted modernity has been the subject of much recent debate, and scholars such as Egil Asprem, Wouter Hanegraaff, and Jason Josephson-Storm have pushed back, arguing that "enchanted" understandings of the world continued throughout the early modern and modern periods.[44] Responding to their criticisms of the theory of disenchantment, Edward Bever and Randall Styers, as noted above, have posited that European modernity is defined by "a double gesture" that reinscribes and revitalizes the sets of knowledge/practice that it seeks to banish.[45] Although the specific meanings that European elites ascribed to the terms "magic" and "science" do not apply to the context of the Kunta, the Kunta were very much involved in the discursive "double gesture" of disavowal and reinscription that these scholars have attributed to Western modernity.

The remainder of this chapter situates the Kunta's classificatory system within two larger, etic contexts and seeks to destabilize the assumption that this "double gesture" is restricted to modern Europe. I begin by mapping Sīdi al-Mukhtār's and Sīdi Muḥammad's engagement with the sciences of the unseen onto the current state of knowledge concerning the history of these sciences in West Africa through the nineteenth century. Although research on this topic is still nascent, there is evidence that the classifications of the Kunta scholars represented a shift in Muslim views on the legitimacy of these practices in the region. This analysis suggests that the Kunta's classifications of certain practices as sorcery and others as impermissible sciences responded to changing developments in the formation of racial identities in the region. I then turn to the transregional context and examine the works of the Kunta in relation to the history of "magic discourses" that began in ancient Greece, were absorbed by Arabic-Islamic philosophy, and went on to influence early modern Europeans and West Africans alike. It is this historical discourse about knowledge, practice, and legitimacy that connects the Kunta scholars to both ancient Mediterranean and early modern European epistemologies—as well as to those nineteenth-, twentieth-, and now twenty-first-century movements that rejected, and continue to reject, the rhetorical categories of the Enlightenment. Both of these etic engagements situate the work of the Kunta within diachronic fields, and although one approach looks at the region and the other explores the transregional context, it should be remembered that they are two snapshots from within the same wide frame. The

Sahara of the late eighteenth and early nineteenth centuries represented one arena in which debates on these topics played out across Africa, the Middle East, and Europe.

Science and Sorcery in West Africa

There is evidence of a long historical presence of some of the first-order disciplines discussed by the Kunta scholars in West Africa. Very recently, Zachary Wright has described a manuscript attributed to the scholar Muḥammad al-Kābarī, who settled in Timbuktu in the fifteenth century, where he trained ʿUmar Aqīt, "whose descendants (including Aḥmad Bābā of later fame) provided the chief jurists and judges for the city throughout the sixteenth century."[46] Al-Kābarī's text, the *Bustān al-fawāʾid wa l-manāfiʿ* (The Garden of Excellences and Benefits), contains powerful prayers and invokes various names of God.[47] Archaeological excavations in the Middle Niger Valley have also unearthed magic squares along with Qurʾānic inscriptions dating from approximately the seventeenth century.[48] And from at least the fourteenth century, Muslim communities dispersed throughout the region along trade routes and established their own towns within rural areas and distinct quarters within larger cities, from which they would direct trade, advise rulers, and provide professional services to Muslims and non-Muslims alike. Many of these services seem to have focused specifically on producing talismans and providing healing and protective services.[49] One example of this trend is the network of Muslim teachers called the Jakhanke, a group of Mande (or Manding) speakers who migrated outward from the city of Dia in the Niger River Valley and established enclaves along pilgrimage and commercial routes throughout the region. Lamin Sanneh's study of the Jakhanke network draws on oral traditions and family chronicles that describe the production of amulets and the use of supplicatory prayers and litanies for healing. The Jakhanke referred to vocational training in these disciplines as *taṣrīf*, which literally means "freedom of action." In this case, *taṣrīf* also referred to knowledge of the principles required to adjust local customs (*ʿādāt*) so that they conformed to accepted Muslim practice (*taqlīd*) according to an Islamic legal framework.[50] The Jakhanke ascribe the founding of their network to a figure named al-Ḥājj Sālim Suware, whom scholars have dated to as early as the twelfth and as late as the fifteenth century.[51] Certainly, enclaves of Mande-speaking Muslim scholars living in communities in majority-non-Muslim areas had spread all the way down to the Akan forest region and the Asante kingdom by the nineteenth century.[52] David Owusu-Ansah's analysis of talismans produced by these Muslim scholars for use by the Asante reveals many charts and tables composed of letters and numbers in Arabic, including magic squares very similar to the ones in the Kunta texts.[53]

The first written reference to the second-order category of sorcery (*siḥr*) in a regionally produced text appears at the turn of the sixteenth century, in a work known as the "Replies" to Askia Muḥammad. In this text, a Saharan scholar named Muḥammad ibn ʿAbd al-Karīm al-Maghīlī responds to a set of questions from the new ruler of the Songhay Empire, Askia al-Ḥājj Muḥammad. In 1493, Askia Muḥammad deposed the son of Sonni ʿAlī, the founder and previous ruler of Songhay, and sent a series of questions to al-Maghīlī to ask whether Sonni ʿAlī's participation in non-Muslim practices justified deposing him in order to establish correct Muslim rule.[54] Al-Maghīlī's "Replies" confirm this position, labeling Sonni ʿAlī and his immediate followers "the most unjust oppressors and miscreants" and declaring that "the *jihād* of the *amīr* Askia against them and his seizure of power from their hands [was] one of the most worthy and important of *jihāds*."[55] Askia Muḥammad also expresses worry about "how people behave in some parts of these lands." His main concern is that "there are among them some who claim to have some knowledge of the unseen (*al-ghayb*) through sand divining and the like, or through the disposition of the stars, information gathered from the jinn or the sounds and movements of birds and so on. Some assert that they produce writings to bring good fortune, such as material prosperity or love, and to ward off ill fortune by defeating enemies, preventing steel from cutting or poison from taking effect and [they make] other similar claims and perform actions such as sorcerers are wont to do."[56] In his response to this statement, al-Maghīlī leaves no room for ambiguity. He writes that anyone who claims knowledge of the unseen "is a liar and an unbeliever and whoever gives him credit is an unbeliever," adding, "Such people must be forced to recant on pain of death."[57] As John Hunwick has noted, al-Maghīlī's opinions on issues ranging from the treatment of Jewish minorities to the declaration of Muslims as unbelievers were considered extreme in the Sahara during his time.[58] We thus cannot assume that his rejection of all knowledge of the unseen represented the predominant, or even a common, scholarly opinion during the late fifteenth and early sixteenth centuries. However, this brief exchange does provide evidence that some West Africans of the fifteenth century claimed to be able to alter material circumstances by accessing the realm of the unseen—the practices mentioned by Askia Muḥammad overlap with many of the first-order disciplines discussed by the Kunta, including communicating with the jinn, sand writing, and divination according to the stars and the sounds and movements of birds. Indeed, Sīdi al-Mukhtār and Sīdi Muḥammad were familiar with al-Maghīlī and included him in their Sufi lineage. The exchange between Askia Muḥammad and al-Maghīlī thus represents evidence that West Africans were making claims to access disciplines related to the unseen from as early as the fifteenth century, and that the Kunta would have had access to at least one Muslim scholar's rejection of these practices. The Kunta's defense of the sciences of the unseen thus represents a deliberate choice that placed them at odds with at least one authoritative writer from the region.

Closer to the Kunta's own time, an eighteenth-century Fulānī scholar named Muḥammad ibn Muḥammad al-Ghallānī al-Kashnāwī[59] left his home in the kingdom of Katsīnā in Hausaland sometime before the year 1730 to make the pilgrimage to Mecca. He settled in Cairo, where he composed several major works and taught students before his death in 1741 at the house of one of his students, Ḥasan al-Jabartī. Dahlia Gubara's recent examination of al-Kashnāwī's life and work situates his engagement with "the sciences of secrets" (*ʿulūm al-asrār*) within a larger episteme and "embodied ethics of learning" that he shared with Egyptian, Arabian, and other African scholars of his day.[60] According to al-Jabartī's account, al-Kashnāwī had five direct teachers in his homeland of Katsīnā, including Muḥammad al-Wālī ibn Sulaymān al-Birnāwī al-Baghiramāwī[61] and Muḥammad Fūdū (or Fūdī), who might be the father of ʿUthmān ibn Fūdī, the founder of the Sokoto movement.[62] With these teachers he studied theology, *ḥadīth*, law, grammar, arithmetic, astrology, sand writing, magic squares, rhetoric, eloquence, and logic. Al-Kashnāwī arrived in the *ḥijāz* and then in Egypt as an accomplished and learned scholar and was subsequently sought as a teacher by local pupils. From his educational history, Gubara rightly argues against hiving off the sciences of secrets from other domains of learning, concluding that "neither al-Kashnāwī nor his teachers could be differentiated by strict fields of specialization, but are reported to have been fluent in many domains of scholarship."[63]

During al-Kashnāwī's period in Egypt he composed several works, including three treatises on "the sciences of secrets" (*ʿulūm al-asrār*): a work on the science of letters and names, a text on numerology and magic squares, and a work called *Al-Durr al-manẓūm wa khulāṣat al-sirr al-maktūm fī ʿilm al-ṭalāsim waʾl-nujūm* (The String of Pearls and the Summary of the Hidden Secret in the Science of Talismans and the Stars), a didactic commentary on a text about talismans, *siḥr*, and *nīranj* called *Al-Sirr al-maktūm fī mukhāṭabāt al-nujūm* (The Hidden Secret in the Correspondences of the Stars), which was composed by the thirteenth-century theologian Fakr al-Dīn al-Rāzī (d. 1209).[64]

In the *Durr al-manẓūm*, al-Kashnāwī directly states that he and his students were engaged in finding and reading works on *nīranj*—a Persian term of varying meaning that became associated with magic discourses—and that this project eventually led him to summarize al-Rāzī's work for didactic purposes.[65] In his discussion of *siḥr*, he describes "four major schools," which Gubara summarizes as "the Indian method . . . based on . . . the purification of the soul and the suspension of illusion; the Nabatean method [which] revolved principally around the invitation and supplication of the planetary spirits by way of fasting and sacrifices . . . ; and finally, the way of the Hebrews, the Copts and the Arabs . . . which amalgamated the above three and was in al-Kashnāwī's estimation superior."[66] Al-Kashnāwī further described talismans as powerful seals that drew on the causal efficacy of the planets, and he described knowledge of astronomy as a basic prerequisite for practicing the sciences of the secrets. Indeed, al-Kashnāwī includes *siḥr* as part of the sciences of the secrets and praises those disciplines for their ability to connect people to the spirits of the planetary spheres and for their useful applications to the daily lives of practitioners.[67] Unlike the Kunta scholars, al-Kashnāwī did not consider any type of knowledge to be intrinsically illegitimate; rather, he argued that the sciences of the secrets needed to be kept secret because they could be used for amoral purposes. And although he composed his works on the sciences of the secrets in Egypt during the last decade of his life, the sources indicate that he was thoroughly trained in these disciplines before he left his homeland of Katsīnā. Al-Kashnāwī's education in Hausaland indicates the establishment of the disciplines of astrology, sand writing, divination, and the sciences of letters and magic squares in that region,[68] and there is every reason to conclude that he participated in the general episteme in which he was educated.

The Kunta scholars' rejection of the category of *siḥr* as prohibited sorcery thus represents a clear divide between their work and al-Kashnāwī's. Moreover, by classifying sand writing, astrology, and divination as prohibited disciplines among the sciences of the unseen, they also rejected bodies of knowledge and practice that were apparently established and flourishing among the Fulānī scholars of Hausaland, a population with which they had direct and ongoing interactions. Sīdi Muḥammad's classification of the sciences of the unseen and sorcery in the *Ṭarāʾif waʾl-talāʾid* and the *Fawāʾid nūrāniyya* might reflect a discomfort with the growing popularity of the sciences of the unseen among elite Muslim scholars in northwestern Africa. This unease is visible in the career of Aḥmad al-Tijānī, a Moroccan contemporary of Sīdi al-Mukhtār. Zachary Wright has demonstrated that al-Tijānī collected powerful supplicatory prayers and that he had knowledge of the sciences of the secrets, but that he also adopted a more reserved opinion concerning these disciplines than his Moroccan contemporaries. Specifically, al-Tijānī "restricted and deemphasized the use of such sciences" and limited their use "to one of two types of people: gnostics (*ʿārifūn*) and saints (*awliyāʾ*)."[69] There is no evidence that Sīdi al-Mukhtār or Sīdi Muḥammad knew of, or were in contact with, the early Tijānī movement, and they did not restrict the sciences to the Sufi friends of God to the same extent. Rather, the works of Sīdi Muḥammad reveal a tension between two modalities for understanding the sciences of the unseen. On the one hand, he presents the sciences of the unseen as a set of techniques available to, and efficacious for, anyone with the requisite knowledge, but on the other hand he positions them as a series of Sufi exercises (*riyāḍāt*) whose efficacy depends on the spiritual status of the practitioner. In the latter mode, the sciences of the unseen become a stage along the Sufi path to God, and a stage that the most advanced practitioners will ultimately abandon, even as they become able to achieve the same effects merely by exerting their will and intention.[70]

The engagement of the Kunta scholars in the sciences of the unseen thus emerges from a long history of the popularity of these disciplines among West African Muslims, even as their writings indicate the beginning of new trends in regional approaches to the sciences. First, while writers like al-Kashnāwī had associated the sciences with the Sufi friends of God, the Kunta also represent the beginning of a growing regional trend among Sufi leaders of presenting these sciences as falling into the exclusive purview of the friends of God. These trends would continue in the region, as the sciences increasingly became associated with Sufi leaders, who expressed reservations about their use by anyone outside the spiritual elite. This attitude toward the sciences was perhaps most pronounced within the Tijānīyya but was also apparent among the leaders of the Sokoto movement.[71] Of course, there is no evidence that these attempts by Sufi leaders and scholars to limit the use of the sciences were effective. On the contrary, Benjamin Soares's ethnographic work in Mali in the 1990s demonstrated the widespread use of these disciplines across all sectors of society, from religious figures, to civil servants, to truck drivers.[72]

Second, aside from al-Maghīlī's blanket condemnation of anything having to do with the unseen, there is no previous evidence that West African Muslims classified any of the first-order disciplines associated with the sciences of the unseen as intrinsically illicit, and the Kunta's texts are also the first in the region to systematically integrate those sciences into Sufi cosmological and metaphysical frameworks. This trend toward the classification of the sciences and their integration with philosophical thought would continue in the region. ʿUthmān ibn Fūdī and his son Muḥammad Bello also appear to have followed the example of the Kunta in rejecting astrology, divination, and litanies or talismans that incorporated non-Arabic speech.[73] Oludamini Ogunnaike has recently examined some of the works of ʻAbd al-Qādir ibn Muṣṭafā al-Turūdī (d. 1864/1280), better known as Dan Tafa, a grandson of ʿUthmān ibn Fūdī. In a poem called "Shukr al-wāhib," Dan Tafa categorizes the types of knowledge he acquired over the course of his education into six sections: (1) the "sciences of the *sharīʿa*"; (2) "the sciences of the ancients" (*ʿulūm al-awā'il*), which included "medicine, arithmetic, logic, the wisdom (*ḥikma*) of the stars (astrology) and physics, the science of magic squares and letters, [and] various forms of divination"; (3) "the sciences/knowledge of realities" (*ʿulūm al-ḥaqāʾiq*), which included knowledge of the divine essence and attributes, the divine names, and the realms of *al-malakūt* and *al-jabarūt*; (4) "the sciences/knowledge of the saints" (*awliyāʾ*), which included details of the states and stations along the Sufi path; (5) "the sciences/knowledge of secrets/mysteries from outside of the Sufi path," which he alluded to through symbolic titles such as "the place of ascent of the luminous elements" but which also included "the knowledge of the letters of His Tremendous Name"; and (6) the sciences "received from . . . the greatest unveiling."[74] With respect to the relationship between the various sciences and the Sufi path, this system of classification is more thorough and specific than Sīdi Muḥammad's. Dan Tafa clearly distinguishes a category of disciplines that lie outside the Sufi path. His classification scheme also categorizes the sciences by their mode of acquisition, distinguishing among those acquired by "textual study," "spiritual realization," "spiritual wayfaring and attraction," "divine bestowal," and "true visions during dreams." In another work, called *ʿUhūd wa mawāthīq* and composed in the last decade of his life, Dan Tafa lists various oaths that he took to remind himself of proper ethical comportment, and he included among these oaths the prohibition on teaching anyone "the sciences of the ancients" and the vow not to use *al-simīyāʾ*, adjurations (*al-ʿazāʾim*), or evocations of the jinn (*istikhdām al-jinn*), or to "search into the unseen by means of divination [*al-ajfār*], divinatory tables [*al-ziyārij*], [or] astrology."[75] These apologetic oaths suggest that Dan Tafa had received criticism for his open engagement with some of these categories of knowledge/practice. Moreover, although most of the disciplines that he vows to abstain from, such as *al-simīyāʾ*, evocations of the jinn, divination, and astrology, are among those sciences rejected by the Kunta, Dan Tafa also includes an oath to abandon adjurations of the jinn (*al-ʿazāʾīm*), which the Kunta permitted. The inclusion of the adjurations among practices abandoned by Dan Tafa indicates that Muslim scholars were increasing the number of sciences that they categorized as prohibited.

Finally, the Kunta's classification of the sciences and sorcery are related to a trend of increasing racialization in the region. In his discussion of the uses of the special properties (*khawāṣṣ*) that fall under the category of sorcery, Sīdi Muḥammad refers to practices that he associates with "a kind of people who predominate in the land of the blacks [*al-sūdān*] and who are called, in the Songhay language 'Karkū' and in the language of the people of the far West [*al-maghrib al-aqsā*] '*al-sallāla*' and in the language of their blacks '*saghnī*.'" He adds that these people increase the evil of their own selves "by sucking the blood from the veins inside the body until the one who is sucked dies or is on the brink of death" (2:187–88). The idea of sorcerers, called *sallāla*, who drain the blood or life force from their victims while they sleep has been documented during the colonial and postcolonial periods in Mauritania, where it became one of many practices associated with blackness and non-Muslimness.[76] The appearance of this idea in the works of the Kunta illustrates its circulation in the region prior to French colonialism, but, more important, it indicates that the Kunta's discussion of sorcery was related to the development of racialized categories along the desert and desert edge. Beginning in the seventeenth century, nomadic desert elites like the Kunta increasingly came to identify as white (*biḍān*) and to identify sedentary agriculturists that lived to the south as black (*sūdān*). From the seventeenth century onward, these white elites developed ideological tools such as genealogies and local chronicles that asserted the superiority of white identity. These tools increasingly came to associate blackness with non-Muslimness and thus with permanent enslaveability (see chapter 1).

The Kunta were very much a part of the development of the racial categories of blackness and whiteness during this period, and they too produced improved genealogies and family chronicles tying themselves to an Arab lineage. Moreover, they overtly characterized the practices of people "in the land of the blacks" as sorcery. Sīdi Muḥammad's rejection of astrology, divination, and sand writing as prohibited sciences may also be tied to this new racial context, as those practices were widespread among Muslims who lived in Hausaland before the rise of Sokoto. While he does not go so far as to describe the practices of Fulānī Muslim scholars like al-Kashnāwī as sorcery, he does associate them with the prohibited practices of the pre-Islamic Arabians. By assigning the knowledge and practices of Fulānī Muslims living in "the land of the blacks" to the category of prohibited sciences and classifying practices that he identifies with blackness as "sorcery," Sīdi Muḥammad furthered the association of blackness with non-Muslimness. The classification of knowledge thus became yet another ideological tool that asserted the superiority of groups who identified as white. However, although the Kunta associate sorcery with the peoples "of the land of the blacks," they do not follow al-Maghīlī's position that all claims to access the unseen constitute sorcery. Instead, the Kunta texts reflect two pressures—first, to offer practices that yielded tangible results, and second, to maintain a line between the practices of Muslims and the practices of non-Muslims. To that end, Sīdi Muḥammad prohibited certain practices, including those, like divination and sand writing, that were in use "in the land of the blacks" to the south during his time, while producing Islamic justifications for the sciences that he does permit.

Islamic Magic Discourses

While Sīdi Muḥammad roots the sciences of the unseen in Islamic sacred history, the historical roots of this discourse stretch all the way back to ancient Greece. And while the term "magic," as it was defined in the twentieth century by religious studies scholars, has been widely criticized, scholars of the ancient and late antique Mediterranean have reconstructed a very old history of the word itself. Kimberly Stratton, in particular, has focused on the production and development of magic as a discourse of alterity that aimed to "other" specific populations while enforcing gender norms and sexual conformity. However, in addition to elite discourses, abundant material evidence indicates that ancient and late antique Greco-Romans did indeed engage in some of the practices that elites labeled "magic" (*mageia*), fashioning binding curses (*katadesmoi, defixiones*) that they deposited in graves, in wells, and at crossroads. An abundance of texts from the fifth century BC to the second century AD, referred to collectively as the Greek magical papyri, contain instructions and recipes for the production of curses and potions.[77] Moreover, Bernd-Christian Otto has pointed out that some of these material artifacts indicate that the practitioners who produced them identified their own practice as "magic."[78] Since then, Otto has posited the existence of a heterogeneous but continuous textual-ritual tradition of "Western learned magic" from the Greek period to the present. This magic "discourse of inclusion" draws its potency and appeal from the "discourse of exclusion" maintained by elites, and the two traditions thus developed together in parallel.[79]

Important aspects of the relationship between Islamic traditions and this history of Western learned magic remain unclear; indeed, scholars working in Islamic studies have yet to take up the theoretical or methodological challenges posed by Otto and Stratton (among others), despite a groundswell of research into Islamic "magic" and "occult sciences" in the past decade.[80] The remainder of this section reads this growing body of literature about the medieval development of Arabo-Islamic debates about *siḥr* and the sciences through the theoretical lens of magic discourses of inclusion and exclusion. For although Islamic studies scholars have yet to adopt this theoretical framework, the evidence strongly indicates the presence of Islamic magic discourses of both inclusion and exclusion between the ʿAbbāsid period and the rise of the Kunta in the eighteenth century. Rather than attempt a complete overview of such a long history, this discussion focuses on discrete moments of particular relevance to the Kunta's own classification of the sciences, beginning with the development of a magic discourse of inclusion during the early ʿAbbāsid period; highlighting the growing association between Sufi scholars and the sciences of letters and names, magic squares, and talismans in the twelfth and thirteenth centuries; and examining the evidence for the presence of magic discourses of inclusion in seventeenth- and eighteenth-century West Africa.

The word *siḥr* itself appears twenty-three times in the Qurʾān, particularly during the encounter between Moses and Pharaoh's sorcerers (Qurʾān 7:112–26, 10:76–81, 20:57–76, 26:37–51) and in a verse that records how some Meccans accused Muḥammad of being a poet, a madman, or a sorcerer (51:52). In one verse, the disbelieving devils (*shayāṭīn*) are described as tempting people by teaching them sorcery (2:102). And while the Qurʾān itself does not condemn *siḥr* (although it does present it as a falsehood), there are numerous *ḥadīth* that call for the death of sorcerers.[81] However, despite this negative portrayal of *siḥr* in the Qurʾān and *ḥadīth*, scholars have shown that by the ʿAbbāsid period, Muslims had come to read the term through new scholarship produced during the Greek translation movement, the multigeneration effort, patronized by the ʿAbbāsid caliphs, to translate the received works of the ancient Greeks into Arabic. The absorption of these classical works ultimately led to the production of a synthesis of Neoplatonic, neo-Pythagorean, and Aristotelian cosmologies and metaphysics. Contributions to this philosophical and metaphysical synthesis include Abū Maʿshar's (d. 886) influential works on astronomy, which outlined the causal effects of planetary rotations on the physical world and the human body.[82] Meanwhile, his contemporary and mentor, al-Kindī (d. 873), identified that causal agent of material change as the astral rays emitted by each heavenly body. Al-Kindī described legally permitted *siḥr* as acts that drew on and harnessed the power of these astral rays. A Pseudo-Aristotelian work from the same period contains a chapter titled "Sirr al-asrār" (The Secret of Secrets), which summarizes the theories of astral influence outlined by Abū Maʿshar and al-Kindī and adds instructions for operationalizing this knowledge in practice.[83] Finally, the tenth century saw the production of the encyclopedic compendium known as the *Rasāʾil Ikhwān al-Ṣafāʾ* (*The Epistles of the Brethren of Purity*) and the *Ghāyat al-ḥakīm* (The Goal of the Sage), by Maslama ibn Qurṭubī (d. 964). Composed by an enigmatic group of scholars devoted to esoteric knowledge, the *Rasāʾil* situates the practice of *siḥr* as the culmination of human learning within the Aristotelian/Neoplatonic curriculum and locates the causal effect of the heavenly bodies in their celestial spirits (*rūḥāniyyāt*), for which they provide names and invocations.[84] According to the Brethren, these spirit beings affect the material world either through their correspondences to material natures or "by way of their souls and volition."[85] Meanwhile, the *Ghāyat* "expands and systematizes" both the theories of causality found in the works of Abū Maʿshar and al-Kindī and the practical applications presented in the "Sirr al-asrār."[86]

While the Kunta scholars refer to *siḥr* only in the pejorative sense, as "sorcery," discussions of *siḥr* during this early period follow the same pattern as magic discourses described by Stratton and Otto for the Hellenistic world. Liana Saif has demonstrated that these early scholars argued for the legitimacy of magic by presenting it as a subset of natural philosophy, an educated manipulation of the forces of cause and effect set in motion by God. Meanwhile, some writers explicitly contrasted this with prohibited magic based on alliances with the Devil or devils.[87] As late as the turn of the thirteenth century, the theologian Fakr al-Dīn al-Rāzī argued that knowledge of magic was not only permitted but obligatory because it allowed Muslims to correctly identify the miracles of the prophets.[88] Thus, for the early ʿAbbāsid period, *siḥr* can be accurately translated as "magic" in the Greek sense of *mageia*.

Although scholars like al-Kindī who wrote in defense of magic were sometimes criticized as demonic, more often they were attacked as deterministic for positing that the natures and fates of individuals were controlled by the movement of the stars. The developing Ashʿarī school of theology, in particular, denounced the idea that secondary causes, such as the movement of the stars, exercised effects in and of themselves without the direct will and action of God.[89] Partly as a result of the success of Ashʿarism, Muslim scholars writing in Arabic gradually ceased to apply the category of *siḥr* to their own work, and by the thirteenth century, works of self-professed *siḥr* are hard to find.[90] Indeed, it became more common from the thirteenth century onward to see a discourse of exclusion in which Sufi scholars leveled accusations of magic against other Sufis whom they viewed as exceeding the boundaries of a new orthodoxy.[91]

However, the twelfth and thirteenth centuries also witnessed the crystallization of the association between Sufism and the sciences of secrets owing to the work and reputations of al-Ghazālī (d. 1111), Ibn al-ʿArabī (d. 1240), and Aḥmad al-Būnī (d. ca. 1232).[92] Both the historical work of these figures and their legacies furthered the growing assimilation of talismans, magic squares, and the sciences of names and letters into Sufism after the fourteenth century.[93] Speculation on the hidden and secret meanings of the letters of the Arabic alphabet and their inscription into cosmological and cosmogonical frameworks may have roots in early Shi'ism, whence it entered Sufi thought.[94] And although the early Sufis of the ʿAbbāsid-era movement based in Baghdad recognized "the sacred and symbolic nature of the Arabic alphabet," the idea that God created the universe from his names, and that the letters of the alphabet form the underlying structure of the universe, appears to have taken root and developed in the Andalusian mystical tradition, particularly through the works of Ibn Masarra and Ibn Barrajān.[95] Al-Ghazālī does not himself engage in the sciences of letters, names, and magic squares; however, his references to these disciplines provide evidence of their popularity in the East during his time. In fact, al-Ghazālī appears concerned about people who consider these practices to be more efficacious than prayer. He specifically condemns those who would abandon "prayer or judge it 'ineffective' while putting their faith in the efficacy of a three-by-three magic square."[96]

It was Aḥmad al-Būnī and Ibn al-ʿArabī—both of them linked to Ibn Barrajān and the Andalusian and North African mystical tradition through their mutual teacher al-Mahdawī—who brought cosmological lettrism together with philosophical currents that developed within the Eastern Sufi tradition.[97] Ibn al-ʿArabī positioned the divine names and letters of the alphabet at the center of his cosmogonical and cosmological schemes. He understood the names and letters to act as generating principles, each one realizing an aspect of created existence according to God's command.[98] Scholars disagree on the extent to which Ibn al-ʿArabī embraced the operational potential of the names and letters. Denis Gril points out that Ibn al-ʿArabī condemned the practical application of the "science of letters" as "detestable in both reason and law."[99] Pierre Lory concurs, describing Ibn al-ʿArabī's "science of letters" as a process of preparing the self and the heart for revelatory knowledge by contemplating the symbolic meanings of the names. He concludes that this "science of letters has no real connection with the magical significance of letters."[100] However, Liana Saif's more recent work highlights the "operational aspect" of Ibn al-ʿArabī's discussion of the letters, through which the worshipper "is able to know the human essence, the universe, and ultimately God." Moreover, the person who acquires "experiential knowledge of the letters and Divine Names" receives "extraordinary feats," including the ability to "*act upon* the realm of the unknown (*ʿālam al-ghayb*) and the *malakūt*."[101]

However, if Ibn al-ʿArabī appeared to equivocate concerning the practical implementation of lettrism, his contemporary, the North African scholar Aḥmad al-Būnī, set down in writing the specific techniques of applied lettrism.[102] His works incorporate the applied sciences into more standard topics of Sufi thought and practice, including metaphysics, cosmology, sacred history, and ritual practice. Indeed, his *Laṭāʾif al-ishārāt* (The Subtleties of the Signs) is organized in much the same fashion as Sīdi Muḥammad's *Fawāʾid nūrāniyya*, consisting of a "rather theoretical and general first part on creation, cosmology, and the insertion of the letters into analogous systems," which leads "to a description of the letters one by one."[103] Moreover, when al-Būnī did engage openly with the sciences of the letters and names, he presented them consistently as a method of spiritual training designed to lead a believer closer to God, or as a means of better understanding the revelation of the Qurʾān.[104] Al-Būnī's decision to openly discuss this science and the related fields of magic squares and talismans was groundbreaking for his day, and later Muslims—both followers and critics—came to associate his name almost exclusively with these disciplines. Scholars today thus consider his works the medieval "culmination of the instrumentalisation of letters."[105] And while al-Būnī engaged the applied sciences of the letters much more directly than Ibn al-ʿArabī, Jean-Charles Coulon concludes that "it is easy to see that the two individuals issued from the same training through their cosmology, in which the divine verb manifests through its letters in all of creation."[106]

The reputations of all three of these scholars only became more closely associated with the applied sciences of the unseen after their deaths, a trend that is most apparent in the receptions of al-Ghazālī and al-Būnī.[107] Thus, in his work, al-Ghazālī refers to a three-by-three magic square composed of the digits one through nine (sometimes referred to as *budūḥ*) only to chastise those who depend on it instead of prayer. However, after his death, his reputation was associated with this magic square to such an extent that it became known as "the magic square [literally 'triangle'] of al-Ghazālī" (*muthallath al-Ghazālī*). A text titled *Mustawjabat al-maḥāmid fī sharḥ khātam Abī Ḥamid* (The Praiseworthy: A Commentary on the Seal of Abū Ḥāmid) by Abū ʿAnd Allāh al-Anṣārī (also known as Ibn Bint Abī Saʾd) seems to have played a pivotal role in spreading this association. The text presents a long chain of transmission connecting al-Ghazālī's knowledge of this seal back to Āṣaf ibn Barakhiyā, Solomon's vizier, and continuing to al-Ghazālī by means of "a Greek sage."[108] Meanwhile, works falsely attributed to al-Būnī circulated across the Arabo-Islamic world in the centuries following his death. The seventeenth century saw the emergence of the most influential of these pseudo-Būnian works, a bricolage of selections from al-Būnī's manuscripts interpolated with later additions called the *Shams al-maʿārif al-kubrā*.[109] Scholars accepted the attribution of the *Shams al-maʿārif al-kubrā* until very recently, when Noah Gardiner began sifting genuine al-Būnī works from later forgeries. And while al-Būnī certainly did not apply the label of "sorcery" to his own works, many of the people who copied, distributed, and purchased al-Būnī forgeries probably understood these texts as works of operational *siḥr*.

Closer to the Kunta scholars' own time, there are two main sources of evidence for the presence of magic discourses in West Africa. The first is the career of Muḥammad al-Kashnāwī, the Muslim scholar from Hausaland (see above), who composed a didactic commentary on Fakr al-Dīn al-Rāzī's text on astral magic, *Al-Sirr al-maktūm*. Al-Kashnāwī was involved in a magic discourse of inclusion, and he intentionally engaged *siḥr* as a permitted category of knowledge and practice. The second is the reputation of al-Būnī and the pseudo-Būnian manuscript tradition, references to which appear in the Kunta's own texts. Sīdi Muḥammad refers to al-Būnī by name, agreeing with another scholar's adjuration to "abandon al-Būnī and his forms."[110] However, although the Kunta writer would have rejected the association, his work bears the unmistakable imprint of the pseudo-Būnian manuscript tradition. Specifically, two folios of his *Fawāʾid nūrāniyya* are copied almost word for word from the fifteenth-century work *Shams al-āfāq fī ʿilm al-ḥurūf wa'l-awfāq* (The Sun of the Horizons: The Science of Letters and Magic Squares), by ʿAbd al-Raḥmān al-Bisṭāmī (d. 1454). This passage provides an Islamic history of the sciences of secrets that begins with Adam and stretches through all of the Muslim prophets down to Muḥammad and from him to ʿAlī.[111] As Coulon has demonstrated, al-Bisṭāmī played an important role in consolidating and spreading al-Būnī's reputation, and passages from this very work were subsequently incorporated into the pseudo-Būnian *Shams al-maʿārif al-kubrā*.[112]

Sīdi Muḥammad's rejection of al-Būnī, his prohibition of sand writing and astrology, and his pejorative description of the process of propitiating the planetary spirits mark his participation in a magic discourse of exclusion. He was clearly aware of traditions that accepted and discussed *siḥr* as a permitted category. Thus his understanding of "the evocation of the planets" as a process of enlisting the aid of the "perceptive faculties" of the planetary spheres is a generally accurate summary of the theory and practice of astral summoning described in the *Epistles of the Brethren of Purity*, the *Ghāyat al-ḥakīm*, and al-Kashnāwī's commentary on the *Sirr al-maktūm*. His disparagement of these practices as involving "sodomy" and other prohibited acts places him in a long history of associating magic practice with sexual deviancy. Unlike al-Kashnāwī, for whom no kind of knowledge was intrinsically illegitimate, the Kunta were involved in demarcating the two separate spheres of illicit and licit knowledge and practice and relating them to each other. For Sīdi Muḥammad, the illicit included sorcery but also prohibited sciences such as sand writing and evocations of the planets. Therefore, the Kunta scholars of West Africa can be said to have participated in the development of parallel discourses of inclusion and exclusion that we find in societies that inherited Hellenistic magic discourses.

Moreover, the tandem development of inclusive and exclusive magic discourses described by Otto is related to the discursive pattern of the "double gesture" that Bever and Styers described as unique to the codevelopment of scientific discourses and magic traditions in western Europe. In effect, the process of designating a sphere of valid, legitimate knowledge and practice constantly reinscribes and reinvigorates those categories that have been rejected and marginalized, leaving them open to powerful reappropriation. Sīdi Muḥammad's categorizations display this same "double gesture"; he first distances himself from magic discourses of inclusion by engaging in a discourse of *exclusion* that derogates sorcery as the practice of sinful Muslims and unbelievers, which appear to be associated, respectively, with Muslim scholars living in pre-Sokoto Hausaland and groups racialized as black. However, rather than categorically exclude all disciplines historically associated with *siḥr*, Sīdi Muḥammad carefully culls from that historical tradition acceptable bodies of knowledge/practice for inclusion in the permissible sciences of the unseen. The most prominent example of this process is his inclusion of the history of the sciences copied from the pseudo-Būnian *Shams al-maʿārif al-kubrā*. Sīdi Muḥammad also cites specific, and historically documented, authors who shaped these magic discourses, such as al-Ṭughrāʾī (d. 1121), a prominent composer of alchemical texts (2:223).[113] Moreover, his understanding of the applied science of the names and letters owes much to the development of these disciplines by al-Būnī and his later followers. His chart of correspondences between the letters, the four elements, and the degrees (see fig. 1), for example, is laid out almost identically to the chart in al-Būnī's *Kitāb Laṭāʾif al-ishārāt fī asrār al-ḥurūf al-ʿulwiyya* (The Subtleties of the Signs: The Secrets of the Celestial Letters).[114] Sīdi Muḥammad's sciences of the unseen thus rely on the development of magic discourses of inclusion—indeed, he inextricably binds himself to those discourses—even as he engages in his own discourse of exclusion and marginalization.

Research on the development of these discourses in the colonial and postcolonial periods is ongoing, but some studies indicate that Muslim discourses of exclusion have also shaped the development of non-Muslim traditions in West Africa. Thus Benjamin Soares's work on the widespread collection and trade in "secrets" (*siru*) in the Malian city of Nioro indicates that non-Muslim practitioners have adopted some forms of Islamic ritual practice—including spoken and chanted words (including Arabic words) and the use of amulets. Both Muslims and non-Muslims identify certain practices as non-Islamic—as outside the fold of Islam. Some self-identified Muslims engage in these practices even while identifying them as non-Islamic. And while some Muslims also classify them as sorcery (*siḥr*), Muslims and non-Muslims alike continue to consider them both powerful and effective. Thus the development of the Islamic sciences of secrets in the region, in conjunction with discourses that exclude sorcery as prohibited, appears to have effectively reinforced the perceived power and efficacy of those practices identified as non-Islamic.[115] The development of an Islamic discourse of exclusion and disavowal simultaneously transformed, reshaped, and reinscribed practices perceived as non-Islamic or rejected as sorcery.

The development of the sciences of the unseen thus illustrates that the discursive "double gesture" of disavowal and reinscription cannot be limited to European modernity and was present in Islamicate contexts. Not only did Muslims, such as the Kunta, participate in this discursive pattern in a variety of contexts, but, I would argue, this "double gesture" most probably characterizes all epistemic systems that attempt to separate the "true" knowledge of elites from a purportedly false and illegitimate knowledge of marginalized groups. And although this discourse was deployed under the rubric of "science" and "magic" in western Europe, and within the categories of "sorcery" and the "sciences of the unseen" in West Africa and the Sahara, both frameworks engage in the same pattern of legitimating and channeling access to true knowledge, and thus correct and efficacious practice, while ironically reinforcing the salience and power of rejected categories of knowledge and practice.

Sīdi al-Mukhtār and Sīdi Muḥammad tied their authority as Sufi friends of God to their mastery of the sciences of the unseen, and they understood those sciences as concrete bodies of knowledge that served as the theoretical foundation of discrete practices that yielded predictable and tangible results. The task of presenting these disciplines as both efficacious and legitimate, according to Islamic law and Ashʿarī orthodoxy, fell to Sīdi Muḥammad, and required that he mobilize a host of historical discourses about cosmology, sacred history, and Muslim practice. In doing do, Sīdi Muḥammad categorized the various fields of potential knowledge and practice into the uneasy categories of the charismata, the sciences of the unseen, and sorcery. And his categorization of these practices reflects the tensions—and the incongruities—of his particular social and historical position: his attempts to balance the ability of humans to exert a meaningful influence over their surroundings with the tenets of Ashʿarī theology, and to maintain a divide between Muslim and non-Muslim practices while presenting himself and his family as the masters of powerful disciplines. These texts thus provide us with a particular window into how Muslims in this precolonial context used debates over practice to fashion and maintain their identity. But, more than that, these texts also illustrate a discursive move that cannot be limited to modern Europe. In trying to hold the thin line between the knowledge/practices he valorizes and those he rejects, Sīdi Muḥammad al-Kuntī illustrates a dynamic involved in all discourses of inclusion and exclusion, by which people bind themselves all the more closely to the knowledge and practices of those they reject as other.

4

BRIDGING THE WORLDS IN PRAYER

In the *Fawāʾid nūrāniyya*, Sīdi Muḥammad argues for the efficacy and legitimacy of the sciences of letters and names, including the use of the greatest name of God, by positioning them as a form of supplicatory prayer (*duʿāʾ*). He defends the practice of calling on God for help by referring to the Qurʾānic verse "Your Lord said, 'Call on me [*adʿūnī*] and I will answer you, but those who think themselves above my devotion [*ʿibādatī*] shall enter Jehenna utterly abject'" (40:60). This verse allows Sīdi Muḥammad to make two arguments. First, prayer works—God responds to the supplications of his creations—and second, supplicatory prayer constitutes an act of devotional worship (*ʿibāda*) that acknowledges the relationship of servanthood (*ʿubūdiyya*) between the servant (*ʿabd*) and God.[1] Within the Arabic Islamic tradition, supplications, or personal requests to God, are referred to as *duʿāʾ* (pl. *duʿāt* or *adʿiyya*). While supplicatory prayer is distinguished in theory from formal, obligatory prayer (*ṣalāt*), recent scholarship has called attention to the ambiguity of the boundaries separating supplicatory from formal prayer and other devotional practices.[2] On the one hand, personal supplication is included as one of the prescribed components of *ṣalāt*. On the other, the plural form of the word—*ṣalawāt*—is often used to refer to supplicatory prayer. Supplicatory prayer can be performed at any time, and while Muslims may choose their own words or formulas, specific prayers became associated with certain authoritative figures and were known to be particularly effective. Set litanies associated with specific Sufi teachers, and meant to be recited at specific times or for specific occasions, were sometimes known as *ḥizb* (pl. *aḥzāb*). The *aḥzāb* are themselves a form of supplication, a type of *duʿāʾ*. In the Kunta texts, as in other Arabic-speaking Sufi contexts, the *adʿiyya* and *aḥzāb* are associated with each other and also with the genres of *wird* (pl. *awrād*) and *dhikr* (pl. *adhkār*). The *awrād* refer to different arrangements of standard formulas whose exact order, pattern, number of repetitions, and timing of recitation are associated with particular teachers. *Dhikr* can refer to remembrance in general or to the Sufi ritual of individually or collectively reciting names of God and devotional formulas. Additionally, the term, particularly in the plural form, can also refer to the specific formulas used during the ritual, and those formulas were, again, often associated with specific Sufi teachers.[3] This chapter takes seriously the Kunta claim that the sciences of letters and names specifically, and the sciences of the unseen more broadly, constitute a form of supplication. Specifically, I interrogate the meaning of supplicatory prayer within Sīdi al-Mukhtār's and Sīdi Muḥammad's works by analyzing written devotional aids, a popular genre of Islamic textual production that has received very little treatment in academic scholarship.

The Kunta not only discussed supplicatory prayer as an aspect of devotional practice; they also produced and circulated their own prayers. These short texts, both single prayers and collections of prayers, are attributed to Sīdi al-Mukhtār, including one collection of prayers for the Prophet, a subgenre of supplicatory prayers that beseech God to pray upon Muḥammad.[4] Judging from the manuscript record, this last work, the *Nafḥat al-ṭīb fī'l-salāt ʿalā'l-nabī al-ḥabīb* (Sweet Breath Concerning Prayer for the Beloved Prophet), was more popular than any of the Kunta's narrative treatises.[5] Muslims in West Africa and elsewhere in the world continue to use devotional texts like these in a variety of contexts and a variety of ways. Supplicatory prayers, including *aḥzāb* and prayers for the Prophet, are recited both individually and in collective rituals. Prayers are sometimes folded and bound into amulets or "erased" when a worshipper soaks them in water and then drinks or washes with that water. Anthropologists working in a variety of contexts have documented how contemporary Muslims discuss and debate the meaning of these texts.[6] In contrast, the research supporting this book is historical and is based on the theoretical position that drawing evidence from the present into the past anachronistically inscribes contemporary debates and struggles for authority onto historical contexts. Studies that make use of such methodologies also risk obscuring the historical contours and development of a tradition. In this case, the possibility of change and development over time becomes hidden beneath an imposed sense of continuity and timelessness.

How, then, can scholars determine how these works acquired meaning within their historical context? This chapter proposes a methodology of reading that situates the Kunta's devotional texts within two contemporaneous intertextual contexts in order to reveal the social logic that shaped and animated these works. The first two sections examine supplicatory prayer texts attributed to Sīdi al-Mukhtār against the background of the Kunta scholars' longer discursive works. Set against the context of Sīdi al-Mukhtār and Sīdi

Muḥammad's discussions of cosmology, metaphysics, and sacred history, these prayer texts appear as a series of encoded references intended for didactic expansion. After demonstrating this reading in the first section, the second situates these devotional aids against the larger theory of efficacious devotional practice that emerges from the Kunta texts. Within this ideology of practice, devotional texts emerge as the link connecting the bodies of believing Muslims to the structure of the cosmos, allowing them to alter the material conditions surrounding them. While the first two sections situate the supplicatory prayers within the larger Kunta corpus, the third turns to other supplicatory texts circulating in the region at the time. Read against a backdrop of proliferating textual devotional aids, the Kunta's contributions to this genre suggest an attempt to regulate the religious practice of Muslims in the region—to bring these practices under the authority of the Kunta scholars. In contrast to the first two sections of this chapter, which portray the Kunta scholars' supplicatory prayers as a manifestation of an ideology of practice, the third section understands this ideology of practice as a secondary effect, produced in order to explain and justify the Kunta's participation in local Muslim religious practices. Both of these readings are equally correct and equally necessary—practice shapes ideology even as ideology shapes practice. Moreover, whether read in one direction or the other, these texts reveal that both the Kunta specifically and Saharan Muslims generally understood Arabic devotional texts as a fundamental component of efficacious religious practice. For eighteenth-century Saharan Muslims, prayer was based in, and driven by, textuality.

By textuality, I refer not solely to the production of written works but rather to the production of "instances of discourse" that, "by being rendered detachable from their immediate context of emission, are made available for repetition or recreation in other contexts."[7] Texts are products of human discourse that can travel from their original sites of production and become available for recontextualization and reinterpretation elsewhere. Karin Barber formulated this definition with the explicit intention of including oral texts equally within a theory of textuality. Her work and the many publications of Ruth Finnegan have drawn attention not only to oral literature but also to the complex interrelationship between oral and written genres. "Written and oral forms can overlap and intermingle," Finnegan writes, with writing serving "as performance score, dictated transcription, crib sheet, memory cue, hearing aid, prompt book, calligraphic representation, ceremonial memento, notes for a speech, printed version of a memorized poem, medium for scholarly exegesis, tool for helping audiences understand a performance as it develops, script for recreating or remembering a past performance—and multiple possible combinations and sequences of all of these and more."[8] The development and spread of rhyming and rhythmic prose (*saj'*) offers one window into the relationship between written and oral forms in the early development of Arabic literature. *Saj'* developed out of the pre-Islamic oral tradition, was legitimized through its use in the Qur'ān—itself a written text embedded in oral performative contexts—and then developed during the literary efflorescence of the 'Abbāsid period, when it "invaded all domains of literature," from the secretarial to the philosophical.[9] And despite this reinscription of what had been an oral mnemonic device into a new literate written context, the foundational unit of the *saj'* developed during this period was a set of syllables, "the length of which remain[ed] within the limit beyond which the breath is exceeded," indicating that even these written compositions were "intended to be recited before an audience, aloud."[10]

While much of the oral performative context surrounding the Kunta's devotional texts has been lost, these works contain evidence that they are examples of precisely the oral/written hybridity described by Finnegan. The prayer texts discussed here all include elements long recognized as constitutive of oral genres, including rhyming and rhythmic prose (*saj'*) and the repetition of formulaic phrases, all of which aid in memorization.[11] Moreover, Sīdi Muḥammad provides explicit instructions for reciting devotional texts, and particularly the *aḥzāb*, as part of a ritual performance in the *Fawā'id nūrāniyya*, while the *Ṭarā'if wa'l-talā'id* describes the recitation of *awrād*, *aḥzāb*, *ad'iyya*, and *adhkār* as part of the pious devotions of his mother, Lalla 'Ā'isha (see below). Thus, although these texts were written down and circulated in manuscript form, they were also intended for oral memorization, transmission, and recitation. Writing and orality serve different purposes and allow for the transmission of texts to different, if often overlapping, populations. Thus written texts demonstrate superior geographic mobility—they can travel *farther* and faster from their points of origin, while oral texts extend a text *deeper* into a society's social fabric, reaching populations that would not have access to a written work. One of the central arguments of this chapter is that the production of these texts in a dual written/oral form allowed Sīdi al-Mukhtār and Sīdi Muḥammad to fix the form of these works and attach them to their names and authority, while also encoding and transmitting their ideas to a wider audience than they could reach by manuscript alone.

Arabic manuscripts and the paper needed to produce them were valuable commodities in the eighteenth and nineteenth centuries and were a central part of inter- and intraregional trade networks. Manuscript books were widely sought and collected, and individuals often amassed impressive personal libraries. However, both books and paper remained limited luxury goods, and the teaching of students revolved around reading groups that shared a text or worked from pieces copied onto wooden boards.[12] Knowledge of the Arabic alphabet and basic literacy during this period may have been unusually high relative to other regions.[13] However, we can presume the presence of both illiterate individuals and a spectrum of literacy ranging from knowledge of the alphabet to fluent reading of classical Arabic manuscripts. Producing short devotional texts intended for memorization would have allowed the Kunta scholars to spread complex metaphysical and cosmological ideas to Muslims who did not have access to, or could not read, written manuscripts. These references to literate or less literate audiences should in no way be confused with "literariness," however. Scholars of orality have stressed the importance of including oral texts in any definition of "literature," and Arab and African literatures have flourished in both low-literacy and highly literate contexts. The devotional works of Sīdi al-Mukhtār al-Kuntī are masterly examples of an Arabic African literature that was simultaneously written and oral.

Supplication

The manuscript libraries of West and North Africa include dozens of supplicatory prayers and devotional texts attributed to Sīdi al-Mukhtār. In addition to the *Nafḥat al-ṭīb*, these include various poems (*qaṣīdāt*); single texts called either *duʿāʾ* or *ḥizb*; and compilations labeled "*dhikr*s and supplications" (*adhkār wa duʿāt*) or "supplications and prayers" (*al-adʿiyya wa'l-ṣalawāt*), and so on. Of the texts titled *ḥizb*, the manuscript catalogues include the names of half a dozen separate works, including *Ḥizb al ʿisrāʾ* (The Prayer of the Night Journey), *Ḥizb al-nūr* (The Prayer of Light), and *Ḥizb al-ikhlāṣ* (The Prayer of Sincerity), among others. What follows is a close reading of, first, the eponymous *Ḥizb sīdī al-mukhtār al-kuntī*, which is representative in its forms and themes of the Kunta's other prayer texts, and, second, of the *Nafḥat al-ṭīb*, the most popular of the Kunta's devotional works. While these two texts do not encompass the entire range of this devotional literature, they do represent a good cross section of the major genres of prayer texts produced and circulated by this community.

The Ḥizb sīdī al-mukhtār al-kuntī

As a single prayer, the *Ḥizb sīdī al-mukhtār* is the shorter of the two works by far—short enough to quote and treat here in its entirety. The text begins with short, rhythmic lines and grows gradually more prosaic. The supplication also begins on a personal note, asking God to add divine or cosmological qualities to the narrator, switches to the plural, addressing the relationship between God and a group of believers, and, finally, asks God to grant those believers victory over, and protection from, their enemies. Within this framework, two repeated devices maintain a sense of continuity and motion. The chiastic structure borrowed from Qur'ān 3:27, "you make the night to enter into the day and you make the day to enter into the night," patterns many of the reversals throughout the text, while lists of dependent clauses following the same grammatical pattern (and ending with the same syllable or vowel) keep the reader moving toward the resolution of the sentence. However, while these general structures provide a loose sense of repeating or evolving patterns, the prayer is not tightly organized, and it contains brief thematic and structural excurses that reflect on the nature of God or sacred history.

> O God, strike me with the veil of light,
> And veil from me the canopy of fire,
>
> And make the greatest name a garment of mine,
> And the largest secret hair of mine,
>
> And the talismanic altar [*al-haykal al-muṭalsam*] a veil of mine,
> And the deeply dark clouds a wall of mine,
> And the perfected radiance light of mine,
>
> And the subduing *jabarūt*,
> And the overcoming *nāsūt*,
> And the gathering forms, a dwelling of mine.
> To you belong the amulets [*kaḥāl*] that compel,
> And the beauty that dazzles,
> And the might that manifests.
>
> Draw me close by bringing me near, near to you as the length of your bow [*qāb qawsik*][14]
> And distant to you as the lasting of your intimacy.
>
> O God, fill our needs with you
> And bring us away from ourselves until we see nothing but you.
>
> O God, hurl your truth against our falsehood[15] and overwhelm it—for thus it perishes, thrown from us into the seas of your knowledge—
> And snatch us from the sea of ignorance and darkness,

And inhabit our secrets with your proximity,
And our hearts with your love,
And our spirits with your concern,
And our intellects with your kindness,
And our chests with your [unintelligible] and your faith,
And our sight with submission to you and watering with the water of your certainty.

For what you have prohibited is not given,
Nor what you have given prohibited.
There is no increase for what you have decreed.
And one who has wealth from you does not benefit from chance.
You are the one who goes before and the one who goes behind.
You are *the first and the last,*
The apparent and the hidden [Qurʾān 57:3].

The greatness of your essence is surrounded by what is above the throne,
And your *jabarūt* by what is beneath the footstool.

You rise above the "how,"
And transcend the "how much."
You are destroyed with "where,"
And you cannot be encompassed by the eye.

O God, make me among those whom you chose before creating,
You singled them out with your mercy after upon them gazing,
And you made the striking of the droplets of your light the cause that led them by the reins to strengthening.
Without strengthening, neither Iblīs nor Balʿām[16] could do anything. They were free from the singling out of mercy and a preexistent lot and so their deeds turned upon them, corrupted.
The abundance of their sciences only increased them in defects.
And gift us, O God, with the manifestation of guidance,
And repel from us the causes of perishing,
And make us victorious over our enemies—
For victory is by your hand. You said—and your speech is truth—"*if God helps you to victory then none can overcome you*" [Qurʾān 3:160]. And we have enemies who see us while we cannot see them. So when we learn that there is no meeting with them we ask you to help us overcome them because you see them while they cannot see you. Then you cover

us with victory out of preference for us—for you said to the chief of tricksters: "*Over my servants you have no power*" [Qur'ān 15:42].

O God, just as you honored us with victory without our deserving it, so honor us with the realization of devotion. *Say*: "*Surely favor is in the hand of God, he gives it to whom he wills*" [Qur'ān 3:73]. May you be exalted. You make weakness mighty when it is from you and to you and you make might weakness when it is to other than you. *Say*: "*O God, king of the kingdom* [*al-mulk*], *you give the kingdom to whom you will and you seize the kingdom from whom you will and you magnify whom you will and you abase whom you will. In your hand is the good, and you are powerful over all things. You make the night to enter into the day and you make the day to enter into the night. You bring forth the living from the dead and you bring forth the dead from the living and you give provision to whomever you will without reckoning*" [Qur'ān 3:26–27].

O God, plunder, with the intensity of your position, those who would plunder us and overcome, with the might of your power, those who would overcome us and destroy the high pillar of those who would abase us, and rend with your force those who would seek to rout us and do not entrust us to our selves in either our smallness or our greatness.

O Most Merciful of the Merciful! O Possessor of Majesty and Nobility. Amen.[17]

The opening of the *Ḥizb* evokes a mélange of allusions to Sufi cosmological and metaphysical principles. The beginning lines of this section first posit and then invert Sufi tropes of veiling and light as the narrator asks for a brutal, direct encounter with the divine light standing between the supplicant and God, while requesting a continued veiling from light in its negative aspect—the fires of hell. From this metaphysical position between divine light and hellfire, the prayer moves on to request that God add divine or cosmological aspects to the body of the supplicant. Some of these, such as the greatest name and secret, and the realms of existence, *al-jabarūt* and *al-nāsūt* (or *al-mulk*), directly recall elements from other texts by Sīdi al-Mukhtār and Sīdi Muḥammad (see chapter 2), while others, such as "the talismanic altar" and the "deeply dark clouds," are more opaque. The next section again asks for the addition of divine qualities to the bodies of what is now a group of supplicants. However, while the previous list added to the body from the outside (clothing, hair, veil, and wall), this section moves into the interior bodies of the believers, asking God to instill his characteristics within them: "our secrets with your proximity / And our hearts with your love / And our spirits with your concern / And our intellects with your kindness / And our chests with your . . . faith." Within these two sections, the *Ḥizb* thus presents exterior and interior aspects of the idealized human body: composed without of clothes, hair, veil, shelter, and illumination, and within of sight, chest, intellect, spirit, heart, and secret. By asking God to inhabit these aspects of the human body with his own characteristics, the narrator engages a familiar Sufi trope that reveals the microcosm of the believing human body as the site of divine manifestation.

In a later section, the *Ḥizb* connects these Sufi metaphysical themes to sacred history. Returning briefly to a single narrator, the text asks God to include the speaker among those chosen for a predetermined but unspecified fate: "O God, make me among those whom you chose before creating / You singled them out with your mercy after upon them gazing." Other texts by Sīdi al-Mukhtār and Sīdi Muḥammad suggest that this fate could refer either to the guarantee of entry into paradise or to reaching the goal of the annihilation of the self in knowledge of the divine (*fanāʾ*). In works composed by both the Kunta scholars and earlier Sufi authors, this direct experience of God represents a return to the day, before creation, when God called forth the future spirits of humankind and asked them to witness him directly.[18] The *Ḥizb* alludes to this cycle of primordial predestination and ultimate return with the line "you made the striking of the droplets of your light the cause that led them by the reins to strengthening." If Sīdi al-Mukhtār only evokes this sacred history in the *Ḥizb*, however, he references it explicitly in the *Nafḥat al-ṭīb*: "You placed him [Muḥammad] in the world of the progeny before the sons of Adam when you manifested yourself to them. Then you said: *Am I not your lord?* (7:172) and he was the first to respond with the utterance—*but yes!*"[19] In this passage, Sīdi al-Mukhtār directly quotes the Qurʾānic verse that forms the basis for this sacred history of predestination and adds the interpretation that on that primordial day, Muḥammad stood before Adam's gathered progeny and was the first among them to testify to God's lordship.

Immediately following the lines in the *Ḥizb* that request this predetermined blessing from God, Sīdi al-Mukhār cites the names of two figures who reappear in Kunta sacred histories: Iblīs and Balʿām. Iblīs, or Satan, the angel who disobeyed God's command to bow down before Adam and was cast out of heaven as a result, appears as a complex figure in Sufi poetics. Classical Sufi authors, beginning with al-Hallāj, cast him in the tragic role of the ultimate monotheist and lover of God, who refused his beloved's command to worship another and found himself forever bereaved as a result.[20] However, despite the familiarity of this portrayal to scholars of Sufism, the Kunta do not make use of this typology of Iblīs, who appears only as a negative character in their writings. In the *Ṭarāʾif waʾl-talāʾid*, Sīdi Muḥammad presents the story of Iblīs as an angel who spent thousands of years in continuous worship of God but grew arrogant as a result. This arrogance led to his refusal of God's order to bow before Adam, a single act of disobedience that erased countless years of devotion and serves as a cautionary tale for the dangers of complacence and the consequences of even one lapse.[21] Elsewhere in the same text, Sīdi Muḥammad claims that his father spent four years battling Iblīs/Satan, establishing his resistance to corruption and his character as a friend of God through this period of resistance and defiance.[22] Iblīs also appears in an important role in a short, untitled text attributed to Sīdi al-Mukhtār and labeled *Khalwa* in manuscript catalogues, which discusses the visions that might appear to followers of the Sufi path.[23] In this context, Iblīs/Satan appears as a purveyor of false visions who manifests himself to a paradigmatic friend of God, ʿAbd al-Qādir al-Jīlānī,[24] and claims to be God himself. In this account, al-Jīlānī proves his status as a friend of God and a Sufi shaykh by correctly identifying and rejecting Satan.[25]

The same text that presents Satan as an impersonator who brings false visions of God also includes one of the longest descriptions of Balʿām by the Kunta scholars, who occasionally mention his name in connection with corrupt practitioners of the sciences of the unseen. In *Khalwa*, the Kunta provide a rare discursive elaboration of this character, writing, "It is narrated that Jesus, peace be upon him, said: 'O God! Why did you bereave Balʿām of [your] friendship . . . ?' So Allāh said to him that he had not [been humble],[26] and for that reason he was recompensed with bereavement. And had he said one day: 'O God! All praise is to you for what you have conferred upon me, which I have not deserved, neither for my essence nor as an imperative of my attributes,' then I would not have expelled him from my presence, nor distanced him. However, he undervalued my favor, so my punishment descended on him."[27] This passage presents a dialogue between God and Jesus, in which the latter asks the reason for Balʿām's punishment. This text suggests that Balʿām, like Iblīs, was punished for his arrogance. However, at no point does *Khalwa* mention exactly what crime Balʿām's arrogance led him to commit and suggests only that a show of proper humility might have averted his fate. Both al-Thaʿlabī and al-Ṭabarī, two early chroniclers of Muslim histories, briefly mention a figure named Balʿām ibn Bāʿurā, a Canaanite who was persuaded by the giants to use the greatest name of God to curse the Israelites. But when he launched his curse, he ended up cursing the giants instead, and God caused his tongue to fall from his mouth.[28] While we cannot be sure that this story corresponds to accounts circulating among the Kunta community, the reference to Balʿām as a corrupt user of the greatest name of God certainly evokes concerns that the Kunta raise about the misappropriation of the sciences of the unseen. In this context, the references in the *Ḥizb* suggest that both Iblīs and Balʿām possessed the sciences, but that their attempts to employ that knowledge only turned against them. Moreover, the *Ḥizb* adds an additional layer of interpretation, linking this failure not to the crime of arrogance in these figures' lifetimes but rather to a withdrawal of God's mercy in the pre-eternity before creation.

Each reference in the *Ḥizb sīdī al-mukhtār* contains the potential for this type of discursive elaboration, evoking an array of intertexts both within and outside the Kunta corpus. The line "Make the greatest name a garment of mine" could easily lead to a long conversation about the greatest name of God, which, in written form, might look similar to the *Fawāʾid nūrāniyya*, discussed in the previous chapter. Similarly, even an apparently simple request, such as "inhabit . . . our hearts with your love," could provide the occasion for a long discourse about the nature and components of the human heart, not to mention the nature and role of God's love for his believers. And if the *Ḥizb* contains this potential for discursive elaboration in every line, the *Nafḥat al-ṭīb* encodes an even denser array of topics, from sacred history and geography to personal ethics, anthropology, cosmology, and metaphysics.

The Nafḥat al-ṭīb

Although both the *Ḥizb sīdī al-mukhtār* and the *Nafḥat al-ṭīb* belong to the overall category of supererogatory devotional prayers, the two works display some distinct genre conventions. Unlike the category of single short prayers known alternately as *ḥizb*, *dhikr*, *wird*, or *duʿāʾ*, the *Nafḥat al-ṭīb* partakes in a genre of literature known as *taṣliyya*, or "prayers for the Prophet." These supplications ask God to pray upon Muḥammad and involve the repetition of some version of the *taṣliyya*, the phrase "prayer and peace be upon the prophet, Muḥammad, and his family and his companions" (*ṣalā wa salām ʿalā al-nabī Muḥammad wa ālihi wa ṣaḥbihi*). This form of benediction stems from Qurʾān 33:43, which describes God as "He who prays upon you, and His angels," and uses the word for formal liturgical prayer (*ṣalā*).[29] The *Nafḥat al-ṭīb* and other collections of prayers for the Prophet add this phrase to the invocation "O God!" (*Allāhuma*), effectively asking God to pray upon the Prophet. In his commentary on the *Nafḥat al-ṭīb*, Sīdi Muḥammad affirms that God does indeed pray. He relates a report that the tribes of Israel asked Moses, "does our Lord pray?," prompting God to respond to Moses, "Say to them, 'Indeed I pray and my prayer is a mercy and my mercy encompasses everything.'"[30] Sīdi Muḥammad states that God's prayer is a mercy, while the prayers of the angels are a supplication (*du'ā'*), asking God to have mercy on his believers. God's prayer is a way of singling out and showing favor to a believer, "a divulgence of his remembrance [*dhikr*] of the beauty in his servants," and a method of praising them. When specifically addressing the *taṣliyya*, Sīdi Muḥammad emphasizes that all members of the community of believers (*umma*) share in God's prayer upon his Prophet.[31] Thus, while some scholars translate *ṣalā* and *yuṣallī* in this context as "blessing" and "to bless," I have decided to use the more literal translation, while taking into account the rich layers of meaning that the Kunta scholars read into this word. This choice reflects an overall methodology of focusing on and clarifying the specific emic terminology used in the Kunta texts (see chapter 3) and highlights the many and overlapping meanings of the different terms used for devotional practice within this context.

As a collection of prayers, rather than a single prayer, the *Nafḥat al-ṭīb* possesses more formal structure than the *Ḥizb*. The text is divided into four "quarters," and many (though not all) of the manuscript witnesses are preceded by a short preface or pre-text that describes a dream encounter between Sīdi al-Mukhtār and Muḥammad, in which the latter demands that the Kunta scholar produce a work of dedicated prayers for the Prophet and then approves the final version of that work. Generally, the first quarter treats the topic of the supplicant's prayer itself, enjoining God repeatedly to call down the greatest possible prayer upon the Prophet; the second quarter refers most consistently to Muḥammad's position in human history and the physical and human geography of the earth; and the final two quarters address the Prophet in terms of his cosmological and metaphysical significance.[32] However, within this general structure, no organized narrative takes shape. Each supplication contains its own host of references and allusions, which may borrow from any of these themes and others. Indeed, the *Nafḥat* contains so many themes and references that one witness to Sīdi Muḥammad's commentary on the text ends after addressing a little more than half of the text and still amounts to almost four hundred manuscript pages.[33] Since even one quarter of the *Nafḥat al-ṭīb* contains too many references to address fully in one chapter, the following analysis addresses a selection of excerpts that illustrate the text's treatment of one theme—Muḥammad's role in human history. For this purpose, selections are grouped thematically and thus are out of order; however, any sense of narrativization gained from this arrangement is illusory. The progressive rhyming supplications in the *Nafḥat al-ṭīb* never add up to a narrative discourse; rather, they pile allusion on top of allusion, making possible a potentially infinite number of discursive expansions.

The second quarter of the *Nafḥat al-ṭīb* opens with a series of supplications, referring to Muḥammad not by name but by genealogy.

O God, pray upon and bring peace to the son of Ibrāhīm who most resembles Ibrāhīm, honored with adornments and intimacies.
O God, pray upon and bring peace to the one sent from the line of Ismāʾīl, ennobled by revelation and sending down.
O God, pray upon and bring peace to the one prophesied from an established seed, whose honoring and remembering and extolling is established in all eras.
O God, pray upon and bring peace to the one chosen from Ḍīʾḍīʾ ʿAdnān, the one who was brought the *seven oft-repeated* [*verses*] and the criterion [Qurʾān 15:87].
O God, pray upon and bring peace to the elected from a destined lineage [ʿ*unṣur*], the one specified by the *sūra*: "*Say, He is God, the One*" [Qurʾān 112:1].
O God, pray upon and bring peace to the best of the Nizār, the one who leads to calling upon the truth of the emigrant and the helpers. (9)

The references in these supplications trace Muḥammad's genealogy in a line of descent from Ibrāhīm, through his son Ismāʿīl, and then into the mythologized origins of the Arabs, represented here by ʿAdnān, the legendary ancestor of the northern Arab tribes, and his grandson Nizār.[34] More than a simple pedigree, the *Nafḥat al-ṭīb* grants the descent of this line through history a teleological force, guided by fate through the "established seed" of Ibrahīm and Ismāʾīl and the "destined lineage" of the Arabs toward the prophesied birth of Muḥammad.[35]

Even as the *Nafḥat al-ṭīb* collapses humanity before Muḥammad into a single descending lineage, it slowly expands the pool included in Muḥammad's community of believers (*umma*), mentioning, at various points, all the peoples reached by his mission. The passage above concludes with a reference to the emigrants (*al-muhājirīn*) who accompanied Muḥammad on his flight from Mecca, and the helpers (*al-anṣār*) who welcomed him to Medina. Elsewhere, the text refers to Muḥammad as "the master of Qaḥṭān and ʿAdnān, by whose call all the types of people and jinn were led" (12). This supplication begins by portraying Muḥammad's prophetic mission as including all Arabs—metonymically represented here by Qaḥṭān and ʿAdnān, the legendary ancestors of both the northern and southern Arab tribes—and ultimately of not only all people but all jinn as well.[36] At other points, supplications portray the Slavs and the Turks as responding to his call (*daʿwa*) (13), and people with red and black skin as joining his community of believers (*umma*) (13).[37] Finally, these references spill out from the human into the nonhuman realm. Above, we saw Muḥammad's mission as reaching both all humans and all jinn, and other lines portray angels, all animals, and inanimate objects as recognizing his prophethood. One set of supplications reads, "O God, pray upon our master Muḥammad, upon him be peace, whom all of the animals addressed with [their] types of speech. . . . O God, pray upon our master Muḥammad, upon him be peace, whom all inanimate objects saluted with greetings. O God, pray upon our master Muḥammad, upon him be peace, for whom the noble angels spread their wings" (14). In contrast to the verses that portray Muḥammad as the end goal of the human history that preceded him, these passages depict the human and nonhuman populations of the world joining his community in ever-expanding and more encompassing categories: emigrants and helpers, Arabs and non-Arabs, and, finally, the nonhuman categories of jinn, angels, animals, and inanimate objects.

Just as some supplications in the *Nafḥat al-ṭīb* look backward to human history before Muḥammad, or to the community of believers after his death, other passages look forward into the future and depict the eschaton. However, while Muḥammad is depicted as the teleological goal of history and as the undisputed center of living Muslims communities, he plays a critical, but not solitary, role at the end of time. In passages referring to the Day of Judgment, Muḥammad appears primarily as the intercessor between God and the believers: "O God, pray for and bring peace to . . . the intercessor on the Day of Judgment, when anxiety will intensify and fear and faintheartedness increase, and the throats constrict and people are choked by sweat" (10–11). This passage refers to the gathered throngs of humanity on the Day of Judgment, conjures up affectively their fear of punishment and retribution, and presents Muḥammad as interceding on their behalf before God. But while Muḥammad appears as the central figure during the encounter between humans and their lord, the end of the world itself evokes the presence of another persona, the *mahdī*: "O God, pray upon and bring peace to our master Muḥammad the effacer, through whom God effaces disbelief and the worship of idols. The effacing of disbelief in his community will continue until his son, the *mahdī*, and ʿIsā emerge, may peace be upon them, and his family, and his companions" (26). This prayer identifies the *mahdī* as Muḥammad's "son," or descendent, and his appearance along with ʿIsā signals an end to Muḥammad's mission and the call to monotheism. In another important passage, the *Nafḥat al-ṭīb* lists the people from Muḥammad's family who served as "seals," bringing closure to key historical periods. "O God, pray upon him whose house you made the sealing house—thus with him you sealed the message, and with his uncle, ʿAbbās, the *hijra*; and with his circumcision and his education the vice-regency; and with his two sons—the lords of the youth of the people of the garden, al-Ḥassan and al-Husayn, the pure, the noble—[you sealed] the grandsons; and with his son, the *mahdī*, you sealed the nation of Islam and the authority (*wilāya*) of men—and upon his family and his companions, and bring peace [to them]" (31). Here, the appearance of the *mahdī*, again identified as a descendent of Muḥammad, signals the end of the growth of the Muslim community, just as Muḥammad signaled the end of the period of prophecy. Bookmarked between these two figures appear Muḥammad's only surviving grandsons, al-Ḥassan and al-Husayn, and ʿAbbās, who joined Muḥammad's followers as they returned from Medina to Mecca, signaling an end to the exile of the early community. Unlike Muḥammad, the *mahdī*, and even ʿAbbās, it is not clear from the passage what historical era al-Ḥassan and al-Husayn served to seal. However, their inclusion here alongside Muḥammad's uncle calls attention to the importance of Muḥammad's relatives—a key point for the Kunta, who also claimed descent from the Prophet's tribe of Quraysh.

These selections do not exhaust the references in the *Nafḥat al-ṭīb* to Muḥammad's life and personal history—other passages treat his night journey, the purification of his heart as a child, and his death. Nor does the text limit its understanding of Muḥammad's roles to the human or the historical, and many supplications deal with his cosmological and cosmogonical significance as well as his status as an exemplar of ethical human behavior. Looking beyond the particular personage of Muḥammad, many supplications in the *Nafḥat al-ṭīb* evoke the characteristics or names of God, and at least one passage enumerates the many components of the world:

> O God, pray upon him the number of revolutions of the spheres. Pray upon him the number of praises of the kings. Pray upon him the number of lights and of darknesses. Pray upon him the reach of perception and pray upon him the number of souls and of progeny. Pray upon him the number of mountaintops and pray upon him the number of the dead and the sleeping. Pray upon him the number of drops in the swelling seas. Pray upon him the number of exquisite flowers and pray upon him the number of lofty waterfalls. Pray upon him the number of sand grains and stones and pray upon him the numbers that can be neither reckoned nor fathomed. Pray upon him the number of raindrops from the clouds. Pray upon him the number of the seen and the unseen. (4–5)

Taken together, the supplications of this relatively short work, written in easily memorized rhyming prose, allude to all the major elements of the Kunta's understanding of the world: its creation and inhabitants, human history and communities, the nature of God and the Prophet, the relationship between God and his believers, and the end of the world. The text discusses none of the references fully, but through its list of allusions it provides a platform for infinite intellectual elaboration, a condensed encoding of an entire worldview.

With their webs of references and allusions to sacred history, Sufi cosmology, metaphysics, and ethics, texts like the *Ḥizb sīdī al-mukhtār* and the *Nafḥat al-ṭīb* could easily have served as mnemonic, didactic texts, memorized by students and then expanded upon in lessons by teachers. However, such an analysis says little about how these texts functioned as *prayers*, that is, about their use in, or relation to, devotional practice. And although we might not know how these prayers were used by Saharan Muslims of the period, one text does suggest how the Kunta scholars understood the application of these texts and how they prescribed their use in Sufi devotional practice.

A Theory of Practice

In the *Fawāʾid nūrāniyya*, as we saw in chapter 3, Sīdi Muḥammad discusses at length the use of the letters of the Arabic alphabet and the greatest name of God to exert control over the world and its inhabitants. In this text, he links the names of God, and the letters that make up those names, to the structure of the cosmos, explaining that each name and letter performs a specific function within the created world, and that whoever connects to and activates that name or letter controls that function—sending down rain, quieting the seas, or healing the sick, for example. Moreover, the greatest name, *AHM SQK ḤLʿ YṢ*, includes the properties of all the other names of God. By extension, anyone who can establish a connection to that greatest name gains control over the entire structure of the cosmos. Finally, the text argues that use of the greatest name constitutes a form of supplicatory prayer, and thus a type of devotion to God (*ʿibāda*). On its own, this discussion of the theory underlying the sciences of the names and letters provides a useful window into the Kunta's understanding of the relationships among cosmology, metaphysics, and devotional worship. But the *Fawāʾid nūrāniyya* moves beyond this theoretical discussion to provide practical instructions on how to use the greatest name in combination with supplicatory prayers to achieve any desired goal. By providing both supplicatory prayers that invoke the greatest name of God and instructions on how to deploy those prayers in ritual, the *Fawāʾid nūrāniyya* depicts the texts of these prayers as part of a larger performance, that is, as a devotional practice.

In one example, Sīdi Muḥammad provides a four-by-four table associated with the greatest name of God and the following instructions:

Put it [the table] on a lead tablet and fumigate it with aloewood and purify your heart with sincerity and your body with the water purification. Then bring it to your special place of retreat [*khalwa*]. First, you become part of the category of the elite, and your eyes darken. Next, you are present of mind. Then you are stricken by the greatness of the remembered, believing that this name is from His hidden absence, and is part of God's grace for the lords of emanation. Then, if He flashes before you a flash of light and pervades your secret with the coolness of happiness and joy, then say with the tongue of brokenness, humility, and poverty:

God witnessed that there is no God but He until *the All-Wise*
[i.e., Qur'ān 59:22–24].
At your service, O God! May you be happy!
All goodness flows from you to you by your hand, and I desire
what comes from you.
O, He who is named by the names!
Though I am in blindness, I ask you by your name of the names
and your most protected secret.

O AHM SQK ḤL' YṢ!
I call to you with the *alif* of the composing of the cosmos,
And with the *hā'* of divinity in the presence of witnessing and
the essences,
And with the *mīm* of sovereignty and the elongating of might
and power,
And with the *sīn* of the encompassing and protecting secret,
And with the *qāf* of subsistence with the sustaining of the cosmos,
And with the *kāf* of the complete sufficing of wants,
And with the *ḥā'* of wisdom with justice and *iḥsān*,
And with the *lām* of the friendship of the people of certainty
and faith,
And with the *'ayn* of concern for the lords of sincerity and
knowing [*'irfān*],
And with the *yā'* of auspiciousness and ease and easing of the
people of need through *iḥsān*,
And with the *ṣād* of everlastingness through the preserving of
the universes from the injuring of order and from greed,
And with the secret of He-ness, concealed by the cloak of greatness
and mightiness.

> O Strongest of pillars!
> O Constant in *iḥsān*!
> O Needless of agents!
> O He who is in every place yet contained by no place!
> O Possessor of might and *al-jabarūt*!
> O He whose hand holds *al-mulk* and *al-malakūt*!
>
> Compel objects to me and strengthen me from the registers of the spirits until neither human nor jinn nor angel from the agents nor benefit nor power nor seeker nor devil nor time nor place—nor any thing that includes the property of existing is beyond the encompassing of my freedom of action, or emerges from the grip of my imposing.[38]

This supplication, with its accompanying instructions, constitutes the primary invocation provided by the *Fawāʾid nūrāniyya*. Many of the elements familiar from the *Ḥizb* and the *Nafḥat al-ṭīb* recur in this prayer, including the references to the realms of *al-mulk*, *al-malakūt*, and *al-jabarūt*. However, the brief instructions at the beginning of the passage situate these references within a larger ritual setting that includes a purified body; a physical object—a lead tablet inscribed with a table; a physical location—a place of withdrawal or spiritual retreat (*khalwa*); and a progression of mental states that lead up to the pronouncement of the prayer itself. These mental states serve as conditions for the performance of the described ritual, ensuring that only those gifted with the exact series of spiritual signs can effectively follow the instructions and achieve the stated goal of the prayer, which is nothing less than complete control over the cosmos.

This goal, while striking in its scope, correlates with the Kunta's depiction of the world as created from, and controlled by, the names of God and their constituent letters. The prayer above invokes the greatest name of God both in full and letter by letter, linking each letter in the name to specific divine characteristics. Moreover, these divine characteristics correspond to the more commonly referenced names of God that begin with the same letter. Thus the letter *kāf*, linked to the characteristic of sufficing, evokes the name *al-Kāfī*, "the Sufficient," while the letter *ḥāʾ*, linked to the characteristic of wisdom, evokes the name *al-Ḥakīm*, "the Wise," and so forth. In this fashion, the prayer calls on God through both his greatest name and all the names invoked by each letter composing it. Since the names of God control the physical and spiritual worlds, invoking them in the proper ritual setting and proper spiritual state allows a believer to exert complete control over those worlds and their inhabitants.

Although this prayer in the *Fawāʾid nūrāniyya* provides instructions for total control over the cosmos, the text goes on to provide alternative prayers with instructions for responding to more specific needs. In one example, the text provides the following variation:

> O God, I ask you with the *alif* of your cleverness—O *Allāh*!
> And with the *hāʾ* of your guidance—O *Hādī*![39]
> And with the *mīm* of your sovereignty—O *Mālik*!
> And with the *sīn* of your peace—O *Salām*!
> And with the *qāf* of your compelling—O *Qahhār*!
> And with the *kāf* of your sufficiency—O *Kāfī*!
> And with the *ḥāʾ* of your forbearance—O *Ḥalīm*!
> And with the *lām* of your subtlety—O *Laṭīf*!
> And with the *ʿayn* of your knowledge—O *ʿAlīm*!
> And with the *yāʾ* of your auspiciousness—O *Yamīn*!
> And with the *ṣād* of your everlastingness—O *Ṣamad*!
>
> O *Allāh*! O *Aḥad*! O *Kāfī*!
> You are the god of those in the heavens and on the earth.
> You are their Guide and you are their Judge.
> O *Muʾmin*! O *Muhaymin*!
> Answer O *Hulmayāʾīl*!
>
> O God! O *Salām*!
> Preserve me from the calamities of this world and the next!
> O *Fahār*!
> Subdue for me my enemies and make me a subduer and not one subdued!
> And make sufficient for me the worst of what you have spread out!
> O *Karīm*! O *Kafīl*!
> Answer O *Musqayāʾīl*!
>
> O God! O *Ḥalīm*! O *ʿAlīm*!
> O Most Kind, be kind to me and teach me the obscurities.
> Restrain me and put compassion for me into the hearts of your servants and give me tenderness toward them.
> Answer O *Qatqayāʾīl*!
>
> O God! O Creator [*Mukawwan*] of created beings! O Easer of hardships!
> O Former of forms! O Creator [*Khāliq*] of the earth and Raiser of the heavens!

O Descender of rain! O Grower of plants!
Make my enemies die.
O Intensely Valorous!
Answer O *Ṭaghayāʾīl*!

By the truth of these names,
O *Allāh*! O *Hādī*! O *Muʾmin*! O *Salām*!
O *Qāhir*! O *Kāfī*! O *Ḥalīm*! O *Laṭīf*!
O *ʿAlīm*! O *Yamīn al-Yaman*! O *Ṣamad*!

All praise belongs to God, Lord of the worlds.[40]

This supplicatory prayer does not directly refer to God as AHM SQK ḤLʿ YṢ but instead lists each of the eleven letters composing that name in turn, connecting them both to one of God's attributes and to one of his more commonly known names. The conclusion of the prayer then invokes each of those eleven names in order, spelling out the greatest name through its component letter-names. Between the first and last sections of this prayer, the text invokes God through his roles in creating and sustaining the earth and through four unexplained epitaphs: *Hulmayāʾīl*, *Musqayāʾīl*, *Qatqayāʾīl*, and *Ṭaghayāʾīl*. Modeled on a naming pattern often used for angel names in Arabic (*Mīkāʾīl*, *ʿAzāʾīl*), these four names do not appear elsewhere in the *Fawāʾid nūrāniyya*, but they do bear striking similarities to the names for the spirits of the planets listed in pseudo-Būnian works.[41]

In contrast to the first prayer, which requested control over every existing thing, this supplication makes more specific requests of God. These more limited requests—for divine protection and secret knowledge for the supplicant, goodwill between him and others, and death to the supplicant's enemies—punctuate the invocations of God by his roles and through the four unexplained names. However, while these embedded requests point to possible reasons for deploying this prayer in practice, the instructions that follow this passage suggest other goals as well:

> And whoever wants to request something from God Most High, let him pray [*yuṣallī*] two *rakʿas* [repeating] the statement, *He is Allāh, One* (112:1) three times after the *fātiḥa*, while remembering the name اا during each prostration. Then, when he finishes the two *rakʿas*, let him pray [*yadʿū*] with the supplicatory prayer. Then let him ask God his request and the answer will come to him quickly from God Most High.

And whoever wants to walk upon the sea, let him do the same and he will obtain his desire with the blessing of the noble name. . . .

And whoever wants to fold up a distant space, let him pray two *rakʿas* and then recite the name | | | | and pray the supplicatory prayer and God Most High will fold up space for him and he will reach [his destination] unharmed.

And whoever wants to reconcile people of the greatest hatred and disorder and dispute, let him pray two *rakʿas* and recite the name | | | and pray the supplicatory prayer. Then let him say, "I have bound your tongues and your hands from dispute and evil deeds, and I have reversed your hearts and changed your natures by this name and the call of God, the lord of the worlds."

And whoever writes | | | | along with the supplicatory prayer and erases it [with water] and washes with it, iron will not work on his body. And in this fashion, sorcery [*siḥr*] will not work on him who drinks it, nor the evil eye, and he will be protected from all hatred.[42]

This list of possible applications (which continues for another page), explains how to use this supplicatory prayer in combination with formal prayer (*ṣalāt*) to make a generic request of God and then to obtain more specific results, including walking on water, traveling instantaneously between two distant places, reconciling two conflicting groups, and protecting a body from iron weapons, sorcery, the evil eye, and other manifestations of hatred. The text provides these instructions in their entirety, except that the specific names of God needed to complete each ritual have been replaced with sets of two, three, or four vertical lines. By leaving this information in code, Sīdi Muḥammad reserves the final deployment of these instructions to himself and his students, and prevents the transmission of this knowledge by manuscript alone. Indeed, elsewhere in the same text, Sīdi Muḥammad displays an awareness of the fact that physical manuscripts, once created, become available for unsupervised use and interpretation. He thus offers up the negative example of a sect of people who "imitate what the people of secrets recorded in their written records" in order to gain secrets and hidden powers. Their obsession with obtaining secrets actually weakens the results of their practice and occludes their perceptive faculties.[43] The coded information embedded in these supplicatory prayers thus serves as a method of limiting the final operation to individuals within the Kunta's pedagogical network.[44]

While lacking the names needed to implement these rituals, the instructions that accompany these prayers depict the supplicatory invocations in connection with the specific sequences of bodily postures indicated by formal prayer and with other physical objects (lead tablets, incense, etc.) and a physical space. Moreover, the *Fawāʾid nūrāniyya* establishes an explicit link between the content of these prayers and their function. Rather than mnemonic or didactic tools written in rhyming shorthand, these prayers invoke the metaphysical structure of the cosmos in order to alter the material conditions surrounding the supplicant. According to these passages, when a believing human body correctly performs her relationship to the world around her—and particularly her relationship to the creator and controller of that world—she gains the ability to physically alter it: folding up space, walking on water, repelling iron, and dispelling hatred. The instructions for these prayers demonstrate that when the text states that any believer who "connects to" the greatest name of God assumes control over the functions exercised by all the names,[45] it means this in a physical, corporeal sense. When a believer correctly enacts, physically and verbally, the greatest name of God, she embodies that name and thus assumes control over its function within the cosmos. By providing supplicatory prayers in combination with instructions and a discursive theory of practice, the *Fawāʾid nūrāniyya* provides a connection between three elements: metaphysics, supplicatory prayers, and the bodies of believing Muslims. By establishing this connection, the text depicts these prayers as performances, as part of a reenactment of the relationship among God, the cosmos, and a believer. Moreover, by withholding a last key piece from many of the instructions, these texts also reinscribe a particular social performance—a reenactment of the relationship between secret knowledge, a teacher, and his students.

The contextualization provided by this theory of devotional practice allows for the identification of corresponding structures in Sīdi al-Mukhtār's other devotional prayers. For example, in addition to cosmological and metaphysical principles, both the *Ḥizb sīdī al-mukhtār* and the *Nafḥat al-ṭīb* include references to practices discussed at length in the Kunta's more prosaic works. The *Ḥizb* refers to both the production of amulets and to the greatest name of God.[46] The *Nafḥat al-ṭīb* even includes a long section calling on God through an apophatically unnamed name:

> O God!
> I call on you by the name in which you lodged the symbols of the realities,
> And with which you opened up the treasuries of the refinements,
> And with which you manifested the manifest in the world of your *mulk*,
> And with which you concealed the concealed in the world of your *malakūt*,
> And made flow the seas of your secret upon *al-mulk* and *al-malakūt*,
> And lit with the flood of its lights the gardens of *al-jabarūt*. (22)

In contrast to the rest of the *Nafḥat al-ṭīb*, this section does not mention or invoke the Prophet but calls on God directly through his unnamed greatest name in a fashion that evokes the structure and content of both the *Ḥizb sīdī al-mukhtār* and the supplicatory prayers of the *Fawāʾid nūrāniyya*. Moreover, many sections of the *Nafḥat al-ṭīb* ascribe to Muḥammad exactly the sorts of extraordinary feats that the *Fawāʾid nūrāniyya* claims to provide: walking on water, speaking to animals and inanimate objects, and folding up space. In this sense, Muḥammad serves as the paradigmatic believing body, an exemplar and a model for the practice of other Muslims. These parallels among the prayers in the *Fawāʾid nūrāniyya*, the *Ḥizb sīdī al-mukhtār*, and the *Nafḥat al-ṭīb* suggest that the Kunta scholars understood all of these supplicatory texts as fulfilling a similar role in relation to Muslim devotional practice—in other words, all three texts are artifacts of a Kunta theory of prayer.

Technologies of Devotion

Situating devotional texts such as the *Ḥizb sīdī al-mukhtār* and the *Nafḥat al-ṭīb* within the Kunta corpus of texts illuminates the role that these short devotional works play within a larger Kunta theory of prayer and devotional practice. However, by granting discursive texts the authority to explain the role of devotional works, this analysis has necessarily privileged the intellectual context of these texts over their social context, and thus also the scholars who composed these works over the practitioners who might have performed them. Indeed, the reading given in the previous section was, necessarily, a reading *down*—it gave priority to longer philosophical and metaphysical discourses and then saw those concepts re-encoded in the format of supplicatory prayers. To put this in social terms, the previous discussion understood supplicatory prayers as a vehicle used by scholars to convey and enact their ideologies. I am not suggesting that this reading was incorrect, but rather that it tells only half of the story.

This section investigates the other half of this story by prioritizing the social context of devotional practice in the Sahara and Sahel at the turn of the nineteenth century. This reading begins by examining other popular works concerned with devotional Sufi practice circulating in the region at the time—and then works *upward*, arguing that the Kunta produced their own works in response to this devotional context. Reading upward privileges the social context of Muslim religious devotion and sees the Kunta's production of supplicatory prayers as a response to, and attempt to shape, that context. Finally, this section argues that, conceptually, the Kunta's longer narrative treatises served to justify this engagement with local devotional practice with reference to established Sufi intellectual traditions, and thus with attention to larger regional and global networks of Muslim scholars.

The Dalāʾil al-khayrāt *of al-Jazūlī*

The internal Kunta accounts provide a few hints concerning the devotional life of the members of their community, including one passage in Sīdi Muḥammad's hagiography of his parents that describes his mother's engagement with Muslim devotional rituals.

> And the *shaykha* . . . was ascetic, devoted, pious, religious, generous, and beloved. You would hardly ever see one of her breaths empty from remembrance of, or reflection on, or recitation of, the book of God, the Mighty and Exalted, or from reciting her *awrād* from the *aḥzāb* and the *adʿiyya* or the *adhkār* handed down from the righteous ancestors, or from supererogatory prayers, or from reading the *Dalāʾil al-khayrāt wa'l-shawāriq al-anwār*—with the appearance of a breaking of the norm that could hardly have happened to anyone other than her.[47]

This passage roots the pious and praiseworthy qualities of Sīdi Muḥammad's mother, Lalla ʿĀʾisha, in a near-continuous outpouring of devotional words, drawn from recitation of the Qurʾān, *dhikrs*, and various supplicatory prayers. The continuity of these devotions, which flow out along with her breath itself, constitutes a breaking of the norm and thus a sign of friendship with God. However, while the *Ṭarāʾif wa'l-talāʾid* abounds with claims of extraordinary piety, this passage uniquely depicts a hagiographic persona in a particular devotional context. Sīdi Muḥammad informs his readers not only that Lalla ʿĀʾisha was extraordinarily pious but, more important, that she manifested that piety through specific acts of reading and recitation. For the most part, the non-Qurʾānic texts referred to in this passage are nameless—*dhikr*s and supplicatory prayers attributed to anonymous Muslim forebears—but Sīdi Muḥammad does mention one text specifically by name: the *Dalāʾil al-khayrāt wa shawāriq al-anwār fī dhikr al-ṣalāt ʿalā'l-nabī al-mukhtār* (*Guide to Goodness and Rays of Lights in Remembering Prayer for the Chosen Prophet*).[48]

This compendium of prayers for the Prophet, attributed to the fifteenth-century Moroccan Sufi Abū ʿAbd Allāh Muḥammad al-Jazūlī (d. 1465),[49] achieved widespread influence across the Muslim world, from West Africa, to India, to Indonesia.[50] Because the *Dalāʾil al-khayrāt* played a pivotal role in establishing the genre characteristics for prayers for the Prophet across the

Muslim world, it unsurprisingly shares many stylistic features with Sīdi al-Mukhtār's *Nafḥat al-ṭīb*. Most manuscript witnesses of the *Dalāʾil al-khayrāt* include markers for the four quarters and three thirds of the text. Modern printed copies also divide the text into eight sections, each labeled for a day of the week, beginning and ending on a Monday. In addition to these divisions of the main text, the work is often prefaced by several short paratexts that vary from witness to witness but usually include an introductory prayer, a list of the Prophet's names, and a description of the Prophet's tomb in Medina.[51] Like the *Nafḥat al-ṭīb*, the main text consists of a list of requests that God pray upon the Prophet Muḥammad, each beginning with the phrase "O God" and including some version of the *taṣliyya*. While most compendia of prayers for the Prophet composed after the *Dalāʾil al-khayrāt* share these genre conventions, al-Jazūlī's compendium is one of the few known with certainty to have circulated in pre-colonial West Africa. The known presence of this work in the region, the fact that Sīdi Muḥammad refers to it by name in the *Ṭarāʾif waʾl-talāʾid*, and the stylistic parallels between the two texts suggest that the *Dalāʾil al-khayrāt* served as the model for Sīdi al-Mukhtār's *Nafḥat al-ṭīb*.

Indeed, in addition to sharing formal genre conventions, the content and even the wording of the two works bear striking similarities. Both texts repeatedly enjoin God to pray for the Prophet with prayers of hyperbolically infinite glory and length, and, just like the *Nafḥat al-ṭīb*, the *Dalāʾil al-khayrāt* often uses these descriptions as an opportunity to enumerate all the facets and components of the world:

> O God, pray upon our master Muḥammad . . . to the number of your creations, to the extent of your pleasure, in the decoration of your throne, and in the ink of your words, and as often as your creations have remembered you in the past and as often as they will remember you throughout the rest of time, and pray upon him in every year, in every month, in every week, in every day, in every night, in every hour, in every sniff, in every breath, in every blink and in every glance, for ever and ever, for the duration of this world and the duration of the next world, and for longer than this, with a beginning which never ends and an end which never finishes![52]

Moreover, the enumeration of the components of the world often overflows into references to the various inhabitants—human, demonic, angelic, and jinn—of the cosmos, and to the end of the world and the Day of Judgment.[53] Other passages refer to Muḥammad's role as intercessor on that day,[54] to episodes from his biography, and to his place among the prophets and his role in sacred history. Finally, the *Dalāʾil al-khayrāt* includes references to the unseen realm and to the greatest secret name of God:

> O God, I ask you—by the truth that carries your seat from your might and your power and your majesty and your glory and your authority, and by the truth of your secret and hidden name by which you named yourself and which you took exclusively for yourself from yourself in knowledge of the unseen [*ʿilm al-ghayb*]—that you pray upon our master Muḥammad, your servant and your messenger.
>
> And I ask you, by your name in which, were one to call upon you, you would answer, and by which, were one to ask you something, you would grant it.
>
> And I ask you by your name which, when you lay it upon the night, darkness falls; and which, when you lay it upon the day, light arises; and which, when you lay it upon the heavens, they are raised up; and which, when you lay it upon the earth, it becomes solid; and which, when you lay it upon the mountains, they form peaks; and which, when you lay it upon difficulties, they become trivial; and which, when you lay it upon the water of the sky, it pours down; and which, when you lay it upon the clouds, they rain.[55]

In its depiction of a secret, all-powerful name—a name that both ensures God's response and directly controls the functioning of the material world—this passage strongly evokes the Kunta's theory of the greatest name of God as described in the *Fawāʾid nūrāniyya*. Al-Jazūlī was certainly not the first, or the only, Sufi author to discuss the idea of God's greatest name and its relationship to the realm of the unseen (*al-ghayb*). However, the resemblance in both content and structure to the *Nafḥat al-ṭīb* and the fact that Sīdi Muḥammad both knew and named the *Dalāʾil al-khayrāt* strongly indicate that this work may have served as one of the key texts shaping the Kunta's theory of God's greatest name.

However, despite the influence of this work in the greater region and in the Kunta's own writings, Sīdi al-Muktār's *Nafḥat al-ṭīb* exhibits significant departures from the *Dalāʾil al-khayrāt.* First of all, despite the high level of mimesis, Sīdi al-Mukhtār never reproduces verbatim any of the prayers included in al-Jazūlī's work. Moreover, the absence of such direct borrowing contravenes the conventions of this genre. Compendia of prayers for the Prophet often, even usually, include prayers attributed to famous Sufi forebears such as al-Shādhilī and Ibn Mashīsh, or to the Prophet himself.[56] The *Dalāʾil al-khayrāt* itself includes numerous repetitions of a prayer known as "the Ibrāhimic prayer" (*al-ṣalāt al-ibrāhimiyya*):

> O God, pray upon our master Muḥammad and the family of our master Muḥammad just as you prayed upon our master Ibrāhīm and the family of our master Ibrāhīm, for you are the Praised, the Good.
>
> O God, bless our master Muḥammad and the family of our master Muḥammad just as you blessed our master Ibrāhīm and the family of our master Ibrāhīm, for you are the Praised, the Good.
>
> O God, have mercy upon our master Muḥammad and the family of our master Muḥammad just as you had mercy upon our master Ibrāhīm and the family of our master Ibrāhīm, for you are the Praised, the Good.
>
> O God, be kind to our master Muḥammad and the family of our master Muḥammad just as you were kind to our master Ibrāhīm and the family of our master Ibrāhīm, for you are the Praised, the Good.[57]

Ḥadīth traditions hold that the Prophet Muḥammad certified this prayer himself, and consequently it is a common element in compendia of prayers for the Prophet throughout the Muslim world.[58] In addition to this nearly ubiquitous prayer, al-Jazūlī reproduces prayers with more specific regional circulation or Sufi affiliations, including the "Ṣalāt al-ṣughrā" (the minor prayer), attributed to ʿAbd al-Qādir al-Jīlānī. "O God, pray upon our lord Muḥammad, whose light precedes creation and whose appearance is a mercy to the worlds, to the number of your creatures who have gone before and who remain and [to the number of] those among them who are fortunate and those who are not; a prayer which exceeds enumeration and that encompasses all limits; a prayer without limitation, end, or conclusion; an eternal prayer through your eternal nature; and protect his family and companions for all time."[59] Because this prayer was attributed to ʿAbd al-Qādir al-Jīlānī, inclusion of this prayer in the *Dalāʾil al-khayrāt* suggests that al-Jazūlī identified with al-Jīlānī's social and spiritual legacy.[60] However, although Sīdi al-Mukhtār identifies al-Jīlānī as the founder of his Sufi lineage, the *Nafḥat al-ṭīb* does not include this or other well-known prayers from this lineage. This omission suggests that while Sīdi al-Mukhtār drew on the familiarity of the form of the *Dalāʾil al-khayrāt* among Saharan Muslims, he chose to set the content of the *Nafḥat al-ṭīb* definitively apart from previous compendia of prayers for the Prophet.

Additionally, despite the great thematic overlap between the two works, the *Nafḥat al-ṭīb* displays a radically heavier emphasis on the cosmological and metaphysical role of Muḥammad and his lights. For example, the fourth quarter of the text begins:

> O God, pray upon our master Muḥammad—from droplets of his light the prophets were created and from him they received, during the first

> determination of fates, the vestments of his beauty and his likeness—and for his family and his companions, and bring him peace.
>
> O God, pray upon our master Muḥammad—whose light prostrated and bent in prayer in all of the holy presences, and thus the angels sing his praises and he is pastured in the gardens of intimacy—and for his family and his companions, and bring him peace.
>
> O God, pray upon our master Muḥammad—the reason for existence and the cause of its appearance after nonexistence, and whose lights shone out from the sea of his light in preexistence—and for his family and his companions, and bring him peace. (24)

This passage depicts Muḥammad's light as the cause and source of creation, and as the wellspring from which all the other prophets received their light. These ideas have a long history within the Sufi intellectual tradition. The depiction of Muḥammad's light as he prays in prostration before God can be traced back to al-Tustarī's tenth-century commentary on the Qurʾān.[61] The idea that God created Muḥammad before, and as the source of, the rest of creation developed gradually within the early Sufi tradition and was consolidated in the concept of the *ḥaqīqa muḥammadiyya* by Ibn al-ʿArabī in the thirteenth century.[62] The presence of these ideas in Sīdi al-Mukhtār's compendium of prayers for the Prophet, along with copious references to the three realms of *al-mulk*, *al-malakūt*, and *al-jabarūt*, reflects the importance of cosmology to the Kunta's understanding of Muslim prayer and devotional practice.

In contrast, al-Jazūlī borrows many themes and terms from the Sufi intellectual tradition, but very rarely those that deal with Muḥammad's cosmological and cosmogonical roles. Instead, al-Jazūlī's compendium depicts Muḥammad as the pinnacle of the Sufi path. Many prayers ask God to grant him what he deserves for having reached the most advanced "rank" and "station," and to bring him to "a place of proximity." Other passages draw on traditions that reflect on the love between God and his believers by referring to the mutual love between Muḥammad and God, and by beseeching God to let the reciters drink "from his drinking bowl" and to "avail us of his love."[63] One prayer describes Muḥammad as "the sea of your lights, the mine of your secrets, the tongue of your proof, and the bridegroom of your kingdom."[64] These references grant Muḥammad a preeminent role in God's regard, place him at the pinnacle of the Sufi path, and draw attention to his importance in guiding humanity out of ignorance and toward the light of God. However, they do not grant him or his light a cosmological or cosmogonical function. Indeed, the reference in the "Ṣalāt al-ṣughrā" to "Muḥammad, whose light precedes creation," represents a rare mention of preexistence, while cosmological realms such as *al-mulk*, *al-malakūt*, and *al-jabarūt* are never mentioned at all. This doesn't mean that al-Jazūlī did not believe that Muḥammad had a cosmological or cosmogonical function, much less that he rejected that concept: various prayers that include references to God's throne, footstool, and tablet, and to various named angels, and to Muḥammad's light may have served as touchstones for cosmological elaboration, either orally or in other writings. However, the contrast with the *Nafḥat al-ṭīb* is striking and suggests that al-Jazūlī did not triangulate cosmology, veneration of Muḥammad, and supplicatory prayer in the same fashion as Sīdi al-Mukhtār. These departures serve as a reminder that we should not equate mimesis with copying, or reduce the complex play of intertextual traditions to the simple transmission of knowledge.

Other Saharan Sources

Although Sīdi Muḥammad's description of his mother's devotional recitations mentions only the the *Dalāʾil al-khayrāt*, we can draw inferences from other sources about the devotional literature available to Saharan Muslims in the late eighteenth century. Zachary Wright's recent examination of Aḥmad al-Tijānī's "travel notebook," the *Kunnāsh al-riḥla*, has demonstrated how eighteenth-century Muslims circulated powerful supplicatory prayers through networks that connected South Asia, the Middle East, and North Africa.[65] And both the catalogues of regional manuscript libraries and commentaries composed by other regional Muslim leaders indicate that West African Muslims also participated in the circulation of devotional works, both prior to the rise of the Kunta and then, increasingly, from the eighteenth century onward. The contents of these collections point to three works that occupied a prominent place among regional collections during the period of Sīdi al-Mukhtār's ascendancy: al-Shādhilī's *Ḥizb al-baḥr*, al-Fāzāzī's *Al-ʿIshrīnīyāt*, and al-Būṣīrī's *Al-Burda*.[66] These titles certainly do not exhaust the body of devotional literature available to Saharan Muslim communities at the time, but they all have clear resonances with the Kunta's own works and provide a template for understanding what kinds of *aḥzāb*, *adʿiyya*, and *adhkār* Lalla ʿĀʾisha and other members of the early Kunta community might have recited.

Of these three sources, al-Shādhilī's *Ḥizb al-baḥr* (Litany of the Sea) most resembles the *aḥzāb* attributed to Sīdi al-Mukhtār. While al-Shādhilī's various devotional works became popular throughout West and North Africa, the *Ḥizb al-baḥr* stands out for the number of copies made of it and the commentaries it inspired. Indeed, several regional contemporaries of Sīdi Muḥammad—Muḥammad Bello in Sokoto and Aḥmad Lobbo and his son Aḥmad Aḥmad in Macina—composed commentaries on the *Ḥizb al-baḥr*.[67] Finally, while the

Kunta do not specifically refer to the *Ḥizb al-baḥr*, they do make numerous references to al-Shādhilī, and both the *aḥzāb* attributed to Sīdi al-Mukhtār and the supplicatory prayers in the *Fawāʾid nūrāniyya* display striking similarities to al-Shādhilī's litany, particular regarding the use of the names of God and the letters of the Arabic alphabet.

In the name of God, the Merciful, the Compassionate.
May the prayers and peace of God be upon our master Muḥammad and his family.

O God,
O Exalted One,
O Gentle One,
O All-Knowing One,
You are my lord, and your knowledge is sufficient for me.
What an excellent lord is my lord!
What a wonderful sufficiency is my sufficiency!

. . . .

Even so, make us firm, aid us, and subject to us this sea, as you did subject the sea to Moses, and the fire to Ibrāhīm, and the mountains and iron to David, and the wind, the devils, and the jinn to Solomon.
Put in subjugation to us every sea of yours in earth and in heaven, in this domain and in the celestial, the sea of this world and the sea of the next. Render subservient to us every thing,
O Thou, whose hand holds sovereignty over every thing [Qurʾān 23:88].

Kaf hāʾ yāʾ ʿayn ṣād [Qurʾān 19:1]
Kaf hāʾ yāʾ ʿayn ṣād
Kaf hāʾ yāʾ ʿayn ṣād
Help us, for you are the best of helpers.
Open to us the hand of mercy, for you are the best of openers.
Pardon us, for you are the best of pardoners.
Be compassionate toward us, for you are the best of those who show compassion.
Sustain us, for you are the best of sustainers.
Guide us and rescue us from the unjust people.

Send us a gentle breeze, as you know how to do, and let it blow on us from the storehouses of your mercy. Let it bear us along as if by miraculous intervention, with security and well-being, in religion, worldly affairs, and the hereafter.

You are powerful over all things.

God, facilitate for us our affairs, with ease of mind and body, with security and well-being in religious and worldly matters. Be a companion for us on our journey, and a substitute for our households.

Blot out the countenances of our enemies, and transform them where they stand, disabling them from leaving or coming to us. *If we willed, we would blot out their eyes. Yet they would race forward to the path. But how would they see? If we willed, we should transform them where they stand. Thus they would be unable to leave or return* [Qur'ān 36:66–67].

. . . .

May their faces be deformed!

May their faces be deformed!

May their faces be deformed!

Let their faces be submissive before the Living, the Self-Subsistent, for he who is laden with wrong has already met frustration.

Tā' sīn ḥā' mīm 'ayn sīn qaf [Qur'ān 27:1, 42:1–2].

. . . .

Ḥā' mīm [Qur'ān 41:1], *ḥā' mīm, ḥā' mīm, ḥā' mīm, ḥā' mīm, ḥā' mīm!*

The affair has been decreed. The triumph has come. Over us they shall not triumph.

Ḥā' mīm!

The sending down of the scripture from God,

The Mighty, the All-Knowing,

Forgiver of sin,

Receiver of penitence,

Severe in punishing,

Forbearing,

No god is there except Him.

To Him is the returning [Qur'ān 40:1–3].

In the name of God is our door.

May he bless our walls.

Yā' sīn [Qur'ān 36:1] is our ceiling.

Kāf hā' yā' 'ayn ṣād [Qur'ān 19:1] is our sufficiency.

Ḥā' mīm 'ayn sīn qāf [Qur'ān 42:1] is our shelter.

So God is sufficient for you against them, for He hears all, knows us.

[Repeat three times]

. . . .

In the name of God, by whose name nothing in the earth or sky can do harm, for He is the All-Hearer, All-Knower.
[Repeat three times]

There is no force and no power save with God, the Most High, the Almighty.[68]

Like the supplicatory prayers of the *Fawāʾid nūrāniyya*, this litany invokes the mysterious letters that begin certain suras of the Qurʾān. Moreover, in his *Durrat al-asrār*, Ibn al-Ṣabbāgh relates the following statement from al-Shādhilī: "By God, I only uttered it because it came from the Prophet of God, from whose instruction I learned it. 'Guard it,' he said to me, 'for it contains the greatest name of God.'"[69] Although the *Ḥizb al-baḥr* itself never refers explicitly to the greatest name of God, this statement suggests that al-Shādhilī's followers believed that the text contained the greatest name of God—perhaps as some arrangement of the various letters invoked by the text. The invocation of these letters closely parallels Sīdi Muḥammad's use of the mysterious letters as stand-ins for God's lesser names when invoked individually, and for God's greatest name when invoked together in the proper sequence. Al-Shādhilī's *Ḥizb al-baḥr* even asks God to make everything in existence subservient to the supplicant, again, in a fashion highly reminiscent of the litanies of the *Fawāʾid nūrāniyya*. Although the Kunta scholars chose different letters for their litanies and their version of the greatest name, they clearly selected and combined specific elements from the earlier *aḥzāb* tradition when fashioning their own supplicatory prayers.

In addition to the *Dalāʾil al-khayrāt* and the *Ḥizb al-baḥr*, evidence suggests that other devotional texts were circulating in the Sahara and Sahel at the turn of the nineteenth century. One such work was the *ʿIshrīnīyāt* of al-Fāzāzī (d. 1230), a poem in praise of the Prophet that is mentioned in the seventeenth-century chronicle *Tārīkh al-Sūdān* and in al-Bartilī's eighteenth-century biographical dictionary, the *Fatḥ al-shakūr*. This poem inspired a tradition of written commentary by scholars such as al-Kashnāwī (d. 1667) and al-Ḥājj ʿUmar Tāl and is listed as one of the major works that ʿUthmān ibn Fūdī and his brother studied as part of their Islamic education.[70] Another work in the same genre, *Al-Kawākib al-durriyya fī madḥ khayr al-bariyya*, more commonly known as *Al-Burda*, by al-Būṣīrī (d. 1295/96), appears in almost all major manuscript collections from the region and contributed greatly to the Islamic poetic tradition of Hausaland and the Sokoto Caliphate.[71] There is also evidence that Saharan Muslims had just begun to compose their own devotional works in the early eighteenth century. The Saharan scholar al-Yadālī, who died in 1753, just before Sīdi al-Mukhtār's rise, composed a poem in praise of the Prophet that had a lasting impact on the development of praise poetry in the region.[72]

This evidence indicates that devotional texts of various genres were proliferating in the region in the late eighteenth century and that Saharan Muslims were increasingly interested in using these texts as devotional aids. Within this context, the prayers attributed to Sīdi al-Mukhtār indicate an attempt to engage with, and contribute to, existing practice by producing new texts in genres already familiar to and popular with local Muslims. The Kunta, moreover, argued that personal supplication to God was closely linked to other devotional practices, such as spiritual retreat, formal prayer, the crafting of amulets, and the use of magic squares, which they described under the rubric of "the sciences of the unseen." They did not simply provide new devotional aids; they sought to teach devotional practice. Against this backdrop, the cosmological and metaphysical theories attached to the *Fawāʾid nūrāniyya*, and explained in greater length in treatises like the *Ṭarāʾif wa'l-talāʾid* and the *Kitāb al-minna*, appear less like theoretical precursors and more like ex post facto productions. If the primary goal of the Kunta scholars was to teach efficacious religious practice to local Muslims, then these treatises can be understood as an attempt to attach existing practice to a larger Sufi intellectual tradition.

As discussed above, the *Fawāʾid nūrāniyya* displays an awareness that Muslims might use texts on religious practice on their own, without the guidance of the Kunta shaykhs. Were Saharan Muslims actively engaged in individual text-based practices during this period? It is impossible to answer this question from works composed by the Kunta scholars alone. However, those texts do suggest that the Kunta were concerned about this possibility and that they responded to that concern by attempting to shape the devotional religious landscape of the Sahara on two levels. First, Sīdi al-Mukhtār and Sīdi Muḥammad produced and circulated written devotional aids. These texts evoked works of devotional literature that were already popular in the region, but without directly citing or referencing the supplicatory prayers of earlier figures. Instead, these new compositions were fixed in written form and attached solely to the name and authority of Sīdi al-Mukhtār. As written works in manuscript form, they could travel by caravan across the region and into the teaching circles of other shaykhs, but as easily memorized oral texts they could also reach a broader cross section of West African society than the manuscripts alone. Next, didactic works like the *Fawāʾid nūrāniyya* suggested that when used in the appropriate ritual context—and under the supervision of Sufi shaykhs—these prayers could alter the material conditions surrounding the supplicant.

Finally, these hybrid teaching texts also began the work, continued in longer treatises, of connecting these practices to a larger Sufi theoretical framework, and thus justifying them from an intellectual perspective. At the same time, however, the relationship between these layers of texts can be flipped. Sīdi al-Mukhtār and Sīdi Muḥammad were indisputably highly educated Muslim scholars and fully engaged and conversant with cosmological and metaphysical discussions. The theories of efficacious religious practice that emerge from their longer works demonstrate not only their fluency but also their investment in these concepts. Their short, supplicatory prayers fit neatly into the framework of their theories, encoding their religious worldview and pointing to the deep relationship between their understanding of God and the cosmos, on the one hand, and of practice, on the other. Devotional practice, for the Kunta scholars, was the performance of cosmology, metaphysics, and sacred history—a reenactment of the relationship among supplicating believers, the world around them, and God.

These two readings are not contradictory. Sīdi al-Mukhtār and Sīdi Muḥammad were products and producers of an intellectual heritage and a social landscape. They applied the textual traditions they studied to their local context, and they sought to shape their context in accord with their scholarship. Ultimately, the ability of these scholars to connect these two kinds of texts demonstrates the degree to which practice, for eighteenth-century Saharan Muslims, was based on and driven by Arabic texts, which were transmitted in both written and oral form. The ideally pious Muslim is represented in the Kunta texts by the image of Lalla ʿĀʾisha, reciting the Qurʾān, the *Dalāʾil al-khayrāt*, and other supplicatory prayers—that is, reading texts. In the *Ṭarāʾif waʾl-talāʾid*, the image of Lalla ʿĀʾisha's devotions is paradigmatic, but it is also concerning. Behind her stands the specter of other Muslims performing similar devotions, but without a marital or family connection to Sīdi al-Mukhtār. The Kunta's devotional aids and didactic works on religious practice address these spectral believers and attempt to bring their practice in line with the Kunta's doctrines and into the sphere of their teaching—to make them, in other words, members of their community.

CONCLUSION

The association of the Kunta scholars with the sciences of the unseen continues to the present day. A popular Saharan saying holds that "wisdom [*ḥikma*] belongs to the Kunta or the Fūtiyya," and scholars acknowledge that "wisdom" refers here both to learning and to secret and powerful disciplines. Moreover, the joint invocation of the Kunta and the people of the Futa Toro (*al-fūtiyya*) simultaneously refers to the ongoing associations of these groups with Islamic learning and to the historic battle between the forces of al-Ḥājj ʿUmar Tāl (of the Futa Toro) and Aḥmad al-Bakkāʾī al-Kuntī, which was portrayed in later oral accounts as a clash between two powerful adepts of the sciences of secrets.[1] In her research on intraregional networks in the contemporary Sahara, Judith Scheele notes that the Malian Kunta are known for "the writing of amulets . . . the curing of mental illnesses and disquiet," and for serving as "fortune-tellers, healers, and soothsayers."[2] At gatherings of Saharan Muslim scholars, Kunta family members from Mali are liable to show up with manuscripts attesting to the sciences of the unseen, much to the embarrassment of their Algerian neighbors, who dismiss them as "mere sorcerers."[3] This discomfort with the physical reminder of the history of these sciences, along with the ongoing engagement of the Malian Kunta with these traditions, attests to the continuing debates among West African Muslims about the legitimacy of these practices. In her research on *l'ḥjāb*, "a secret Islamic wisdom of healing and protecting" in Mauritania, Erin Pettigrew confirms that debates over the legality of these practices continued through the colonial and postcolonial periods, and that Mauritanians continue to refer to the Kunta as a source of knowledge for these disciplines.[4]

This historical and ongoing association of the Kunta family with powerful practices capable of altering the material world originated with the investment of Sīdi al-Mukhtār and Sīdi Muḥammad al-Kuntī in presenting themselves as masters of the sciences of the unseen. This book has sought to locate those sciences within the writings of these two Saharan scholars and within the social and historical context that gave them shape and was shaped by them in return. These two men depicted a world composed of two interlocking realms, the visible world of the senses and the invisible world of the unseen. And, while not identical, the dichotomy of this presentation mirrors the scholarly division between social and economic history, on the one hand, and the history of ideas, on the other—the divide between the accounts of human material and social circumstances and the reconstruction of past worldviews. Indeed, this book has followed just such a pattern in presenting both the visible and invisible worlds of the Kunta scholars—the social and material world in which they lived and the intellectual realm in which they articulated sacred history, described cosmological and metaphysical structures, and classified knowledge. And just as the Kunta imagined constant connection and mutual interaction between the visible and invisible worlds, so too has this book sought to illustrate the reciprocal interactions between their ideas and arguments and the society in which they lived.

For Sīdi al-Mukhtār and Sīdi Muḥammad, that visible world of material and social circumstances was the West African Sahara Desert, and they occupied a particularly privileged position within that world. In the absence of centralizing state structures, Saharans of the eighteenth century developed a series of social charters that provided historical rationales for a society organized around occupational divisions. Within this social organization, the Kunta presented themselves as members of the *zwāya*, religious specialists who devoted themselves to learning while ceding political control to the warrior *ḥassān*. In the occupational hierarchy of the Sahara, this position also indicated wealth, as embodied by the ownership of herds—often placed with tributary clients for caretaking—and slaves. According to the Kunta's own accounts, Sīdi al-Mukhtār acquired much of his wealth through involvement with regional trade. Recent scholarship on the Sahara has stressed the mutually reinforcing bonds between social institutions and the material environment, pointing, for example, to the ways in which people used the trade routes to spread pedagogical networks, and how the presence of a renowned teacher provided the founding story for many wells and their surrounding settlements. Sīdi al-Mukhtār and Sīdi Muḥammad helped reinforce these links between the Saharan environment and Muslim social institutions, particularly through their participation in desert institutions of learning. However, although these scholars acquired wealth and successfully asserted their status as *zwāya* religious specialists, Sīdi al-Mukhtār may have begun as a tributary client of the Kunta family, presenting a revised genealogy after his rise in socioeconomic fortune. Such ex post facto transformations were part and parcel of the Saharan world, where social positions—and their accompanying genealogies and ethnic identities—shifted along with a family's economic fortunes.

The hagiographic accounts and chains of transmission provided by Sīdi Muḥammad indicate that his father studied with teachers among the Kel al-Sūq, particularly the Sufi shaykh Sīdi ʿAlī al-Najīb. The hagiographies also suggest that Sīdi al-Mukhtār competed with Sīdi ʿAlī's children—particularly his daughter and son-in-law—for the right to inherit Sīdi ʿAlī's authority. Sīdi al-Mukhtār was ultimately acknowledged as a Sufi friend of God, partly owing to the efforts of his son and hagiographer Sīdi Muḥammad, and the reputation and authority of the Kunta family expanded outward from the Azawād—particularly to the south and to the west. By the early nineteenth century, Muslim scholars from the Senegal River Valley, the Mauritanian Hodh, and the Inner Niger Delta claimed the Kunta scholars as their teachers or sent their children to them to study. This pedagogical network resulted in the establishment of Shaykh Sīdiyya's community in the Hodh, while Sīdi Muhammad's hagiography of his father served as the template for the hagiography of Aḥmad al-Fādil. By the time ʿUmar Tāl began his campaign in the Niger Delta, the Kunta family exercised de facto control over Timbuktu and the desert to the north. It was thus one of Sīdi al-Mukhtār's grandsons, Aḥmad al-Bakkāʾī, who opposed the ʿUmarian armies and ended the northern expansion of the *jihād*.

However, Aḥmad al-Bakkāʾī's identification of Sīdi al-Mukhtār as the leader of an organized Qādiriyya Sufi order does not reflect the writings of his father and grandfather, who imagined themselves much differently. Prior to the rise of the Kunta, West African Sufis of the seventeenth and early eighteenth centuries made up relatively small communities of isolated ascetics who engaged in devotional practices handed down from a paradigmatic friend of God like ʿAbd al-Qādir al-Jīlānī or Abū Ḥasan al-Shādhilī. Evidence from those periods indicates that participation in these communities was not exclusive—students could and did travel from one to the other—and nothing suggests the presence of the specific organizational hierarchies that would predominate in later centuries. Sīdi al-Mukhtār and Sīdi Muḥammad's writings demonstrate that the Kunta community developed within this model of Sufism. These shaykhs identified their community as "Qādirī," according to their practice of reciting litanies (*awrād*) traced back to al-Jīlānī, even as they abundantly referenced earlier Shādhilī authorities. Sīdi al-Mukhtār's spiritual lineage (*silsila*) also carefully ties him to historical Muslim authorities in the region, including Aḥmad al-Bakkāʾī al-Kuntī al-Kabīr, al-Maghīlī, al-Suyūṭī, and Aḥmad al-Raqqād. Sīdi al-Mukhtār and Sīdi Muḥammad broke from this earlier model of Sufism not through organizational hierarchy or exclusive corporate identity but by renouncing ascetic withdrawal from the social and political realms. They used their acquired wealth to place tributary families under their "protection" and then leveraged their economic resources and the military force of their allies to insert themselves into the political realm—supporting contenders for leadership among the Barābīsh and the Kel Tadamakkat, negotiating with the Iwellemmedan Tuareg, resisting the economic claims of the Moroccan sultanate to the north, and occasionally warring directly with surrounding "warrior" groups. Sīdi al-Mukhtār and Sīdi Muḥammad could enforce their authority by leveraging the military force of their tributary clients; however, they employed the rhetoric that the support of these "students" stemmed from voluntary submission to their authority as Sufi shaykhs.

The texts composed by Sīdi al-Mukhtār and Sīdi Muḥammad also indicate that they located their authority as Sufi friends of God in their privileged access to, and mastery over, the realm of the unseen. The hagiographies composed by Sīdi Muḥammad present the friends of God as the site at which the divine realm, with all of its force and power, erupts into the material and human world. These spectacular breakings of the norm indicate the special position that the friends of God occupy between the world as perceivable to the senses and the realm of the unseen. Indeed, it is this alternate realm that provides the framework for all of the Kunta's arguments about the authority of the friends of God in the social realm. Across the Kunta's many texts, the unseen realm appears as the scaffolding that undergirds material existence. But while all believing Muslims partake in this realm to some degree, the friends of God rise within it to a position of ultimate cosmic importance. Arriving at the end of the Sufi path, these individuals participate in the simultaneous destruction of both their selves and the created universe, only to be re-created as the source of creation and the gateway between the manifest and unseen realms. Finally, because it is the physical hearts and bodies of all believers in general, and of these elite believers in particular, that serve as the connection between these two realms, the purification of the heart and body through devotional practice assumes a position of central importance in the Kunta texts.

For Sīdi al-Mukhtār and Sīdi Muḥammad, it was privileged access to the realm of the unseen that granted them mastery over powerful practices. They referred to these practices, and the bodies of knowledge on which they were based, as "the sciences of the unseen." These sciences lie at the heart of the legacy of the Kunta family in West Africa. The Kunta scholars, and Sīdi Muḥammad in particular, acknowledged the apparent proximity between these sciences and prohibited acts of sorcery and went to great lengths to present the sciences of the unseen as legitimate engagements for Muslims. To accomplish this goal, Sīdi Muḥammad categorized the various fields of potential knowledge/practice into the uneasy categories of the charismata, the sciences of the unseen, and sorcery, and employed a bricolage of rationales to distinguish between these various classifications. Rather than a neat epistemic map, these classificatory efforts reflect a series of tensions, including his attempts to balance the ability of humans to exert a meaningful influence over their surroundings with the tenets of Ashʿarī theology, and his desire to maintain a divide between Muslim and non-Muslim practices while presenting himself and his family as the masters of powerful disciplines.

There is evidence that several of the first-order disciplines that make up the Kunta's sciences of the unseen were widespread and established in West Africa in the fifteenth through eighteenth centuries. This evidence points to the widespread use of the sciences of letters and names, magic squares, and talismans by networks of Muslim clerics throughout the region. Muḥammad al-Kābarī, a fifteenth-century scholar from Timbuktu, produced a work on using supplicatory prayers and names of God to effect tangible results in the material world. And the sciences of sand writing (geomancy), astrology, letters, and magic squares were established among the Fulānī in Hausaland by the eighteenth century. There is much less evidence, however, for the development of second-order classifications that sought to use Islamic justifications for grouping disciplines into prohibited and permitted categories. One exception occurs in the work of al-Maghīlī, whose "Replies" to Askia Muḥammad at the turn of the sixteenth century associate writings "that bring good fortune . . . [or] ward off ill fortune" with the actions of "sorcerers," while proclaiming that anyone who claims knowledge of the unseen is an unbeliever. However, al-Maghīlī's categorical rejection of any knowledge or practice associated with the unseen does not appear to have been taken up by any later writer. The Kunta scholars are thus the first in the region to compose written works organizing the sciences into second-order classifications of prohibited and permitted disciplines and integrating them into Sufi cosmological and metaphysical frameworks. The Kunta appear to have initiated a trend of increasing systemization of these disciplines as well as an increasing association between the sciences of the unseen and Sufi shaykhs. Indeed, following the rise of the Kunta, Sufi scholars and leaders in the region increasingly worked to restrict the sciences of the unseen to the purview of the Sufi friends of God.

Finally, this examination of the Kunta's sciences of the unseen illustrates a new approach to the study of contested Islamic bodies of knowledge/practice. Earlier works on these types of practices traditionally begin by taking terms such as "magic" or "the occult," which are laden with negative meanings in the contemporary West, and applying them anachronistically to non-Western cultures and other historical contexts. More recently, Islamic studies scholars attempting to avoid this error often resort to abandoning second-order categories in their entirety and dealing exclusively with first-order disciplines (alchemy, astronomy, etc.). The former method has received much criticism for its roots in colonial-era approaches and for its inaccurate portrayal of the emic terminology used by Muslims. However, while the latter approach has yielded more accurate results, it has also resulted in a fragmentation of knowledge about these disciplines. And neither approach has engaged with the rich scholarship on the development of traditions of self-professed magic in the ancient Mediterranean and medieval Europe. In contrast, this study reveals that the Kunta scholars engaged in historical discourses about magic that began in ancient Greece and influenced Islamic thought and culture as well as medieval and early modern Europe.

Specifically, the Kunta's classification of the sciences of the unseen participated in what Kimberly Stratton has called a "discourse of alterity" and Bernd-Christian Otto has labeled a "magic discourse of exclusion." Sīdi Muḥammad in particular associated the condemned practice of "sorcery" with racialized others in "the land of the blacks," and he included practices prevalent among Muslims living in Hausaland in the prohibited sciences of the unseen. His approach stands in marked contrast to "the discourse of inclusion" demonstrated by the eighteenth-century Fulānī scholar Muḥammad al-Kashnāwī, for whom no type of knowledge was considered intrinsically illicit. Al-Kashnāwī composed, among other works on the sciences of secrets, a didactic commentary on Fakr al-Dīn al-Rāzī's *Al-Sirr al-maktūm*. This commentary directly engages with both *siḥr* and *nīranj* as legitimate sources of beneficial knowledge and practice. As such, al-Kashnāwī's work demonstrates a magic discourse of inclusion. The dialectical codevelopment of magic discourses of inclusion and exclusion also tie the Kunta to the "double gesture" of disavowal and reinscription by which the process of rejecting categories of knowledge/practice in fact reinscribes those practices as both generative and meaningful. And while this "double gesture" has previously been described as a unique feature of European modernity, this study indicates that this discursive move applies to all contexts in which people in authority attempt to reject and delegitimize the knowledge and practices of those they describe as other.

Finally, Islamic studies scholarship has traditionally considered the disciplines that the Kunta describe as the sciences of the unseen as categorically distinct from other aspects of Muslim devotional practice, such as seclusion (*khalwa*), the recitation of the names of God (*dhikr*), and prayer. However, the works of Sīdi al-Mukhtār and Sīdi Muḥammad consistently associate the sciences with these types of ritual action, and particularly with the use of various forms of supplicatory prayer. This study thus situates the sciences of the unseen within the devotional landscape of West Africa during the eighteenth and nineteenth centuries. The evidence suggests that West African Muslims were recopying and composing textual devotional aids in greater and greater numbers during this period, and that the Kunta participated in this trend by composing their own Arabic texts for use as supplicatory prayers. Sīdi al-Mukhtār's and Sīdi Muḥammad's production of these texts stemmed from their overall understanding of devotional practice as a performance of the relationships among God, the cosmos, and the believer, while allowing them to condense and transmit their understanding of cosmology, metaphysics, and sacred history to a wider audience through oral transmission. However, comparison to other devotional aids circulating in the region at the time, such as the *Dalāʾil al-khayrāt* of al-Jazūlī and the *Ḥizb al-baḥr* of al-Shādhilī indicate that Sīdi al-Mukhtār and Sīdi Muḥammad also intentionally produced prayers that would have been familiar to a Saharan audience but were attached to their own name and authority. In this fashion, the Kunta scholars sought to shape the larger landscape of Saharan devotional practice and to legitimize that practice in reference to Islamic intellectual traditions.

Returning to the social context of the Kunta scholars' intellectual output brings this study full circle by linking their intellectual production back to the material conditions of Saharan devotional practice—in this case through the production of manuscript texts. Just as scholars such as Judith Scheele and James McDougall have documented how human populations and social formations shaped the physical environment of the Sahara, this study demonstrates the bi-directional influence of the social and material circumstances of Muslim practices and the ideational, intellectual production of elites. Educated Muslim scholars like Sīdi al-Mukhtār and Sīdi Muḥammad invested their economic and intellectual resources in attempts to shape Saharan society and practice through the material production and circulation of written Arabic texts, even as their own ideologies and philosophies were shaped by both the preexisting social landscape of the Sahara and the circulation of material goods. Ultimately, this study of the works of Sīdi al-Mukhtār and Sīdi Muḥammad once again demonstrates the inextricable relationship between the material and the ideational, the world of ideas and the visible realm of material history and culture.

NOTES

INTRODUCTION

1. McDougall and Scheele, "Introduction"; Horden, "Situations Both Alike"; Scheele, "Traders, Saints, and Irrigation." For a discussion of the "economics of scarcity" of the desert, see Webb, *Desert Frontier*, 10–14, 52–55.

2. For webs of interconnectivity across this region, see Scheele, "Traders, Saints, and Irrigation" and *Smugglers and Saints of the Sahara*.

3. Hall, *History of Race*, 36–39. For an extensive account of the Moroccan conquest of Timbuktu, see Abitbol, *Tombouctou et les Arma*.

4. Webb, *Desert Frontier*.

5. Ibid.; Lovejoy, *Transformations in Slavery*; for the Senegambia, see Searing, *West African Slavery and Atlantic Commerce*; for the central Sudan, see Levtzion, "Urban and Rural Islam" and "Merchants vs. Scholars and Clerics."

6. Curtin, "Jihad in West Africa."

7. Last, *Sokoto Caliphate*.

8. Robinson, *Holy War of Umar Tal*.

9. Brenner, "Histories of Religion in Africa," 148–49; Bakkāʾī, letter to ʿUmar Tāl; C. Stewart, "Frontier Disputes and Problems"; Robinson, *Holy War of Umar Tal*, 303–16.

10. Louise Marlow, "Advice and Advice Literature," *EI2*. For the application of this category in a modern context, see Asad, *Genealogies of Religion*, 214–23.

11. Ould Cheikh, "Man of Letters in Timbuktu," 239–45; Nobili, *Sultan, Caliph, and the Renewer*, 160–61.

12. Brenner, *Controlling Knowledge*, 29.

13. Ibid., 29–32; Ould Cheikh, "Tribu comme volonté"; Nouhi, "Society of the Southwestern Sahara," 45–51.

14. C. Stewart, *Islam and Social Order in Mauritania*; Ould Cheikh, "Tribu comme volonté."

15. Boubrik, *Saints et société en Islam*, 13.

16. McLaughlin, "Sufi, Saint, Sharif," 176–94; Robinson, *Paths of Accommodation*, 161–93.

17. Scheele, *Smugglers and Saints of the Sahara*, 158–62.

18. Marty, *Kounta de l'est*.

19. Baṭrān, "Sidi al-Mukhtar al-Kunti," 47–52; Kuntī, *Ṭarāʾif waʾl-talāʾid* (2013), 1:217 (unless otherwise noted, all citations of this source refer to the four-volume version edited by Yaḥyā Ould Sayyid Aḥmad and published in 2013); Kuntī, *Risāla al-ghallāwiyya*, 185.

20. Marty, *Kounta de l'est*, 3–11; Baṭrān, "Sidi al-Mukhtar al-Kunti," 32, 47–48. See also Ould Cheikh, "Man of Letters in Timbuktu," 232.

21. Baṭrān, "Sidi al-Mukhtar al-Kunti," 43–45, 52–54, 94–96, 105–25, 241–64; Baṭrān, "Kunta." See also McDougall, "Ijil Salt Industry," 93–107, and "Economics of Islam."

22. For the development of the Sufi movement in Baghdad during the ʿAbbāsid era, see Karamustafa, *Sufism*.

23. Bashir, *Sufi Bodies*, 9–11.

24. Karamustafa, *Sufism*, 2, 6; Bernd Radtke, Pierre Lory, Thierry Zarcone, Devin DeWeese, Marc Gaborieau, F. M. Denny, Françoise Aubin, John O. Hunwick, and Neil Mchugh, "Walī," *EI2*.

25. For an introduction to al-Ghazālī's life and thought, see Garden, *First Islamic Reviver*; Griffel, "Al-Ghazali"; W. Montgomery Watt, "Al-Ghazālī," *EI2*.

26. Ibn al-ʿArabī has received more scholarly attention than perhaps any other Sufi figure. Key publications on his life and work include Chittick, *Ibn ʿArabi*; Chodkiewicz, *Seal of the Saints* and *Ocean Without Shore*; Corbin, *Creative Imagination*; Shaikh, *Sufi Narratives of Intimacy*.

27. Karamustafa, *Sufism*, 114–34; Ohlander, *Sufism in an Age of Transition*.

28. Jacqueline Chabbi, "ʿAbd al-Qādir al-Jīlānī," *EI2*.

29. Baṭrān, "Kunta" and *Qadiryya Brotherhood in West Africa*; Brenner, "Concepts of Ṭarīqa in West Africa"; Ould Cheikh, "Man of Letters in Timbuktu."

30. Brenner, in "Concepts of Ṭarīqa in West Africa," provides a useful examination of how the leaders of the Sokoto Caliphate understood their relationship to ʿAbd al-Qādir al-Jīlānī and institutionalized Sufism. However, I disagree with his portrayal of Sīdi al-Mukhtār's understanding of the Qādiriyya in the first half of his essay.

31. Brown, "Faithful Dissenters"; Louis Gardet, "Karāma," *EI2*. For a discussion of these debates in North Africa, see Fierro, "Polemic About the Karāmāt al-Awliyā."

32. Zadeh, "Magic, Marvel, and Miracle," 246–47.

33. Amanullah, "Debate over the Karāmah."

34. Joseph Laycock discusses the interactions between these different modes of understanding of magic in *Dangerous Games*, 1–28. For a now classic study of self-professed magic practitioners, see Luhrmann, *Persuasions of the Witch's Craft*; for more recent studies, see the essays in Bever and Styers, *Magic in the Modern World*.

35. James George Frazer was instrumental in suggesting that magic should be considered a lower form of religion and then later classifying it as flawed science.

36. Edward B. Tylor is usually credited with the introduction of this idea.

37. Evans-Pritchard, *Witchcraft, Oracles, and Magic*.

38. Important exceptions include the works of Toufic Fahd, whose meticulous efforts to trace the philological origins of Arabic terms relating to sorcery and divination still serve as key reference works in the field. See his *Divination Arabe*, "Magic in Islam," and "Connaissance de l'inconnaissable."

39. Hanegraaff, "Magic," 396; see also Hanegraaff, *Esotericism and the Academy*.

40. Styers, *Making Magic*, 223.

41. Stratton, *Naming the Witch*.

42. Otto, "Towards Historicizing 'Magic' in Antiquity."

43. Otto, "Historicising 'Western Learned Magic.'"

44. For an introduction to these texts, see Fierro, "Bāṭinism in al-Andalus"; Saif, "Ġāyat al-Ḥakīm to Šams al-Maʿārif," *Arabic Influences*, 36–45, and "Ikhwān al-Ṣafāʾ's Religious Reform"; and De Callataÿ, *Ikhwan al-Safa* and "Classification of Knowledge."

45. Gril, "Science of Letters"; Lory, *Science des lettres en Islam*.

46. Gardiner, "Forbidden Knowledge" and "Esotericist Reading Communities."

47. Saif, *Arabic Influences*.

48. Hanegraaff, "Magic," 401.

49. Ibid., 402; Bergunder, "What Is Esotericism?"

50. Josephson, "God's Shadow," 315.

51. Pels, "Introduction," 3–4.

52. Bever and Styers, "Introduction," 3–4, 12.

53. Brenner, "Introduction," 7.

54. Melvin-Koushki, "Introduction," 288–89; Doostdar, *Iranian Metaphysicals*, 9.

55. Brenner, *Controlling Knowledge*, 7–9, 17–38; Tamari, "Caste Systems in West Africa"; Brooks, *Landlords and Strangers*, 39–46.

56. Contributors to the Timbuktu Manuscripts Project estimated that there were three hundred thousand Arabic manuscripts "in Timbuktu and the surrounding areas" and up to one million in Mali. Farouk Ali, "Timbuktu's First Private Manuscript Library"; Haidara, "State of Manuscripts in Mali," 266. Charles Stewart has recently suggested that these estimates are probably wildly inflated and that the Arabic manuscript holdings in Timbuktu should be numbered "merely" in the tens of thousands. Stewart, "Rethinking the Missing Manuscripts."

57. El Hamel, "Transmission of Islamic Knowledge," 70–74.

58. Merolla, "Orality and Technauriture," 80–81; Finnegan, "How of Literature," 173–75.

59. Barber, *Anthropology of Texts*, 22–29.

60. Messick, *Shariʿa Scripts*, 41.

61. The one manuscript that I consulted from this collection was made available as part of the Islamic Manuscripts from Mali Collection through the Library of Congress, at http://memory.loc.gov/intldl/malihtml//malihome.html.

62. The BnF has since made the complete contents of this collection available digitally at http://gallica.bnf.fr.

63. Other searchable library catalogues that contain Kunta manuscripts include the Institut mauritanien de recherche scientifique (IMRS) in Nouakchott (some of its holdings are available online through the Oriental Manuscript Resource at http://omar.ub.uni-freiburg.de; the Institut des hautes études et de recherches islamiques–Ahmed Baba in Timbuktu (IHERI-AB); and the Fondation du Roi Abdul-Aziz Al Saoud in Casablanca, the manuscript holdings of which are available digitally at http://www.fondation.org.ma/green/homdigital_en.htm. The catalogues of the IMRS in Nouakchott, the IHERI-AB in Timbuktu, the Boutilimit Collection, and the Segou Collection now held at the BnF (along with five other West African manuscript libraries) can be searched online at http://www.westafricanmanuscripts.org.

64. My witness to the *Kitāb al-minna fī ʿitiqād ahl al-sunna* is held by the BNRM in Rabat. The copy appears to be complete at 140 folios, but the writing from the last folio—and thus any trace of a colophon—has been completely washed out. Kuntī, *Kitāb al-minna*, BNRM 2573d.

65. My main witness to the commentary is a copy held at the BNRM. The witness appears to be complete at 119 folios, but unfortunately the writing from the last folio has been completely washed out, and if there was a colophon, it is not extant. I also consulted a copy held by the library of the Great Mosque of Meknes. While complete at 157 folios, the colophon of the Meknes copy lacks either a date or the name of a copyist. Kuntī, *Sharḥ al-qaṣīda al-fayḍiyya*, BNRM 4469d; Kuntī, *Sharḥ al-qaṣīda al-fayḍiyya*, Meknes 502.

66. I located a copy of the nineteen-line poem *al-Qaṣīda al-fayḍiyya* in an untitled poem in the BnF's collection. Kuntī, untitled, BnF 5623, fol. 103a–b.

67. Pollock quoted in Messick, *Shariʿa Scripts*, 26.

68. References to the *Jidhwat al-anwār* in this book cite a witness held by the BNRM. This witness is complete and comprises sixty-three folios, is in excellent condition, is written in a clear hand, and includes a colophon. The colophon does not name the copyist but claims that Sīdi al-Mukhtār finished composing the original work on the evening of October 17, 1810 (Monday, the 19th of Ramaḍān, 1225) and that the copy was completed forty-one years later in 1849–50 (1266). I also consulted two other witnesses, one held at the BnF and the other made available online at the Library of Congress by the Cheik Zani Baye Library in Timbuktu. The BnF witness contains a colophon reading, "completed on 20 December 1825 (10 Jumādā al-Awwal 1241) by the scribe Muḥammad ibn Sayyid al-Amīn al-Būsīfī for his brother in God, Sayyid ibn Sālim al-Tishītī." This date makes this the earliest verifiable witness to this text that I have accessed. Unfortunately, at least the first twenty folios were bound out of order, and pages appear to be missing. Pages from the witness from the Cheik Zani Baye Library are also misordered, with the date of copying given as 1858. Kuntī, *Jidhwat al-anwār*, BNRM 2579k; *Jidhwat al-anwār*, BnF 5429, fols. 232a–293b; *Jidhwat al-anwār*, Cheik Zani Baye Library.

69. The hostilities between these two scholars is recorded in Shinqīṭī, *Wasīṭ fī tarājim udabāʾ shinqīt*, 277–83, 361.

70. My primary witness for the *Kitāb zawāl al-ilbās* is a copy held at the BnF, which contains a colophon giving the date of completion of the original composition as July 31, 1803 (12 Rabīʿ al-Thānī 1218) and the date of completion of the copy as December 4, 1830 (19 Jumādā al-Thānī 1246). I also consulted a second witness from the University of Illinois Archives (62/7), which contains a colophon identifying the copyist as Maḥmūd ibn Amhīb, a student of Shaykh Sīdiyya (1775–1868). Ibn Amhīb gives the date for his completion of the copy as November 30, 1865. Kuntī, *Kitāb zawāl al-ilbās*, Arabe 5452, BnF, fols. 73b–99a; *Kitāb zawāl al-ilbās*, MS 62/7, Charles C. Stewart Papers.

71. I consulted three witnesses of the *Fawāʾid nūrāniyya* for this study. My primary witness is held at the MH in Rabat, the second is at the BNRM, and the third is in the Hamdan Diadié Bocoum Collection at the Bibliothèque des manuscrits de Djenne in Mali. Kuntī, *Fawāʾid nūrāniyya*, BNRM 209d; *Fawāʾid nūrāniyya*, MH 12221; *Fawāʾid nūrāniyya*, Hamdan Diadié Bocoum 04.

72. Kuntī, *Ḥizb sīdī al-mukhtār*, 250–53. This witness is part of an undated bound collection of supplicatory prayers attributed to many different Sufi figures.

73. Kuntī, *Ḥizb al-nūr*, 6–8. This prayer is included in a large collection of both named and unnamed supplicatory prayers attributed to Sīdi al-Mukhtār.

74. Kuntī, *Ḥizb al-isrāʾ*.

75. This is the only one of Sīdi al-Mukhtār's devotional aids that has been published. Ould Wadādī's 1990 published edition has the order of the "second" and "third" quarters reversed from the ordering found in the two manuscript witnesses consulted for this study.

76. Asad, "Idea of an Anthropology of Islam," 10.

77. Ibid., 22.

78. The word "marabout" originated as a pejorative (mis)translation of the word *murābiṭ* by French colonial scholars and administrators. However, it is now widely used as a label of self-identification across West Africa. Robinson, *Paths of Accommodation*, 241n4; Soares, *Islam and the Prayer Economy*, 129.

CHAPTER 1

1. McDougall and Scheele, "Introduction," 5.

2. Ibid., 5–7, 12–15; Scheele, "Traders, Saints, and Irrigation." For the applicability of Mediterranean frameworks to the Sahara, see Horden, "Situations Both Alike."

3. See in particular McDougall, "Research in Saharan History" and "Salts of the Western Sahara"; Scheele, *Smugglers and Saints of the Sahara*; McDougall and Scheele, *Saharan Frontiers*; and Lydon, "Writing Trans-Saharan History" and *On Trans-Saharan Trails*.

4. Webb, *Desert Frontier*, 3–4.

5. Ibid., 3–14; Brooks, *Landlords and Strangers*, 1–13, 167–74.

6. Webb, *Desert Frontier*, 10–14.

7. McDougall and Scheele, "Introduction," 10.

8. Scheele, "Traders, Saints, and Irrigation."

9. Ibid., Webb, *Desert Frontier*, 52–55. Ann McDougall's work has been definitive for determining the patterns and significance of the precolonial salt trade. See McDougall, "Salts of the Western Sahara" and "Ijil Salt Industry."

10. Baṭrān, "Sidi al-Mukhtar al-Kunti," 241–47.

11. Ibid., 247–58; McDougall, "Salts of the Western Sahara" and "Snapshots from the Sahara."

12. Nobili, *Sultan, Caliph, and the Renewer*, 51; McDougall, "Economics of Islam," 53.

13. Scheele, "Traders, Saints, and Irrigation."

14. Ware, "Slavery in Islamic Africa," 55–56.

15. Hall, *History of Race*, 36.

16. Ibid., 36–39.

17. Webb, *Desert Frontier.*

18. Hall, *History of Race*. For Hall's relationship to Webb's work, see 37.

19. Ibid., 39–49; see also Cleaveland, *Becoming Walāta*; Norris, *Arab Conquest of the Western Sahara*, 12–15; and Taylor, "Of Disciples and Sultans," 23.

20. Hall, *History of Race*, 55.

21. Ibid., 39–40; Norris, "Znāga Islam"; Curtin, "Jihad in West Africa," 14–17; Ould Cheikh, "Nomadisme, Islam et pouvoir politique," 832–50.

22. The European sources include the diary of a French traveler named La Courbe, who arrived in the Gebla in 1686 and described the society he saw there as the result of a great war concluded about ten years earlier, and the report of a French administrator of St. Louis, Chambonneau, who wrote about a religious movement to the north of the Senegal River led by "the so-called Marabou or Presbyter of the Superstition of Muhammad." Chambonneau reported that the leader of this movement died in 1674, while his brother, Munīr al-Dīn, was on a mission to meet with the French in St. Louis. Norris, "Znāga Islam," 501; Ould Cheikh, "Nomadisme, Islam et pouvoir politique," 839–40.

23. Lovejoy and Baier, "Desert-Side Economy"; Lovejoy, *Salt of the Desert Sun*, 252–55.

24. Webb, *Desert Frontier*, 68–90. See McDougall's response, "Research in Saharan History," 476–77.

25. Research has not improved on Austen's tentative census; see Austen, "Mediterranean Islamic Slave Trade." For an assessment of current estimates, see Ware, "Slavery in Islamic Africa," 51–54.

26. Brenner, *Controlling Knowledge*, 24.

27. For the development of these occupation groups in the region, see Tamari, "Caste Systems in West Africa."

28. Brenner, *Controlling Knowledge*, 28–29.

29. Ould Cheikh, "Nomadisme, Islam et pouvoir politique" and "Tribu comme volonté."

30. Bonte, "Tribus, factions et état"; see also Ould Cheikh, "Herders, Traders, and Clerics," 213–15.

31. While this was always the case to some extent, *amīrs*' control over tributary warrior groups diminished over the first half of the nineteenth century before disintegrating altogether in the face of French expansion in the Senegal River Valley. Taylor, "Warriors, Tributaries, Blood Money."

32. Webb, *Desert Frontier*, 16, 48.

33. Abitbol, *Tombouctou et les Arma.*

34. Saad, *Social History of Timbuktu.*

35. Norris, *Arab Conquest of the Western Sahara*, 78–86.

36. Grémont, *Touaregs Iwellemmedan*, 15, 110n113, 73–76, 93–94.

37. Ibid., 9–10, 14–16, 135–39, 149–211; Norris, *Arab Conquest of the Western Sahara*, 105–10.

38. Norris, *Arab Conquest of the Western Sahara*, 78, 82–83.

39. Saad, *Social History of Timbuktu*, 215.

40. Houdas, *Tedzkiret En-Nisiān fī Akhbār Molouk as-Soudān*, 172–74.

41. Norris, *Arab Conquest of the Western Sahara*, 113–14; Grémont, *Touaregs Iwellemmedan*, 243–57; Baṭrān, "Sidi al-Mukhtar al-Kunti," 301–71.

42. Brenner, *Controlling Knowledge*, 22.

43. The trading of free Muslims into slavery was an explicit motivation for the revolution of the Torobbe in Futa Toro and ʿUthmān ibn Fūdī's revolution in Hausaland. Ware, "Slavery in Islamic Africa," 65–67.

44. Curtin, "Jihad in West Africa," 18–22.

45. Last, *Sokoto Caliphate.*

46. The most recent and complete account of Aḥmad Lobbo and the founding of Macina is found in Nobili, *Sultan, Caliph, and the Renewer.*

47. Robinson, *Holy War of Umar Tal*; Last, "Reform in West Africa."

48. Nobili, *Sultan, Caliph, and the Renewer*, 131, 160–70; C. Stewart, "Frontier Disputes and Problems"; Saad, *Social History of Timbuktu*, 214–18.

49. Brenner, *Controlling Knowledge*, 29. I have altered the orthography of the Arabic words in this quotation.

50. Moraes Farias, "Oldest Extant Writing"; Pettigrew, "History of Islam in Mauritania," 2.

51. Hunwick, "Aḥmad Bābā on Slavery"; Hunwick and Harrak, *Miʿrāj al-Suʿūd*; see both ʿUthmān ibn Fūdī's *Taʿlīm al-ikhwān* and Martin's introduction and commentary in Martin, "Unbelief in the Western Sudan."

52. The earlier work of Yahya Ould al-Bara was critical for establishing this field. See Bara, "Milieu culturel."

53. Warscheid, *Droit musulman et société*.

54. Lydon, *On Trans-Saharan Trails*.

55. Kuntī, *Ṭarāʾif waʾl-talāʾid*, 1:222–23, hereafter cited parenthetically in the text in this chapter. Again, all citations of this source refer to the 2013 published version edited by Yaḥyā Ould Sayyid Aḥmad, unless otherwise noted. All English translations are my own unless otherwise noted.

56. J. M. Landau, "Kuttāb," *EI2*.

57. Jacqueline Chabbi, "ʿAbd al-Qādir al-Jīlānī," *EI2*.

58. Shinqīṭī, *Wasīṭ fī tarājim udabāʾ shinqīṭ*. See also Miské, *Wasīṭ*; Fortier, "Pédagogie coranique"; Ould Ahmedou, *Enseignement traditionnel en Mauritanie*; and El Hamel, "Transmission of Islamic Knowledge."

59. Renard, *Friends of God*, 47–48.

60. El Hamel, "Transmission of Islamic Knowledge," 70–71; for the term *dawla*, see Shinqīṭī, *Wasīṭ fī tarājim udabāʾ shinqīṭ*, 519.

61. Shinqīṭī, *Wasīṭ fī tarājim udabāʾ shinqīṭ*, 519.

62. Cf. El Hamel, "Transmission of Islamic Knowledge," 70–74.

63. C. Stewart, "Rethinking the Missing Manuscripts."

64. Al-Bartilī gives his name as Aḥmad ibn Āg ibn al-Shaykh al-Sūqī. El Hamel, *Vie intellectuelle islamique*, 201–2. See also Saad, *Social History of Timbuktu*, 71.

65. While this And-Agh Muḥammad is not attested, al-Bartilī includes an entry for his father, And ʿAbd Allāh, and records that he died in 1675. El Hamel, *Vie intellectuelle islamique*, 350.

66. Saad, *Social History of Timbuktu*, 60–67; El Hamel, "Transmission of Islamic Knowledge," 78, and *Vie intellectuelle islamique*, 167–68.

67. According to Saad, Sīdi al-Mukhtār's *isnād* seems to confuse Aḥmad Bābā's teacher, Muḥammad Baghayughu al-Wangarī, with another Muḥammad Baghayughu (Ibn Muḥmmad Gurdu al-Fulānī) two generations later. Saad, *Social History of Timbuktu*, 67.

68. El Hamel, "Transmission of Islamic Knowledge," 74–76; Pettigrew, "History of Islam in Mauritania," 10.

69. Shinqīṭī, *Wasīṭ fī tarājim udabāʾ shinqīṭ*, 517.

70. Frede, "Arabic Manuscripts," 75–78.

71. Lydon, *On Trans-Saharan Trails*, 217–19, 232–42.

72. The same work claims that Sīdi ʿAlī's own teacher was a grandson of Aḥmad al-Raqqād, and thus makes an indirect claim that by inheriting the authority of Sīdi ʿAlī, Sīdi al-Mukhtār consolidated the lines of biological and spiritual descent within this teaching lineage. But all of these claims, for both biological and educational genealogies, should be interpreted in light of Timothy Cleaveland's evidence that Saharan scholars actively manipulated and rewrote their genealogies as they assumed new social and political roles. Kuntī, *Ṭarāʾif waʾl-talāʾid*, 1:262; Cleaveland, *Becoming Walāta*.

73. Brenner, "Concepts of Ṭarīqa in West Africa," 36–43; Ould Cheikh, "Nomadisme, Islam et pouvoir politique," 396; Nouhi, "Religion and Society," 14.

74. Baṭrān, "Sidi al-Mukhtar al-Kunti," 67–71, 156; see also Baṭrān, "Kunta."

75. McLaughlin, "Sufi, Saint, Sharif," 2–10.

76. Soares, "Rethinking Islam and Muslim Societies."

77. El-Rouayheb, *Islamic Intellectual History*, 150–53. For the expansion of these rural *zāwiyas* during this period, see Cornell, *Realm of the Saint*; for the Nāṣiriyya, see Gutelius, "Path Is Easy" and "Sufi Networks and the Social Contexts."

78. Warscheid, *Droit musulman et société*, 40–43.

79. El-Rouayheb, *Islamic Intellectual History*, 151.

80. Norris, *Ṣūfī Mystics of the Niger Desert*, 1–7.

81. Nouhi, "Religion and Society," 176–213.

82. For the growing importance of the title of *mujaddad* in the region, see Nobili, *Sultan, Caliph, and the Renewer*, 111–14.

83. Kuntī, *Kawkab al-waqqād*, 11; cf. Ibn al-ʿArabī's understanding of the relationship between the prophets and the saints in Chodkiewicz, *Seal of the Saints*.

84. Kuntī, *Kawkab al-waqqād*, 11, 16, 1.

85. Norris, *Ṣūfī Mystics of the Niger Desert*, xvi, 21.

86. A published edition of this text has been provided by Kota Kariya; see Yadālī, "Khātima (fī) al-taṣawwuf"; this text is discussed in Nouhi, "Religion and Society," 180–90.

87. Wright, "Islamic Intellectual Tradition."

88. Hall and Stewart, "Historic 'Core Curriculum,'" 110–11. This increase in the production of local written texts was linked to the increased availability of paper during this period. Lydon, "Thirst for Knowledge," 48, 43.

89. He did this by introducing into the *Tarīkh al-Fattāsh* a legend about the prophesied arrival of a spiritual heir to Askia Muḥammad. For a biography of Nūḥ ibn Ṭāhir and a detailed description of the changes he added to the *Tārikh ibn al-Mukhtār* to produce the *Tārikh al-Fattāsh*, see Nobili, *Sultan, Caliph, and the Renewer*, 84–121.

90. C. Stewart, *Islam and Social Order in Mauritania*; Ould Cheikh, "Tribu comme volonté."

91. Robinson, *Holy War of Umar Tal*, 65.

92. McLaughlin, "Sufi, Saint, Sharif," 84–87; Boubrik, *Saints et société en Islam*, 13.

93. Brenner, "Histories of Religion in Africa," 148–49.

94. Robinson, *Holy War of Umar Tal*, 112.

95. Ould Abdellah, "'Passage au sud,'" 72–84.

96. Syed, "Al-Ḥājj ʿUmar Tāl," 4–5, 60–79; Robinson, *Holy War of Umar Tal*, 94–99.

97. Syed, "Al-Ḥājj ʿUmar Tāl," 75–76; Robinson, "Between Hashimi and Agibu," 106–7.

98. Brenner, "Concepts of Ṭarīqa in West Africa," 49; Robinson, *Holy War of Umar Tal*, 282–83, 303–10.

99. Bashir, *Sufi Bodies*, 9–11; Ernst, "Between Orientalism and Fundamentalism"; Ogunnaike, "Philosophical Sufism in the Sokoto Caliphate," 147.

100. This dynamic has been revealed most recently in revisionist scholarship that emphasizes the erudition of Aḥmad Lobbo and his community and situates ʿUmar Tāl as a scholar who sought to demonstrate mastery through the production of his own written compositions. Nobili, *Sultan, Caliph, and the Renewer*, 141–48; Syed, "Al-Ḥājj ʿUmar Tāl," esp. 24–25.

101. Nobili, "Back to Saharan Myths"; Norris, *Tuaregs*, 19; Kuntī, *Risāla al-ghallāwiyya*, 185–94.

102. Baṭrān, "Sidi al-Mukhtar al-Kunti," 43–45, 52–54, 94–96.

103. Both Marty and Baṭrān present the figure of Sīdi Muḥammad al-Kuntī al-Kabīr as the point at which the history of the Kunta emerges from "legend" into "history." Marty, *Kounta de l'est*, 3–11; Baṭrān, "Sidi al-Mukhtar al-Kunti," 32, 47–48.

104. Baṭrān, "Sidi al-Mukhtar al-Kunti," 34–39, 105–8; Ould Cheikh, "Généalogie et les capitaux flottant."

105. Martin, *Oasis sahariennes*, 122–23.

106. Martin, *Quatre siècles d'histoire marocaine*, 33–34.

107. Whitcomb, "Origins of the Kunta—I" and "Origins of the Kunta—II."

108. El Hamel, *Vie intellectuelle islamique*, 337–40.

109. Shinqīṭī, *Wasīṭ fī tarājim udabāʾ shinqīṭ*, 361.

110. Cleaveland, *Becoming Walāta.*

111. Marty, *Kounta de l'est.*

112. This process mirrors the development of racial categories in the region, as colonial administrators adopted the racial assumptions of self-identified "white" Muslims like the Kunta. Hall, *History of Race.*

113. Baṭrān, "Sidi al-Mukhtar al-Kunti," 105–13.

114. Ibid., 114–17.

115. Ibid., 265–76, 305–11.

116. Ibid., 323–30.

117. Ibid., 330–40.

118. Shinqīṭī, *Wasīṭ fī tarājim udabāʾ shinqīṭ*, 277–83, 361.

119. Ould Abdellah, "'Passage au sud,'" 87.

120. These materials have been analyzed, respectively, in Ibn al-Shaykh Sīdi Bab, *Kitāb al-akhbār*, 1:161–216, and Ould Cheikh, "Man of Letters in Timbuktu."

121. Saad, *Social History of Timbuktu*, 215.

122. Caillié, *Travels Through Central Africa*, 1:44.

123. Ibn al-Shaykh Sīdī Bāb, *Kitāb al-akhbār*, 1:216. Hārūn ibn al-Shaykh Sīdi Bāb's *Kitāb al-akhbār* is based on the manuscript records of his great-grandfather Shaykh Sīdiyya. He provides this date only according to the Gregorian calendar.

124. Ould Cheikh, "Man of Letters in Timbuktu," 237–45. Lovejoy attests to the dominance of the Kel Awayʾ in the Aïr Massif and the Kel Dinnig in the Azawaq. Lovejoy, *Salt of the Desert Sun*, 225.

125. Ould Cheikh, "Man of Letters in Timbuktu," 237–38; Norris, *Arab Conquest of the Western Sahara*, 39–40; Kuntī, *Risāla al-ghallāwiyya.*

CHAPTER 2

1. The three stories appear in Kuntī, *Ṭarāʾif waʾl-talāʾid* (all citations, again, are to the 2013 published version unless otherwise noted), 1:220–21, 1:234–35, and 2:45–46, respectively.

2. Kuntī, *Jidhwat al-anwār*, BNRM 2579k, 7, 13, 15.

3. Chabbi, *Seigneur des tribus*, 124.

4. Meir M. Bar-Asher, "Hidden and the Hidden," *EQ.*

5. Stefania Cunial, "Spiritual Beings," *EQ.* For the transformation of invisible entities from the pre-Islamic to the Qurʾānic context, see Jacqueline Chabbi, "Jinn," *EQ*, and *Seigneur des tribus*, 182–83, 190–95, 221; and Welch, "Allah and Other Supernatural Beings." For the ongoing relevance of the jinn in the modern context, see Siegel, *Shadow and Sound*; Taneja, *Jinnealogy.*

6. Louis Gardet and D. B. MacDonald, "Al-Ghayb," *EI2.*

7. For more in-depth discussion of these philosophical frameworks, see Netton, *Muslim Neoplatonists*; Nasr, *Islamic Cosmological Doctrines*; Fakhry, *History of Islamic Philosophy*; Davidson, *Alfarabi, Avicenna, and Averroes on Intellect.* For a history of the translation of Greek texts into Arabic, see Gutas, *Greek Thought, Arabic Culture.*

8. Orthmann, "Lettrism and Magic in an Early Mughal Text," 228–29; Gardiner, "Stars and Saints," 39–40; Gril, "Science of Letters."

9. Christian Lange describes this eschatological space as an "every-when" that exists, synchronically, alongside life in "this world" (*al-dunyā*). Lange, *Paradise and Hell in Islamic Traditions*, 11–12; see also Louis Gardet, "Ḳiyāma," *EI2.* For a treatment related to Sufism, see Chittick, "Death and the World of Imagination." For the ongoing importance of these ideas in a modern context, see Hirschkind, *Ethical Soundscape*, 173–204.

10. Kuntī, *Jidhwat al-anwār*, BNRM 2579k, 3, 5–6.

11. Ibid., 3–4.

12. For more on the history of these terms, see Wensinck, Ghazālī's *Cosmology and His Mysticism*. See also Louis Gardet, "ʿĀlam," *EI2*; Roger Arnaldez, "Lāhūt and Nāsūt," *EI2*.

13. Nakamura, "Imām Ghazālī's Cosmology Reconsidered," 38–43.

14. Kuntī, *Sharḥ al-qaṣīda al-fayḍiyya*, BNRM 4469d, fol. 15a.

15. The word the Kunta use in this context for heaven or heavens (*samāʾ* or *samawāt*) refers to the region above the earth, "the sky" or "the celestial spheres," and is not the same word they use for heaven in the sense of "paradise" or "the garden" (*al-jinna*).

16. Kuntī, *Jidhwat al-anwār*, BNRM 2579k, 19–20.

17. Ibid., 83, 85.

18. A term mentioned eight times in the Qurʾān: 3:45, 4:172, 7:114, 26:42, 56:11, 56:88, 83:21, 83:28.

19. Toufic Fahd offers an overview of these various angel figures in "Génies, anges et demons en Islam."

20. Literally, a woman whom he could permissibly have married. Kuntī, *Ṭarāʾif wa'l-talāʾid*, 1:236.

21. In this, the Kunta align themselves with the Ashʿarī theological position on angelic inviolability. See Street, "Medieval Islamic Doctrine on the Angels."

22. For more on the relationship between the *jinn* and the devils in Islamic intellectual history, see Fahd, "Génies, anges et demons en Islam."

23. Kuntī, *Khalwa*, fol. 2a–b.

24. Kuntī, *Sharḥ al-qaṣīda al-fayḍiyya*, BNRM 4469, fol. 9b.

25. Kuntī, Kitāb zawāl al-ilbās, Arabe 5452, BnF, fol. 78b.

26. Ibid.

27. Kuntī, *Jidhwat al-anwār*, BNRM 2579k, 2.

28. For more on the relationship between the spirit and the body in Islamic thought, see Bashir, *Sufi Bodies*, 34–35.

29. Kuntī, *Ṭarāʾif wa'l-talāʾid*, 1:96, 98.

30. For an overview of these categories in Ashʿarī Sufi theology, see Murata, *Beauty in Sufism*, 55–68.

31. Kuntī, *Kitāb al-minna*, 14–15.

32. Kuntī, *Fawāʾid nūrāniyya*, MH 12221, fol. 19b.

33. Clément Huart and Joseph Sadan, "Kursī," *EI2*; Arent Jan Wensinck and C. E. Bosworth, "Lawḥ," *EI2*; Gardiner, "Stars and Saints," 49.

34. Kuntī, *Kitāb zawāl al-ilbās*, Arabe 5452, BnF, fol. 79a.

35. Ibid., fol. 78b.

36. For more on the human heart in Sufi intellectual traditions, see Bashir, *Sufi Bodies*, 43–45.

37. Kuntī, *Ṭarāʾif wa'l-talāʾid*, 2:139.

38. Kuntī, *Sharḥ al-qaṣīda al-fayḍiyya*, BNRM 4469d, fol. 5b.

39. For an introduction to the states and stages in Sufi mystical writings, see Sells, *Early Islamic Mysticism*, 97–150, 197–211.

40. Kuntī, *Jidhwat al-anwār*, BNRM 2579k, 55. See also Kuntī, *Sharḥ al-qaṣīda al-fayḍiyya*, BNRM 4469d, fol. 4a.

41. Sells, *Early Islamic Mysticism*, 257–65.

42. Kuntī, *Ṭarāʾif wa'l-talāʾid*, 1:126.

43. Kuntī, *Sharḥ al-qaṣīda al-fayḍiyya*, BNRM 4469d, fols. 13b–14a.

44. Ibid., fol. 14a–b.

45. Kuntī, *Khalwa*, fol. 1b.

46. Kuntī, *Sharḥ al-qaṣīda al-fayḍiyya*, BNRM 4469d, fol. 16b.

47. Davidson, *Alfarabi, Avicenna, and Averroes on Intellect*.

48. Kuntī, *Sharḥ al-qaṣīda al-fayḍiyya*, BNRM 4469d, fol. 14b.

49. Ibid.

50. Ibid., fol. 16a.
51. Ibid., fol. 16b.
52. Ibid., fol. 11b.
53. Ibid., fols. 11b–12a.
54. Ibid., fol. 12b. For more on Abū Yazīd al-Bisṭāmī and his importance to early Islamic mystical thought, see Sells, *Early Islamic Mysticism*, 212–50; and Karamustafa, *Sufism*, 3–6.
55. Kuntī, *Jidhwat al-anwār*, BNRM 2579k, 19.
56. Kuntī, *Sharḥ al-qaṣīda al-fayḍiyya*, BNRM 4469d, fol. 2b.
57. Kuntī, *Kitāb zawāl al-ilbās*, Arabe 5452, BnF, fol. 78b.
58. Kuntī, *Sharḥ al-qaṣīda al-fayḍiyya*, BNRM 4469d, fol. 9b.
59. I have found no further references to this figure in either reference works or the Kunta texts, but the context of the passage indicates that Sīdi al-Mukhtār considers him one of the friends of God.
60. Kuntī, *Sharḥ al-qaṣīda al-fayḍiyya*, BNRM 4469d, fol. 8b.
61. Kuntī, *Ṭarāʾif wa'l-talāʾid*, 1:256.
62. Kuntī, *Kitāb zawāl al-ilbās*, Arabe 5452, BnF, fol. 87a.
63. For a thorough treatment of the topic of formal prayer, its components, and its importance in Islamic thought and history, see Katz, *Prayer in Islamic Thought*.
64. Kuntī, *Jidhwat al-anwār*, BNRM 2579k, 19.
65. Ibid.
66. Kuntī, *Kitāb zawāl al-ilbās*, Arabe 5452, BnF, fol. 78b.
67. Kuntī, *Ṭarāʾif wa'l-talāʾid*, 1:229.
68. Kuntī, *Sharḥ al-qaṣīda al-fayḍiyya*, BNRM 4469d, fol. 9a.
69. Kuntī, *Kitāb zawāl al-ilbās*, Arabe 5452, BnF, fols. 78b–79a.
70. Kuntī, *Sharḥ al-qaṣīda al-fayḍiyya*, BNRM 4469d, fol. 7a–b.
71. Kuntī, *Jidhwat al-anwār*, BNRM 2579k, 54.
72. Ibid.; Kuntī, *Sharḥ al-qaṣīda al-fayḍiyya*, BNRM 4469d, fol. 6a.
73. Kuntī, *Jidhwat al-anwār*, BNRM 2579k, 54.
74. Kuntī, *Sharḥ al-qaṣīda al-fayḍiyya*, BNRM 4469d, fol. 11a.
75. For the metaphor of the polished mirror of the heart in Sufi thought, see Sells, *Mystical Languages of Unsaying*, 63–89.
76. Kuntī, *Ṭarāʾif wa'l-talāʾid*, 1:51.
77. Kuntī, *Jidhwat al-anwār*, BNRM 2579k, 8–9. On al-Khidr, see Arent Jan Wensinck, "Al- K͟haḍir (al-K͟hiḍr)," *EI2*.
78. See, for example, Karamustafa, *Sufism*, 42, 46, 127–28.
79. The authors of regional biographical dictionaries followed Sīdī Muḥammad in referring to Sīdī al-Mukhtār as the *ghawth* of his age. See El Hamel, *Vie intellectuelle islamique*, 337; Shinqīṭī, *Wasīṭ fī tarājim udabāʾ shinqīṭ*, 361.
80. Kuntī, *Jidhwat al-anwār*, BNRM 2579k, 89.
81. Kuntī, *Kitāb zawāl al-ilbās*, Arabe 5452, BnF, fol. 79a.
82. Kuntī, *Ṭarāʾif wa'l-talāʾid*, 1:58.

CHAPTER 3

1. See Otto, "Towards Historicizing 'Magic' in Antiquity" and "Historicising 'Western Learned Magic.'"
2. The term "double gesture" comes from Bever and Styers, "Introduction," 3–4. Bever and Styers draw on earlier work by Pels, who also locates this relationship between magic and science as a function of modernity. Pels, "Introduction."
3. Kuntī, *Ṭarāʾif wa'l-talāʾid*, 2:135, hereafter cited parenthetically in the text in this chapter. Again, all citations of this text are to the 2013 published version unless otherwise noted.
4. The 2013 edition edited by Yaḥyā Ould Sayyid Aḥmad spells this word *al-sīmiyā*, which is closer to the standard orthography of *al-sīmiyāʾ*. However, both manuscripts consulted in

this study spell it *al-sīmā* (السيما), which seems to reflect local orthography. Kuntī, *Ṭarāʾif wa'l-talāʾid*, 1:96; compare Arabe 5334, BnF, fol. 13a, and Arabe 6755, BnF, fol. 26b. Sīdi Muḥammad's definition of *al-sīmā/al-sīmiyāʾ* is notably different from earlier definitions. Prior to the thirteenth century, *al-sīmiyāʾ* was associated with the use of seals and talismans, while thirteenth-century writers such as Ibn al-ʿArabī and al-Būnī increasingly associated *al-sīmiyāʾ* with the science of letters and the use of powerful words. Coulon, *Magie en terre d'Islam*, 103, 145, 213–14.

5. El Hamel, *Vie intellectuelle islamique*, 367–69; Shinqīṭī, *Wasīṭ fī tarājim udabāʾ shinqīṭ*, 37–38.

6. The term *firāsa* is sometimes used in Arabic texts to refer to physiognomy, "the technique of reading people's character (and sometimes even their future actions) on the basis of physical appearance," but this is clearly not the meaning that Sīdi Muḥammad ascribes to the term. Mavroudi, "Islamic Divination," 225.

7. For a detailed analysis of this work, see Marcus-Sells, "Science, Sorcery, and Secrets."

8. Kuntī, *Fawāʾid nūrāniyya*, MH 12221, fol. 20a–b.

9. Ibid., fol. 20a; the insertion "for what He wishes" is found only in BNRM 209d, fol. 198a.

10. Kuntī, *Fawāʾid nūrāniyya*, MH 12221, fol. 19b.

11. This could also be translated as "the spirits of *al-mulk*" if it is read as *arwāḥ al-mulkiyya* rather than *arwāḥ al-malakiyya*.

12. Kuntī, *Fawāʾid nūrāniyya*, MH 12221, fol. 19b.

13. Ibid. Another version of this passage can be found in Kuntī, *Ṭarāʾif wa'l-talāʾid*, 2:176.

14. Kuntī, *Fawāʾid nūrāniyya*, MH 12221, fol. 20b.

15. Gimaret, *Noms divins en Islam*; Ibrahim-Lizzio and González, "Al-Asma al-Husna"; Gerhard Böwering, "God and His Attributes," *EQ*.

16. Gimaret, *Noms divins en Islam*, 87.

17. Ibn al-Ṣabbāgh, *Mystical Teachings of al-Shadhili*, 75; Wright, "Secrets on the Muhammadan Way," 89–93.

18. Kuntī, *Fawāʾid nūrāniyya*, MH 12221, fol. 19a. Other variations include "the greatest name is that which, if He is called by it, He answers, and if He is asked by it, He gives" (ibid., fol. 36b), and "the name by which, if you call Him by it, He answers" (*Ṭarāʾif wa'l-talāʾid*, 2:190).

19. Kuntī, *Fawāʾid nūrāniyya*, MH 12221, fols. 23b–24a.

20. Ibid., fol. 24a.

21. Ibid., fols. 33a, 36a–b.

22. Ibid., fols. 31b–32b.

23. Ibid., fol. 32a.

24. Ibid., fol. 31b.

25. Historians often refer to these symbols as "the seven signs" or "the seven seals of Solomon," although the Kunta do not use either of these designations. Porter, Saif, and Savage-Smith, "Medieval Islamic Amulets," 541–42; Canaan, "Decipherment of Arabic Talismans," 169–70. The most thorough research on these symbols can be found in the works of Lloyd D. Graham. Note that this exact table can be found in a nineteenth-century Ottoman manuscript. See Lloyd D. Graham, "The Seven Seals of Judeo-Islamic Magic: Possible Origins of the Symbols" (2012), 7, https://www.academia.edu/1509428/The_Seven_Seals_of_Judeo-Islamic_Magic_Possible_Origins_of_the_Symbols; Lloyd D. Graham, "Qurʾānic Spell-Ing: Disconnected Letter Series in Islamic Talismans" (2011), 11–14, https://www.academia.edu/516626/Qur_anic_Spell-ing_Disconnected_Letter_Series_in_Islamic_Talismans. Some of these characters continue to be used in talismanic rings, seals, and pendants in Mali; see Lloyd D. Graham, "The Magic Symbol Repertoire of Talismanic Rings from East and West Africa" (2014), https://hcommons.org/deposits/item/hc:32405/.

26. Savage-Smith, "Introduction," xxv–xxvii; Sesiano, "Construction of Magic Squares"; Jacques Sesiano, "Wafḳ," *EI2*; Muehlhaeusler, "Math and Magic."

27. Kuntī, *Fawāʾid nūrāniyya*, MH 12221, fol. 33b.

28. Ibid., fol. 30b.

29. Kuntī, *Fawā'id nūrāniyya*, BNRM 209d, fols. 33a, 36a.

30. The BNRM witness reads: "compel the forms to your servant [ʿ*abīdika*]." Ibid., fol. 215b.

31. Kuntī, *Fawā'id nūrāniyya*, MH 12221, fol. 38a–b.

32. Ibid., fols. 39a–46a.

33. Van Bladel, *Arabic Hermes*; Kevin van Bladel, "Hermes and Hermetica," *EI3*.

34. O'Brien, "Spirit Discipline"; Toufic Fahd, "Rukya," *EI2*.

35. Fierro, "Polemic About the Karāmāt al-Awliyā"; Zadeh, "Magic, Marvel, and Miracle," 246–47.

36. Louis Gardet, "Allāh," *EI2*.

37. See also Kuntī, *Jidhwat al-anwār*, BNRM 2579k, 6. This understanding of *istadrāj* adheres to Ashʿarī typologies of different kinds of breakings of the norm as described in Brown, "Faithful Dissenters," 134.

38. Louis Gardet, "Dhikr," *EI2*.

39. In medieval Islamic treatises, the *khawāṣṣ* were often linked to the celestial spheres, a connection that Sīdi Muḥammad does not discuss. Manfred Ullman, "Khāssa," *EI2*; Gannagé, "Between Medicine and Natural Philosophy"; Saif, "Ġāyat al-Ḥakīm to Šams al-Maʿārif," 300.

40. This term usually appears in Arabic textual traditions as *khaṭṭ al-raml*, which is often translated as "geomancy" and refers to an astrological process of divining the future by drawing lines in the sand. For the development of this discipline within Islamic intellectual traditions and its spread to sub-Saharan Africa, see Brenner, "Muslim Divination."

41. Reading omens from the flight of birds is more commonly referred to as *al-ṭayr* or *al-ṭīr* in Arabic texts. Sīdi Muḥammad does refer once to *al-ṭayra* in the context of prohibited practices associated with the *jāhiliyya*, but he does not define it. *Ṭarāʾif wa'l-talāʾid*, 2:181.

42. Smith, *Map Is Not Territory*, 294.

43. Kim, "Max Weber."

44. Hanegraaff, "How Magic Survived"; Asprem, *Problem of Disenchantment*; Josephson-Storm, *Myth of Disenchantment*.

45. Bever and Styers, "Introduction," 3–4; Bever and Styers build on earlier work in Meyer and Pels, *Magic and Modernity*.

46. Wright, "Islamic Intellectual Tradition," 62–63.

47. Wright, "Islamic Esotericism in West Africa."

48. One magic square inscribed on the foundation of a house included a date of 519/1125–26 but was found in a layer deposited at a much later date. Roderick McIntosh has thus expressed uncertainty regarding the date of the deposits. McIntosh, *Ancient Middle Niger*, 179–80; see also 161.

49. Levtzion, "Patterns of Islamization in West Africa"; Brooks, *Landlords and Strangers*, 115–19, 61–77; Loimeier, *Muslim Societies in Africa*, 96–103.

50. Sanneh, *Jakhanke Muslim Clerics*, esp. 158–59, 181–213. See also Wright, *Living Knowledge in West African Islam*, 47–48.

51. Wilks, "Transmission of Islamic Learning," 177–78; Sanneh, *Jakhanke Muslim Clerics*, 2, 15–21; Loimeier, *Muslim Societies in Africa*, 105–7.

52. Wilks, *Northern Factor in Ashanti History*, 15, 20–21; Loimeier, *Muslim Societies in Africa*, 101–3.

53. Owusu-Ansah, "Islamic Influence in a Forest Kingdom," 117–30.

54. For the history of Sonni ʿAlī, the rise of the Songhay Empire, and Askia Muḥammad's revolt, see Hunwick's commentary in Maghīlī, *Sharīʿa in Songhay*, 3–28; and Saʿdī, *Timbuktu and the Songhay Empire*, xxxviii–xliv.

55. Maghīlī, *Sharīʿa in Songhay*, 72. This exchange between al-Maghīlī and Askia Muḥammad revolves almost entirely around the distinctions among good Muslims, bad Muslims, and non-Muslims. In his first question, the Askia presents the problem of scholars "who are reputed to be learned" but "[understand] nothing of the Arabic language . . . [and] do not understand the arguments of the scholars" (60–61). In his response, al-Maghīlī admits that

false "scholars and pietists (*ʿubbād*)" have spread corruption through the community, but he rejects the possibility of a complete vacuum of correct religious knowledge (64). According to al-Maghīlī, God ensures that guides appear to every community of believing Muslims to lead them in proper behavior, that these guides are manifestly distinct from corrupt scholars, and that it is the duty of every Muslim ruler to seek them out and question them concerning every action. This text marks the earliest written evidence in West Africa for the idea that God sends specific guides, or "renewers," to lead each community of Muslims, an idea that Sīdi al-Mukhtār and Sīdi Muḥammad expand on centuries later (see chapter 1).

56. Ibid., 89. I have made slight changes to John Hunwick's translation of this passage (see Arabic text on p. 39).

57. Ibid., 91.

58. See Hunwick's introductory commentary on al-Maghilī's text in ibid., 32–39.

59. This is how al-Kashnāwī wrote his own name, adding the *nisbas* "al-Ashʿarī al-Mālikī," but there are many variations on his name in the Arabic sources. Gubara, "Al-Azhar and the Orders of Knowledge," 249n5. Bivar and Hiskett call him "Muḥammad ibn Muḥammad al-Fulānī al-Katsināwī" in "Arabic Literature of Nigeria," 135.

60. Gubara, "Al-Azhar and the Orders of Knowledge," 333. For earlier work on al-Kashnāwī, see Gwarzo, "Theory of Chronograms"; Bivar and Hiskett, "Arabic Literature of Nigeria," 135–37.

61. There is some scholarly debate surrounding the figure of Muḥammad al-Wālī, particularly concerning the attribution to him of a poem titled *Rāʾīyah fī dhamm al-Munajjimīm* that attacks astrology, the science of letters, and the science of magic squares. Brenner has suggested either that the attribution was inaccurate or that al-Wālī was attacking only those who abused these sciences. Gubara follows the latter hypothesis and accepts the attribution of this poem to al-Wālī. Meanwhile, Dorrit van Dalen follows the former interpretation and believes that the poem should be attributed to ʿUthmān ibn Fūdī. For Van Dalen, al-Wālī was not engaged (as either supporter or critic) in astrology, magic squares, or the science of letters, but dedicated most of his career to the discipline of theology (*kalām*). Brenner, "Three Fulbe Scholars in Borno," 110; Gubara, "Al-Azhar and the Orders of Knowledge," 260–61, 320–22; Van Dalen, *Doubt, Scholarship, and Society*, 65–68.

62. Gubara, "Al-Azhar and the Orders of Knowledge," 258–62; Bivar and Hiskett, "Arabic Literature of Nigeria," 136n5.

63. Gubara, "Al-Azhar and the Orders of Knowledge," 321.

64. Ibid., 263–65. While the attribution of *al-Sirr al-maktūm* was previously debated, Michael-Sebastian Noble has definitely identified al-Rāzī as the author. His thorough analysis of this text was published during the final preparation of this manuscript. Noble, *Philosophising the Occult.*

65. Gubara, "Al-Azhar and the Orders of Knowledge," 324; Toufic Fahd, "Nīrandj," *EI2*.

66. Gubara, "Al-Azhar and the Orders of Knowledge," 327.

67. Ibid., 328–33.

68. See also Kani, "Arithmetic in Pre-Colonial Central Sudan," 35.

69. Wright, *Living Knowledge in West African Islam*, 233–34; see also Wright, "Secrets on the Muhammadan Way," esp. 88–90.

70. Marcus-Sells, "Science, Sorcery, and Secrets," 454–59.

71. Wright, *Living Knowledge in West African Islam*, 235–39; Wright, "Secrets on the Muhammadan Way," 88.

72. Soares, *Islam and the Prayer Economy*, 127–52.

73. Last, "Note on Attitudes to the Supernatural," 6–7. Last's article is outdated in that he associates these disciplines with "the irrational," applies the term "magic" to all the disciplines under discussion, and makes repeated uncritical references to synchronism with Hausa practices. However, he also cites specific textual evidence for ʿUthmān ibn Fūdī's and Muḥammad Bello's rejection of these first-order disciplines.

74. Ogunnaike, "Philosophical Sufism in the Sokoto Caliphate," 145–46.

75. Ibid., 149. I am indebted to Dr. Ogunnaike for sharing with me an early version of this chapter and for clarifying the technical Arabic terms that Dan Tafa used in the text.

76. Pettigrew, "Heart of the Matter."

77. Stratton, *Naming the Witch* and "Early Greco-Roman Antiquity."

78. Otto, "Towards Historicizing 'Magic' in Antiquity."

79. Otto, "Historicising 'Western Learned Magic.'"

80. Otto notes that this topic remains underinvestigated. Ibid., 184.

81. Toufic Fahd, "Siḥr," *EI2*.

82. For Abū Maʿshar, see Saif, *Arabic Influences*, 9–26; Charles Burnett, "Abū Maʿshar," *EI3*.

83. Saif, *Arabic Influences*, 17, 27–31, 36–37; see also Burnett, "Al-Kindī on Judicial Astrology."

84. Saif, "Ikhwān al-Ṣafāʾ's Religious Reform" and "Ġāyat al-Ḥakīm to Šams al-Maʿārif," 303–8; De Callataÿ, *Ikhwan al-Safa* and "Classification of Knowledge"; Netton, *Muslim Neoplatonists*.

85. Saif, "Ġāyat al-Ḥakīm to Šams al-Maʿārif," 306. Saif clarifies: "Despite the personal names and prescribed invocations . . . the *rūḥāniyyāt* must be perceived as tools that impel volitional forces to facilitate natural processes for the benefit of the operator. . . . These must remain distinct from those (supernatural) beings, referred to as jinn and devils, who belong 'to a mysterious world that cannot be seen, [and who] breed and die'" (308).

86. Saif, *Arabic Influences*, 37. A new translation of the Latin version, known in the West as "Picatrix," has recently been published as Attrell and Porreca, *Picatrix*; the correct attribution for this text was determined by Maribel Fierro. See Fierro, "Bāṭinism in al-Andalus."

87. Saif, *Arabic Influences*, 27–28. Centuries later, medieval European practitioners of "image magic" used the same defense, classifying their knowledge/practices as natural science even as their critics accused them of demonic activities. Klaassen, *Transformations of Magic*; Collins, "Learned Magic"; Bailey, "Diabolic Magic."

88. Coulon, *Magie en terre d'Islam*, 162–65.

89. Saif, *Arabic Influences*, 22–26, and "Ġāyat al-Ḥakīm to Šams al-Maʿārif," 315.

90. However, magic discourses of inclusion during this period may have shifted to other terms, such as *nīranj*, or into other linguistic spheres, such as Persian.

91. Coulon, *Magie en terre d'Islam*, 176. Coulon cites Ibn Taymiyya and al-Shaʿrānī (d. 1565) as examples of this trend, although it should be noted that some scholars would not identify Ibn Taymiyya as a Sufi.

92. The date of al-Būnī's death is usually given as 1225 or 1232, but Noah Gardiner's careful work with the Būnian manuscript corpus has revealed problems with both of these dates. Gardiner, "Forbidden Knowledge," 89–93, 102–3; see also Constant Hamès, "Al-Būnī," *EI3*.

93. Melvin-Koushki, "Powers of One"; Burak, "Section on Prayers," 342.

94. Coulon, *Magie en terre d'Islam*, 173.

95. Ebstein and Sviri, "So-Called Risālat al-Ḥurūf," 214; Casewit, *Mystics of al-Andalus*, 33–39, 136–57.

96. Coulon, *Magie en terre d'Islam*, 189.

97. Ibid., 211–12; Casewit, *Mystics of al-Andalus*, 4.

98. Saif, "Ġāyat al-Ḥakīm to Šams al-Maʿārif," 323–24; Lory, "Symbolism of Letters and Language"; Gril, "Science of Letters."

99. See Gril's commentary in "Science of Letters," 123.

100. Lory, "Symbolism of Letters and Language," unpaginated.

101. Saif, "Ġāyat al-Ḥakīm to Šams al-Maʿārif," 333.

102. Gardiner, "Forbidden Knowledge," 94. For an excellent analysis of operational lettrism in al-Būnī's works, see Saif, "Ġāyat al-Ḥakīm to Šams al-Maʿārif," 333–34.

103. Coulon, *Magie en terre d'Islam*, 222.

104. Ibid.; Gardiner, "Forbidden Knowledge," 98–99, 103–10.

105. Saif, "Ġāyat al-Ḥakīm to Šams al-Maʿārif," 344.

106. Coulon, *Magie en terre d'Islam*, 215.

107. Astrological works falsely attributed to Ibn al-ʿArabī did circulate after his death. Morris, "Ibn ʿArabi and His Interpreters," 741n19.

108. Coulon, *Magie en terre d'Islam*, 190–91. For the presence of this attribution in West Africa, see Kane, *Beyond Timbuktu*, 92; Ogunnaike, "Ousmane Oumar Kane."

109. Gardiner, "Forbidden Knowledge," 123–29; Saif, "Ġāyat al-Ḥakīm to Šams al-Maʿārif," 334. Published well before scholars concluded that this work was a seventeenth-century forgery, all of Pierre Lory's conclusions about al-Būnī's understanding of the sciences of the letters (see Lory, "Magie des lettres") can be accurately applied to the unknown authors of the *Shams al-maʿārif al-kubrā*.

110. Kuntī, *Fawāʾid nūrāniyya*, MH 12221, fol. 28a.

111. Compare ibid., fols. 29b–31a, to Coulon, "Building al-Būnī's Legend," 17–19.

112. Coulon, "Building al-Būnī's Legend."

113. F. C. de Blois, "Al-Ṭug̲h̲rāʾī," *EI2*.

114. Būnī, *Kitāb Laṭāʾif al-ishārāt*, fol. 13a. Both Noah Gardiner and Jean-Charles Coulon accept the attribution of this text to al-Būnī. Gardiner, "Forbidden Knowledge," 96; Coulon, *Magie en terre d'Islam*, 220–23.

115. Soares, *Islam and the Prayer Economy*, 129–31, 134–37.

CHAPTER 4

1. Kuntī, *Fawāʾid nūrāniyya*, MH 12221, fol. 24b.

2. Katz, *Prayer in Islamic Thought*, 30–31.

3. For the overlap and relationship between these various genres, see McGregor, "Sufi Legacy in Tunis," 263–71; Padwick, *Muslim Devotions*, 12–25; Louis Gardet, "Duʿāʾ" and "Dhikr," both in *EI2*; Hamid Algar, "Doʿā," *EIr*; F. M. Denny, "Wird," *EI2*. Kunta devotional texts—including *adhkār*, *adʿiyya*, and *aḥzāb*—were often compiled together in untitled collections.

4. Padwick, *Muslim Devotions*, 152–66; Puente, "Prayer upon the Prophet Muhammad."

5. I have identified twenty-eight manuscript witnesses to the *Nafḥat al-ṭīb*, in contrast to fifteen witnesses to the *Fawāʾid nūrāniyya* and twenty to the *Ṭarāʾif wa'l-talāʾid*. This work has previously been misidentified as a *sira* text (a biography of the prophet); see Hall and Stewart, "Historic 'Core Curriculum,'" 125, 161; Kane, *Beyond Timbuktu*, 86.

6. Excellent examples include Bowen, *Muslims Through Discourse*; Flueckiger, *In Amma's Healing Room*; and Doostdar, *Iranian Metaphysicals*.

7. Barber, *Anthropology of Texts*, 22.

8. Finnegan, "How of Literature," 168–69.

9. Toufic Fahd, W. P. Heinrichs, and Ben Abdesselem, "Sad̲j̲ʿ," *EI2*. For the oral context of the Qurʾān, see Graham, *Beyond the Written Word*.

10. Fahd, Heinrichs, and Abdesselem, "Sad̲j̲ʿ," *EI2*. Samer Ali has provided a refreshing discussion of private literary salons (*mujālasāt*) that served as the oral performative stage for both professional and amateur litterateurs in the medieval period. Ali, *Arabic Literary Salons*, esp. 3–5, 15–32.

11. Merolla, "Orality and Technauriture," 80–81; Finnegan, "How of Literature," 173–75.

12. Lydon, "Inkwells of the Sahara," 52–62; Hall and Stewart, "Historic 'Core Curriculum.'"

13. Writing in the late nineteenth century, al-Shinqīṭī boasted that all men and women among the clerical lineages learned to read and write (see chapter 1). *Wasīṭ fī tarājim udabāʾ shinqīṭ*, 517.

14. A reference to the vision depicted in Qurʾān 53:6–9, in which something "draws near . . . two bows' length away."

15. A reference to Qurʾān 21:18: "We hurl the truth against falsehood."

16. This name is spelled "Bāl'ām" (with an *alif* after the *bā'*) in this witness of the *Ḥizb sīdī al-mukhtār*, but in *Khalwa* the name is spelled "Bal'ām." For consistency, I have adopted the latter orthography throughout.

17. Kuntī, *Ḥizb sīdī al-mukhtār*, 250–53.

18. This episode takes Qur'ān 7:172 as its reference. See, for example, Tustarī, *Tafsīr al-Tustarī*, 68.

19. Kuntī, *Nafḥat al-ṭīb*, 4. All citations of the *Nafḥat al-ṭīb* refer to Ould Wadādī's 1990 published edition unless otherwise noted.

20. Awn, *Satan's Tragedy and Redemption.*

21. Kuntī, *Ṭarā'if wa'l-talā'id*, 2:148–49.

22. Ibid., 1:228.

23. For an analysis of this work, along with a transcription and translation of the text, see Marcus-Sells, "Poised on the Higher Horizon."

24. Sīdi al-Mukhtār and Sīdi Muḥammad traced their spiritual lineage (*silsila*) to the Prophet Muḥammad back through al-Jīlānī, who correspondingly features frequently in their writings.

25. Kuntī, *Khalwa*, fol. 1b.

26. This sentence literally reads: "He did not set in the west beneath the ground of the west," and it plays with the verb *khaḍa'a*, which means both "to be humble" and "to set," as in "the sun sets in the west."

27. Kuntī, *Khalwa*, fol. 2b.

28. Tha'labī, *'Arā'is al-majālis*, 392–96; Ṭabarī, *Children of Israel*, 91–95.

29. For an overview of issues concerning the *taṣliyya*, see Puente, "Prayer upon the Prophet Muhammad"; and Padwick, *Muslim Devotions*, 152–64.

30. Kuntī, *Rawḍ al-khaṣīb*, 7.

31. Ibid., 7–8.

32. This description of the four quarters follows the arrangement in the printed version edited by Muḥammad Maḥmūd Ould Wadādī and published in 1990 (hereafter cited parenthetically in the text). Ould Wadādī's edition reverses the order of the "second" and "third" quarters found in the manuscript witnesses consulted for this study. One witness, Manuscrits Orientaux, Arabe 5675, BnF, fols. 28b–58a, is also marked according to "thirds."

33. Kuntī, *Rawḍ al-khaṣīb*. Additional manuscript witnesses will be required to determine whether this copy is incomplete or whether the work ends at this point.

34. Werner Caskel, "'Adnān," *EI2*; Giorgio Levi Della Vida, "Nizār b. Ma'add," *EI2*.

35. Another line in the *Nafḥat al-ṭīb* specifies that the birth of Muḥammad was prophesied in the Torah. Kuntī, *Nafḥat al-ṭīb*, 18.

36. Caskel, "'Adnān," *EI2*; A. Fischer and A. K. Irvine, "Ḳaḥṭān," *EI2*.

37. This refers to a *ḥadīth* in which the prophet says, "I have been sent to all the red and the black" (Saḥīḥ Muslim book 4, *ḥadīth* 1058). Classical commentators sometimes interpreted "the red" to mean non-Arabs (whose skin turned red in the sun) and "the black" to mean Arabs (whose skin was darkened by the sun). This *ḥadīth* might also have had local resonance, as the Tuareg today sometimes refer to themselves as "red." Hall, *History of Race*, 6.

38. Kuntī, *Fawā'id nūrāniyya*, MH 12221, fol. 38a–b.

39. I established the word *Hādī* by reference to a different manuscript witness—BNRM 209d, fol. 218a.

40. Kuntī, *Fawā'id nūrāniyya*, MH 12221, fols. 41b–42a.

41. Saif, "Ġāyat al-Ḥakīm to Šams al-Ma'ārif," 341–42.

42. Kuntī, *Fawā'id nūrāniyya*, MH 12221, fol. 42a–b.

43. Ibid., fol. 29a.

44. Noah Gardiner has described similar practices used to limit the circulation of works among the followers of Aḥmad al-Būnī. Gardiner, "Esotericist Reading Communities."

45. Kuntī, *Fawā'id nūrāniyya*, MH 12221, fol. 19b.

46. Kuntī, *Ḥizb sīdī al-mukhtār*, 250.

47. Kuntī, *Ṭarā'if wa'l-talā'id*, 1:218.

48. Published in facing Arabic and English translation as Jazūlī, *Guide to Goodness*.

49. For al-Jazūlī's life, works, and influence, see Cornell, *Realm of the Saint*, 155–271; Mohamed Bencheneb, "Al-Djazūlī," *EI2*.

50. The wide circulation of copies of the *Dalā'il al-khayrāt* is attested to in Witkam, "Battle of the Images"; Cornell, *Realm of the Saint*, 157; Padwick, *Muslim Devotions*, 163; and Trimingham, *Sufi Orders in Islam*, 85–86; for the *Dalā'il al-khayrāt* in West African manuscript traditions, see Johnson, "Amuletic Manuscript"; Hall and Stewart, "Historic 'Core Curriculum,'" 126.

51. Witkam, "Battle of the Images," 69.

52. Jazūlī, *Guide to Goodness*, 62–63. This and other translations from the *Dalā'il al-khayrāt* are based on the translations in Rosowsky's edition, which I have modified.

53. Ibid., 90–93.

54. Ibid., 80–81.

55. Ibid., 94–97.

56. Padwick, *Muslim Devotions*, 163–65.

57. For example, Jazūlī, *Guide to Goodness*, 32–35, 66–67, 102–5.

58. Puente, "Prayer upon the Prophet Muhammad," 124; Padwick, *Muslim Devotions*, 167.

59. Jazūlī, *Guide to Goodness*, 62–65; see also Cornell, *Realm of the Saint*, 175–76.

60. As Vincent Cornell suggests in *Realm of the Saint*, 175.

61. Sells, *Early Islamic Mysticism*, 11, 89–96; Böwering, *Mystical Vision of Existence*.

62. D. Stewart, "Prophecy," 299–300.

63. Jazūlī, *Guide to Goodness*, 102–3.

64. Ibid., 47.

65. Wright, "Secrets on the Muhammadan Way."

66. For the presence of the *Dalā'il al-khayrāt*, *Al-'Ishrīnīyāt*, and *Al-Burda* in the "core curriculum" for the region, see Hall and Stewart, "Historic 'Core Curriculum,'" 125–28.

67. There are various manuscript witnesses to these commentaries, including Fūdī, *Sharḥ ḥizb al-baḥr*"; Muḥammad, *Sharḥ ḥizb al-baḥr*; and Aḥmad, *Sharḥ ḥizb al-baḥr*.

68. Translation adapted from Ibn al-Ṣabbāgh, *Mystical Teachings of al-Shadhili*, 75–78.

69. Ibid., 75.

70. Syed, "Al-Ḥājj 'Umar Tāl," 118–31; Ogunnaike, *Poetry in Praise of Prophetic Perfection*, 96–100; Hiskett, "Material Relating to the State of Learning," 563; Hunwick, "'Uthmān b. Fodiye's So-Called 'ishrīniyya."

71. For a thorough treatment of al-Busīrī's poem, see Stetkevych, *Mantle Odes*, 90–147; and Thomas Emil Homerin, "Al-Būṣīrī," *EI2*. For the relevance of al-Būṣīrī's poem to West Africa, see Hunwick, "Arabic Literary Tradition of Nigeria," 217; and Hiskett, *History of Hausa Islamic Verse*, 43–44.

72. Ogunnaike, *Poetry in Praise of Prophetic Perfection*, 125–28.

CONCLUSION

1. Pettigrew, "Muslim Healing, Magic, and Amulets," 112. The saying is also recorded in Kane, *Beyond Timbuktu*, 60, 93.

2. Scheele, *Smugglers and Saints of the Sahara*, 161.

3. Ibid., 162.

4. Pettigrew, "Muslim Healing, Magic, and Amulets," 9, 112–15.

BIBLIOGRAPHY

UNPUBLISHED PRIMARY SOURCES

Aḥmad, Aḥmad ibn. *Sharḥ ḥizb al-baḥr.* Manuscrits Orientaux, Arabe 5355, BnF.

Bakkā'ī, Aḥmad al-. Letter to 'Umar Tāl. Manuscrits Orientaux, Arabe 5259, fols. 66a–68b, BnF.

Būnī, Abū al-'Abbās Aḥmad ibn 'Alī al-. *Kitāb Laṭā'if al-ishārāt fī asrār al-ḥurūf al-'ulwiyya.* Manuscrits Orientaux, Arabe 2657, BnF.

Fūdī, Muḥammad ibn 'Uthmān al-. *Sharḥ ḥizb al-baḥr.* MS 394, Institut des hautes études et de recherches islamiques Ahmed Baba, Timbuktu, Mali.

Kuntī, Muḥammad ibn al-Mukhtār al-. *Fawā'id nūrāniyya wa farā'id sirriyya raḥmāniyya.* Hamdan Diadié Bocoum 04, Bibliothèque des manuscripts de Djenne, Djenne, Mali.

———. *Fawā'id nūrāniyya wa farā'id sirriyya raḥmāniyya.* MS 209d, BNRM.

———. *Fawā'id nūrāniyya wa farā'id sirriyya raḥmāniyya.* MS 12221, MH.

———. *Al-Rawḍ al-khaṣīb fī sharḥ nafḥat al-ṭīb.* MS 164k, BNRM.

———. *Al-Ṭarā'if wa'l-talā'id min karāmāt al-shaykhayn al-wālida wa'l-wālid.* Manuscrits Orientaux, Arabe 5334, BnF.

———. *Al-Ṭarā'if wa'l-talā'id min karāmāt al-shaykhayn al-wālida wa'l-wālid.* Manuscrits Orientaux, Arabe 6755, BnF.

Kuntī, Al-Mukhtār ibn Aḥmad ibn Abī Bakr al-. *Ḥizb al-isrā'.* MS 77/3, Charles C. Stewart Papers, University of Illinois Archives, Urbana, IL.

———. *Ḥizb al-nūr.* MS 1130, MH.

———. *Ḥizb sīdī al-mukhtār al-kuntī.* MS 1053, MH.

———. *Jidhwat al-anwār fī dhabb 'an munāṣib awlīyā' allāh al-khiyār.* December 20, 1825. Manuscrits Orientaux, Arabe 5429, BnF.

———. *Jidhwat al-anwār fī dhabb 'an munāṣib awlīyā' allāh al-khiyār.* 1849. MS 2579k, BNRM.

———. *Jidhwat al-anwār fī dhabb 'an munāṣib awlīyā' allāh al-khiyār.* 1858. Cheik Zani Baye Library, African and Middle Eastern Division, U.S. Library of Congress, Washington, DC. http://memory.loc.gov/intldl/malihtml//malihome.html.

———. *Al-kawkab al-waqqād fī dhikr faḍl al-mashāyik wa ḥaqīqat al-awrād.* MS 2644, Institut mauritanien de recherche scientifique, Nouakchott, Mauritania.

———. *Khalwa.* MS 61/10, Charles C. Stewart Papers, University of Illinois Archives, Urbana, IL.

———. *Kitāb al-minna fī 'itiqād ahl al-sunna.* MS 2573d, BNRM.

———. *Kitāb zawāl al-ilbās wa ṭard wasāwas al-khannās.* November 30, 1865. MS 62/7, Charles C. Stewart Papers, University of Illinois Archives, Urbana, IL.

———. *Kitāb zawāl al-ilbās wa ṭard wasāwas al-khannās.* April 12, 1830. Manuscrits Orientaux, Arabe 5452, BnF.

———. *Nafḥat al-ṭīb fī'l-salāt 'alā'l-nabī al-ḥabīb.* Manuscrits Orientaux, Arabe 5519, BnF.

———. *Nafḥat al-ṭīb fī'l-salāt 'alā'l-nabī al-ḥabīb.* Manuscrits Orientaux, Arabe 5675, BnF.

———. *Sharḥ al-qaṣīda al-fayḍiyya*. MS 502, Library of the Great Mosque of Meknes, Meknes, Morocco.
———. *Sharḥ al-qaṣīda al-fayḍiyya*. MS 4469d, BNRM.
———. Untitled. Manuscrits Orientaux, Arabe 5623, BnF.
Muḥammad, Aḥmad ibn. *Sharḥ ḥizb al-baḥr*. Manuscrits Orientaux, Arabe 4296, BnF.

PUBLISHED PRIMARY SOURCES

Caillié, René. *Travels Through Central Africa to Timbuctoo, and Across the Great Desert, to Morocco, Performed in the Years 1824–1828*. 2 vols. London: Frank Cass, 1968.
El Hamel, Chouki. *La vie intellectuelle islamique dans le Sahel ouest-africain, XVI–XIX siècles: Une étude sociale de l'enseignement islamique en Mauritanie et au nord du Mali (XVI–XIX siècles) et traduction annotée de Fatḥ ash-shakūr d'al-Bartilī al-Walātī (mort en 1805)*. Paris: L'Harmattan, 2002.
Gril, Denis, trans. "The Science of Letters." In *The Meccan Revelations*, by Muḥyī al-Dīn ibn al-ʿArabī. Edited by Michel Chodkiewicz, 2 vols., 2:105–219. New York: Pir Press, 2004.
Houdas, O. *Tedzkiret En-Nisiān fī Akhbār Molouk as-Soudān*. Paris: Librairie de la Société Asiatique, 1901.
Hunwick, John O., and Fatima Harrak, trans. *Miʿrāj al-Ṣuʿūd: Aḥmad Bābā's Replies on Slavery*. Rabat: Institut des Études Africaines, Université Mohamed V, 2000.
Ibn al-Ṣabbāgh, Muḥammad ibn Abī al-Qāsim. *The Mystical Teachings of al-Shadhili: Including His Life, Prayers, Letters, and Followers; A Translation from the Arabic of Ibn al-Sabbagh's Durrat al-Asrar Wa Tuhfat al-Abrar*. Edited by Ibrahim M. Abu-Rabiʿ. Translated by Elmer H. Douglas. SUNY Series in Islam. Albany: State University of New York Press, 1993.
Ibn al-Shaykh Sīdī Bāb ibn al-Shaykh Sīdī Muḥammad ibn al-Shaykh Sīdiyya al-Kabīr, Hārūn. *Kitāb al-akhbār: Fī akhbār al-Mawrītāniīn wa-man jāwrihim min al-nawāḥī al-muḥīṭa bihim*. 2 vols. [Nouakchott]: Bāb ibn Hārūn, 1998.
Jazūlī, Abū ʿAbd Allāh Muḥammad ibn Sulaymān al-. *Guide to Goodness (Dalāʾil al-khayrāt)*. Edited and translated by Andrey Rosowsky. Great Books of the Islamic World. Chicago: Kazi Publications, 2000.
Kuntī, Muḥammad ibn al-Mukhtār al-. *Al-Risāla al-ghallāwiyya*. Edited by Hamāhullah Ould al-Sālim. Beirut: Dār al-Kutub al-ʿIlmiyya, 2013.
———. *Al-Ṭarāʾif wa'l-talāʾid min karāmāt al-shaykhayn al-wālida wa'l-wālid*. Edited by Yaḥyā Ould Sayyid Aḥmad. 4 vols. N.p.: Dār al-maʿrifa, 2013.
Kuntī, Al-Mukhtār ibn Aḥmad ibn Abī Bakr al-. *Nafḥat al-ṭīb fī'l-salāt ʿalā'l-nabī al-ḥabīb*. Edited by Muḥammad Maḥmūd Ould Wadādī. Damascus: Maṭbaʿat al-Jamhūriyya, 1990.
Maghīlī, Muḥammad ibn ʿAbd al-Karīm al-. *Sharīʿa in Songhay: The Replies of al-Maghīlī to the Questions of Askia al-Ḥājj Muḥammad*. Edited and translated by John O. Hunwick. Oxford: Oxford University Press, 1985.
Martin, Bradford G., trans. "Unbelief in the Western Sudan: ʿUthmān Dan Fodio's 'Taʿlīm al-Ikhwān.'" *Middle Eastern Studies* 4, no. 1 (1967): 50–97.
Saʿdī, ʿAbd al-Raḥmān ibn ʿAbd Allāh. *Timbuktu and the Songhay Empire: Al-Saʿdi's Taʾrikh al-Sudan Down to 1613, and Other Contemporary Documents*. Edited and translated by John O. Hunwick. Leiden: Brill, 1999.
Shinqīṭī, Aḥmad ibn al-Amīn al-. *Al-Wasīṭ fī tarājim udabāʾ shinqīṭ wa al-kalām ʿalā tilka'l-bilād taḥdīdan wa-takhṭīṭan wa-ʿādātihim wa-akhlāqihim wa-mā yataʿallaq bi-dhālika*. Cairo: Maktaba al-Khānajī, 1989.
Ṭabarī, Abū Jaʿfar al-. *The Children of Israel*. Vol. 3 of *Tārīkh al-Rusul Wa'l-Mulūk*. Edited by E. Yar-Shater. Translated by William M. Brinner. Albany: State University of New York Press, 1991.

Thaʿlabī, Aḥmad ibn Muḥammad al-. *ʿArāʾis al-majālis fī qiṣaṣ al-anbiyā*. Translated by William M. Brinner. Leiden: Brill, 2002.
Tustarī, Abū Muḥammad Sahl b. ʿAbd Allāh al-. *Tafsīr al-Tustarī*. Edited by Muḥammad Bāsil ʿUyūn al-Sūd. Beirut: Dār al-Kutub al-ʿIlmiyya, 2002.
Yadālī, Muḥammad al-. "Khātima (fī) al-taṣawwuf: An Arabic Work of a Western Saharan Muslim Intellectual." Edited by Kota Kariya. *Journal of Asian and African Studies* 81 (2011): 133–46.

SECONDARY SOURCES

Abitbol, Michel. *Tombouctou et les Arma: De la conquête marocaine du Soudan nigérien en 1591 à l'hégémonie de l'empire Peulh du Macina en 1833*. Paris: Maisonneuve et Larose, 1979.
Ali, Samer M. *Arabic Literary Salons in the Islamic Middle Ages: Poetry, Public Performance, and the Presentation of the Past*. Notre Dame: University of Notre Dame Press, 2010.
Amanullah, Muhammad. "Debate over the Karāmah of Allah's Friends." *Arab Law Quarterly* 18 (2003): 365–74.
Asad, Talal. *Genealogies of Religion: Discipline and Reasons of Power in Christianity and Islam*. Baltimore: Johns Hopkins University Press, 2009.
———. "The Idea of an Anthropology of Islam." *Qui parle* 17, no. 2 (2009): 1–30.
Asprem, Egil. *The Problem of Disenchantment: Scientific Naturalism and Esoteric Discourse, 1900–1939*. Leiden: Brill, 2014.
Attrell, Dan, and David Porreca, trans. *Picatrix: A Medieval Treatise on Astral Magic*. University Park: Penn State University Press, 2019.
Austen, Ralph A. "The Mediterranean Islamic Slave Trade out of Africa: A Tentative Census." *Slavery and Abolition* 13, no. 1 (1992): 214–48.
Awn, Peter J. *Satan's Tragedy and Redemption: Iblīs in Sufi Psychology*. Leiden: Brill, 1983.
Bailey, Michael. "Diabolic Magic." In *The Cambridge History of Magic and Witchcraft in the West from Antiquity to the Present*, edited by David J. Collins, 361–92. New York: Cambridge University Press, 2015.
Bara, Yahya Ould al-. "Le milieu culturel et social des fuqahâ maures." *Nomadic Peoples* 2, nos. 1–2 (1998): 198–214.
Barber, Karin. *The Anthropology of Texts, Persons, and Publics: Oral and Written Culture in Africa and Beyond*. Cambridge: Cambridge University Press, 2007.
Bashir, Shahzad. *Sufi Bodies: Religion and Society in Medieval Islam*. New York: Columbia University Press, 2011.
Baṭrān, ʿAbd al-ʿAzīz. "The Kunta, Sīdī al-Mukhtīr al-Kuntī, and the Office of Shaykh al-Ṭarīqa'l-Qādiriyya." In *The Cultivators of Islam*, edited by John Ralph Willis, 113–46. Studies in West African Islamic History 1. London: Frank Cass, 1979.
———. *The Qadiryya Brotherhood in West Africa and the Western Sahara: The Life and Times of Shaykh al-Mukhtar al-Kunti (1729–1811)*. Rabat: Publications de l'Institut des études africaines, 2001.
———. "Sidi al-Mukhtar al-Kunti and the Recrudescence of Islam in the Western Sahara and the Middle Niger, c. 1750–1811." PhD diss., University of Birmingham, 1971.
Bergunder, Michael. "What Is Esotericism? Cultural Studies Approaches and the Problems of Definition in Religious Studies." *Method and Theory in the Study of Religion* 22, no. 1 (2010): 9–36.
Bever, Edward, and Randall Styers. "Introduction." In *Magic in the Modern World: Strategies of Repression and Legitimization*, edited by Edward Bever and Randall Styers 1–14. University Park: Penn State University Press, 2017.
———, eds. *Magic in the Modern World: Strategies of Repression and Legitimization*. University Park: Penn State University Press, 2017.

Bivar, Adrian D. H., and Mervyn Hiskett. "The Arabic Literature of Nigeria to 1804: A Provisional Account." *Bulletin of the School of Oriental and African Studies* 25, no. 1 (1962): 104–48.

Bladel, Kevin van. *The Arabic Hermes: From Pagan Sage to Prophet of Science.* Oxford: Oxford University Press, 2009.

Bonte, Pierre. "Tribus, factions et état: Les conflits de succession dans l'émirat de l'Adrar." *Cahiers d'études Africaines* 22, nos. 87–88 (1982): 489–516.

Boubrik, Rahal. *Saints et société en Islam: La confrérie ouest saharienne Fâdiliyya.* Paris: CNRS Editions, 1999.

Bowen, John Richard. *Muslims Through Discourse: Religion and Ritual in Gayo Society.* Princeton: Princeton University Press, 1993.

———. *The Mystical Vision of Existence in Classical Islam: The Qur'anic Hermeneutics of the Sufi Sahl At-Tustarī.* Berlin: De Gruyter, 1980.

Brenner, Louis. "Concepts of Ṭarīqa in West Africa: The Case of the Qādiriyya." In *Charisma and Brotherhood in African Islam,* edited by Donal B. Cruise O'Brien and Christian Coulon, 33–52. Oxford: Oxford University Press, 1988.

———. *Controlling Knowledge: Religion, Power, and Schooling in a West African Muslim Society.* Bloomington: Indiana University Press, 2001.

———. "Histories of Religion in Africa." *Journal of Religion in Africa* 30, no. 2 (2000): 143–67.

———. "Introduction." In *Coran et talismans: Textes et pratiques magiques en milieu musulman,* edited by Constant Hamès, 7–15. Paris: Karthala Editions, 2007.

———. "Muslim Divination and the History of Religion of Sub-Saharan Africa." In *Insight and Artistry in African Divination,* edited by John Pemberton, 45–59. Washington, DC: Smithsonian Institution Press, 2000.

———. "Three Fulbe Scholars in Borno." *Maghreb Review* 10, nos. 4–6 (1985): 107–13.

Brooks, George. *Landlords and Strangers: Ecology, Society, and Trade in West Africa, 1000–1630.* Boulder: Westview Press, 1993.

Brown, Jonathan A. C. "Faithful Dissenters: Sunni Skepticism About the Miracles of Saints." *Journal of Sufi Studies* 1, no. 2 (2012): 123–68.

Burak, Guy. "The Section on Prayers, Invocations, Unique Qualities of the Qur'an, and Magic Squares in the Palace Library Inventory." In *Treasures of Knowledge: An Inventory of the Ottoman Palace Library,* edited by Gülru Necipoğlu, Cemal Kafadar, and Cornell H. Fleischer, 2 vols., 1:341–66. Leiden: Brill, 2019.

Burnett, Charles. "Al-Kindī on Judicial Astrology: 'The Forty Chapters.'" *Arabic Sciences and Philosophy* 3, no. 1 (1993): 77–117.

Canaan, Tewfik. "The Decipherment of Arabic Talismans." In *Magic and Divination in Early Islam,* edited by Emilie Savage-Smith, 125–77. Aldershot: Ashgate, 2004.

Casewit, Yousef. *The Mystics of al-Andalus: Ibn Barrajān and Islamic Thought in the Twelfth Century.* Cambridge: Cambridge University Press, 2017.

Chabbi, Jacqueline. *Le Seigneur des tribus: L'Islam de Mahomet.* 3rd ed. Paris: CNRS Éditions, 2013.

Chittick, William C. "Death and the World of Imagination: Ibn al-'Arabī's Eschatology." *Muslim World* 78, no. 1 (1988): 51–82.

———. *Ibn 'Arabi: Heir to the Prophets.* London: Oneworld, 2012.

Chodkiewicz, Michel. *An Ocean Without Shore: Ibn Arabi, the Book, and the Law.* Albany: State University of New York Press, 1993.

———. *Seal of the Saints: Prophethood and Sainthood in the Doctrine of Ibn 'Arabī.* Translated by Liadain Sherrard. Golden Palm Series. Cambridge: Islamic Texts Society, 1993.

Cleaveland, Timothy. *Becoming Walāta: A History of Saharan Social Formation and Transformation.* Portsmouth, NH: Heinemann, 2002.

Collins, David J. "Learned Magic." In *The Cambridge History of Magic and Witchcraft in the West from Antiquity to the Present,* edited by David J. Collins, 332–60. New York: Cambridge University Press, 2015.

Corbin, Henri. *Creative Imagination in the Sufism of Ibn Arabi*. London: Routledge, 2013.
Cornell, Vincent J. *Realm of the Saint: Power and Authority in Moroccan Sufism*. Austin: University of Texas Press, 1998.
Coulon, Jean-Charles. "Building al-Būnī's Legend: The Figure of al-Būnī Through ʿAbd al-Raḥmān al-Bisṭāmī's Shams al-Āfāq." *Journal of Sufi Studies* 5, no. 1 (2016): 1–26.
———. *La magie en terre d'Islam au Moyen Âge*. N.p.: Éditions CTHS, 2017.
Curtin, Philip D. "Jihad in West Africa: Early Phases and Inter-Relations in Mauritania and Senegal." *Journal of African History* 12, no. 1 (1971): 11–24.
Davidson, Herbert A. *Alfarabi, Avicenna, and Averroes on Intellect: Their Cosmologies, Theories of the Active Intellect, and Theories of Human Intellect*. Oxford: Oxford University Press, 1992.
De Callataÿ, Godefroid. "The Classification of Knowledge in the Rasāʾil." In *The Ikhwān al-Ṣafāʾand Their Rasāʾil: An Introduction*, edited by Nader El-Bizri, 58–82. Oxford: Oxford University Press in association with the Institute of Ismaili Studies, 2008.
———. *Ikhwan al-Safa: A Brotherhood of Idealists on the Fringe of Orthodox Islam*. Oxford: Oneworld, 2012.
Doostdar, Alireza. *The Iranian Metaphysicals: Explorations in Science, Islam, and the Uncanny*. Princeton: Princeton University Press, 2018.
Ebstein, Michael, and Sara Sviri. "The So-Called Risālat al-Ḥurūf (Epistle on Letters) Ascribed to Sahl al-Tustarī and Letter Mysticism in al-Andalus." *Journal asiatique* 299, no. 1 (2011): 213–70.
El Hamel, Chouki. "The Transmission of Islamic Knowledge in Moorish Society from the Rise of the Almoravids to the 19th Century." *Journal of Religion in Africa* 29, no. 1 (1999): 62–87.
El-Rouayheb, Khaled. *Islamic Intellectual History in the Seventeenth Century: Scholarly Currents in the Ottoman Empire and the Maghreb*. Cambridge: Cambridge University Press, 2015.
Ernst, Carl. "Between Orientalism and Fundamentalism: Problematizing the Teaching of Sufism." In *Teaching Islam*, edited by Brannon Wheeler, 108–23. Oxford: Oxford University Press, 2002.
Evans-Pritchard, E. E. *Witchcraft, Oracles, and Magic Among the Azande*. Oxford: Clarendon Press, 1976.
Fahd, Toufic. "La connaissance de l'inconnaissable et l'obtention de l'impossible dans la pensée mantique et magique de l'islam." *Bulletin d'études orientales* 44 (1992): 33–44.
———. *La divination Arabe: Études religieuses, sociologiques et folkloriques sur le milieu natif de l'Islam*. Leiden: Brill, 1966.
———. "Génies, anges et demons en Islam." In *Génies, anges et demons*, 155–214. Sources Orientales 8. Paris: Éditions du Seuil, 1971.
———. "Magic in Islam." In *Hidden Truths, Magic, Alchemy, and the Occult: Selections from the Encyclopaedia of Religion*, edited by Lawrence E. Sullivan, 122–30. New York: Macmillan, 1989.
Fakhry, Majid. *A History of Islamic Philosophy*. 2nd ed. New York: Columbia University Press, 2004.
Farouk Ali, Aslam. "Timbuktu's First Private Manuscript Library." *ISIM Review* 15 (Spring 2005): 51.
Fierro, Maribel. "Bāṭinism in al-Andalus: Maslama b. Qāsim al-Qurṭubī (d. 353/964), Author of the 'Rutbat al-Ḥakīm' and the 'Ghāyat al-Ḥakīm (Picatrix).'" *Studia Islamica* 84 (1996): 87–112.
———. "The Polemic About the Karāmāt al-Awliyā and the Development of Ṣūfism in al-Andalus (Fourth/Tenth–Fifth/Eleventh Centuries)." *Bulletin of the School of Oriental and African Studies* 55, no. 2 (1992): 236–49.
Finnegan, Ruth H. "The How of Literature." *Oral Tradition* 20, no. 2 (2005): 164–87.
Flueckiger, Joyce Burkhalter. *In Amma's Healing Room: Gender and Vernacular Islam in South India*. Bloomington: Indiana University Press, 2006.

Fortier, Corinne. "'Une pédagogie coranique': Modes de transmission des savoirs islamiques (Mauritanie)." *Cahiers d'études africaines* 43, nos. 169–70 (2003): 235–60.

Frede, Britta. "Arabic Manuscripts of the Western Sahara: Trying to Frame an African Literary Tradition." *Journal of Islamic Manuscripts* 8, no. 1 (2017): 57–84.

Gannagé, Emma. "Between Medicine and Natural Philosophy: Avicenna on Properties (Khawāṣṣ) and Qualities (Kayfiyyāt)." In *The Occult Sciences in Pre-Modern Islamic Cultures*, edited by Nader El-Bizri and Eva Orthmann, 41–66. Beirut: Ergon Verlag Würzburgh, 2018.

Garden, Kenneth. *The First Islamic Reviver: Abū Ḥāmid al-Ghazālī and His Revival of the Religious Sciences*. Oxford: Oxford University Press, 2014.

Gardiner, Noah. "Esotericist Reading Communities and the Early Circulation of the Sufi Occultist Aḥmad al-Būnī's Works." *Arabica* 64, nos. 3–4 (2017): 405–41.

———. "Forbidden Knowledge? Notes on the Production, Transmission, and Reception of the Major Works of Aḥmad al-Būnī." *Journal of Arabic and Islamic Studies* 12 (2012): 81–143.

———. "Stars and Saints: The Esotericist Astrology of the Sufi Occultist Aḥmad al-Būnī." *Magic, Ritual, and Witchcraft* 12, no. 1 (2017): 39–65.

Gimaret, Daniel. *Les noms divins en Islam: Exégèse lexicographique et théologique*. Paris: Les Éditions du Cerf, 1988.

Graham, William A. *Beyond the Written Word: Oral Aspects of Scripture in the History of Religion*. Cambridge: Cambridge University Press, 1993.

Grémont, Charles. *Les Touaregs Iwellemmedan (1647–1896): Un ensemble politique de la Boucle du Niger*. Paris: Karthala Editions, 2010.

Griffel, Frank. "Al-Ghazali." In *The Stanford Encyclopedia of Philosophy*, edited by Edward N. Zalta. Winter 2016 ed. https://plato.stanford.edu/entries/al-ghazali/.

Gubara, Dahlia el-Tayeb M. "Al-Azhar and the Orders of Knowledge." PhD diss., Columbia University, 2014.

Gutas, Dimitri. *Greek Thought, Arabic Culture: The Graeco-Arabic Translation Movement in Baghdad and Early ʿAbbāsid Society (2nd–4th/5th–10th c.)*. London: Routledge, 1998.

Gutelius, David. "The Path Is Easy and the Benefits Large: The Nāṣiriyya, Social Networks, and Economic Change in Morocco, 1640–1830." *Journal of African History* 43 (2002): 27–49.

———. "Sufi Networks and the Social Contexts for Scholarship in Morocco and the Northern Sahara, 1660–1830." In *The Transmission of Learning in Islamic Africa*, edited by Scott Reese, 15–38. Islam in Africa 2. Leiden: Brill, 2004.

Gwarzo, Hassan Ibrahim. "The Theory of Chronograms as Expounded by the 18th-Century Katsina Astronomer-Mathematician Muhammad B. Muhammad." *Research Bulletin of the Center of Arabic Documentation* 3, no. 2 (1967): 116–23.

Haidara, Abdel Kader. "The State of Manuscripts in Mali and Efforts to Preserve Them." In *The Meanings of Timbuktu*, edited by Shamil Jeppie and Souleymane Bachir Diagne, 265–70. Cape Town: HSRC Press, 2004.

Hall, Bruce. *A History of Race in Muslim West Africa, 1600–1960*. Cambridge: Cambridge University Press, 2011.

Hall, Bruce, and Charles Stewart. "The Historic 'Core Curriculum' and the Book Market in Islamic West Africa." In *The Trans-Saharan Book Trade: Manuscript Culture, Arabic Literacy, and Intellectual History in Muslim Africa*, vol. 3, edited by Krätli Graziano and Ghislaine Lydon, 109–74. Leiden: Brill, 2011.

Hanegraaff, Wouter J. *Esotericism and the Academy: Rejected Knowledge in Western Culture*. Cambridge: Cambridge University Press, 2012.

———. "How Magic Survived the Disenchantment of the World." *Religion* 33, no. 4 (2003): 357–80.

———. "Magic." In *The Cambridge Handbook of Western Mysticism and Esotericism*, edited by Glenn Alexander Magee, 393–404. New York: Cambridge University Press, 2016.

Hirschkind, Charles. *The Ethical Soundscape: Cassette Sermons and Islamic Counterpublics.* New York: Columbia University Press, 2006.

Hiskett, Mervyn. *A History of Hausa Islamic Verse.* London: University of London School of Oriental and African Studies, 1975.

———. "Material Relating to the State of Learning Among the Fulani Before Their Jihād." *Bulletin of the School of Oriental and African Studies* 19, no. 3 (1957): 550–78.

Horden, Peregrine. "Situations Both Alike? Connectivity, the Mediterranean, the Sahara." In *Saharan Frontiers: Space and Mobility in Northwest Africa*, edited by James McDougall and Judith Scheele, 25–38. Bloomington: Indiana University Press, 2012.

Hunwick, John O. "Aḥmad Bābā on Slavery." *Sudanic Africa* 11 (2000): 131–39.

———. "The Arabic Literary Tradition of Nigeria." *Research in African Literatures* 28, no. 3 (1997): 210–23.

———. "A Note on ʿUthmān b. Fodiye's So-Called ʿishrīniyya." *Sudanic Africa* 10 (1999): 169–72.

Ibrahim-Lizzio, Celene, and Teresa Soto González. "Al-Asma al-Husna (Allah's Most Beautiful Names)." In *Islam: A Worldwide Encyclopedia*, edited by Cenap Çakmak, 98–101. Santa Barbara: ABC-CLIO, 2017.

Johnson, Kitty. "An Amuletic Manuscript: Baraka and Nyama in a Sub-Saharan African Prayer Manual." In *The Islamic Manuscript Tradition: Ten Centuries of Book Arts in Indiana University Collections*, edited by Christiane J. Gruber, 251–72. Bloomington: Indiana University Press, 2010.

Josephson, Jason A. "God's Shadow: Occluded Possibilities in the Genealogy of 'Religion.'" *History of Religions* 52, no. 4 (2013): 309–39.

Josephson-Storm, Jason A. *The Myth of Disenchantment: Magic, Modernity, and the Birth of the Human Sciences.* Chicago: University of Chicago Press, 2017.

Kane, Ousmane. *Beyond Timbuktu: An Intellectual History of Muslim West Africa.* Cambridge: Harvard University Press, 2016.

Kani, Mohammad. "Arithmetic in Pre-Colonial Central Sudan." In *Science and Technology in African History, with Case Studies from Nigeria, Sierra Leone, Zimbabwe, and Zambia*, edited by Gloria Thomas-Emeagwali, 33–39. Lewiston, NY: Edwin Mellen Press, 1992.

Karamustafa, Ahmet T. *Sufism: The Formative Period.* Berkeley: University of California Press, 2007.

Katz, Marion Holmes. *Prayer in Islamic Thought and Practice.* New York: Cambridge University Press, 2013.

Kim, Sung Ho. "Max Weber." In *The Stanford Encyclopedia of Philosophy*, edited by Edward N. Zalta. Summer 2021 ed. https://plato.stanford.edu/entries/weber/.

Klaassen, Frank. *The Transformations of Magic: Illicit Learned Magic in the Later Middle Ages and Renaissance.* University Park: Penn State University Press, 2013.

Lange, Christian. *Paradise and Hell in Islamic Traditions.* New York: Cambridge University Press, 2015.

Last, Murray. "A Note on Attitudes to the Supernatural in the Sokoto Jihad." *Journal of the Historical Society of Nigeria* 4, no. 1 (1967): 3–13.

———. "Reform in West Africa: The Jihād Movements of the Nineteenth Century." In *History of West Africa*, edited by J. F. Ajayi and Michael Crowde, 2 vols., 2:1–29. London: Longman, 1974.

———. *The Sokoto Caliphate.* Harlow: Longmans, 1967.

Laycock, Joseph P. *Dangerous Games: What the Moral Panic over Role-Playing Games Says About Play, Religion, and Imagined Worlds.* Berkeley: University of California Press, 2015.

Levtzion, Nehemia. "Merchants vs. Scholars and Clerics: Differential and Complementary Roles." *African and Asian Studies* 20 (1986): 27–44.

———. "Patterns of Islamization in West Africa." In *Conversion to Islam*, edited by Nehemia Levtzion, 207–16. New York: Holmes and Meier, 1979.

———. "Urban and Rural Islam in West Africa: An Introductory Essay." *African and Asian Studies* 20 (1986): 7–26.

Loimeier, Roman. *Muslim Societies in Africa: A Historical Anthropology*. Bloomington: Indiana University Press, 2013.

Lory, Pierre. "La magie des lettres dans le 'Šams al-Ma'arif' d'al-Būnī." *Bulletin d'études orientales* 39–40 (1987): 97–111.

———. *La science des lettres en Islam*. Paris: Dervy, 2004.

———. "The Symbolism of Letters and Language in the Work of Ibn 'Arabī." Translated from the French by Karen Holding. *Journal of the Muhyiddin Ibn al-Arabi Society* 23 (1998). http://www.ibnarabisociety.org/articles/symbolism-of-letters-and-language.html.

Lovejoy, Paul E. *Salt of the Desert Sun: A History of Salt Production and Trade in the Central Sudan*. Cambridge: Cambridge University Press, 1986.

———. *Transformations in Slavery: A History of Slavery in Africa*. 3rd ed. New York: Cambridge University Press, 2012.

Lovejoy, Paul E., and Stephen Baier. "The Desert-Side Economy of the Central Sudan." *International Journal of African Historical Studies* 8, no. 4 (1975): 551–81.

Luhrmann, Tanya M. *Persuasions of the Witch's Craft: Ritual Magic in Contemporary England*. Cambridge: Harvard University Press, 1991.

Lydon, Ghislaine. "Inkwells of the Sahara: Reflections on the Production of Islamic Knowledge in Bilād Shinqīṭ." In *The Transmission of Learning in Islamic Africa*, edited by Scott Reese, 39–71. Leiden: Brill, 2004.

———. *On Trans-Saharan Trails: Islamic Law, Trade Networks, and Cross-Cultural Exchange in Nineteenth-Century Western Africa*. Cambridge: Cambridge University Press, 2009.

———. "A Thirst for Knowledge: Arabic Literacy, Writing Paper, and Saharan Bibliophiles in the Southwestern Sahara." In *The Trans-Saharan Book Trade: Manuscript Culture, Arabic Literacy, and Intellectual History in Muslim Africa*, edited by Krätli Graziano and Ghislaine Lydon, 35–72. Leiden: Brill, 2011.

———. "Writing Trans-Saharan History: Methods, Sources, and Interpretations Across the African Divide." *Journal of North African Studies* 10, nos. 3–4 (2005): 293–324.

Marcus-Sells, Ariela. "'Poised on the Higher Horizon': Seeing God in the Sahara." *Journal of Islamic and Middle Eastern Multidisciplinary Studies* 6, no. 1 (2020): 1–37.

———. "Science, Sorcery, and Secrets in the Fawā'id Nūrāniyya of Sīdi Muḥammad al-Kuntī." *History of Religions* 58, no. 4 (2019): 432–64.

Martin, Alfred Georges Paul. *Les oasis sahariennes*. Vol. 1. Paris: L'Imprimerie Algérienne, 1908.

———. *Quatre siècles d'histoire marocaine au Sahara de 1504 à 1902, au Maroc de 1894 à 1912*. Paris: Librairie Félix Alcan, 1923.

Marty, Paul. *Les Kounta de l'est, les Berabich, les Iguellad*. Vol. 1 of *Études sur l'Islam et les tribus du Soudan*. Paris: Leroux, 1920.

Mavroudi, Maria. "Islamic Divination in the Context of Its 'Eastern' and 'Western' Counterparts." In *Falnama: The Book of Omens*, edited by Massumeh Farhad and Serpil Bağci, 222–29. London: Thames and Hudson, 2009.

McDougall, E. Ann. "The Economics of Islam in the Southern Sahara: The Rise of the Kunta Clan." In *Rural and Urban Islam in West Africa*, edited by Nehemia Levtzion and Humphrey J. Fisher, 39–54. Boulder: Lynne Rienner, 1987.

———. "The Ijil Salt Industry: Its Role in the Precolonial Economy of the Western Sudan." PhD diss., University of Birmingham, 1980.

———. "Research in Saharan History." *Journal of African History* 39, no. 3 (1998): 467–80.

———. "Salts of the Western Sahara: Myths, Mysteries, and Historical Significance." *International Journal of African Historical Studies* 23, no. 2 (1990): 231–57.

———. "Snapshots from the Sahara: 'Salt,' the Essence of Being." In *The Libyan Desert: Natural Resources and Cultural Heritage*, edited by David J. Mattingly, Sue McLaren, Elizabeth Savage, Yahya al-Fasatwi, and Khaled Gadgood, 295–303. London: London Society for Libyan Studies, 2006.

McDougall, James, and Judith Scheele. "Introduction: Time and Space in the Sahara." In *Saharan Frontiers: Space and Mobility in Northwest Africa*, edited by James McDougall and Judith Scheele, 1–24. Bloomington: Indiana University Press, 2012.

———, eds. *Saharan Frontiers: Space and Mobility in Northwest Africa*. Bloomington: Indiana University Press, 2012.

McGregor, Richard J. A. "A Sufi Legacy in Tunis: Prayer and the Shadhiliyya." *International Journal of Middle East Studies* 29, no. 2 (1997): 255–77.

McIntosh, Roderick J. *Ancient Middle Niger: Urbanism and the Self-Organizing Landscape*. Cambridge: Cambridge University Press, 2005.

McLaughlin, Glen Wade. "Sufi, Saint, Sharif, Muhammad Fadil Wuld Mamin: His Spiritual Legacy, and the Political Economy of the Sacred in Nineteenth Century Mauritania." PhD diss., Northwestern University, 1997.

Melvin-Koushki, Matthew. "Introduction: De-Orienting the Study of Islamicate Occultism." *Arabica* 64, nos. 3–4 (2017): 287–95.

———. "Powers of One: The Mathematicalization of the Occult Sciences in the High Persianate Tradition." *Intellectual History of the Islamicate World* 5, nos. 1–2 (2017): 127–99.

Merolla, Daniela. "Introduction: Orality and Technauriture of African Literatures." *Tydskrif Vir Letterkunde* 51, no. 1 (2014): 80–90.

Messick, Brinkley. *Shariʿa Scripts: A Historical Anthropology*. New York: Columbia University Press, 2018.

Meyer, Birgit, and Peter Pels, eds. *Magic and Modernity: Interfaces of Revelation and Concealment*. Stanford: Stanford University Press, 2003.

Miské, Aḥmad Bābā. *Al-Wasīṭ: Tableau de la Mauritanie à la fin du XIXe siècle*. Paris: Klincksiek, 1970.

Moraes Farias, Paulo F. de. "The Oldest Extant Writing of West Africa: Medieval Epigraphs from Issuk, Saney, and Egeg-n-Tawaqqast (Mali)." *Journal des Africanistes* 60, no. 2 (1990): 65–113.

Morris, James Winston. "Ibn ʿArabi and His Interpreters, Part II: Influences and Interpretations." *Journal of the American Oriental Society* 106, no. 4 (1986): 733–56.

Muehlhaeusler, Mark. "Math and Magic: A Block-Printed Wafq Amulet from the Beinecke Library at Yale." *Journal of the American Oriental Society* 130, no. 4 (2010): 607–18.

Murata, Kazuyo. *Beauty in Sufism: The Teachings of Rūzbihān Baqlī*. Albany: State University of New York Press, 2017.

Nakamura, Kojiro. "Imām Ghazālī's Cosmology Reconsidered, with Special Reference to the Concept of 'Jabarūt.'" *Studia Islamica* 80 (1994): 29–46.

Nasr, Seyyed Hossein. *An Introduction to Islamic Cosmological Doctrines: Conceptions of Nature and Methods Used for Its Study by the Ikhwān al-Ṣafāʾ, al-Bīrūnī, and Ibn Sīnā*. 2nd ed. Albany: State University of New York Press, 1993.

Netton, Ian Richard. *Muslim Neoplatonists: An Introduction to the Thought of the Brethren of Purity (Ikhwān al-Ṣafāʾ)*. London: RoutledgeCurzon, 2002.

Nobili, Mauro. "Back to Saharan Myths: Preliminary Notes on ʿUqba al-Mustajab." *Annual Review of Islam in Africa* 11 (2012): 79–84.

———. *Sultan, Caliph, and the Renewer of the Faith: Aḥmad Lobbo, the Tārīkh al-Fattāsh, and the Making of an Islamic State in West Africa*. Cambridge: Cambridge University Press, 2020.

Noble, Michael-Sebastian. *Philosophising the Occult: Avicennan Psychology and "the Hidden Secret" of Fakhr al-Dīn al-Rāzī*. Berlin: De Gruyter, 2021.

Norris, H. T. *The Arab Conquest of the Western Sahara: Studies of the Historical Events, Religious Beliefs, and Social Customs Which Made the Remotest Sahara a Part of the Arab World*. Harlow, UK: Longman, 1986.

———. *Ṣūfī Mystics of the Niger Desert: Sīdī Maḥmud and the Hermits of Aïr*. Oxford: Clarendon Press, 1990.

———. *The Tuaregs: Their Islamic Legacy and Its Diffusion in the Sahel*. Warminster: Aris and Phillips, 1975.

———. "Znāga Islam During the Seventeenth and Eighteenth Centuries." *Bulletin of the School of Oriental and African Studies* 32, no. 3 (1969): 496–526.

Nouhi, Mohamed Lahbib. "Approaches to the History and Society of the Southwestern Sahara: The Study of Sufi Culture as an Alternate Paradigm." *Religious Studies and Theology* 32, no. 1 (2013): 31–56.

———. "Religion and Society in a Saharan Tribal Setting: Authority and Power in the Zwaya Religious Culture." PhD diss., University of Alberta, 2009.

O'Brien, Susan. "Spirit Discipline: Gender, Islam, and Hierarchies of Treatment in Postcolonial Northern Nigeria." In *Discipline and the Other Body: Correction, Corporeality, Colonialism*, edited by Steven Pierce and Anupama Rao, 273–302. Durham: Duke University Press, 2006.

Ogunnaike, Oludamini. "Philosophical Sufism in the Sokoto Caliphate: The Case of Shaykh Dan Tafa." In *Islamic Scholarship in Africa: New Directions and Global Contexts*, edited by Ousmane Kane, 136–68. London: Boydell and Brewer, 2021.

———. *Poetry in Praise of Prophetic Perfection: A Study of West African Arabic Madīḥ Poetry and Its Precedents*. Cambridge: Islamic Texts Society, 2020.

———. Review of *Beyond Timbuktu: An Intellectual History of Muslim West Africa*, by Ousmane Oumar Kane. *Journal of Religion* 99, no. 3 (2019): 388–90.

Ohlander, Erik. *Sufism in an Age of Transition: 'Umar al-Suhrawardī and the Rise of the Islamic Mystical Brotherhoods*. Leiden: Brill, 2008.

Orthmann, Eva. "Lettrism and Magic in an Early Mughal Text: Muḥammad Ghawth's Kitāb al-Jawāhir al-Khams." In *The Occult Sciences in Pre-Modern Islamic Cultures*, edited by Nader El-Bizri and Eva Orthmann, 223–48. Beirut: Ergon Verlag Würzburgh, 2018.

Otto, Bernd-Christian. "Historicising 'Western Learned Magic.'" *Aries* 16, no. 2 (2016): 161–240.

———. "Towards Historicizing 'Magic' in Antiquity." *Numen* 60 (2013): 308–47.

Ould Abdellah, A. Dedoud. "Le 'passage au sud': Muhammad al-Hafiz et son héritage." In *La Tijâniyya: Une confrérie musulmane à la conquête de l'Afrique*, edited by Jean-Louis Triaud and David Robinson, 69–100. Paris: Karthala Editions, 2000.

Ould Ahmedou, El Ghassem. *Enseignement traditionnel en Mauritanie: La Mahadra ou l'école "à dos de chameau."* Paris: Harmattan, 1997.

Ould Cheikh, Abdel Wedoud. "La généalogie et les capitaux flottant: Al-Shaykh Sîd al-Mukhtâr (c. 1750–1811) et les Kunta." In *Emirs et présidents: Figures de la parenté et du politique dans le monde arabe*, edited by Pierre Bonte, Edouard Conte, and Paul Dresch, 137–61. Paris: CNRS Editions, 2001.

———. "Herders, Traders, and Clerics: The Impact of Trade, Religion, and Warfare on the Evolution of Moorish Society." In *Herders, Warriors, and Traders: Pastoralism in Africa*, edited by John G. Galaty and Pierre Bonte, 199–221. Boulder: Westview Press, 1991.

———. "A Man of Letters in Timbuktu: Al-Shaykh Sidi Muhammad al-Kunti." In *The Meanings of Timbuktu*, edited by Shamil Jeppie and Souleymane Bachir Diagne, 231–48. Cape Town: HSRC Press, 2004.

———. "Nomadisme, Islam et pouvoir politique dans la société maure precoloniale (XIème siècle–XIXème siècle): Essai sur quelques aspects du tribalisme." PhD diss., Université Paris V, 1985.

———. "La tribu comme volonté et comme représentation: Le facteur religieux dans l'organisation d'une tribu maure, les Awlâd Abyayri." In *Al-Ansâb: La quête des origines; Anthropologie historique de la société tribale arabe*, edited by Pierre Bonte, Edouard Conte, Constant Hamès, and Abdel Wedoud Ould Cheikh, 201–38. Paris: Éditions de la Maison des Sciences de l'Homme, 1991.

Owusu-Ansah, David. "Islamic Influence in a Forest Kingdom: The Role of Protective Amulets in Early 19th-Century Asante." *Transafrican Journal of History* 12 (1983): 100–133.

Padwick, Constance Evelyn. *Muslim Devotions: A Study of Prayer-Manuals in Common Use*. London: SPCK, 1961.

Pels, Peter. "Introduction: Magic and Modernity." In *Magic and Modernity: Interfaces of Revelation and Concealment*, edited by Birgit Meyer and Peter Pels, 1–38. Stanford: Stanford University Press, 2003.

Pettigrew, Erin. "The Heart of the Matter: Interpreting Bloodsucking Accusations in Mauritania." *Journal of African History* 57, no. 3 (2016): 417–35.

———. "The History of Islam in Mauritania." In *The Oxford Research Encyclopedia of African History*, December 23, 2019, 1–29. https://doi.org/10.1093/acrefore/9780190277734.013.628.

———. "Muslim Healing, Magic, and Amulets in the Twentieth-Century History of the Southern Sahara." PhD diss., Stanford University, 2014.

Porter, Venetia, Liana Saif, and Emilie Savage-Smith. "Medieval Islamic Amulets, Talismans, and Magic." In *A Companion to Islamic Art and Architecture*, edited by Finbarr Barry Flood and Gülru Necipoğlu, 521–57. Hoboken: John Wiley and Sons, 2017.

Puente, Cristina de la. "The Prayer upon the Prophet Muhammad (Taṣliya): A Manifestation of Islamic Religiosity." *Medieval Encounters* 5, no. 1 (1999): 121–29.

Renard, John. *Friends of God: Islamic Images of Piety, Commitment, and Servanthood*. Berkeley: University of California Press, 2008.

Robinson, David. "Between Hashimi and Agibu: The Umarian Tijâniyya in the Early Colonial Period." In *La Tijâniyya: Une confrérie musulmane à la conquête de l'Afrique*, edited by Jean-Louis Triaud and David Robinson, 101–24. Paris: Karthala Editions, 2000.

———. *The Holy War of Umar Tal: The Western Sudan in the Mid-Nineteenth Century*. Oxford: Clarendon Press, 1985.

———. *Paths of Accommodation: Muslim Societies and French Colonial Authorities in Senegal and Mauritania, 1880–1920*. Athens: Ohio University Press, 2000.

Saad, Elias N. *Social History of Timbuktu: The Role of Muslim Scholars and Notables, 1400–1900*. Cambridge: Cambridge University Press, 1983.

Saif, Liana. *The Arabic Influences on Early Modern Occult Philosophy*. London: Palgrave Macmillan, 2015.

———. "From Ġāyat al-Ḥakīm to Šams al-Maʿārif: Ways of Knowing and Paths of Power in Medieval Islam." *Arabica* 64, nos. 3–4 (2017): 297–345.

———. "Ikhwān al-Ṣafāʾ's Religious Reform and Magic: Beyond the Ismaʿili Hypothesis." *Journal of Islamic Studies* 30, no. 1 (2019): 34–68.

Sanneh, Lamin O. *The Jakhanke Muslim Clerics: A Religious and Historical Study of Islam in Senegambia*. Lanham, MD: University Press of America, 1989.

Savage-Smith, Emilie. "Introduction: Magic and Divination in Early Islam." In *Magic and Divination in Early Islam*, edited by Emilie Savage-Smith, xiii–li. Aldershot: Ashgate, 2004.

Scheele, Judith. *Smugglers and Saints of the Sahara: Regional Connectivity in the Twentieth Century.* Cambridge: Cambridge University Press, 2012.

———. "Traders, Saints, and Irrigation: Reflections on Saharan Connectivity." *Journal of African History* 51, no. 3 (2010): 281–300.

Searing, James F. *West African Slavery and Atlantic Commerce: The Senegal River Valley, 1700–1860.* Cambridge: Cambridge University Press, 2003.

Sells, Michael A., trans. and ed. *Early Islamic Mysticism: Sufi, Qur'an, Miraj, Poetic, and Theological Writings.* New York: Paulist Press, 1996.

———. *Mystical Languages of Unsaying.* Chicago: University of Chicago Press, 1994.

Sesiano, Jacques. "Construction of Magic Squares Using the Knight's Move in Islamic Mathematics." *Archive for History of Exact Sciences* 58, no. 1 (2003): 1–20.

Shaikh, Sadiyya. *Sufi Narratives of Intimacy: Ibn 'Arabī, Gender, and Sexuality.* Chapel Hill: University of North Carolina Press, 2012.

Siegel, James T. *Shadow and Sound: The Historical Thought of a Sumatran People.* Chicago: University of Chicago Press, 1979.

Smith, Jonathan Z. *Map Is Not Territory: Studies in the History of Religions.* Chicago: University of Chicago Press, 1978.

Soares, Benjamin F. *Islam and the Prayer Economy: History and Authority in a Malian Town.* Edinburgh: Edinburgh University Press, 2005.

———. "Rethinking Islam and Muslim Societies in Africa." *African Affairs* 106, no. 423 (2007): 319–26.

Stetkevych, Suzanne Pinckney. *The Mantle Odes: Arabic Praise Poems to the Prophet Muḥammad.* Bloomington: Indiana University Press, 2010.

Stewart, Charles C. "Frontier Disputes and Problems of Legitimation: Sokoto-Masina Relations, 1817–1837." *Journal of African History* 17, no. 4 (1976): 497–514.

———. *Islam and Social Order in Mauritania: A Case Study from the Nineteenth Century.* Oxford: Clarendon Press, 1973.

———. "Rethinking the Missing Manuscripts of Timbuktu." Paper presented at the Symposium on Muslim Africa, Duke University, April 13, 2016.

Stewart, Devin. "Prophecy." In *Key Themes for the Study of Islam*, edited by Jamal J. Elias, 281–303. Oxford: Oneworld, 2010.

Stratton, Kimberly B. "Early Greco-Roman Antiquity." In *The Cambridge History of Magic and Witchcraft in the West from Antiquity to the Present*, edited by David J. Collins, 83–112. New York: Cambridge University Press, 2015.

———. *Naming the Witch: Magic, Ideology, and Stereotype in the Ancient World.* New York: Columbia University Press, 2007.

Street, Tony. "Medieval Islamic Doctrine on the Angels: The Writings of Fakhr al-Dīn al-Rāzī." *Parergon* 9, no. 2 (1991): 111–27.

Styers, Randall. *Making Magic: Religion, Magic, and Science in the Modern World.* New York: Oxford University Press, 2004.

Syed, Amir. "Al-Ḥājj 'Umar Tāl and the Realm of the Written: Mastery, Mobility, and Islamic Authority in 19th-Century West Africa." PhD diss., University of Michigan, 2017.

Tamari, Tal. "The Development of Caste Systems in West Africa." *Journal of African History* 32, no. 2 (1991): 221–50.

Taneja, Anand Vivek. *Jinnealogy: Time, Islam, and Ecological Thought in the Medieval Ruins of Delhi.* Stanford: Stanford University Press, 2017.

Taylor, Raymond M. "Of Disciples and Sultans: Power, Authority, and Society in the Nineteenth-Century Mauritanian Gebla." PhD diss., University of Illinois at Urbana-Champaign, 1996.

———. "Warriors, Tributaries, Blood Money, and Political Transformation in Nineteenth-Century Mauritania." *Journal of African History* 36, no. 3 (1995): 419–41.

Trimingham, J. Spencer. *The Sufi Orders in Islam.* New York: Oxford University Press, 1998.

van Dalen, Dorrit. *Doubt, Scholarship, and Society in Seventeenth-Century Central Sudanic Africa*. Leiden: Brill, 2016.

Ware, Rudolph T. "Slavery in Islamic Africa, 1400–1800." In *The Cambridge World History of Slavery*, vol. 3, *AD 1420–AD 1804*, edited by David Eltis and Stanley L. Engerman, 47–80. New York: Cambridge University Press, 2011.

Warscheid, Ismail. *Droit musulman et société au Sahara prémoderne: La justice islamique dans les oasis du Grand Touat (Algérie) aux XVIIe–XIXe siècles*. Leiden: Brill, 2017.

Webb, James L. A. *Desert Frontier: Ecological and Economic Change Along the Western Sahel, 1600–1850*. Madison: University of Wisconsin Press, 1995.

Welch, Alford T. "Allah and Other Supernatural Beings: The Emergence of the Qur'anic Doctrine of Tawḥīd." *Journal of the American Academy of Religion* 47, no. 4 (1980): 733–58.

Wensinck, Arent Jan. *On the Relation Between Ghazālī's Cosmology and His Mysticism*. Amsterdam: Noord-Hollandsche Uitgevers-Maatschappij, 1933.

Whitcomb, Thomas. "New Evidence on the Origins of the Kunta—I." *Bulletin of the School of Oriental and African Studies* 38, no. 1 (1975): 103–23.

———. "New Evidence on the Origins of the Kunta—II." *Bulletin of the School of Oriental and African Studies* 38, no. 2 (1975): 403–17.

Wilks, Ivor. *The Northern Factor in Ashanti History*. Accra: Institute of African Studies, University of Ghana, 1961.

———. "The Transmission of Islamic Learning in the Western Sudan." In *Literacy in Traditional Societies*, edited by Jack Goody, 162–97. Cambridge: Cambridge University Press, 1968.

Witkam, Jan Just. "The Battle of the Images: Mekka vs. Medina in the Iconography of the Manuscripts of al-Jazūlī's Dalā'il al-Khayrāt." In *Theoretical Approaches to the Transmission and Edition of Oriental Manuscripts: Proceedings of a Symposium Held in Istanbul, March 28–30, 2001*, edited by Judith Pfeiffer and Manfred Kropp, 67–82. Beirut: Orient-Institut Beirut, 2007.

Wright, Zachary Valentine. "Islamic Esotericism in West Africa: From Timbuktu to Senegal, 15th to 20th Centuries." Paper presented at the conference "Islamic Esotericism in Global Contexts," European Network for the Study of Islam and Esotericism, held via Zoom, December 4, 2020.

———. "The Islamic Intellectual Tradition of Sudanic Africa, with Analysis of a Fifteenth-Century Timbuktu Manuscript." In *The Palgrave Handbook of Islam in Africa*, edited by Fallou Ngom, Mustapha H. Kurfi, and Toyin Falola, 55–76. London: Palgrave Macmillan, 2020.

———. *Living Knowledge in West African Islam: The Sufi Community of Ibrāhīm Niasse*. Leiden: Brill, 2015.

———. "Secrets on the Muhammadan Way: Transmission of the Esoteric Sciences in 18th-Century Scholarly Networks." *Islamic Africa* 9, no. 1 (2018): 77–105.

Zadeh, Travis. "Magic, Marvel, and Miracle in Early Islamic Thought." In *The Cambridge History of Magic and Witchcraft in the West from Antiquity to the Present*, edited by David J. Collins, 235–67. New York: Cambridge University Press, 2015.

INDEX

al-Abayirī al-Intishā'ī, Sīdiyya ibn al-Mukhtār (Shaykh Sīdiyya al-Kabīr), 6, 51–52, 58–59, 90, 163
'Abbās, 140–41
'Abbāsid period, 9, 11, 99, 101, 119, 120–21, 130
abiding (*baqā'*), 9, 73, 74, 75, 83
Abraham (Ibrāhīm), 139, 156
Abtītī, 56
Abū Ma'shar, 119, 120
acquisition, doctrine of (*kasb*), 101
Active Intellect (*al-'aql al-fa'aliyya*), 74–75
Adam, 67, 98, 123, 135–36
adhkār. *See* prayer, supplicatory; recitation of names of God; remembrance
ad'iyya. *See* prayer, supplicatory
adjurations (*al-'azā'im*), 90, 102, 106, 108, 116
'Adnān, 139
Adrār, 4, 8, 28, 30, 36, 54
Agadez, 30, 48
Aghlāl, 7, 59
agriculture and agriculturalists, 4, 29, 30, 32, 33
Ahaggar Mountains, 4, 28, 30, 31, 37–38, 60
aḥwāl (states), 9, 38, 43, 72, 80, 116, 144
aḥzāb or *ḥizb*, 104, 127, 128, 130, 150, 155–56, 158
  See also prayer, supplicatory
Aïr Massif, 4, 28, 30, 37, 48, 60
'Ā'isha (Ibn al-Najīb's daughter), 45–46
al-ākhira (next world), 64–65
  See also *al-malakūt*
'ālam al-ghayb. *See* realm of the unseen
'ālam al-shahāda. See *al-mulk*; visible world
al-'Alawī, 'Abd Allāh ibn Ibrāhīm, 91
Algeria, 7, 31, 161
'Alī ibn Abī Ṭālib, 49
Allāh. *See* God
Almamates, 5, 39
alterity, discourse of, 118, 166
  See also exclusion and inclusion, discourse of
amenoukal (leader or sultan), 37, 38
al-Amīn, Muḥammad (Dua-Dua), 58
amīrs, 36, 37, 173n31
amulets
  devotional practice and, 148, 159
  and exclusion, discourse of, 124
  and knowledge, hierarchy of, 16
  sciences of the unseen and, 25, 87, 99, 111, 161
  Sufism and, 23
  supplicatory prayer and, 128
Andalusian mystical tradition, 121
angels, 63, 66–67, 70, 78–79, 91–92, 177n21
annihilation (*fanā'*), 9, 72–73, 74, 75, 83, 85, 135, 164
al-Anṣārī, Abū 'Abd Allāh (Ibn Bint Abī Sa'd), 122
al-'aql al-fa'aliyya (Active Intellect), 74–75
Arawān, 28, 37
Aristotle, 63
Arma pashalic, 36, 38
Asad, Talal, 20–21
Āṣaf ibn Barakhiyā, 122
Asante, 111–12
ascetism, 9, 163, 164
Ash'arī theology, 69, 101, 105, 120, 125, 165
Askia Muḥammad, 40, 112–13, 165, 180n55
al-asmā' al-ḥusnā. *See* names of God
Asprem, Egil, 110
asrār. *See* sciences of the unseen
astral magic, 13, 14, 119–20, 123
astrology (*'ilm al-nujūm*), 107, 108, 114, 116, 117, 165
astronomy, 119
Atlantic slave trade, 35
  See also slavery
authority, 2, 5–6, 10, 24, 38–39, 130–31, 175n100
  See also Kunta authority
awfāq or *wafq*. *See* magic squares
Awlād al-Nāṣir, 60
Awlād Bella, 57–58, 60
awliyā'. *See* friends of God
awrād or *wird* (litanies), 50, 87, 127, 127–28, 130, 163
  See also prayer, supplicatory

al-ʿazāʾim (adjurations), 90, 102, 106, 108, 116
Azawād, 4–5, 8, 28, 29–31, 36–37, 54–55

Baghayuʿu, Muḥammad, 45
al-Baghdadī, Maḥmūd, 48
al-Baghiramāwī, Muḥammad al-Wālī ibn Sulaymān al-Birnāwī, 113, 181n61
Baier, Stephen, 33
Balʿām, 133, 135, 136–37
al-Balkhī, Abū Maʿshar ibn Jaʿfar ibn Muḥammad ibn ʿUmar, 119, 120
baqāʾ (abiding), 9, 73, 74, 75, 83
Barābīsh, 6, 36, 56, 57, 60, 164
Barber, Karin, 17, 129
al-Bartilī, 54, 158
al-Bāsha Bū Farīra, 57
basīra (insight), 91
al-Baṣrī, al-Ḥasan, 49
al-bāṭin (hidden), 89–90
  See also sciences of the unseen
Baṭrān, ʿAbd al-ʿAzīz, 7–8, 10, 55
The Believer's Model (Lamtūnī), 51
Bever, Edward, 14, 15, 89, 110, 124
Bible, Hebrew, 99
Bint ʿAlī ibn al-Najīb, ʿĀʾisha, 45–46
Bint Sīdi al-Mukhtār ibn Sīdi al-Amīn al-Azraq, Lalla ʿĀʾisha, 56, 130, 150, 155, 160
al-Bisṭāmī, ʿAbd al-Raḥmān, 123
al-Bisṭāmī, Abū Yazīd, 78
blackness, 4, 32, 88, 117–18, 124, 139, 166
  See also racial discourses
bodies
  angels and interactions with, 66
  God and existence of, 69–70, 75, 76–77
  in Kunta texts, importance of, 24–25
  and Muḥammad, perfection of, 82, 149
  numerology and, 94
  purification of, 144
  supplicatory prayer and, 134–35, 148
  unseen realm and perfection of, 64, 77–86, 164
  visible and unseen realms, mediation of, 67–69
Bonte, Pierre, 36
The Book of Dispelling Confusion (al-Mukhtār al-Kuntī), 19–20, 68, 79, 80–81, 82, 85, 172n70
The Book of Grace (al-Mukhtār al-Kuntī), 18, 55, 69–70, 159, 171n64
Bornu empire, 32
Brākna, 36
breakings of the norm (*khawāriq al-ʿādā*), 11, 101–2, 108–9, 150, 164
Brenner, Louis, 16, 35, 38, 170n30, 181n61
Brothers of Purity (Ikhwān al-Ṣafāʾ), 13
Bū Jbayha, 37
Bundu, 5, 39
al-Būnī, Aḥmad, 14, 120–23, 124, 178n4, 182n92
Al-Burda (Būṣīrī), 155, 158
al-Burnāwī, ʿAbdullah, 48, 49
The Burning Stars (al-Mukhtār al-Kuntī), 50
al-Būṣīrī, Abū ʿAbd Allāh Muḥammad ibn Saʿīd, 155, 158
Bustān al-fawāʾid (Kābarī), 51, 111

Caillié, René, 59
camels, 29, 30, 32, 34–35, 60, 62
canals, underground (*fagāgīr*), 30
caravans, 30, 41, 45, 56, 57, 60, 159
  See also trade and commerce
caste systems, 16
  See also racial discourses
cavalry states, 34–35
cereal trade, 30, 31, 33
  See also trade and commerce
Chabbi, Jacqueline, 63
chains of transmission (*isnād*), 44–45, 46, 50, 174n72
chains or lineages (*silsila*)
  of Kunta scholars, 6–7, 19, 49–51, 53, 59, 141, 153, 163
  of Muḥammad, 139–41
  racial discourses and, 4, 117
  Saharan history and, 4–5, 32–33, 35–37, 38–39, 41
  and Sufism, history of, 10–11, 48–49
charismata (*karāmāt*)
  classification of, 100–102, 103, 109, 165
  definition and translation, 11
  historical context, 13
  Kunta scholars and, 62–63
  sciences of the unseen and, 88, 103–4
  Sīdi al-Mukhtār, 41–42
  sorcery vs., 15
  See also sciences of the unseen
chronicles, local, 32–33, 34, 53–54, 55, 117
class categories, 4, 11, 12, 33, 34, 35, 37
  See also racial discourses
Cleaveland, Timothy, 55, 174n72
clerical lineages (*zwāya*)
  Kunta scholars and, 57–58, 162
  literacy and, 183n13
  Saharan history and, 4, 33, 34, 35–36, 37, 38, 39
  sciences of the unseen and, 165
  women's education and, 45
colonialism, 2, 3, 6–7, 11–12, 27, 55, 117
consultation (*istikhāra*), 91
The Conveyer of the Biographies (Shinqīṭī), 43, 54

false charismata (*istidrāj*), 88
  See also charismata
fanā' (annihilation), 9, 72–73, 74, 75, 83, 85, 135, 164
fasting, 79–80, 81–82
fate, 105, 135, 136, 139
Fatḥ al-shakūr (Bartilī), 54, 158
fatwas, 41
Fawā'id nūrāniyya (Muḥammad al-Kuntī)
  Būnian manuscript tradition and, 122, 123
  Dalā'il al-khayrāt and, 152
  on devotional aids, 130
  on God, 70
  on greatest name of God, 93–94
  Ḥizb al-baḥr, compared, 156, 158
  on magic squares, 97
  manuscript, 172n71
  overview, 3, 19, 20, 91
  on sciences of letters and names, 91–92, 127, 142
  on sciences of the unseen, 114
  study and challenges of, 2
  supplication and devotional practice in, 142–48, 149, 159
  on world, manipulation of, 1–2
al-Fāzāzī, 155, 158
Ficino, Marsilio, 14
al-Fihrī, 'Uqba ibn Nafi', 7, 53
Finnegan, Ruth, 17, 129
al-firāsa (perception), 91, 179n6
folding up space (*ṭayy al-arḍ*), 103, 148, 149
Frazer, James George, 170n35
Frede, Britta, 45
free cities, 38–39
  See also Timbuktu
friends of God (*awliyā'*)
  ascent to God and, 73, 74, 77–78, 81, 84–86, 164
  charismata and, 11, 62–63, 101
  knowledge of God and, 83
  Kunta authority and, 8, 10, 24–25, 26, 60, 163, 164
  realm of the unseen and, 66, 76–77
  and revelation, continued, 84
  Sahara and history of, 27–28, 37
  sciences of the unseen and, 87, 104, 115, 165
  self and spirit of, 68
  Sīdi al-Mukhtār's defense of, 19
  and Sufism, history of, 9, 10
Fulānī scholars, 114, 117, 165
Fulbe (Pulaar) identity, 39
Futa Jallon, 5, 39
Futa Toro, 5, 39, 52, 161

Gabriel (Jibrīl), 49, 66
  See also angels
Gao, 36, 38
The Garden of Excellences and Benefits (Kābarī), 51, 111
Gardiner, Noah, 122–23
Gebla, Mauritanian, 6, 28, 33, 51–52, 60
gender roles, 45–46
genealogies, 6–7, 32–34, 53–61, 117, 139–40, 162–63, 174n72
  See also chains or lineages
geomancy, 107, 112, 114, 117–18, 165, 180n40
Ghadames, 30
al-Ghālī, Muḥammad, 52
al-ghawth (succor), 84, 85, 178n76
Ghāyat al-ḥakīm (Qurṭubī), 13, 120, 123
al-ghayb (the unseen), 63
  See also realm of the unseen
al-Ghazālī, Abū Hamīd Muḥammad, 10, 49, 65–66, 120–21, 122, 123
al-Ghumayrī, 56, 57
globalization, 22, 23
The Goal of the Sage (Qurṭubī), 13, 120, 123
Gobir, 39
God
  charismata and, 101
  creation of realms and, 91
  devotional practice and, 78, 81
  essence, attributes, and actions of, 69, 70, 72–73, 75, 76, 116, 143
  friends of God and, 84–85
  greatest name of, 92–95, 96–98, 99, 137, 142–43
  heart and knowledge of, 70–77
  knowledge of, as flood, 82–83
  Kunta scholars on, 69–70
  prayers for the Prophet and, 137–38
Greek magic discourse, 118
  See also magic
Greek philosophy, 63, 75
Greek translation movement, 119
Gril, Denis, 121
Gubara, Dahlia, 113, 114, 181n61
Guide to Goodness (Jazūlī), 150–53, 154–55, 167, 185n50

ḥadīth, 89, 92, 119, 153
  See also Qur'ān
al-Ḥāfiz, Muḥammad, 52
hagiographies. *See* chains or lineages; genealogies
Hall, Bruce, 32, 41
al-Hallāj, 135
Hamdullahi, 5, 39
al-Hāmiliyya, Lalla Ambārika, 55
Ḥammāda ibn Muḥammad ibn Amalan, 58, 60
Hanegraaff, Wouter J., 12, 110
ḥaqīqa muḥammadiyya, 154

Harāmisa, 98, 99
Ḥasan ibn ʿAlī ibn Abī Ṭālib, 140–41
ḥassan (warrior lineages), 33, 34, 35–36, 38–39, 162
Ḥassaniyya dialect, 32
Hausaland, 5, 39, 114, 117, 158, 165
al-Ḥayūnī, ʿAbd al-Mālik ibn Aḥmad, 31
heart
  ascent to God and, 70–72, 73, 74
  existence and, 73, 76
  realm of the unseen and, 64, 76–77
  unseen realm and perfection of, 77–86
  visible and unseen realms, mediation of, 67–68, 69, 78–79, 85, 164
heaven and hell, 64–65, 66
  See also eschaton
herding, 29, 30
  See also pastoralism
Hermes Trismegistus, 14, 98, 99
hidden (*al-bāṭin*), 89–90
  See also sciences of the unseen
The Hidden Secret (Rāzī), 113, 123, 166, 181n64
ḥikma (wisdom), 161
al-Ḥilla, 56, 60
hīmā, 90, 102–3, 107, 108
  See also sorcery
Ḥizb al-baḥr (Shādhilī), 155–58, 167
Ḥizb al-ikhlāṣ (al-Mukhtār al-Kuntī), 131
Ḥizb al-isrāʾ (al-Mukhtār al-Kuntī), 20, 131
Ḥizb al-nūr (al-Mukhtār al-Kuntī), 20, 131
ḥizb or *aḥzāb*, 104, 127, 128, 130, 150, 155–56, 158
  See also prayer, supplicatory
Ḥizb sīdī al-mukhtār al-kuntī (al-Mukhtār al-Kuntī)
  close reading of, 134–37
  devotional practice and, 148–49
  Ḥizb al-baḥr, compared to, 155–56
  overview, 20, 131–32
  text of, 132–34
Hodh, 6, 7, 8, 28, 30, 52
horses, 34, 35
  See also trade and commerce
Hunwick, John, 112
Ḥusayn ibn ʿAlī ibn Abī Ṭālib, 140–41

Iblīs (Satan), 67, 133, 135–36, 137
Ibn ʿAbbās, ʿAbd Allah, 64
Ibn ʿAbd Allāh, Muḥammad (sultan), 31
Ibn Abī Ṭālib, ʿAlī, 49
Ibn Alād, ʿUwar (Ughmar), 38
Ibn al-ʿArabī, Muḥyī al-Dīn, 10, 13, 49, 120–21, 122, 154, 178n4
Ibn ʿAlī ibn Abī Ṭālib, Ḥasan, 140–41
Ibn ʿAlī ibn Abī Ṭālib, Ḥusayn, 140–41
Ibn al-Najīb, ʿAlī, 8, 43, 44–45, 54, 55, 62, 163, 174n72
Ibn al-Ṣabbāgh (Muḥammad ibn Abī al-Qāsim al-Ḥimyarī), 158
Ibn Amma, Kāwa, 59
Ibn Barrajān (Abū al-Ḥakam ʿAbd al-Salām al-Ifrīqī al-Ishbīlī), 121
Ibn Bint Abī Saʿd (Abū ʿAbd Allāh al-Anṣārī), 122
Ibn Būnā al-Jakanī, al-Mukhtār, 19, 45, 58
Ibn Fūdī, ʿUthmān
  education of, 158
  Kunta scholars and, 51, 52, 59
  Muslimness and, 40
  Rāʾīyah fī dhamm and, 181n61
  Saharan history and, 5, 39
  sciences of the unseen and, 115–16
  Sokoto movement and, 113
Ibn Intiqād, Bāsha, 57
Ibn Masarra al-Jabalī, Muḥammad ibn ʿAbd Allāh, 121
Ibn Mashīsh, ʿAbd al-Salām, 49, 51
Ibn Muḥammad ibn Amalan, Ḥammāda, 58, 60
Ibn Muḥammad ibn Riḥāl ibn Daḥmān, ʿAlī, 57
Ibn Riḥāl ibn Daḥmān ibn al-Ḥājj, Muḥammad, 57
Ibn Sharīf, Rashīd (sultan), 48
Ibn Sīdi Aḥmad, ʿAbd Allāh, 54
Ibn Sīdi Hamū, ʿAlī, 56
Ibn Sīdi Muḥammad ibn Sīdi ʿAlī ibn Sīdi Muḥammad ibn Sīdi al-Mukhtār al-Shaykh, ʿAbd al-Qādir, 55
Ibn Ṭāhir, Nūḥ, 51, 175n89
Ibn ʿUthmān ibn Fūdī, Muḥammad, 5, 6, 115–16, 155
Ibn Yūsuf, Muḥammad, 57
Ibrāhīm (Abraham), 139, 156
Ibrāhimic prayer (*al-salāt al-ibrāhimiyya*), 152–53
Idaw ʿAlī, 52
Idaw al-ʿIsh, 59
identity, 40, 52, 53, 60, 125–26
idolatry, 105–6, 107, 108
Idrīs, 98, 99, 107
ijāza, 44
  See also chains of transmission
Ijjil salt mine, 28, 31
  See also trade and commerce
Ikhwān al-Ṣafāʾ (Brothers of Purity), 13
The Illuminated Benefits (Muḥammad al-Kuntī). See *Fawāʾid nūrāniyya*
ʿilm al-ḥurūf wa'l-asmāʾ. *See* science of letters and names
ʿilm al-nujūm (astrology), 107, 108, 114, 116, 117, 165
immaterial plane (*al-malakūt*), 65–66, 68, 70, 76, 91, 144, 148, 154

inclusion. *See* exclusion and inclusion, discourses of
initiation, 16, 52, 93
insight (*basīra*), 91
institutions, Islamic, 40–46
See also Sufi orders
intellectuals, Muslim, 35, 36, 37, 38, 39, 111–12, 167
interdependence, commercial, 29, 31
intermediary realm (*al-jabarūt*), 65–66, 70, 91, 134, 144, 148, 154
intertextuality, 18, 20
See also texts and textuality
irrigation, 30
ʿIsā (Jesus), 136, 140
Ishmael (Ismāʿīl), 139
Al-ʿIshrīnīyāt (Fāzāzī), 155, 158
Islamicate magic, 13, 14, 118–26
See also magic
Islamic law, 40–41, 106, 108, 125
Islamic studies, 12, 22, 165–66
Ismāʿīl (Ishmael), 139
isnād (chains of transmission), 44–45, 46, 50, 174n72
See also chains or lineages
istadrāj, 101
See also sorcery
istakhdāmāt (evocations), 106–7, 107, 108, 116
istidrāj (false charismata), 88
See also charismata
istikhāra (consultation), 91
Iwellemmedan Tuareg, 6, 37, 38, 56, 57, 59, 60, 164

al-Jabartī, Ḥasan, 113
al-jabarūt (intermediary realm), 65–66, 70, 91, 134, 144, 148, 154
jadāwil (tables), 94, 95–97, 99, 112, 142–43, 144
See also sciences of letters and names
Jakhanke, 111
al-Jazūlī, Abū ʿAbd Allāh Muḥammad, 150–51, 152, 153, 154–55, 167
Jesus (ʿIsā), 136, 140
Jibrīl (Gabriel), 49, 66
See also angels
Jidhwat al-anwār (al-Mukhtār al-Kuntī), 19, 58, 64–65, 66, 68, 72–73, 84, 171n68
jihāds, 5, 10, 39, 52, 163
al-Jīlānī, ʿAbd al-Qādir
Iblīs and, 136
Kunta scholars and, 10–11, 28, 43, 46, 49, 53
minor prayer of, 153
West African Sufism and, 163
jinn
believers and, 67, 78
Muḥammad and, 139
realm of the unseen and, 63, 66
ruqyā and, 100
sciences of the unseen and, 87, 102, 106–7, 112, 116
shayāṭīn and, 63, 67
Josephson-Storm, Jason, 110
al-Juhanī, ʿUqba ibn ʿAmīr, 53
al-Junayd, Abū Qāsim, 49
jurisprudence (*fiqh*), 42, 89

Kaarta, 39
al-Kābarī, Muḥammad, 51, 111, 165
al-kahāna (divination), 107, 112–13, 114, 116, 117–18
Kajoor, 34
al-Kalḥurmī, Āḥḥ, 42, 44, 46
karāmāt. *See* charismata
Karidenna, 37, 38
kasb (acquisition, doctrine of), 101
al-Kashnāwī, Muḥammad ibn Muḥammad al-Ghallānī, 113–14, 115, 117, 123, 158, 166, 181n59
al-kawākib (employment of planets), 106, 107, 108, 114, 123–24
Al-Kawākib al-durriyya (Būṣīrī), 155, 158
Kawkab al-waqqād (al-Mukhtār al-Kuntī), 50
Kel Ahaggar (Huqqār), 37, 38
Kel al-Sūq, 37, 42, 44, 46, 53, 55, 163
Kel Dinnig, 59
Kel Inbalbūsh, 42
Kel Intasār, 37, 55
Kel Tadamakkat, 37, 56, 60, 164
Khalwa (al-Mukhtār al-Kuntī), 67, 136
khalwa (spiritual retreat), 9, 99, 143, 144, 166
"Khātima fī al-taṣawwuf" (Yadālī), 51
al-khaṭṭ (sand writing), 107, 112, 114, 117–18, 165, 180n40
khawāriq al-ʿādā (breakings of the norm), 11, 101–2, 108–9, 150, 164
khawāṣṣ, 101, 102, 105, 107–8, 117, 180n39
See also sorcery
al-Khidr, 84
Khumayka, 56–57
al-Kindī, 119, 120
Kitāb al-minna (al-Mukhtār al-Kuntī), 18, 55, 69–70, 159, 171n64
Kitāb zawāl al-ilbās (al-Mukhtār al-Kuntī), 19–20, 68, 79, 80–81, 82, 85, 172n70
knowledge, mystical (*maʿrifa*), 42, 90
knowledge and practice
access to, 16
ascent to God and, 71–73
classification of, 25, 89–90, 109
contested meanings of, 2–3
devotional aids and, 129
discursive traditions and, 20–21, 109–11, 165–66

Kunta authority and, 3, 26
legitimate vs. illegitimate, 3, 15, 21, 23–24, 88–91, 100–101, 123–26, 161, 166
racial discourses and, 117–18
sciences of the unseen and, 64, 87–88, 116
See also devotional practice
Kunnāsh al-riḥla (Tijānī), 155
Kunta authority
devotional practice and, 2, 26, 64, 129, 149–50, 159–60
friends of God and, 8, 10, 24–25, 26, 60, 163, 164
and genealogies, construction of, 8, 10–11, 34, 53, 56, 163
realm of the unseen and, 63, 64
sciences of the unseen and, 2, 3, 7, 8–9, 21, 64, 125, 165
textual production and, 51–52, 53, 129, 130, 159–60, 167
voluntary submission and, 6, 27, 40, 164
in West Africa, 40, 56, 60
Kunta scholars
on ascent to God, 71, 72
on bodies and unseen realm, 77, 78–79
charismata and, 62–63
contemporary, 22–23
devotional aids and, 25–26, 128–29
devotional practice and, 149–50, 159, 159–60, 167
discourses of inclusion and exclusion, 15, 25, 123–24, 126, 166
on divination, 107
education and, 43–44, 46
emic terminology of, 15–16, 88
on friends of God, 83–84
genealogies of, constructed, 53–61
on greatest name of God, 152
history and political context of, 4–8, 24, 27–28, 30–31, 34, 37–40, 162–63
on Iblīs, 135–36
Islamic institutions and identity and, 40–46
Islamic magic discourses and, 119, 166
lineages of, 6–7, 19, 49–51, 141, 153, 162, 163
manuscript traditions and, 17–18, 19
and prayer, theory of, 149
realm of the unseen and, 24–25, 63–70, 76–77, 85, 162, 164
on *ruqyā*, 100, 105
sciences of the unseen, defense of, 2–3, 11, 15, 25, 87, 113, 125, 164
sciences of the unseen and, 1, 2, 7, 87–88, 109–10, 111–19, 161–62, 165, 167
on al-Shādhilī, 156
on sorcery, 102, 114, 120
Sufism and, 6, 8, 9, 10, 24, 53, 59, 60, 163
supplicatory prayer and, 128–29, 158
trade and wealth of, 30–31
See also Kunta authority
al-Kuntī, Muḥammad ibn al-Mukhtār ibn ʿAḥmad (Sīdi Muḥammad al-Kuntī)
on angels, 66
on ascent to God, 72, 73
authority and influence of, 6, 8, 51–52, 53, 60, 130, 162–63, 164, 165
on believers, 71
on bodies, perfection of, 77
Būnian manuscript tradition and, 123
on charismata, 62
devotional practice and, 80, 130, 142–43, 159–60, 166–67
on education, 41, 43–44
on friends of God, 81–82, 83–84
genealogy of, constructed, 7, 34, 53–61, 163, 175n103
on God, 70
on greatest name of God, 92–95, 158
on Iblīs, 136
and inclusion and exclusion, discourses of, 89, 123–25, 126, 166
Islamic institutions and, 41
on jinn, 107
life of, 27, 28, 58–59
on magic squares, 97, 100, 104–5
on mother, devotional practice of, 150
on *Nafḥat al-ṭīb*, 137–38
political involvement of, 6, 40, 59, 60, 61, 164
racial discourses of, 117–18
on realm of the unseen, 24, 65, 86
on *ruqyā*, 99–100, 105
on sciences of letters and names, 91–92, 97–99, 142
sciences of the unseen, classification of, 100–109, 114–15, 125, 164–65
sciences of the unseen, defense of, 3, 11, 15, 25, 87, 125, 164
sciences of the unseen, first-order disciplines, 89–100
sciences of the unseen and, 1, 3, 87–88, 102, 124, 125, 161–62
on secrets, unsupervised use of, 147
on self (*nafs*), 68, 72
on Sīdi al-Mukhtār, 7–8, 41–43, 163
on sorcery, 15, 90, 100, 101, 102–3, 107–9
on spirit, 69
Sufi lineage of, 49–51, 52, 53, 59
Sufism and, 8–9, 10–11, 24, 27–28, 47, 51, 52
on supplicatory prayer, 127, 128
on tables and talismans, 95
on *tarīqa*, meaning of, 50
texts attributed to, 16–17, 18, 19–20
trade and wealth of, 31, 60–61

al-Kuntī, al-Mukhtār ibn Aḥmad ibn Abī Bakr (Sīdi al-Mukhtār al-Kuntī)
on ascent to God, 65, 66, 72–73, 74
authority and influence of, 6, 34, 51–52, 53, 56, 60, 130, 164
on believers, 64–65, 66, 70–71
on bodies and unseen realm, 68, 77–78, 79
charismata and, 41–42
on creation, 75–76
devotional aids of, 20, 25, 159
devotional practice and, 80–81, 85, 159–60, 166–67
on divine letters, 79
education and training of, 41, 42–43, 44, 46, 55, 89–90, 163
on fasting, 79–80, 81
on friends of God, 83, 85
genealogy of, constructed, 34, 53–61, 162–63
on God, 69–70
on greatest name of God, 93
Ḥizb sīdī al-mukhtār and, 131–37
Iblīs and, 136
Islamic institutions and, 41
on jinn, 67, 106–7
on knowledge of God, 82–83
life of, 7–8, 27, 28, 55–56
magic squares and, 104–5
Nafḥat al-ṭīb, 137–42, 152, 153–54
political involvement of, 6, 34, 40, 56–58, 59, 60, 61, 164
on prophets, 82
on realm of the unseen, 24, 65, 85
on *ruqyā*, 100
Saharan history and, 4, 5, 38, 162–63
sciences of the unseen, defense of, 2–3, 11, 15
sciences of the unseen and, 1, 3, 87, 125, 161–62
on self (*nafs*), 68
Sufi lineage of, 49–51, 52, 53, 59, 163
Sufism and, 8–9, 10–11, 24, 27–28, 46–47, 51, 53
on supplicatory prayer, 128
on *tarīqa*, meaning of, 50
texts attributed to, 16–17, 18–19
trade and wealth of, 30, 31, 60–61
women's education and, 45–46
al-Kuntī, Muḥammad (Sīdi Muḥammad al-Kabīr), 7–8, 163
al-Kuntī, Abū Bakr (Sīdi al-Ḥājj Abū Bakr), 56, 100
al-Kuntī, Aḥmad al-Bakkā'ī (son of Sīdi Muḥammad al-Kabīr), 8, 54, 55
al-Kuntī, Aḥmad al-Bakkā'ī (son of Sīdi Muḥammad-Kuntī), 5, 39, 47, 52, 53, 161, 163
al-Kuntī, Aḥmad ibn Abī Bakr, 55
al-Kuntī, Bābā Aḥmad, 58
kuttāb (local schools), 41, 43

Lalla 'Ā'isha, 56, 130, 150, 155, 160
Lalla Ambārika al-Hāmiliyya, 55
al-Lamtunī, Aḥmad al-Ṣadiq ibn Uwāyis, 48, 51
Lange, Christian, 176n9
language and speech, 31–32, 89–90, 100, 105, 106, 107, 115–16
Laṭā'if al-ishārāt (Būnī), 122, 124
law and punishment, 40–41, 106, 108, 125
The Letter to the Aghlāl (Muḥammad al-Kuntī), 7, 18, 19, 53–54, 59
lettrism, 13–14, 63, 90, 121–22
See also sciences of letters and names
l'ḥjāb, 161
lights (*anwār*), 134, 153–54
litanies (*awrād* or *wird*), 50, 87, 127, 127–28, 130, 163
See also prayer, supplicatory
Litany of Light (al-Mukhtār al-Kuntī), 20, 131
Litany of Sīdi al-Mukhtār (al-Mukhtār al-Kuntī). See *Ḥizb sīdī al-mukhtār al-kuntī*
Litany of Sincerity (al-Mukhtār al-Kuntī), 131
Litany of the Night Journey (al-Mukhtār al-Kuntī), 20, 131
Litany of the Sea (Shādhilī), 155–58, 167
literacy, 131, 183n13
literature, Arabic, 130, 131
See also texts and textuality
al-liwāṭ (sodomy), 106, 123
Lobbo, Aḥmad, 5, 6, 31, 39, 51, 59, 155, 175n100
Lobbo, Aḥmad ibn Aḥmad, 155
local chronicles, 32–33, 34, 53–54, 55, 117
Lory, Pierre, 121, 183n109
love, 9, 154
Lovejoy, Paul E., 33
love poetry, 9, 10
Lydon, Ghislaine, 41, 45

Mabrūk, 55–56
Macina, 5, 39, 40
al-Maghīlī, Muḥammad ibn 'Abd al-Karīm, 49, 112–13, 115, 118, 163, 165, 180n55
Maghẓūf, 60
magic
discourses and usage of term, 3, 11–16, 88–89, 109–11, 118, 165, 170n35
Islamic discourses of, 118–26
sciences of the unseen and, 11, 25, 88
in West Africa, 111–18
See also sciences of the unseen
magic squares (*awfāq* or *wafq*)
archaeological findings of, 111, 180n48
history and usage of, 96–97
Islamic magic discourses and, 119
Sīdi al-Mukhtār and, 104

Sīdi Muḥammad on, 97, 98, 99, 100, 102, 105, 108
Sufism and, 121, 122
in West Africa, 112, 114, 165
maḥāḍra, 44
al-Mahdawī, 121
mahdī, 140–41
Maḥmūdiyya, 48
Majābat al-Kubrā, 36
al-malakūt (immaterial plane), 65–66, 68, 70, 76, 91, 144, 148, 154
Mali, 8, 22–23, 28, 115, 124, 161
Mali Empire, 38
Malikī law, 108
See also law and punishment
al-Manṣūr, Ahmad, 47
manuscripts, 16–18, 130–31, 147, 167, 171n56
See also texts and textuality
Map Is Not Territory (Smith), 109
marabouts, 22, 23, 172n78
ma'rifa (mystical knowledge), 42, 90
Martin, Alfred Georges Paul, 54
Marty, Paul, 7, 8, 55
marvelous occurrences. *See* charismata
Massūfa, 36
material world. See *al-mulk*
matrilineal systems, 37
McDougall, Ann, 31
McDougall, James, 167
McLaughlin, Glen, 47
medicine (*al-ṭibb*), 88
medicine, spiritual (*al-ṭibb al-rūḥānī*), 100
See also *ruqyā* or *ruqiyya*
memorization, 17, 41, 43, 44, 130, 131, 142, 159
Messick, Brinkley, 18, 19
methodology, 16, 17–18, 20–21, 22–24, 88, 128, 138, 165–66
Meyer, Birgit, 88
microcosm, 69, 75, 135, 138
See also cosmology
militarism, 4–5, 6, 39
mimesis, 152, 155
miracles, prophetic (*mu'jizāt*), 11, 15, 88, 101–2, 109
mirrors, 83
mirrors for princes, 5–6
modernity, 89, 110, 125, 166
monotheism, 135, 140
morality, 2, 5–6, 12, 13, 21, 27, 68, 114
Morocco, 28, 31, 32, 34, 36, 47–48, 164
Moses (Mūsā), 50, 119, 137, 156
Muḥammad (prophet)
charismata and, 101
in *Dalā'il al-khayrāt*, 151–52, 154–55
in *Kitāb zawāl al-ilbās*, 82–83
and lineages, construction of, 4, 7, 32, 49, 53
in *Nafḥat al-ṭīb*, 138–41, 153–54
perfection of, 82, 149
spiritual medicine and, 100
supplicatory prayer and, 128, 135, 137
Muḥammad al-Amīn (Dua-Dua), 58
Muḥammad Bello, 5, 6, 115–16, 155
Muḥammad Fūdū (Fūdī), 113
mu'jizāt (prophetic miracles), 11, 15, 88, 101–2, 109
See also charismata
al-mulk (material world)
devotional practice and, 154
in *Fawā'id nūrāniyya*, 144
in *Ḥizb sīdī al-mukhtār al-kuntī*, 134
in Kunta cosmology, 65–66, 68, 70, 76
in *Nafḥat al-ṭīb*, 148
sciences of letters and names and, 91
See also visible world
al-Mursī, Aḥmad Abū 'Abbās, 49
Mūsā (Moses), 50, 119, 137, 156
al-Muṣṭafā, 'Abd al-Mu'min ibn Sīdi Muḥammad, 38
al-Mustajab, 'Uqba, 53–54
Mustawjabat al-maḥāmid (Anṣārī), 122
See also magic squares
Mu'tazīli theology, 101
muthallath al-Ghazālī, 122
See also magic squares

Nafḥat al-ṭīb (al-Mukhtār al-Kuntī)
close reading of, 138–42
Dalā'il al-khayrāt and, 151, 152, 153, 155
devotional practice and, 148–49
on light of Muḥammad, 153–54
manuscript, 183n5
overview, 128, 138
as prayer to the Prophet, 137–38
predestination in, 135
publication of, 172n75
nafs (self), 68, 71–72, 74, 76, 79, 85, 108
names of God (*al-asmā' al-ḥusnā*)
cosmology and, 13–14
creation and, 70, 78–79, 97
in *Dalā'il al-khayrāt*, 152
devotional practice and, 142–43, 144, 146–49
in *Ḥizb al-baḥr*, 156
and jinn, control of, 106–7
in *Nafḥat al-ṭīb*, 141
remembrance and, 104–5
ruqyā and, 100
sciences of letters and names and, 95–99, 142
sciences of the unseen and, 90–93, 100
Sufism and, 9
and world, manipulation of, 1–2
al-Nāqil, 'Abd al-Karīm, 52
Nāṣir al-Dīn, 33, 39, 51

natural philosophy, 120, 182n87
nawāzil, 41
Neoplatonic philosophy, 10, 63, 69
networks, regional, 4
  See also economic relationships
next world (*al-ākhira*), 64–65
  See also *al-malakūt*
Niger River Valley, 28, 35, 37, 39, 111
nīranj, 113–14, 166
  See also sorcery
Nobili, Mauro, 53
Noble, Michael-Sebastian, 181n64
nobles, 4, 33–34, 35, 37, 84
nomadic pastoralism, 4, 29–30, 32, 33, 34
Norris, H. T., 48, 51, 53
Nouhi, Mohamed Lahbib, 48–49
numerology, 93, 94, 98, 113
  See also sciences of letters and names

oasis towns, 4, 30
  See also Sahara Desert
occult sciences, 14, 16, 88, 165
  See also magic
occupation groups, 35, 37, 162
Ogunnaike, Oludamini, 116, 182n75
orality, 2, 17, 129–30, 131, 160, 167
Original and Inherited Knowledge (Muḥammad al-Kuntī). See *Ṭarā'if wa'l-talā'id*
orthodoxy, 13, 21, 22, 23, 120, 125
Otto, Bernd-Christian, 13, 15, 88–89, 118, 124, 166
Ould Cheikh, Abdel Wedoud, 36
Owusu-Ansah, David, 112

paper, 130
  See also texts and textuality
pastoralism, 4, 29–30, 32, 33, 34
path or way (*ṭarīqa*)
  ascent to God and, 70–77
  and bodies, perfection of, 77
  devotional practice and, 85
  friends of God and, 164
  Kunta scholars and, 11, 28, 49–51
  meaning of term, 46–47, 48–49, 50
  Muḥammad and, 154
  prayer and, 80
  sciences of the unseen and, 104–5, 115, 116
  subject and goal of, 89–90
  and Sufism, history of, 9, 48–49
  See also Sufi orders
patrilineal systems, 37
Pels, Peter, 14, 89
perceptible world. *See* visible world
perception (*al-firāsa*), 91, 179n6
performance and performativity, 17, 129–30, 142, 144, 148, 160, 167
  See also devotional practice
Peripatetic philosophy, 105
Pettigrew, Erin, 161
Pico, Giovanni, 14
piety, 9, 150, 160
planets, employment of (*al-kawākib*), 106, 107, 108, 114, 123–24
Plato, 98, 99
poetic traditions, 158–59
political movements, 6, 34–40
Pollock, Sheldon, 19
positionality, 21–24
practice. *See* knowledge and practice
praise poetry, 159
The Praiseworthy (Anṣārī), 122
  See also magic squares
prayer (*ṣalāt*), 80–81, 127, 147, 148
prayer, supplicatory (*du'ā'* or *ad'iyya*)
  devotional practice and, 127, 142–49, 160
  Ḥizb sīdī al-mukhtār and, 131–37
  of al-Kābarī, 165
  and knowledge, discourses of, 16
  Kunta texts and, 131
  methodology and interpretation of, 149
  Nafḥat al-ṭīb and, 137–42
  overview and context, 127–29
  remembrance of God and, 104–5
  in Sahara, history and context of, 149–59, 167
  sciences of letters and names and, 98–99
  sciences of the unseen and, 25, 128, 166
  Sīdi Muḥammad on, 130
  sources, 20
  textuality and, 26
prayers for the Prophet (*taṣliyya*), 128, 137, 141, 150–51, 152–54
predestination, 105, 135
  See also cosmology
princes (*'umarā'*), 5–6
production, economic, 29, 31
  See also economic relationships

qadirī lineages, 48, 49
Qādiriyya order, 8, 10, 11, 28, 52, 163
  See also Sufi orders
The Qadiryya Brotherhood (Baṭrān), 7
Qaḥṭān, 139
Qudwat al-mu'taqid (Lamtūnī), 51
Qur'ān
  angels and devils in, 66–67
  education and, 43
  in *Fawā'id nūrāniyya*, 143
  greatest name of God and, 93
  in *Ḥizb al-baḥr*, 156, 157, 158
  Ḥizb sīdī al-mukhtār and, 132, 133, 134, 135
  Kunta texts and, 40
  light of Muḥammad and, 154
  in *Nafḥat al-ṭīb*, 139
  oral tradition of, 130

prayers for the Prophet and, 137
realm of the unseen and, 63
sciences of letters and names and, 92–94, 99, 122
sciences of the unseen and, 89, 100, 103
and Sīdi al-Mukhtār, education of, 41
siḥr in, 119
supplicatory prayer and, 127
symbols of, 70
Quraysh, tribe of, 7, 141
al-Qurṭubī, Maslama ibn Qāsim, 13, 120

racial discourses
colonialism and, 176n112
knowledge and practice and, 15, 125
magic and, 89
in *Nafḥat al-ṭīb*, 139, 184n37
Saharan history and, 4–5, 31–33
sciences of the unseen and, 88, 110, 117–18, 124, 166
rainfall, 29, 30
al-Raqqād, Aḥmad (sultan), 46, 48, 49, 163, 174n72
Rasāʾil Ikhwān al-Ṣafāʾ, 120
rationalism, 12, 13, 14
al-Rāzī, Fakr al-Dīn, 113–14, 120, 123, 166, 181n64
realm of the unseen (*ʿālam al-ghayb*)
ascent to God and, 70–77
and bodies, perfection of, 77–86
charismata and, 62–63
in *Dalāʾil al-khayrāt*, 152
friends of God and, 85–86, 164
greatest name of God and, 152
Kunta and architecture of, 63–70
Kunta scholars and, 24–25, 76–77, 85, 162, 164
science of letters and, 121
supplication and devotional practice and, 25, 78, 85, 87
visible realm and, 110
recitation of names of God (*dhikr*), 9, 128, 166
See also prayer, supplicatory
reenactment, 148, 160
See also performance and performativity
religion, usage of term, 2, 3, 12, 14, 109–11
religious studies, 3, 12, 22
remembrance (*dhikr*), 104, 127–28, 138
See also prayer, supplicatory
"Replies" (Maghīlī), 112, 165
retreat, spiritual (*khalwa*), 9, 99, 143, 144, 166
revelation, 50, 63, 71, 84, 89, 99, 104, 122
rhyming prose (*sajʿ*), 130
Risāla al-ghallāwiyya (Muḥammad al-Kuntī), 7, 18, 19, 53–54, 59
ritual practice. *See* devotional practice; knowledge and practice
Robinson, David, 52
rūḥ (spirit), 68–69, 71, 74, 76, 78
al-rūḥ al-amīn (faithful spirit), 66
Ruma of Timbuktu, 56
ruqyā or *ruqiyya*, 99–100, 102, 105

Saad, Elias N., 36
sacred history
devotional aids and, 129, 132
devotional practice and, 160, 167
in *Ḥizb sīdī al-mukhtār*, 135, 142
Muḥammad and, 152
in *Nafḥat al-ṭīb*, 137, 142
realm of the unseen and, 63
of sciences of letters and names, 20, 97, 122
sciences of the unseen and, 118, 125
Sahara Desert
devotional aids and practice in, 129, 149–60, 167
history and environment of, 4–8, 27–28, 28–35, 60–61, 162
Islamic institutions and identity in, 40–46
Kunta genealogies in, 53–59
Kunta scholars and, 24, 26, 167
political formations in, 34–40, 59–60
sciences of the unseen in, 88
Sufis and Sufism in, 27–28, 46–53, 60
Sahel, 4, 29, 32, 48, 149
Saif, Liana, 14, 120, 121
sainthood, 9
sajʿ (rhyming prose), 130
al-salāt al-ibrāhimiyya (Ibrāhimic prayer), 152–53
ṣalāt (prayer), 80–81, 127, 147, 148
See also prayer, supplicatory
"Ṣalāt al-ṣughrā" (Jīlānī), 153, 154
sallāla (sorcerers), 117
See also sorcery
salt trade, 28, 30–31
sand writing (*al-khaṭṭ*), 107, 112, 114, 117–18, 165, 180n40
Sanneh, Lamin, 111
Satan (Iblīs), 67, 133, 135–36, 137
al-Sāṭī, Abū ʿAbd Allāh, 80
scarcity, economies of, 30, 31, 33, 60
Scheele, Judith, 30, 31, 161, 167
scholars (*ʿulamāʾ*), 5–6
schools, local (*kuttāb*), 41, 43
science, discourse of, 3, 14, 89, 109–18
sciences of letters and names (*ʿilm al-ḥurūf wa'l-asmāʾ*)
adjurations and, 106–7
creation and, 63, 90–91, 93, 97–98, 99
devotional practice and, 144, 146–49
in *Fawāʾid nūrāniyya*, 20
greatest name of God and, 92–95, 97, 99
hierarchy of practice, 2
in *Ḥizb al-baḥr*, 156, 158

sciences of letters and names *(continued)*
  Islamic magic discourses and, 119
  magic squares and, 96–97, 98–99
  ruqyā and, 99–100
  sciences of the unseen and, 90–94
  Sīdi Muḥammad and, 124
  al-sīmiyā' and, 178n4
  Sufism and, 9, 13–14, 91, 92, 121–22
  supplicatory prayer and, 127, 128
  tables and, 95–96
  and visible world, impact on, 91–92
  in West Africa, 114, 165
sciences of the hidden (*'ulūm al-bāṭin*), 89–90
sciences of the unseen (*'ulūm al-ghayb*)
  and body, perfection of, 64, 77–86, 164
  classification of, 88, 89, 100–109, 116–18, 125, 164–65
  contemporary practitioners of, 22–23
  devotional practice and, 25, 64, 159, 166–67
  discourses and usage of term, 11, 15–16, 88–89, 109–11
  first-order disciplines of, 89–100
  in *Ḥizb sīdī al-mukhtār*, 137
  and inclusion and exclusion, discourses of, 117–18, 123–26, 166
  Islamic magic discourses and, 118–26, 166
  Kunta authority and, 2, 3, 7, 8–9, 21, 64, 125, 165
  Kunta defense of, 2–3, 11, 15, 25, 87, 113, 125, 164
  Kunta scholars and, 1, 87–88, 109–10, 115–18, 161–62, 165
  overview, 25, 87–88
  racial discourses and, 88, 110, 117–18, 124, 166
  sciences of letters and names and, 90–94
  Sufism and, 8–9, 88, 115, 116, 120–21, 165
  supplicatory prayer and, 25, 128, 166
  in West Africa, discourses of, 110, 111–18
"The Seal of Becoming" (Yadālī), 51
seals, 140–41
"The Secret of Secrets," 119, 120
secrets (*asrār*). *See* sciences of the unseen
Segou, 39
self (*nafs*), 68, 71–72, 74, 76, 79, 85, 108
Senegal, 22, 23, 35, 39, 47
seven seals of Solomon, 96, 179n25
sexual deviancy, 106, 123
al-Shādhilī, Abū Ḥasan, 49, 92, 155–56, 158, 167
shādhilī lineages, 48, 49
Shams al-āfāq (Bisṭāmī), 123
Shams al-ma'ārif al-kubrā, 14, 122–23, 124, 183n109
Sharḥ al-qaṣīda al-fayḍiyya (al-Mukhtār al-Kuntī), 18–19, 66, 68, 72–74, 77–79, 81, 163, 171n65
shayāṭīn (devils), 63, 64, 66–67, 68, 92, 99, 119, 120
  See also Iblīs
shaykhs, 47, 50, 53, 71–72
al-Shiblī, Abū Bakr, 49
Shi'ism, 121
al-Shinqīṭī, Aḥmad ibn al-Amīn, 43, 45, 54, 58, 183n13
"Shukr al-Wāhib" (Dan Tafa), 116
Shurr Bubba, 33
Sīdi Bādī, 55
Sīdi al-Ḥājj Abū Bakr, 56, 100
Sīdi Muḥammad (Abū Ḥāmiyya), 55
Sīdi Muḥammad al-Kabīr, 7–8, 163
Sīdi Muḥammad al-Kuntī. *See* al-Kuntī, Muḥammad ibn al-Mukhtār ibn 'Aḥmad
Sīdi al-Mukhtār al-Kuntī. *See* al-Kuntī, al-Mukhtār ibn Aḥmad ibn Abī Bakr
Sīdiyya al-Kabīr (Sīdiyya ibn al-Mukhtār al-Abayirī al-Intishā'ī), 6, 51–52, 58–59, 90, 163
Sīdiyya ibn al-Mukhtār, 6, 51–52, 58–59, 90, 163
siḥr. *See* sorcery
silsila. *See* chains or lineages
sīmā (*sīmiyā'*), 90, 102–3, 107, 108, 116, 178n4
  See also sorcery
"Sirr al-asrār," 119, 120
Al-Sirr al-maktūm (Rāzī), 113, 123, 166, 181n64
slavery
  Kunta scholars and, 30
  racial discourses and, 117
  Saharan history and, 4–5, 31, 32, 33, 34–35, 37, 39, 162, 173n43
Smith, Jonathan Z., 109
Soares, Benjamin, 47, 115, 124
sodomy (*al-liwāṭ*), 106, 123
Sokoto Caliphate, 5, 39, 40, 115, 158, 170n30
Solomon (prophet), 106, 156
Songhay Empire, 27, 32, 34, 36, 38, 112
Sonni 'Alī, 112
sorcerers (*sallāla*), 117
sorcery (*siḥr*)
  classification of, 15, 101–4, 107, 108–9, 165–66
  discourses and usage of term, 13, 14, 109–11
  Islamic discourses of, 119–26
  legal implications of, 108
  magic squares and, 100
  racial discourses and, 117–18, 166
  sciences of secrets and, 114
  sciences of the unseen and, 1, 3, 11, 15, 25, 88, 90, 100–101, 164
  Sufism and, 11
  in West Africa, discourse of, 111–18
sources, 18–21, 171n63
spirit (*rūḥ*), 68–69, 71, 74, 76, 78

spiritual retreat (*khalwa*), 9, 99, 143, 144, 166
states (*aḥwāl*), 9, 38, 43, 72, 80, 116, 144
Stewart, Charles, 171n56
Stratton, Kimberly B., 12–13, 88, 118, 166
The String of Pearls (Kashnāwī), 113–14
Styers, Randall, 12, 14, 15, 89, 110, 124
subjectivity, 40, 52, 53, 60, 125–26
submission, voluntary, 6, 27, 40, 60, 164
The Subtleties of the Signs (Būnī), 122, 124
succession, 36, 37, 56, 57
succor (*al-ghawth*), 84, 85, 178n76
Sufi lodges (*zāwiyas*), 47–48
Sufi orders (*ṭurūq*), 10, 22, 23, 40, 41, 46–48, 52
Sufism
  contemporary, 22–23
  cosmological realms in, 65–66
  friends of God, 84
  God and, 69
  history and description of, 8–11
  Iblīs and, 135
  Kunta scholars and, 6, 8, 9, 10, 24, 53, 59, 60, 163
  light of Muḥammad and, 154
  meaning of, conflicted, 53
  miracles and magic and, 11–16
  Sahara and history of, 27–28
  sciences of letters and names and, 9, 13–14, 91, 92, 121–22
  sciences of the hidden and, 90
  sciences of the unseen and, 8–9, 88, 115, 116, 120–21, 165
  in West Africa, 46–53, 163
al-Suhrawardī, Abū Najīb, 49
The Sun of the Horizons (Bisṭāmī), 123
The Suns of Knowledge, 14, 122–23, 124, 183n109
superstition, 3, 12, 14
supplicatory prayer. *See* prayer, supplicatory
al-Sūqī, Aḥmad ibn al-Shaykh al-Hīyūnīkal, 44–45, 174n64
Suware, Sālim, 111
al-Suyūṭī, Jalāl al-Dīn, 49, 163
Sweet Breath Concerning Prayer (al-Mukhtār al-Kuntī). See *Nafḥat al-ṭīb*

al-Ṭabarī, 136
tables (*jadāwil*), 94, 95–97, 99, 112, 142–43, 144
  See also sciences of letters and names
"Tadhkirāt al-nisyān," 38
Taghāzā, 30–31
Tagnīt, 36
Tāl, ʿUmar, 5, 10, 39, 47, 52, 158, 161, 163, 175n100
talismans (*al-ṭilasmāt*)
  Islamic magic discourses and, 119
  Kunta cosmology and, 68, 79, 83
  sciences of letters and names and, 95
  sciences of secrets and, 114
  sorcery and, 102, 108
  Sufism and, 121, 122
  in West Africa, 111–12, 165
Ṭarāʾif waʾl-talāʾid (Muḥammad al-Kuntī)
  on angels, 66
  charismata in, 62
  devotional practice and, 159, 160
  on education, 41, 43–44, 46
  on friends of God, 84
  on Iblīs, 136
  influence of, 52, 55
  on Lalla ʿĀʾisha, 150
  overview, 7, 19
  publication of, 18
  on recitation, 130
  on *ruqyā*, 99–100
  on sciences of the unseen, 89–91, 102, 103, 105, 114
  on Sīdi al-Mukhtār, 41–43, 55–58, 89
  on sorcery, 102, 103, 107, 108
  on tables and talismans, 95
  on women's education, 45–46
Tārīkh al-Sūdān, 158
ṭarīqa. *See* path or way
taṣawwuf, meaning of, 9
  See also Sufism
taṣliyya (prayers for the Prophet), 128, 137, 141, 150–51, 152–54
  See also prayers, supplicatory
taṣrīf, 111
Tawdennī, 30–31
tawḥīd (unity of God), 18
  See also annihilation
ṭayy al-arḍ (folding up space), 103, 148, 149
texts and textuality
  authority and production of, 51–52, 53, 129, 130, 159–60, 167
  definitions, 129
  devotional aids and practice and, 2, 17, 20, 129, 159, 160
  history and production of, 130–31
  interpretation and use of, 147
  Kunta scholars and, 16–21
  orality and, 17, 129–30
  religious practice and, 26
  Sufism and, 51, 53, 175n88, 175n100
al-Thaʿlabī, 136
this world (*al-dunyā*), 64, 68, 71, 79, 176n9
  See also *al-mulk*; visible world
al-ṭibb (medicine), 88, 100
  See also *ruqyā or ruqiyya*
al-Tijānī, Aḥmad, 52, 92, 114–15, 155
Tijānī Sufis, 10, 52

al-ṭilasmāt. *See* talismans
al-Timbuktī, Aḥmad Bābā, 40, 45
Timbuktu
  Abtītī assassination and, 56
  education and scholarship in, 42–43, 44–45
  as free city, 38–39
  Iwellemmedan confederation and, 38
  Kunta scholars and, 163
  Moroccan invasion of, 32, 34, 36, 47
  Saharan economy and, 28, 30
  ʿUmar Tāl's *jihād* and, 5, 39
Timbuktu Manuscripts Project, 171n56
Tishīt, 57–58
tobacco trade, 31
The Torch of Lights (al-Mukhtār al-Kuntī), 19, 58, 64–65, 66, 68, 72–73, 84, 171n68
Torobbe scholars, 52
trade and commerce
  Kunta scholars and, 30–31, 60, 162
  of literature and manuscripts, 41, 130
  Saharan history and, 4, 28, 30–31, 47, 111
  sciences of secrets and, 124
Trārza, 36
tsetse flies, 29, 34–35
Tuareg, 32, 33, 36–37, 38, 48
  See also Iwellemmedan Tuareg
al-Ṭughrāʾī, 124
al-Turūdī, ʿAbd al-Qādir ibn Musṭafā, 116
ṭurūq (Sufi orders), 10, 22, 23, 40, 41, 46–48, 52
al-Tustarī, 154
Tuwāt, 30, 48, 54

ʿUhūd wa mawāthīq (Dan Tafa), 116
ʿulamāʾ (scholars), 5–6
ʿulūm al-bāṭin (sciences of the hidden), 89–90
ʿulūm al-ghayb. *See* sciences of the unseen
ʿumarāʾ (princes), 5–6
ʿUmar Aqīt, 111
unity of God (*tawḥīd*), 18
  See also annihilation
unseen, usage of term (*al-ghayb*), 63
  See also realm of the unseen
ʿUqba al-Mustajab, 54–53
Usman dan Fodio. *See* Ibn Fūdī, ʿUthmān

van Dalen, Dorrit, 181n61
visible world (*ʿālam al-shahāda*)
  in Kunta scholarship, 24–25, 162
  realm of the unseen and, 63, 64–65, 68, 76, 110, 164
  sciences of letters and names and, 91–92
  sciences of the unseen and, 88
  See also *al-mulk*
voluntary submission, 6, 27, 40, 60, 164

Waalo, 34
wafq or *awfāq*. *See* magic squares
war drums (*eṭṭebel*), 37
warfare, 34, 35, 36, 38, 39
warrior lineage (*ḥassan*), 33, 34, 35–36, 38–39, 162
Warscheid, Ismail, 41
Wasīṭ fī tarājim udabāʾ shinqīṭ (Shinqīṭī), 43, 54
way. *See* path or way
Webb, James, 32, 35
Weber, Max, 109
wells and water supply, 4, 30
West Africa
  contemporary, 22–23
  devotional aids and practice in, 129, 149–60, 167
  Kunta scholars and, 7
  and sciences of the unseen, discourses of, 16, 88, 110, 111–18, 165
  Sufism in, 46–53, 163
  See also Sahara Desert
Whitcomb, Thomas, 54
whiteness, 4, 32–33, 117
  See also racial discourses
wird or *awrād* (litanies), 50, 87, 127, 127–28, 130, 163
  See also prayer, supplicatory
wisdom (*ḥikma*), 161
witchcraft, 12, 13
  See also sorcery
Wolof kingdoms, 34
women, 11, 12, 13, 45–46, 89
Wright, Zachary, 51, 111, 114, 155
written texts, 51, 53, 60, 129–31, 175n88
  See also texts and textuality
wuld Māmīn, Muḥammad Fādil, 6, 47, 52, 163
wuld Sīdi Maḥmūd, ʿAbd Allāh, 7, 59

al-Yadālī al-Daymānī, Muḥammad ibn al-Mukhtār, 33, 51, 159
al-Yamanī, Aḥmad, 48, 49

zāwiyas (Sufi lodges), 47–48
Zoroaster, 14
zwāya. *See* clerical lineages

www.ingramcontent.com/pod-product-compliance
Lightning Source LLC
Chambersburg PA
CBHW031243290426
44109CB00012B/417
* 9 7 8 0 2 7 1 0 9 2 3 0 0 *